Green Taxation in East Asia

November, 2011

To:

Prof. Johannes Chan S.C.

From:

With thanks &
very best wishes !

Green Taxation in East Asia

Edited by

Richard Cullen

Visiting Professor, The University of Hong Kong

Jefferson VanderWolk

Professor, The Chinese University of Hong Kong

Yan Xu

Post Doctoral Fellow, The University of Hong Kong

Edward Elgar

Cheltenham, UK • Northampton, MA, USA

Published by
Edward Elgar Publishing Limited
The Lypiatts
15 Lansdown Road
Cheltenham
Glos GL50 2JA
UK

Edward Elgar Publishing, Inc.
William Pratt House
9 Dewey Court
Northampton
Massachusetts 01060
USA

A catalogue record for this book
is available from the British Library

Library of Congress Control Number: 2011925784

ISBN 978 1 84980 300 7

Typeset by Servis Filmsetting Ltd, Stockport, Cheshire
Printed and bound by MPG Books Group, UK

Contents

Figures

Tables

Contributors

Professor Arthur J. Cockfield, Faculty of Law, Queen's University, Canada.

Professor Richard Cullen, Faculty of Law, The University of Hong Kong.

Dr Mattias Derlén, Department of Law, Umea University, Sweden.

Shelley Griffiths, Faculty of Law, University of Otago, New Zealand.

Wayne Gumley, Department of Business Law and Taxation, Monash University, Australia.

Dr Johan Lindholm, Department of Law, Umea University, Sweden.

Professor Janet E. Milne, Environmental Tax Policy Institute of Vermont Law School, USA.

Professor Stephen L.H. Phua, National University of Singapore.

Professor Natalie Stoianoff, Faculty of Law, University of Technology, Sydney, Australia.

Professor Jefferson VanderWolk, Faculty of Law, The Chinese University of Hong Kong.

Dr Yan Xu, Faculty of Law, The University of Hong Kong.

Foreword by
Christine Loh, CEO, Civic Exchange, Hong Kong.

Preface

The planning for the conference on which this book is based began in mid-2008. The title for the conference held at Hong Kong University (HKU), was: "Green Taxation in East Asia". This title, which worked well for the conference, has been retained for this book.

It was suggested, in 2008, that it would be sensible to run our conference after, rather than before, the Conference of the Parties (COP15) Climate Change Conference to be held in Copenhagen in December, 2009. The HKU conference, thus, ran in late January, 2010.

From the time when the conference was conceived as the Second International Conference of the Taxation Law Research Programme at HKU, the primary focus was identified as being on taxation systems – and how they should respond (especially in East Asia) to the serious environmental challenges posed by growing greenhouse gas (GHG) emissions. We knew that much international effort had been expended on research and analysis related to the role of other (non-taxation) regulatory measures designed to meet the GHG challenge. Taxation, though, tended to be regarded as being of secondary importance, at best, in the mainstream, post-Kyoto global debate on how best to tackle excessive GHG emissions.

This comparative lack of attention to the role of taxation and related measures as tools to help remedy environmental degradation is unfortunate, we believe, especially in the case of East Asia. China, the largest nation in the world and the key jurisdiction in East Asia has so many environmental challenges and ongoing, regular instances of environmental calamities that it is hard to know where to begin to catalogue them all. But China also presents a remarkable story of economic success probably never before equalled in recorded history. The potential for innovative taxation measures to help build a much more sustainable economic growth model is substantial – and, as we argue, based on the detailed comparative analysis which follows, potentially "doable".

The cut off point for the majority of the legal and political discussion in the book is mid-2010.

We are indebted to a range of persons for helping to turn our project into this book. We received outstanding support from the Faculty of Law at HKU and the Asian Institute of International Financial Law (AIIFL) at HKU. The Think-Tank, Civic Exchange was also strongly supportive. We are most grateful to all the participants in the conference and particularly to all the chapter-writers. Special thanks are given to Flora Leung of AIIFL whose tireless work on all aspects of organization was exemplary.

Foreword

Christine Loh

Human activities are putting pressures on Planet Earth on such a scale that there could be abrupt global environmental change.

Scientists have proposed a new approach to global sustainability by identifying and defining "planetary boundaries" within which humanity can operate safely. Nine planetary boundaries have been identified: climate change; ocean acidification; stratospheric ozone; biogeochemical nitrogen cycle and phosphorus cycle; global freshwater use; land system change; loss of biological diversity; chemical pollution; and atmospheric aerosol loading. The scientists observed that humanity has probably already transgressed three of these planetary boundaries: climate change, biodiversity loss, and changes to the global nitrogen cycle.[1]

Moreover, the scientists noted that these systems are interdependent in the sense that Planet Earth's various systems function as a whole. They put forward the hypothesis that transgressing one or more planetary boundaries may tip Planet Earth into a state which could trigger non-linear, abrupt environmental change within continental-to planetary-scale systems. Moreover, because of the interdependence of these systems, transgressing one may shift the position of, or result in transgressing, other boundaries. The scientists emphasized that changes to Planet Earth's functioning system do not mean that the planet will not survive – it will, but in another state, but humans are the ones who will be affected. The social impact of transgressing planetary boundaries will depend on the social-ecological resilience of the affected societies.[2]

Humans are thus part of a complex web of relationships involving Planet Earth, without which we cannot exist. It is simply not possible to maintain human well-being within degraded ecosystems.

While there are large uncertainties and knowledge gaps that still need to be filled, the concept of there being planetary boundaries lays the

---

[1] Rockstrom, J. et al., "A Safe Operating Space for Humanity", *Nature*, Volume 461, 2009, pages 472–5.

[2] *Ibid.*

groundwork for society to think about a new approach to governance and management of Planet Earth to ensure a safe space for human development. A new approach to avert the environmental crises humans have created requires change on many fronts throughout the world. We need to transform not only our economic and political systems, but also our legal and financial systems.

Cormac Cullinan, the author of *Wild Law*, argues that the law must protect and enforce the rights of Nature as well as those of humans. To date, environmental laws have failed to stop environmental destruction. Cullinan believes today's laws do not work because they were never intended to serve the environment. Our laws are designed to regulate the manner and rate of exploitation of natural resources and not to enforce limitations on human behaviour in the interests of preserving the ecological balance of Planet Earth. He argues, therefore, that recognizing that Nature has legally enforceable rights would enable the machinery of the state to be used to safeguard ecosystems, rivers, mountains and other species against human exploitation and, in so doing, would begin a process of fundamentally restructuring legal and political systems.[3] His view is no longer "pie-in-the-sky". In 2008, Ecuador adopted a constitution which recognized that Nature has legally enforceable rights.

What role can taxation play in this early phase of that transformation? It is clear enough that society needs to discourage certain activities that harm ecosystems and encourage activities that restore and strengthen them. A tax can be imposed on undesirable activities. The question is how to structure such a tax and deal with the politics that inevitably arise as we implement new ways of doing things.

Ideas for new taxes are coming from a variety of sources, including scientists. For example, James E. Hansen, one of the world's best known climate scientists, proposes a special tax to deal with coal. He has repeatedly emphasized that burning fossil fuels (coal, oil, gas) will eventually threaten humanity's survival because fossil fuels produce carbon dioxide (CO_2) that stays in surface reservoirs – atmosphere, ocean, soils and biosphere – for millennia. Climate response to CO_2 begins slowly, because of the inertia of the ocean and the ice sheets on Antarctica and Greenland. He says global warming so far is equivalent to Earth having the sniffles. He points to the events of 2010 – China's droughts followed by floods, Moscow's heat wave, and Pakistan's extensive floods – and while people can get through these problems, the real challenges will

---

[3]   Cullinan, C., "Wild Law and the Challenges of Climate Change", *Soundings*, Issue 37, 2007, pages 116–26.

affect our grandchildren if this generation does not rapidly reduce CO_2 emissions.

Hansen argues that governments must recognize that burning fossil fuels will increase CO_2 and will cause Planet Earth as we know it today to become a different planet – ultimately, a desolate ice-free planet with much higher sea levels than today. For humans, the transition will be painful and out of humanity's control. Hansen wants society to phase out coal burning and leave fossil fuels in the ground. The challenge is cost. Fossil fuels are cheaper than other forms of power in significant part because the companies that sell them and the consumers who use them are not required to cover the real costs of their impact on society. Public health costs, for example, (called "external costs" by economists) are borne by the public through sickness and paying medical bills. The fossil fuel industry is not made to cover these costs. If it were, then fossil fuels would not be as cheap as they are today.

Hansen's idea is to create a special carbon tax to be collected from fossil fuel companies. The money collected should be distributed monthly to the public on a per capita basis as a dividend to allow lifestyle adjustments and spur clean energy innovations. He argues that as the tax rises, it will make fossil fuels more and more expensive, and at some stage, there will be no reason to keep on burning them and they will be phased out and replaced by clean forms of energy. Hansen argues this "fee-and-dividend" approach provides the most rapid economically efficient path to a clean energy future and would cure us of our current fossil fuel addiction.[4]

Economist Richard Sandor, founder of the Chicago Climate Exchange, and known as the "father of financial futures", argues in favour of using market means as another way to change behaviour. He points to the successful sulphur dioxide emissions trading scheme in the United States as an example, and advocates that society should think broadly about all the tools available to push the low carbon transformation. Sandor acknowledges that Hansen's worry about cap-and-trade schemes being exploited by business to line their own pockets is real, but he argues that this is not a reason to "throw the baby out with the bathwater". Properly designed, cap-and-trade schemes have a role to play too.[5]

---

[4] Hansen, J., *Storms of My Grandchildren: The Truth about the Coming Climate Catastrophe and Our Last Chance to Save Humanity*, Bloomsbury, 2009, page 241; Hansen, J., "Tell Barack Obama the Truth – The Whole Truth", http://www.columbia.edu/~jeh1/mailings/2008/20081229_Obama_revised.pdf, 10 November, 2010.

[5] *See,* e.g., "Economics, Innovation and Persistence", http://www.kellogg.northwestern.edu/news_articles/2009/richardsandor.aspx; *see also* "CCX's

It would be comforting to think that the transformation to an ecologically sustainable future has already begun. We see evidence of this in new scientific understanding that Planet Earth is one functioning system, that Planet Earth can be given legally enforceable rights, and that both market systems and taxation can expedite the transition. There is another challenge and that is time. Scientists worry about run-away climate change once a tipping point is reached and that humans will be catapulted from the current climate sweet spot into another state that is unsafe for us.

The macro policy rethinking advocated by commentators such as Hansen and Sandor provides us with frameworks for longer-term reshaping of the fundamentals of making carbon "pay its way" in a comprehensive and proper manner. The authors of the jurisdictional chapters in this book are, of necessity, more focused on analysing the interaction, *today*, between taxation (and related fiscal measures) and the environment. From these studies it is clear that a great deal is amiss in the way this interface works at present across all the jurisdictions under review. But this research also shows positive steps being taken – and great scope for further, positive tax policy development. We can see from this research how smart policy innovation can start right now – and also how it can build better foundations for the introduction of more comprehensive, globally effective policy frameworks such as those advanced by Hansen and Sandor.

Time is of the essence. The scholarship in this volume shows that lawyers and tax experts are engaged in finding solutions. Can green taxation make a difference? The answer is a resounding "yes".

Richard Sandor on Financial Innovation and the Protection of Our Air and Water", http://knowledge.emory.edu/article.cfm?articleid=1338, 10 November 2010. For the *Hansen vs. Sandor* argument, *see also* Cheung, C.F. and Chen, S., "Fiery Exchange at Climate Dialogue", *South China Morning Post*, November 5, 2010.

1. Conspectus

Richard Cullen and Yan Xu[1]

1. INTRODUCTION

Expectations were high with respect to the COP15, Climate Change Conference to be held in Copenhagen in December, 2009.[2] Many hoped that it might resolve a number of the varied problems associated with the implementation of the Kyoto Protocol (COP3). The Kyoto Protocol was

---

[1] For the purposes of this book (and the conference on which it is based), we have used the term *green taxation* as a shorthand expression to include: taxes, fees and charges – similar to traditional taxes, fees and charges – which are directed (at least in part) at generating improved environmental outcomes (some chapter authors have used slightly modified versions of this terminology). By East Asia we mean that part of Asia including China, Japan, Korea and South East Asia – but not including the nations of the former USSR, the Middle East and South Asia (India, Pakistan, Sri Lanka and adjacent smaller States). We have concentrated on particular key jurisdictions in East Asia for this book: China, Hong Kong and Singapore. China due to its combination of extraordinary size and even more extraordinary, long-term economic development is self-evidently crucial in any discussion such as this. Hong Kong and Singapore provide examples of highly developed jurisdictions in East Asia which both face major environmental challenges. Each of them has, in its way (and for various reasons, not least, ethnic linkages and economic investment), been deeply influential in shaping aspects of development policy in Mainland China over several decades. (Limitations of space meant we needed to make certain jurisdictional choices.) The other jurisdictions discussed have been included: (A) to provide a representative, comparative picture of the state of green taxation today; and (B) to let the experience from those jurisdictions inform the ongoing policy discussion about green taxation in East Asia.

[2] "COP15" is an acronym for "Conference of Parties, Number 15". The "United Nations Framework Convention on Climate Change" (UNFCCC or FCCC) is an international environmental treaty produced at the United Nations Conference on Environment and Development (UNCED), informally known as the Earth Summit held in Rio de Janeiro from June 3 to 14, 1992. The objective of the treaty is to stabilize greenhouse gas concentrations in the atmosphere at a level that would prevent dangerous anthropogenic change within the world climate system, http://unfccc.int/essential_background/convention/background/items/1353.php, June 3, 2010. A continuing series of Conference of Parties has run since the Earth Summit.

concluded in 1997. It established binding obligations on all those countries which signed up to limit greenhouse gas (GHG) emissions.[3] Mostly it
affected developed countries plus a range of "post-1989" Central-Eastern
European countries.[4]

> The major feature of the Kyoto Protocol was that it set binding targets for
> 37 industrialized countries and the European Community for reducing GHG
> emissions. These amounted to an average of five per cent against 1990 levels
> over the five-year period 2008–2012.
>   The Kyoto Protocol was generally seen as an important first step towards a
> truly global emission reduction regime that would stabilize GHG emissions,
> and provide the essential architecture for any future international agreement
> on climate change.
>   By the end of the first commitment period of the Kyoto Protocol in 2012,
> a new international framework needed to be negotiated and ratified which
> could deliver the stringent emission reductions the Intergovernmental Panel on
> Climate Change (IPCC) has clearly indicated were needed.[5]

The Kyoto Protocol placed a special burden on developed nations (Annex
1 Countries (which includes Economies-in-Transition from Central-
Eastern Europe)). The Industrial Revolution had begun in these nations
over 150 years ago and heavy industrialization was seen as the primary
cause of the growth in GHGs, which, in turn, were seen as the primary
drivers of dangerous anthropogenic (man-made) global climate change.[6]

Developing nations, including large rapidly industrializing developing
nations like China and India, were not subjected to the same sort of obligations under the Kyoto Protocol. Certain developed nations, including the
USA and Australia refused to sign up to the Kyoto Protocol – although
Australia finally signed the Protocol, after a change of government, in
2007.[7]

The primary means by which the Kyoto Protocol sought to reduce
GHG levels were: Emissions Trading (the carbon market), the Clean
Development Mechanism (CDM) and Joint Implementation (JI).[8] There

---

   [3]   The key details of the Kyoto Protocol are summarized at http://unfccc.int/
kyoto_protocol/items/2830.php, June 6, 2010 (henceforth "KP Key Details").
   [4]   After the fall of the Berlin Wall and the collapse of the USSR these economies began re-engaging with the world in new ways.
   [5]   KP Key Details, *op. cit.*
   [6]   *Ibid.*
   [7]   McGuirk, R., "Australia Signs Kyoto Protocol; US Now Only Holdout",
December 3, 2007, http://news.nationalgeographic.com/news/2007/12/071203-AP-
aus-kyoto.html, June 6, 2010.
   [8]   KP Key Details, *op. cit.*

was only limited focus on the potential direct role of taxation as these primary means of, inter alia, allocating carbon-usage costs were being resolved. The primary means have, as it has turned out, not proved to be very effective in reducing GHG emissions since 1998 – not least because emission levels from major developing nations not covered by the Kyoto Protocol, such as China and India, have increased significantly.[9] The arguably huge "fiscal moral hazard" problems associated with these UN or government-run, "market-based" mechanisms aimed at reducing GHGs have also increasingly been argued. We use the term fiscal moral hazard to mean the way in which markets (or market-related systems) created using formal legislative or similar instruments, in particular, are prone to being exploited for financial advantage in ways usually technically "within the rules" but also often contrary to the aims of the created market.[10]

Great, indeed excessive expectations were placed on the COP15 Meeting in Copenhagen in December, 2010. The serious, continuing impact of climate change (accelerated by massive and increasing carbon-based energy consumption along with a range of other aggravating factors) was widely acknowledged. The "first commitment" period under the Kyoto Protocol (for Annex I countries) is also due to expire in 2012.[11]

The COP15 Meeting brought together the widest range of key world leaders. The hope was that the seriousness of the problems and the presence of key decision-makers could lead to real progress towards crafting a new multi-lateral agreement on tackling climate change.[12] This did not happen.

---

[9] World Bank, *World Development Report 2010 – Overview,* http://siteresources.worldbank.org/INTWDR2010/Resources/5287678-1226014527953/Overview.pdf, June 6, 2010.

[10] *See,* for example, Ng, E., "UN Probes Claim Firms are Faking Carbon Credits", *Sunday Morning Post,* October 10, 2010. A detailed argument of this view was presented on November 3, 2009 at the Hong Kong University (Campbell, I. D., "After Kyoto: International Welfarism and the Impossibility of Global Carbon Trading", notes on file with Richard Cullen). Supporters of the CDM also acknowledge these moral hazard problems, *see* Nigoff, M. G., "The Clean Development Mechanism: Does the Current Structure Facilitate Kyoto Protocol Compliance?", *Georgetown International Environmental Law Review,* Volume 18, 2006, page 249.

[11] KP Key Details, *op. cit.*

[12] *See,* for example, "Great Expectations for COP15 Climate Change Conference", http://www.caricom.org/jsp/pressreleases/pres97_09.jsp, June 7, 2010. The UN climate change negotiating process seems to have made some modest steps towards restored relevance at the UN Climate Conference in Cancun, Mexico, in December, 2010. *See* "Back from the Brink", *The Economist,* December 18, 2010, page 113.

Serious critics of the mainstream approach to tackling climate change, like Bjorn Lomborg both predicted and noted what they said was the failure of the COP15 Meeting.[13] Christine Loh, whilst acknowledging the severe disappointments arising out of the COP15 Meeting, also notes the way in which the COP15 process has potentially helped to create a new "tipping point". In particular the event showed, first that there is now a wide consensus that economies do need to become far less carbon-reliant and secondly, that the seriousness of climate change as a primary global issue was evidenced by the presence of all key world leaders at the COP15 Meeting. She goes on to analyze why the outcomes at COP15 were so below par and notes, for example, entrenched ("locally vital") views and the cumbersome UN discussion system. She also sets out the now clarified negotiating positions post-COP15. There is a basic three-way tension between: (A) vulnerable smaller countries; (B) larger developing countries; and (C) the developed world.[14]

One other consequence of the COP15 process is the way that use of taxation as one key means to tackle the manifest problems associated with climate change has begun to rise up the climate change, serious-discussion-agenda. The Kyoto Protocol itself and what followed from it – not least the very lengthy debate about the position of "stand-outs" like the US and Australia – consumed much climate change political energy. Much of that energy, in turn, was then directed towards the quest of drawing a measurable success from the COP15 Meeting. Despite the post-COP15 disappointment, one benefit of having gotten past this process is that the policy-options discussion has opened up.

Lomborg makes essentially the same point (rather more polemically) when he says:

> After 20 years of wasted effort, we can no longer afford to squander more time continuing on this road to nowhere. We can only hope that December's [COP15] failure will be the jolt we need to once and for all drop the Rio-Kyoto-Copenhagen approach and start tackling climate change effectively.

His primary point is that the best way to tackle climate change is by making a very major effort – significantly public-funded at the outset – to

---

[13] *See* Lomborg, B., "Technology not Talks will Save the Planet", *Finance and Development – International Monetary Fund*, December, 2009, page 13; and Lomborg, B., "Climate Strategy on a Road to Nowhere", *Globe and Mail*, February 1, 2010.

[14] Loh, C., "Copenhagen is not Over", December, 2009, http://www.caricom.org/jsp/pressreleases/pres97_09.jsp, June 7, 2010.

stimulate the highest level of research and development aimed at generating a green-energy technological revolution. This, he argues, would be far more effective – and far less costly – than the mainstream approach, which he characterizes as imposing crippling costs on carbon usage in a likely doomed quest to achieve breakthrough GHG emission reduction targets.[15]

As it happens, Lomborg does support, as part of his program, increased taxation of carbon usage – but at a far lower level than levels suggested by serious supporters of the Kyoto approach to allocating costs to carbon usage.[16]

When we decided to organize the Green Taxation in East Asia Conference (GTC) a core concern was to focus on the potential use of taxation (and related) measures to foster climate-helpful, large-scale, behaviour change. The true quotidian impact of climate awfulness is more apparent in East Asia than any other region of the world. Greater China confronts severe environmental degradation problems as a direct product of several decades of remarkable economic growth. In 2005 it was reported that 16 of the 20 most polluted cities in the world, where "you could chew the air", were in Mainland China.[17] Since then the position has tended to grow worse.[18]

No one before COP15 honestly believed that any sort of "magic bullet" solution existed. But many were persuaded that the fundamentals of the Kyoto Protocol comprised the core of the any "right approach" and alternatives outside that core were thought to be more marginal. In the post-COP15 world, it seems clear that we will see a wider variety of measures designed to tackle climate change problems being seriously studied.

---

[15] Lomborg, *op. cit*. Numbers of commentators have argued that Lomborg, in his new (edited) book (*Smart Solutions to Climate Change. Comparing Costs and Benefits*, Cambridge University Press, 2010) has changed his views so that he is now notably less sceptical about the argued consequences flowing from climate change. Lomborg himself claims his position remains that we need to focus on practical remedies – rather than reaching for (vastly expensive) grand solutions. *See*, for example, Rundle G., "Bjorn Again? Reshaping the Climate Change Debate", *Crikey E-Newsletter*, September 1, 2010, http://www.crikey.com.au/2010/09/01/rundle-bj%C3%B8rn-again-reshaping-the-climate-change-debate/, December 28, 2010.

[16] "Frequently Asked Questions", http://www.lomborg.com/faq/, June 7, 2010.

[17] Watts, J., "Satellite Data Reveals Beijing as Air Pollution Capital of World", the *Guardian*, October 31, 2005, http://www.guardian.co.uk/news/2005/oct/31/china.pollution, June 7, 2010.

[18] Lee, H. Y., "Air Pollution Worsens from World's Biggest Emitter Nation", *World Focus*, March 29, 2010, http://worldfocus.org/blog/2010/03/29/air-pollution-worsens-from-worlds-biggest-emitter-nation/10170/, June 7, 2010.

As this openness to a more multi-factor process unfolds, it is particularly timely to reconsider the role that taxation-related measures can play.

For the purposes of the GTC and this book, we have used the term *green taxation* as a shorthand expression to include: taxes, fees and charges – similar to traditional taxes, fees and charges – which are directed (at least in part) at generating improved environmental outcomes.

A primary aim of the GTC was to generate an academically well-grounded comparative study of the use and misuse of fiscal measures – especially green taxation to:

- encourage environmental protection and improvement in particular jurisdictions (and across jurisdictional borders);
- discourage behaviour leading to environmental damage and degradation in particular jurisdictions (and across jurisdictional borders).

We were also interested in the revenue outcomes of such measures – and the way such outcomes can, in turn, shape later tax and related policy – and social behaviour. Our aim was for the GTC to explore the scope – and limits – of green taxation in depth.

Since 2000, a widely attended and well-respected annual Global Conference on Environmental Taxation (GCET) has been held. To date, the GCET has mainly focused on environmental taxation issues arising in the Americas, the EU and Australia.[19] Thus far, there has been no serious, detailed, comparative study primarily focused on the good – and bad – ways in which green taxation can be utilized in East Asia as one important means to try and shape collective environment-affecting behaviour. The aim of the GTC was to address this space in the public policy debate.

The GTC – and this book – are fundamentally comparative. Our aim is to inform the debate (as it relates to the use of tax and related measures) on meeting environmental challenges in East Asia by drawing on relevant world-wide experience.

2. JURISDICTION CHAPTERS

2.1 Introduction

We invited a number of tax policy specialists and public policy commentators to attend the GTC. They wrote and presented their papers at the

---

[19] *See* further, re the GCET: http://www.worldecotax.org/.

conference and then revised them in the light of conference discussion and further research. Each of the following chapters offers a jurisdiction-based perspective on the development and operation of green taxation measures. Each chapter highlights aspects of jurisdictional experience with green taxation, which relate to key, usually long-term, political-economy considerations particular to the jurisdiction. In sum, the chapters address most of all the positive prospects – and limitations – in developing and applying green taxation measures, today.

Our primary aim is to use a strong comparative discussion to help inform the ongoing policy debate about green taxation in East Asia. For the purposes of the GTC and this book, we have chosen to focus, in East Asia, first on China and next on Hong Kong and Singapore. Limitations of space have meant we have had to make choices.

China, in view of its sheer size and remarkable economic growth – and extraordinary potential – is once again the fundamental key jurisdiction in East Asia. Hong Kong and Singapore are tiny by comparison. But these two very successful jurisdictions face major environmental challenges and they present interesting cases of differing approaches to using green taxation measures. Moreover, they have each had a crucial influence on aspects of public policy development in Mainland China especially since the start of China's "open door" policy around 1978.

In the next part of the book, we have included chapters from North America (the US and Canada); the EU; and Australasia (Australia and New Zealand). These jurisdictions have been incorporated: (A) to provide a representative, comparative picture of the state of green taxation today; and (B) to let the experience from those jurisdictions inform the ongoing policy discussion about green taxation in East Asia.

2.2 China

Dr Yan Xu, from the Faculty of Law at Hong Kong University, faced some major decisions as she began writing her paper for the GTC. China, the most populous nation in the world with a population of some 1.3 billion, has so many environmental challenges (and ongoing, regular instances of environmental calamities) it was hard to know where to focus a single chapter for a book like this. Ultimately, she has concentrated her focus on the development of what she identifies as a consolidated fuel tax for China. This discussion is placed within the context of a quite comprehensive review of the use of taxation and other, related, public policy instruments to address China's manifest and always growing environmental problems.

Dr Xu also notes some of the key "headwind factors" holding back a fully committed public policy assault on environment-damaging behaviour, not least, local government economic growth zealotry and the manifest problems related to central–local, public revenue distribution in China.[20]

Dr Xu bases much of the analysis in her chapter on an essentially Pigouvian understanding of green taxation.[21] Briefly Pigou argued powerfully for the need to "internalize the externalities" of economic actors. By using taxes (and subsidies) market failures which allow economic actors "to pollute and forget" could be corrected. Notwithstanding significant criticism from other economic thinkers, Pigou's key insights remain convincing for many. These insights, as Dr Xu explains, laid the theoretical foundations for the application of green taxation in many countries around the world today.

The focus on fuel taxation arises from several considerations including the key role of fuel, especially for transportation, in the growth of China's vast new economy. Fuel is also vital in terms of energy production. Dr Xu has, however, taken a pragmatic policy review approach: she has narrowed her research attention so as to allow her time and space to develop a prescriptive investigation of how a consolidated fuel tax might be crafted and applied in China. As she points out, direct and indirect taxation of fuel for transport is an area of public policy permeated by much ad hoc complexity. Yet the fundamental need to build a more systematic consolidated system is deeply apparent – not least because of the prodigious growth in car ownership in China over the last decade.[22]

Key elements in the recommended reform of (transport) fuel taxation include: higher rates of taxation (to discourage excessive use and wastage and to encourage much greater fuel-use efficiency); environmen-

---

[20]   As Dr Xu explains, in the Chinese unitary state, one has, based in Beijing, the central government. All governments below this level – from provincial governments down to county governments are typically referred to, collectively, as "local governments". The Mainland PRC has long been beset by major problems – especially as between the central government and provincial governments – related to distribution of rights to tax (and charge) and rights to share centrally collected revenues.

[21]   Pigou, A. C., *The Economics of Welfare*, (4th ed.), Macmillan, 1932.

[22]   Some estimates are that there will be 75 million cars in China by 2011 – up from about 6 million in 2000. China now has more operating motorways than anywhere outside the US. The growth in car ownership – and motorway construction – are set to continue at high rates. Meanwhile air transport and rail transport also are growing at remarkable rates. *See* "Car ownership in China expected to overtake Japan next year", *People's Daily Online,* May 31, 2010, http://english. peopledaily.com.cn/90001/90778/90860/7006415.html, June 10, 2010; and "China Transportation Growth", *Early Warning*, http://earlywarn.blogspot.com/2010/01/ chinese-transportation-growth.html, June 10, 2010.

tally targeted taxation (to encourage the use of cleaner, less scarce carbon-based fuels); market-tracking taxation (to ensure world market prices rises are swiftly passed on to consumers in China); and greater harmonization (and elimination of loopholes and anomalies) in the taxation of fuel. Dr Xu also recommends studying how road-tolling – recently mainly abolished in China (see details in Chapter 2) – could be re-introduced using electronic systems to build an efficient nation-wide congestion charging system.

Dr Xu also discusses the spending side of the above new taxation equation: she recommends that strong consideration be given to at least partial "ear-marking" or hypothecation of funds raised, for example, to redress environmental degradation; and to fund public transport infrastructure. Increased revenues could also be used to reduce economically inefficient taxation.

2.3 Hong Kong

British Hong Kong was first established in 1841. It became the Hong Kong Special Administrative Region (HKSAR) of the People's Republic of China (PRC) on July 1, 1997. The reversion of sovereignty to the PRC proceeded under the Beijing-proclaimed doctrine of "One Country – Two Systems". Under this doctrine, the HKSAR has been maintained as, essentially, a separate first world, remarkably free, "City-State", within the fast-developing but still heavily impoverished PRC with its deeply entrenched, one party, authoritarian system of government.[23] The HKSAR has retained its British common law legal system and a wide array of civic freedoms. The HKSAR, Beijing-enacted mini-Constitution, the Basic Law, does, however, attempt to retain (subject to a slow process of political reform) the essence of the largely non-democratic, "executive-led" system of government perfected by the British in Hong Kong. The One Country – Two Systems doctrine – and the Basic Law – thus combine great economic (and civil society)

---

[23] City-States are typically defined as "an independent political unit consisting of a city and surrounding countryside". They reached their peak in ancient Greece, although a number, like Florence, Venice and Genoa endured in Italy until the middle of the 19th century. Bremen and Hamburg also retained this status until they were absorbed into the modern German State. *See* http://www.answers.com/topic/city-state, July 31, 2010. *See also* Glotz, G., *The Greek City and Its Institutions*, Knopf, 1951 (reprinted 1969); and Ehrenberg, V., *The Greek State* (2nd ed.), Methuen, 1969 (reprinted 1972). Hong Kong is clearly not a separate sovereign State (like, for example, the City-State Singapore). As the HKSAR, it is now plainly a part of the PRC and subject to the sovereignty of Beijing. Such is the level of effective political and economic separation of the HKSAR from the PRC Mainland it retains the appearance and de facto face of a City-State, however.

independence with significant political restraint.[24] A crucial aspect of the separation of the two systems is the way in which the Basic Law has built a "fiscal firewall" between the Mainland PRC and the HKSAR. Basically, the HKSAR is to maintain its low rate, simple tax system; no PRC Mainland taxes are ever to be imposed within the HKSAR; and no HKSAR public revenues are ever to be transferred to Beijing.[25]

The HKSAR has a population of around 7 million. The total land area is approximately 1000 square kilometers. For a range of policy and topographical reasons the heavily built-up area of Hong Kong has remained at around 200 square kilometers. The result is a particularly high density conurbation in those built-up areas.[26]

Professor Jefferson VanderWolk, from the Chinese University of Hong Kong, explains in the introduction to Chapter 3 that:

> After surveying the relevant legal and tax landscape, I will turn to policy proposals for the immediate future. Specifically, I will argue that the Hong Kong government should consider introducing well-designed tax measures related to the use of fossil fuels in the energy and transport sectors, and to the use of water. The benefits of these measures could be significant, including the broadening of Hong Kong's tax base, a reduction of taxes on desirable economic activity, enhancement of Hong Kong's competitive position in the region, and improvement of the environment.

Once more the analysis draws on Pigouvian insights. It also stresses (drawing, *inter alia*, on considered arguments from the Organisation for Economic Co-operation and Development (OECD)) the way in which carbon taxes (or green taxation) can be deployed to achieve positive environmental outcomes. Well-designed green taxes can operate both efficiently and flexibly. Other well-tried adjustment measures can also be used, as the OECD notes, to address problems of regressivity.

Professor VanderWolk notes the well-recognized narrowness of the tax base in Hong Kong; there are no formal consumption or capital gains taxes

---

[24]   The remarkable experiment of maintaining an energetic capitalist enclave within the largest (and most successful and durable) one party state in the modern world is a matter of long established and ongoing discussion: the literature is extensive. For a comprehensive review of the legal implementation of the One Country – Two Systems doctrine – and its political-economy consequences – *see* Ghai, Y., *Hong Kong's New Constitutional Order*, (2nd ed.), Hong Kong University Press, 1999. *See also* Cullen, R., "Hong Kong: The Making of a Modern City-State", *Murdoch E-Law Journal,* Volume 1, 2006, page 24.

[25]   *See* Articles 106, 107 and 108 of the Basic Law.

[26]   *See* "Hong Kong: The Facts", http://www.gov.hk/en/about/abouthk/ factsheets/docs/population.pdf, June 11, 2010.

and the income tax regime is source-based; that is, confined to the territory of the HKSAR. Transaction taxes are generally low and the majority of wage and salary earners are exempt from income tax. The HKSAR Government relies heavily, directly and indirectly, on revenues related to land-transactions. Especially in the post-1997 period, this income source has proved to be highly volatile.[27] Base broadening measures have been more actively considered – in particular, the introduction of a Goods and Services Tax (GST). But, as Professor VanderWolk explains, that initiative now seems to have been removed from the policy-agenda altogether, at least for the foreseeable future.

This chapter moves on from the review of the existing tax regime to consider what existing green taxation measures exist in the HKSAR prior to contemplating the sort of smarter, future green taxation measures Hong Kong should be implementing, including: a comprehensive carbon duty (affecting energy supplies, especially); enhanced taxation of motor fuels; and revised water and sewage charges.

2.4 Singapore

The other outstandingly durable and successful City-State established in East Asia, as part of the British Empire, is Singapore. It was founded as a British enclave, more than 20 years before Hong Kong, in 1819. Today, as the Republic of Singapore, it is, unlike Hong Kong, a fully independent (City-State) jurisdiction – and has been so, since 1965. Both the population and area of Singapore are about 70 per cent of that of the HKSAR, at around 5 million and 700 square kilometers respectively. Like the HKSAR, Singapore is a high-density, small, first-world city-state.

Singapore is a unicameral, parliamentary democracy which has been dominated since independence by a single party, the People's Action Party (PAP). The parliament is made up of a combination of elected and some nominated members. Only the PAP has ever held government since independence. Singapore retains much of the essence of the common law legal system introduced by the British but with some significant modifications – for example, trial by jury has been abolished. Singapore consistently ranks very highly in world-wide comparisons in terms of its infrastructure and stability but less well (including compared to Hong Kong) in terms of civic and political freedom and cultural diversity and the living environment.[28]

---

[27] Cullen, *op. cit.*
[28] Lim, J., "'Software' Areas Hurt Singapore Ranking in Global City Poll", *Straits Times,* February 13, 2010, http://wildsingaporenews.blogspot.com/2010/02/

One area where Singapore does excel is in the way in which it can mobilize and coordinate the resources of the State to drive new public policy development and implementation. It, perhaps better than any other jurisdiction, has shown how to marry political will with effective policy action. Its compact size, strongly perceived need for self-reliance, strong (and continuous single party) political leadership and extensive experience in facing and overcoming an array of governance challenges over more than four decades help to explain this.[29]

As Professor Stephen Phua from the National University of Singapore notes in Chapter 4, Singapore determined some time ago that it must take GHG emissions seriously. Having made that decision, the City-State has put a major effort into developing and implementing an array of medium- to long-term, responsive policies. Thus, policies have been developed to secure long-term, sustainable supplies of water and gas (for electricity) from Malaysia and Indonesia, respectively. Major initiatives have been launched, too, to enhance the "greening" of Singapore's built environment: new building codes governing current developments and the upgrading of existing buildings have also been targeted. These changes are noted in Chapter 4, below, but the main focus in the chapter is on the variety of ways the City-State has set about reforming the mix and operation of its entire approach to regulating internal transportation.

Briefly, Singapore has crafted (and is still creating) a strong mix of often inter-linked policies designed: to limit the growth in private car ownership; encourage low-emission commercial and private road vehicles, reduce road congestion; and rapidly expand the public rail and road transportation system. Serious funding research modeling has been undertaken to show how these programs can be paid for. Additional research on tax and charging systems has been done to show where to target fees so that they produce the greatest (green-friendly) behaviour change.

Although Singapore's per capita car ownership rate is only about 20 per cent of that in Australia, it is still around double the rate in Hong Kong.[30] High initial purchase-related charges and a (usually) expensive

---

software-areas-hurt-singapore-ranking.html, June 11, 2010. This article refers to recent detailed comparative by organizations such as The Economist Intelligence Unit and International Living.

[29] *See* Vasil, R., *Governing Singapore: A History of National Development and Democracy*, Allen & Unwin Academic, 2001; and "Economic History", Ministry of Trade and Industry, Singapore, http://app.mti.gov.sg/default.asp?id=545, July 28, 2010.

[30] *See* "Passenger Cars per 1,000 People", World Bank, http://data.world-bank.org/indicator/IS.VEH.PCAR.P3, July 28, 2010.

"Certificate of Entitlement" (COE) scheme have, however, helped to hold that annual ownership growth rate to less than 2 per cent in Singapore. A combination of prohibitions on high-pollution vehicles and fuel pricing and other schemes have made the use of cleaner fuels, especially for commercial vehicles, all but mandatory. "Off peak" registration of private cars has been introduced, too, to encourage non-use during peak periods.

Most effective of all, perhaps, in shaping better road usage behaviour has been the extensive deployment of Electronic Road Pricing (ERP). ERP currently applies to the busiest areas in the City-State but the system appears to have been so successful in reducing congestion (and modifying usage patterns) that it looks set to be expanded, perhaps right across Singapore.

Unlike Hong Kong, Singapore has a Goods and Services Tax (GST) which has become a key revenue source. Funds flowing from the GST and a number of other sources, including the COE scheme, are now "quasi-ear-marked" to fund the planned massive increase in the public transport system (which includes a doubling of rail-based, public transport service provision). Singapore's integrated policy implementation process does not just envision increased public transport as a "fuzzy green plus" – it sees this as a "must have" factor to complement the transition to a notably lower level of private car usage (if not ownership). The aim is that by 2020, individual daily transits will average 70 per cent by public transport systems – up from 59 per cent today. Singapore is also trying to foster increased bicycle usage as part of the reform mix. Given the compact nature of the city, the generally flat terrain plus the health benefits arising from the exercise involved in cycling, this makes sense. The plans so far include creating dedicated cycling paths on a limited scale.[31]

Another crucial aspect of such integrated policy-making is that significant commercial opportunities are envisaged from this mass transition – across the economy – to much enhanced energy efficiency. The sorts of systems, technical hardware, manufacturing processes, and so on, being developed, can, it is reasoned, be packaged for export. A key substantial, export market – where some Singapore energy-enhancing systems are already being tested – is Mainland China.

Singapore's particular combination of political, economic, social and geographic factors set it apart. That said, the City-State does seem to provide some serious guidance on how, where there is real political will coupled with adequate resources, strong, considered policy making can

---

[31] *See* "Cycling in Singapore", July 23, 2010, http://cyclinginsingapore.blog spot.com/, July 29, 2010.

tackle, at a local level, the huge challenge of GHG emissions, using a multi-factor approach. And it can do so in a way which offers the potential to build a robust platform for developing an array of sturdy commercial applications.

2.5 United States of America

The United States of America (US), population over 300 million, is the single most dominant economy in the world and also the world's second greatest contributor to GHG emissions overall (after China) and the most significant contributor on a per capita basis.[32] As with the case of China, it is basically mandatory to include in a book of this type, a review of the experience of green taxation in the US. First, the US is simply so economically and environmentally important according to any global measure. Next due to its long-term, extensive policy development experience, the US is in a special position to offer lessons (both good and bad) based on its own policy building history.

Professor Janet Milne, from Vermont Law School in the US, like many of our authors, begins her chapter with an analysis of the influence of Pigouvian theory on the use of public policy instruments to shape environment-affecting behaviour. As she makes clear, much public policy aimed at rectifying particular sorts of "market failure" with market economies, builds on the key Pigouvian insight that:

> [It is] possible for the State, if it so chooses, to remove the divergence in any field [between trade and social net product] by "extraordinary encouragements" or "extraordinary restraints" upon investment in that field [giving taxation is an example].[33]

Professor Milne concentrates on the "main game in town" – the federal tax regime. She spends considerable time usefully reviewing the US experience of green taxation. She pays particular attention to the use of "tax expenditures" as well as the imposition of taxes and charges and the uses of revenues derived therefrom. Environmental tax expenditures – that is, system-granted tax concessions aimed at prompting certain kinds of environmentally positive, economic activity – have, as she explains, regularly

---

[32] Netherlands Environmental Assessment Agency, "Which are the Top-20 CO_2 or GHG Emitting Countries?", http://www.pbl.nl/en/dossiers/Climatechange/FAQs/index.html?vraag=10&title=Which%20are%20the%20top-20%20CO2%20or%20GHG%20emitting%20countries%3F#10, June 11, 2010.

[33] Pigou, *op.cit.*, page 168.

been deployed in the US. Large scale environment-based taxation measures have often proved difficult to enact. The example of President Clinton's failed attempt to introduce a broad-based energy tax in 1993 is mentioned. Other measures, introduced at a particularly "ripe time", perhaps, such as the 1978 tax on "gas guzzling" cars have become law, however.

The US, as the world's largest, richest and most diverse, fully federal system presents itself as a very special case, in many ways. Private wealth, great diversity, multitudes of energized special interests and a federally divided power structure are some of the factors which need to be taken account of when considering major policy changes in the US. These many factors rarely make for smooth implementation of new policy initiatives.

Yet, out of this very rich political experience some strong lessons emerge. Professor Milne summarizes these well. Firstly, taxation-based measures – and especially taxation impositions – are almost always the hardest of all policy instruments to use in a day-to-day political sense. Prima facie, the voting public does not like new or increased taxes. This maxim applies to environmental taxes, too. Although, as Professor Milne notes, there are various aspects of green taxes which can be used to help persuade citizens towards acceptance, including the direct environmental good they may secure and the way green taxation revenue can be earmarked for spending to generate positive environmental outcomes.

Environmental tax expenditures are notably less transparent and their fiscal impact is much more obscure to the average citizen. But these "advantages", as Professor Milne notes, often makes their positive impact much more difficult to judge. They can also readily lead to adverse "unforeseen consequences" as taxpayers "game the system" (as taxpayers are inclined to do). Next, once they are in place, a (self-serving) constituency can swiftly grow to lobby for their retention even if their policy impact is limited or negative.

Professor Milne notes that environmentally focused, direct regulatory instruments outside of the tax system altogether are the most likely to leave their full range of impacts disguised.

He also stresses the need to test the effectiveness of all policy measures which set off into the real world waving an environment-friendly flag: whether they comprise direct environmental regulation, tax expenditures or tax impositions. She also notes the need to recognize that environmental problems are often multi-faceted. It follows that solutions will often need to deploy multiple instruments. These lessons do seem to have genuine universal resonance.

Professor Milne concludes by suggesting that green taxation is likely to play a role as the world tackles the task of reducing GHG emissions

– but that the scope of that role is yet to be resolved. In Chapter 5 she makes clear that given the immense difficulties associated with using increased or new taxation measures, generally, in America, the role of green taxation looks set to be heavily constrained in future US policy development. This lesson may, however, be more a lesson for the US than a message of more universal significance. Taxpayers everywhere are usually hostile to new or more taxation. But modern experience *outside of the US* shows that advanced democracies can be persuaded to accept major new taxation initiatives as the introduction of new GST regimes in New Zealand (1986), Canada (1991), and Australia (2000) over the last 25 years demonstrates.

2.6 Canada

Canada is the second largest economy in North America. Canada joined the Group of Seven (G7) (as it became) in 1976.[34] Notwithstanding this international standing, Professor Arthur Cockfield, of Queen's University in Canada, identifies Canada as a "small open economy". This is an accurate characterization. With a population of around 35 million it is less than 12 per cent of the size of the US. Canada is also comfortably the smallest member of the (now) G8 in terms of population.

Professor Cockfield argues that small open economies are best advised to seek and foster international collective action in the quest to reduce GHG emissions and lessen the adverse impact of climate change. Canada, however, has, he argues, failed, on the whole, to adopt such an approach. Canada is a comparatively resource-rich country and it is, within the Western World, well endowed with carbon-based natural resources. The drive to exploit those resources both for domestic use and export has, thus far, tended to dominate the policy-setting agenda.

Professor Cockfield writes in his conclusion that Canada continues to struggle to find an appropriate response to concerns about global warming (notwithstanding certain green taxation initiatives at the provincial level of government). Implicit in this observation is the supposition that Canada is

---

[34] The Group of Six (G6) countries was initially an ad hoc forum established by France in 1975 for the governments of France, Germany, Italy, Japan, the UK and the US. It was subsequently institutionalized. It became the G7 when Canada joined in 1976 and the G8 when Russia joined in 1998. It was conceived as a forum comprising the major advanced democracies formed after the first "oil shock" in 1973. *See* further "The History of the G7 Summit: The Importance of American Leadership", http://www.g7.utoronto.ca/annual/bayne1997/document.html, June 11, 2010.

also constrained in its approach to green taxation in general. The factors which explain this include:

> [F]ears that a significant curtailment of emissions by, say, a carbon tax will reduce economic growth and employment. Moreover, there are reasons fairly unique to the Canadian situation that may help to explain Canadian reluctance to enact a broad-based carbon tax. For example, Canada is a northern country and the second largest country in the world with significant exploitable carbon resources. As a result, despite the growing academic and policy views that carbon taxes are best suited to reducing these emissions, the Canadian government is currently supporting a cap and trade system (similar to the proposed U.S. approach) that will likely permit certain firms to maintain high emissions for some time.

Canada, like the US, also has a federal system of government. Canada's much smaller size reduces the complexity arising therefrom compared to the US. But Canada's federal system adds a special complexity of its own related, primarily, to the presence of the Province of Quebec within that system. Quebec has a strong sense of separate identity bolstered, not least, from having French as its first language. Other Provinces in Canada, in both the west and east of the country have not infrequently, taking a lead from Quebec, tended to stress their own separate identities. Historically, this has often predisposed Canada to special difficulties in crafting taxation and other policies related to energy resources.[35]

Professor Cockfield further demonstrates how yet more limits are placed on what may be possible in terms of green taxation initiatives because of the way the Canadian economy is so closely intertwined with the US economy. Many mainstream Canadian policy makers believe that in order to maintain the vital cross-border trade and investment with the US, the Canadian tax system, *inter alia*, cannot move significantly away from the fundamental tax framework obtaining in the US.

2.7 European Union

The European Union (EU) was established by the Treaty of Maastricht in 1993, building upon the long process of post World War II, cross-national political-community building which began in Western Europe with the establishment of the European Coal and Steel Community in 1951.[36] The

---

[35] *See*, for example, Cullen, R., "Canada and Australia: A Federal Parting of Ways," *Federal Law Review*, Volume 18, 1989, page 53.
[36] "European Union", *CIA – The World Fact Book,* https://www.cia.gov/library/publications/the-world-factbook/geos/ee.html, June 12, 2010.

EU does not qualify to be called a federation as this term is commonly understood. Yet it is far more than a free trade association or some type of purely international association of Nation States. It has its own array of significant executive, legislative and judicial institutions, its own currency and anthem and flag, for example.[37]

The EU is a unique political entity, one which now has 27 distinct Nation States as members, a population of over 500 million and, if taken in totality, it comprises the single largest economy in the world. The EU is, to an extent, a single economy but, even more so, it remains an agglomeration of 27 still separated economies.[38]

In Chapter 7, looking at the EU experience with green taxation, Mattias Derlén and Johan Lindholm, from Umea University in Sweden, provide a clear analysis of why the evolved EU structure has, to a significant extent, reduced the role which taxation can play in addressing environmental challenges. The problem, as they describe it, is, first, that the highly complex EU structure largely places direct taxation measures outside the scope of (centralized) EU decision-making: control of taxation is primarily left with the EU Member States.

Next, however, the EU has an overarching commitment to maximizing economic harmonization within the EU as one of its core functions. The quest to achieve this imposes real restrictions on how Member States may deploy their taxation powers. Thus, there is an EU-wide ban on discriminatory or protective taxes which could adversely affect the EU internal free market. Taxes which might be introduced at the national level with the best intentions in terms of environment-enhancement can still readily be challenged in court, with a real risk that they may be struck down in part or altogether for violating the EU-wide harmonizing exhortations just noted.

Non-tax measures directly aimed at environment protection can also swiftly fall foul of the stipulation that, prima facie, trade must not be impeded. Thus, in the *Danish Bottles* case, the European Court of Justice found that environmental protection could justify imposing certain obstacles to trade – but any such obstacles had to be proportionate and, in this case, they were not.[39]

The two authors provide an array of examples in Chapter 7 of the genuine difficulties which the EU's constitutional structure has imposed

---

[37]   *Ibid.*

[38]   *Ibid.*

[39]   Case 302/86, *Commission of the European Communities v Kingdom of Denmark* [1988] ECR, 4607.

on both taxation-based and other regulatory measures designed to achieve environment-friendly outcomes. They conclude by noting that, without question, implementing green taxes at the EU level is notably more difficult than using non-tax-based EU measures to foster stronger protection of the environment.

At the national level, the reverse is generally true; the EU Member States can develop and apply green taxes. But they still will need to be well crafted and administered to ensure that they do not breach any aspects of the wide assortment of EU directives aimed at preventing discriminatory or protective taxation. The authors note, in this regard, that Sweden's own carbon tax, which has operated since 1991, has proved that national green taxes can work within the EU constitutional framework. This tax has survived Sweden's admission to the EU in 1995. (In fact, the impact of this relatively early carbon tax has, overall, been reduced over the time since its inception through the introduction of special exemptions for certain export-focused industries.)

After reading the chapters on the EU and the US, there is a similar impression that the EU and the US are rather special cases where the deployment of green taxation measures may be more constrained than elsewhere in the developed world – fundamentally because of the political, size-complexity factors applying.

2.8   Australia

Australia, like the US and Canada, has what can be termed a classical federal system of government. The central or federal government is based in Canberra. Both the federal government and the six constituent States with which it co-exists are constitutionally entrenched entities. However, Australia has a federal system where the central government is the overwhelmingly dominant political entity within the federation. This centralizing tendency gathered serious momentum as the nation – and the High Court of Australia – responded to the impact of World War I and its immediate aftermath.[40] It is a process which has been steadily sustained since that time.[41] In 2006, in the *Work Choices* case, certain remaining major constraints on federal government power (the limitation of what

---

[40]   Galligan, B., *Politics of the High Court*, University of Queensland Press, 1987.

[41]   *Ibid. See also* Cullen, R., "Australian Federalism: Its Provenance and Its Prognosis" in P. Häberle, *Jahrbuch des Öffentlichen Rechts der Gegenwart*, J.C.B. Mohr (Paul Siebeck), 1992, page 723.

sort of activities undertaken by corporations could be federally regulated) were largely lifted.[42]

One commentator put the standing of the Australian federal system in the *Work Choices* case in this way:

> In conclusion, the Court's endorsement [in the *Work Choices* case] of an object of command test, the support it gives to laws that regulate the activities of constitutional corporations, and the expansive approach which it adopted to the validity of laws that regulate those whose conduct is or "is capable of affecting" the activities, functions, relationships or business of a constitutional corporation equips the Commonwealth with power to regulate across an enormous range of subject matters, given the ubiquitous role of corporations in our daily lives. The issue is not whether the Commonwealth has the constitutional power to regulate, but whether it has the political desire and will to do so.[43]

Australia is, then, notably less beset by the division of power complexities evident in the federal systems in Canada and the US, discussed above. As the joint authors of Chapter 8 on Australia (Professor Natalie Stoianoff (University of Technology, Sydney) and Wayne Gumley (Monash University, Melbourne) show, however, this comparative enhancement of central power has not produced a well-focused, environmentally positive approach to green taxation.

To be fair, the very complex tax (and tax expenditure) infrastructure put in place in Australia has taken decades to construct. And for much of the time that this rather amazing fiscal and related policy matrix was evolving, the powers of the federal government were circumscribed by a division of power regime then more favourable to the States.

In a comprehensive chapter, Gumley and Stoianoff set a strongly detailed discussion of the relevant Australian experience within a helpful outline of the major international agreements related to GHG emissions and climate change. The chapter also includes an informing discussion of the long-debated comparative merits of Pigouvian-tax-based systems compared to Coase-based emissions-trading systems.[44] The chapter also

---

42   *New South Wales v Commonwealth of Australia* [2006] HCA 52.

43   Applegarth, P., "The Work Choices Case: Corporations Power Aspects", (paper presented at Constitutional Law Conference 2007, Gilbert & Tobin Centre of Public Law, University of New South Wales), http://www.gtcentre.unsw.edu.au/publications/papers/docs/2007/153_PeterApplegarth.pdf , June 13, 2010.

44   Pigouvian systems (already discussed) simply put, aim to internalize "external costs" by imposing a balancing tax or charge on, for example, polluting externalities, *see* Pigou, *op.cit.*; and Baumol, W. J. and Oates, W. E., "The Use of Standards and Prices for Protection of the Environment", *Swedish Journal of Economics*, Volume 73, 1971, page 42. The foundations for a property rights/

discusses the basic market-based trading systems: cap and trade versus baseline and credit.

The history of Australia's initial sceptical approach to the Kyoto Protocol is explained as is Australia's later ratification of the Kyoto Protocol, following a change of federal government, in 2007. Within a year of this ratification, the new Rudd Government had released the "Garnaut Report" and then a White Paper which set out the design features for a comprehensive emissions trading scheme. From this emerged, in May 2009, a set of bills to enact the Carbon Pollution Reduction Scheme (CPRS). The Upper House of the Australian Parliament (the Senate) where the Rudd Government did not have a majority, rejected the CPRS twice – in August 2009 and again in December 2009. Subsequently the government announced that further consideration of the CPRS would be postponed until 2012 – until after the expiry of the Kyoto Protocol commitment period.

The authors explain that the CPRS had broad coverage and sound international integration. But it was also noteworthy (and heavily criticized by many) for its significant concessions to major existing CO_2 generators.

In the latter part of the chapter, the authors set out the astonishing assortment of entrenched – mainly tax-related – impediments to any reforms designed to deal with GHG emissions in Australia. What emerges is an immensely complex mix of primarily federal but also State-sourced taxes, charges and tax expenditures which all have, at least in part, environment-related impact. The Garnaut Report flagged that it was important that this thicket of barriers to reform be addressed. Briefly, special concessions in the tax regime for real estate investment; employer-provided cars and rural fuel tax credits have created tax-driven incentives for activities which all bolster GHG emissions. Predictably, most of these long-established concessions have well-organized, politically vocal, lobby groups focused on resisting all measures which might reduce the perceived benefits.

Tax expenditures, measures embodied in tax legislation which reduce or forgo certain taxes to encourage certain behaviour have been with us for many decades. A long-standing example which can be found in most tax systems is allowing a deduction from income for gifts made to certain, recognized charities. As the authors explain, tax expenditures in Australia

---

trading-based system for addressing the problem of externalities is commonly traced to the 1960 seminal article by Robert Coase where he urges reliance on market-based mechanisms, *see* Coase, R., "The Problem of Social Cost", *Journal of Law and Economics*, Volume 3, 1960, page 1.

now cost the public purse over A$100 billion – or 8.5 per cent of GDP. Worse still, Australia continues to lack robust institutional means to highlight – and provoke proper examination of – the detailed high cost of these massive concessions.

A generous view of the tale told in Chapter 8 is that tackling GHG emissions in Australia remains a work in progress. A less charitable view is that reforms designed to tackle climate change in Australia are very badly bogged down in a rather vast swamp which marries a complex (and combative) political system with a tax system notable for its awesome intricacy.

The authors conclude with an outline of some lessons which can be drawn from the relevant Australian experience in the area of green taxation. First, the attempts to achieve GHG reductions using voluntary or persuasive mechanisms simply have not worked in Australia. Next, introducing market-based measures (such as the CPRS) can be extremely difficult where one is trying to mesh that with a complex tax system. Almost certainly, highly organized and numerous vested interests will organize to protect their favoured patch within the existing tax regime. Finally, few parts of any given tax system are more deserving of forensic scrutiny than tax expenditures – yet, for the most part, such expenditures thrive year after year far removed from mainstream political scrutiny. Specific measures, noted in the chapter, can tackle this quite central tax design problem, however.

In summary, Australia stands out more than it should, perhaps, as an example of how to build a tax regime that combines high compliance costs, immense complexity and deeply embedded barriers to reform. It is worth remembering, however, that, despite this reality, Australia still managed to achieve a high degree of comprehensive tax reform based around the introduction of GST just over a decade ago.

2.9 New Zealand

In certain ways, the final chapter in this book is particularly significant. New Zealand is comparatively small in terms of both population (4.3 million approximately) and also area (around 270,000 square kilometers) and it is more geographically isolated than any other part of the developed world.[45] Yet as Shelley Griffiths (University of Otago) shows in her

---

[45]   New Zealand is located some 2000 kilometres southeast of Australia – which itself is regarded as being comparatively separated from the rest of the developed world, especially.

informative Chapter 9, New Zealand has, since the 1980s, completed a remarkable level of taxation policy reflection *and reform* and this process has included significant deliberation about the role of green taxation. Although, once again, local political-economy factors have deeply shaped this reform process, the ongoing New Zealand "fiscal experiment" has produced statements of policy principle and broad policy commentary which are of general significance.

No other developed jurisdiction has completed so much recent remaking of their tax regime as New Zealand. Being small, stable and relatively homogenous helps to explain some of why this is so. Some key political-economic turning points also need to be noted, however. In the immediate post World War II period, New Zealand grew increasingly prosperous – but off a narrow base. Most of all, it relied on its highly efficient agricultural export sector to power the economy – plus (like in Australia) a raft of protectionist subsidies and other measures which helped to spread the prosperity within a highly controlled, internal economy.

The economic wheels began to "wobble badly", however, when the largest export market, the UK, finally joined the European Common Market (EEC) in 1973.[46] To make matters worse, this happened just as the First Oil Shock, arising from the Arab Oil Embargo hit, following the Yom Kippur War in 1973.[47] New Zealand was severely distressed by the resulting huge increase in the price of oil: it had no significant, known petroleum resources and its geographic isolation made it heavily reliant on access to long-distance transportation. These and related experiences fairly swiftly (in political-time) led to a radical rethinking of the fundamentals of the New Zealand economy.[48]

---

[46]   Nixon, C. and Yeabsley, J., "Overseas Trade Policy – New Zealand, Britain and the EEC" in *Te Ara – the Encyclopedia of New Zealand,* http://www.teara. govt.nz/en/overseas-trade-policy/4, June 14, 2010. Various initial concessions were negotiated with the EEC (a predecessor of the EU) but these faded with time: the UK took 53 per cent of all New Zealand (almost all agricultural) exports in 1960. This figure dropped to 36 per cent in 1970 and around 5 per cent by 2007. *Ibid.*

[47]   For a well-regarded account of the political and economic history of the global oil industry, *see* Yergin D., *The Prize: The Epic Quest for Oil, Money, and Power*, Simon & Schuster, 1991. This book covers the period from 1850 to 1990, with significant analysis of both the First Oil Shock brought on by the unsuccessful Arab Coalition attack on Israel in the Yom Kippur War in 1973 and the Second Oil Shock in 1979, which followed from the overthrow of the Shah of Iran in early 1979.

[48]   The Treasury, "Final Report – Tax Review 2001", October 24, 2001, http://www.treasury.govt.nz/publications/reviews-consultation/taxreview2001/tax review2001-report.pdf, June 14, 2010. Pages 5–17 describe the pre-1984 regime and the changes to it.

The old (UK-dependent) economic model was almost entirely rejected. This had wide-ranging effects, not least for the New Zealand taxation system. The new "tax mantra" which remains determinative today is that New Zealand should stay committed to a "broad-based, low-rate" tax system. The main focus of the reform process was on broadening the tax base and lowering marginal rates of tax, as Shelley Griffiths notes. The three main tax bases were defined as personal income, company income and goods and services consumption (New Zealand introduced a GST in 1986 as a component in the process of fundamental economic reform). New Zealand still has no Capital Gains Tax. Griffiths goes on to make a critical point: a key feature of the old, explicitly rejected system was that the tax system had been widely used, over time, to provide incentives or concessions for activities which were seen, over the longer term, to have social or economic merit. But as the reform process gathered momentum, a powerful belief established itself, that any use of the tax system as a primary policy tool to try and foster or reward particular behaviour had, in future to be approached with extreme caution. Almost all such past measures were seen to have failed the now critical test of "tax efficiency". They also did not measure up well according to the modern tests of tax simplicity and tax equity.

There have been two major government-initiated, committee-based reviews of the New Zealand tax system, post reform in 2001 and 2009. The first committee, the McLeod Committee, released its final report in 2001, shortly before New Zealand ratified the Kyoto Protocol (in 2002). The committee knew that ratification was likely and it recommended the introduction of a broad-based carbon tax, as the key measure to allow New Zealand to meet its Kyoto Protocol obligations (related to controlling GHG emissions). The carbon tax, which was to be revenue neutral, was felt to provide a better approach than relying on a cap and trade, Emissions Trading System (ETS). As it happens, the committee specifically rejected the use of widely applied eco-taxes and behaviour modification taxes in general. They failed, above all, the crucial tax efficiency test, it was argued. Such taxes were, by now, seen to be "tainted" by their close association with the pre-1980s policies which, over several decades, had help to create an economy which grimly evolved, in the eyes of many, into a complex, protected, failure.

The government, acting on this recommendation, finalized the details of the proposed new, general carbon tax by 2005. Serious difficulties with implementation swiftly emerged. Because of the continuing high efficiency (and international competitiveness) of the agriculture sector, New Zealand relies more than most of any other developed economy, on animal-based exports. The very high populations of sheep (33 million) and cattle (10 million) mean that animal-generated methane makes up a remarkably high, 35 per cent of all New Zealand's GHG emissions. The fervent opposition of the powerful farming industry resulted in the carbon tax proposal being modified to exempt methane emissions from animals.

A new, inter-departmental review committee was formed in 2005. Its deliberations led it to conclude that, for a range of reasons, the previously rejected ETS option was now the best way forward. By the end of 2005, the government announced that they were not going to proceed with the carbon tax after all. Since the enactment of the ETS in 2008, it, too, has come in for much review and criticism. Now a number of significant stakeholders are arguing for a carbon tax once more: a tax-based system is more certain and predictable, they say.

New Zealand is a unitary (non-federal) state. It has a British-style, parliamentary system of government. It also only has a single house within the parliament. All these features suggest that, institutionally, policy development and implementation should be able to proceed more smoothly than in other jurisdictions with more complex, democratic political structures. However, in 1996 (following a referendum) the previously used "First Past the Post" (FPP) voting system (which strongly favoured the two largest parties) was replaced by what is known as a Mixed Member Proportional (MMP) voting system. Since then, New Zealand has had a series of coalition governments. This has made policy implementation subject to much greater negotiation and, normally, significantly more difficult to implement than was the case when the FPP system prevailed. A further referendum asking whether the current MMP system should continue and, if not, what might replace it is now planned.

New Zealand has, over the last three decades, provided a "working laboratory study" of real tax reform being developed and applied – and revised. One thing the New Zealand, real-life tax policy experience suggests is that you can always rely on the "Law of Unintended Consequences" to apply itself to any and every reform initiative. In other words, those pursuing reform should expect outcomes (both adverse and sometimes positive) not originally planned for and be ready to react in a sound and timely way.

There looks, also, to be a message about the wisdom of using past experience to close off, too quickly, options for today and a possible further message about the need to allow sufficient time for reform initiatives to take full root and have a settled effect.

3. PRELIMINARY OBSERVATIONS

It is clear both from the comparative input and direct discussion in this book that Mainland China and Hong Kong each badly need to build and deploy superior policies to deal with an array of immense environmental challenges including GHG emissions.

The serious faltering of the globalized, emissions trading model favoured in the Kyoto Protocol, especially post-Copenhagen, has led to policy makers around the world taking a fresh look at alternative strategies for tackling massive and serious, environmentally bad behaviour.[49]

Green taxation does not provide any sort of one-stop solution for dealing with GHG emissions. Nor can we hope that it will single-handedly stop and then reverse the collective human behaviour responsible for degradation of air and water quality, for example, across the globe. Green taxation can play a significant role in helping to meet these challenges, however. That this is now more widely recognized, after Copenhagen, is a good thing.

The jurisdictional reviews in the following chapters are valuable and varied. They offer a wide range of comparative perspectives which can help to inform green taxation policy development and implementation in East Asia.

It is worth noting that our authors show how, ultimately, tax policy is always closely shaped by local political, economic and social circumstances. For example:

- What sort of basic political structure is in place – to what degree does it add layers of complexity to high-level decision making?
- What are the embedded economic interests – and how strong are they in terms of shaping overall public policy?
- What sort of timeframes are realistic for testing out new green taxation policies?
- What sort of green taxes look to be core required taxes?
- How can green taxation policies best be integrated with other, related, regulatory measures?

---

[49] Following the completion of the UN Climate Conference in Cancun, Mexico, in December, 2010, restrained optimism has emerged that the UN negotiating process related to GHGs and climate change has regained some level of rehabilitated acceptance. *See*, for example: "Back from the Brink", *The Economist*, December 18, 2010, page 113, and "China Plays a Quiet Hand but Some Good Cards at Cancun", *Sunday Examiner*, December 24, 2010, page 4.

- What sort of earmarking or hypothecation of green taxation revenues should be looked at?

The following chapters present many good lessons about what to do – and what not to do – as these and other related questions are being addressed. The ensuing deliberations also often foreshadow a need to expect the unexpected once new green taxation policies are put into place – and make ready to respond swiftly and thoughtfully when this happens.

2. Environmental taxation in China: the case of transport fuel taxation

Yan Xu*

1. INTRODUCTION

In the 1960s, due to rapid industrial development, a series of grave environmental pollution accidents occurred in a number of countries. Man-made environmental harm in many regions of the earth, such as dangerous water and air pollution, and destruction and depletion of irreplaceable resources, has posed a major threat to the existence and development of mankind. We have begun to face increasingly severe environmental problems. In 1972, the United Nations Environment Program (UNEP) adopted the Declaration of the United Nations Conference on the Human Environment (The Stockholm Declaration), which, for the first time, raised concerns about the preservation and enhancement of the human environment for the purpose of development of mankind. In 1987, the World Commission on Environment and Development published a report called Our Common Future (The Report). The Report recaptured the spirit of The Stockholm Declaration and helped make the concept of environmentally sustainable development widely accepted, in principle, at least, by many countries. The shorthand characterization of sustainable development means development that meets the needs of the present without compromising the ability of future generations to meet their own needs. The Report called for collective action by all national states to participate in finding solutions to the "tragedy of the commons".

Among various measures for protecting the environment and fairly distributing natural resources across regions and generations, taxation can serve as an important instrument to help achieve this goal. The economic rationale of environmental taxes or green taxes often rests on what Pigou, a British economist, says about the negative externalities,

* The author would like to thank Professor Richard Cullen for his helpful comments. The author also would like to thank the participants at the Green

which are caused by pollution or the misuse of resources.[1] The existence of negative externalities can lead to market failures, for instance, when a company produces too much and at prices too low for the efficient allocation of resources in the economy. Pigou came up with the notion that taxes could be used to combat negative externalities, and in comparison with the alternative measure, regulation, taxes raise revenue and respond automatically to such market changes as the lowered cost of production, as well as providing incentives to reduce pollution.[2] Pigou's idea laid the theoretical foundation for the application of green taxation in many countries today.

Taxation Conference held by the Taxation Law Research Programme of the HKU Faculty of Law's Asian Institute of International Financial Law (AIIFL). A revised version of this chapter was published in *Fordham Environmental Law Review*, Volume 21, Number 2, 2010, pp.295–343.

[1] Pigou, A.C. (1877–1959) is best known for his work in welfare economics. In his book *The Economics of Welfare*, he developed Alfred Marshall's concept of externalities, i.e., costs imposed or benefits conferred on others that are not taken into account by the person taking the action. Pigou maintains that governments can, through a mixture of taxes and subsidies, correct such market failure or "internalize the externalities". These taxes and subsidies are now called Pigouvian taxes and subsidies, respectively. Pigou's analysis was later on attacked by Ronald Coase and Public Choice theorists and other economists as well. However, many economists still advocate Pigouvian taxes as a more efficient way of dealing with pollution than government standards. *See* Pigou, A.C., *The Economics of Welfare*, Macmillan, (4th ed.), 1932; *see* also The Concise Encyclopedia of Economics, "Arthur Cecil Pigou", http://www.econlib.org/library/Enc/bios/Pigou.html, May 13, 2010; and The History of Economic Thought, "Arthur Cecil Pigou", http://homepage.newschool.edu/het//profiles/pigou.htm, May 13, 2010. An externality "is a cost or benefit arising from an economic transaction that falls on a third party and that is not taken into account by those who undertake the transaction." Externalities may take two forms: negative externality (external costs) and positive externality (external benefits). A negative externality exists where consumption or production of a good generates a cost borne by someone outside of the production or consumption of that good. A positive externality occurs where benefits accrues to someone outside of the production or consumption of a good. *See* McTaggart, D., Findlay, C., and Parki, M., *Economics*, Addison Wesley Publishers Ltd, 1992, page 467; Katz, M., and Rosen, H., *Microeconomics*, Irwin Inc., (2nd ed.), 1991, page 611; Leftwich, R. and Eckert, R., *The Price System and Resource Allocation*, The Dryden Press, (9th ed.), 1985, pages 594, 596. Cited in Gibson, H., "Externalities: Implications for Allocative Efficiency and Suggested Solutions", http://users.hunterlink.net.au/~ddhrg/econ/ext1.html, May 13, 2010.

[2] The Pigouvian tax can be understood to mean that some form of state intervention is necessary to correct market failures. *See* Määttä, K., *Environmental Taxes: An Introductory Analysis*, Edward Elgar, 2006, page 4. Basic economic theory recognizes the existence of externalities and their potential negative effects. To the extent that green taxes correct for externalities such as pollution, they

China has also developed significant policies to address environmental and development issues. Contrary to the common view, a variety of domestic programs and policies relating to the environment and natural resources have been formulated and applied seriously by the government in recent years. The central government has put environmental protection at the centre of its macro-policy-making to achieve sustainable economic growth. Although strictly speaking, environmental taxes have not been applied in China, an environmentally-related tax and charge system has been implemented in China for some years.[3] The difficulties of introducing a comprehensive environmental taxation system are caused by various factors, such as the zealotry for economic growth of local governments and conflicting interests produced by the de facto "fiscal federalism" in taxation.[4] This chapter is focused on issues of green taxation in China. Section 2 provides an overview of the concept of green taxes, the current tax law system regarding the environment and resources, and environmental problems in China. Section 3 examines the possibility of applying a consolidated fuel tax in China,[5] beginning with a discussion of the existing tax and charge system on the consumption of petroleum-based products and usage of vehicles. Section 4 goes further to discuss how to impose

---

correspond with mainstream economic theory. In practice, however, setting the correct taxation level or the tax collection system is difficult, and may lead to further distortions or unintended consequences.

[3]   The concept of environmental taxes or green taxes is given below in Section 2. For the general definition and definition within Chinese law context, *see* Part 2.1 of Section 2.

[4]   China is a unitary state. The taxing power is centralized in the central government. But the 1994 tax reform introduced a tax-sharing system and separated tax administration into central and local. For an overview of China's administrative division system, tax administration structure and tax-sharing system, *see* Figure 2.1, 2.2 and Table 2.3 in the Appendix. In political-economic discussion about China, the terms, "central government" and "local government" are typically used to mean the central government in Beijing, and local governments at and below the provincial level, which includes all governments at different levels.

[5]   A fuel tax is also known as a petrol tax, gasoline tax, or a fuel duty. In most countries, it is primarily imposed on and collected from fuel which is intended for road transportation. Fuel is also used for sea transport, industrial production, household heating, and domestic aviation. Such uses are, however, typically taxed at a different, usually lower, rate. This chapter concentrates on discussing road transport fuel taxation including taxes and charges applying to transport fuel (and vehicles). Viewpoints expressed in this chapter may be applied to taxes on the use of fuel in sectors other than transport in the future in China, however. "Consolidated fuel taxation" in this chapter thus means an imposition system bringing all taxes and charges related to the use or consumption of road transport fuel into a single system.

a consolidated fuel tax in China. By drawing on the experience of some developed countries and regions like the UK and Hong Kong, this chapter proposes that in order to introduce such a tax to China, basic issues like the tax base, tax rate, imposition principles and tax administration need to be carefully examined. Section 5 provides the conclusion.

2.   AN OVERVIEW: CONCEPT AND LEGAL FRAMEWORK OF GREEN TAXATION

2.1   What is an Environmental Tax

2.1.1   General definition

Green taxes, also called environmental taxes, pollution taxes, ecological taxes, Pigouvian taxes and ecotaxes,[6] have not been defined unambiguously and unanimously. There have been attempts to create general definitions, for instance, the Organisation for Economic Co-operation and Development (OECD) refers to a green tax as "a tax based on polluting emissions (for example, biological oxygen demand (BOD) discharges) or on disamenities expressed by some appropriate method of measurement (for example, an index of annoyance) or on other parameters such as inputs".[7] The scope of green taxes depends on the specific environmental goal of the taxes. If environment is broadly defined, part of the excise tax on alcohol (in terms of its effect on the social environment), and taxes on tobacco (in terms of improving the air quality of non-smokers), could be perhaps defined as green taxes. Many green taxes are related to pollution, that is, they aim at reducing sulphur dioxide and carbon dioxide emissions, waste and other pollutants in the environment. Moreover, green taxes may be associated with resource utilization, including the use of land or water resources. In this sense, the term "green tax" is an umbrella concept for two kinds of tax, a pollution tax and a resource tax. The broadest definition of green taxes encompass all the taxes that are related to the environment and natural resources, as well as government's tax policies that may have an effect on the environment because those taxes shape certain economic activities.

It is worth noting that there are considerable differences between green taxes and charges. Taxes are unrequited payments in which benefits

---

[6]   Määttä, *op. cit.*, page 15.
[7]   Organisation for Economic Co-operation and Development (OECD), *Pollution Charges in Practice*, OECD Publications and Information Centre, 1980. Cited in Määttä, *op. cit.*, page 15.

provided by governments to taxpayers are not normally in proportion to their payment. Charges are paid by individuals and companies to authorities in return for services received. The revenue generated by green taxes goes to the general budget or is earmarked for a broad range of environmental expenditures. Green charges can roughly be divided into user and administrative charges. User charges have been defined as payments to meet the costs of the collective or public treatment of effluent and waste, whereas administrative charges are payments to authorities for services rendered, for example, for the registration of chemicals and enforcement of regulations. Administrative charges have been divided into license fees and registration or control fees.[8] Nonetheless, it is difficult to draw the borderline between green taxes and green charges precisely.

From a fiscal point of view, green taxes have a double-dividend gain under certain conditions. In addition to increasing welfare due to lower pollution externalities, a "green" dividend, green taxes raise revenues that can be used to lower other pre-existing tax distortions, resulting in welfare gains from a smaller deadweight loss of the tax system, or an "efficiency" dividend.[9] As some economists have said, green taxes stand out from ordinary taxation in that they have the potential to improve the efficiency of the tax system and the wider economy by improving resource allocation. Taxes that encourage better environmental outcomes contribute to sustainability and inter-generational equity, and may often benefit disadvantaged groups of society. For example, a tax differential discouraging the use of leaded petrol contributes to improved air quality and child health outcomes in poor urban areas. It is also clear that some potential green taxes may widen the revenue base and raise significant amounts of revenue, allowing less desirable taxes to be reduced or removed.[10]

The notion of a double dividend for the environment and the economy, even if controversial on theoretical grounds could be an important pillar in promoting fiscal reform. This implies that the environmental effects of fiscal reform should be taken into account from the outset. In the

---

[8] Määttä, *op. cit.*, pages 17–19.
[9] Goulder, L.H., "Environmental Taxation and the Double Dividend: A Reader's Guide", *International Tax and Public Finance*, Volume 2, 1995, pages 157–84; McCoy, D., "Reflections on the Double Dividend Debate" in T. O'Riordan, *Ecotaxation*, Earthscan Publications, 1997, pages 201–214. Cited in Määttä, *op. cit.*, page 87. Bovenberg, A. L., "Green Tax Reforms and the Double Dividend: an Updated Reader's Guide", *International Tax and Public Finance,* Volume 6, pages 421–43.
[10] "China Considers Levying Environmental Tax on Polluters", *Beijing Today*, October 19, 2007, http://bjtoday.ynet.com/article.jsp?oid=24783901&pageno=1, May 13, 2010.

meantime, the introduction of green taxes should be supported by a reduction in distortionary taxes. In this manner general welfare could be increased and negative distributional impacts avoided.

2.1.2 Definition within the Chinese law context

Currently, there are no green taxes in a strict sense in China, though China's tax system applies several categories of taxes related to environmental resources. Under China's existing tax law system, the term "green taxes" or "environmental taxes" is used in this chapter as a generic term for taxes associated with natural resources and the environment.

As with many other countries, taxes and charges are considered two different concepts in China. A tax is levied on the community as a whole, regardless of who captures the benefits of the public goods and services funded thereby. The revenue from taxes goes into the general budget. By contrast, a charge is (at least in theory) imposed on specific beneficiaries in proportion to the services they personally receive. The revenue collected is used for defined purposes. As a result, the application method and the revenue destination which apply to taxes and charges are different in China.

This chapter is focused on green taxes but it also looks at some environmentally-related charges. Although pollution charges are not regarded as a pollution tax by the government, a pollution levy system has been applied in China since 1982.[11] This has played a positive role in reducing pollution and financing environmental protection investments. The levy system has undergone substantial reform recently in order to adapt it to the conditions of a deepening market economy and the new environmental objectives.[12] As reform progresses in this area it would be desirable for most (if not all) pollution charges to be converted to pollution taxes (based on volume, usage, and so on).

---

[11] In 1982, the State Council promulgated the Provisional Method on the Imposing of Pollution Charges. In 1988, the State Council issued the Provisional Method on the Paid Use of Special Funds on Abatement of Pollutant Sources. These two administrative regulations have been replaced with the Regulations on the Collection and Use of Pollution Charges issued by the State Council in 2003.

[12] According to some studies, prior to the recent reform in 2003, the previous levy system had some critical problems, such as no consideration of total amount of pollution discharged, too-low rate schedules on pollutions, and lack of control over the charge yields. Wang, J. N., Ge, C. Z., and Yang, J. T., "Taxation and the Environment in China: Practice and Perspectives" in the OECD, *Environmental Taxes: Recent Developments in China and OECD Countries*, OECD, 1999, pages 83–4, 90. These problems were caused by the ambiguity of relevant regulations and rules as well as other factors. The 2003 reform has addressed some of these problems.

2.2   The Legal System Governing Environmentally-Related Taxes in China

China undertook a major tax reform in 1994, resulting in a policy framework that is more consistent with the needs of a market-based economy. Five environmentally-related taxes have been introduced to China, that is, resource tax, consumption tax, vehicle tax, urban construction and maintenance tax, and land use tax (see Table 2.4 in the Appendix to this chapter). They each have a direct or indirect relationship with environmental protection.

Specifically, the resource tax was adopted on 1 October 1984 as part of the 1984 tax reform. From the beginning of 1994, a new Provisional Regulations on Resource Tax replaced the old regulations.[13] The new regulations govern the imposition of tax on mineral resources in a broad sense and salt. Taxable mineral products include crude oil, natural gas, coal, metal mineral products and other non-metal mineral products. The amount of tax payable by a specific taxpayer, for example a coal mine operator, is dependent, in the main, on the resource type and it is independent of the environmental effects of resource uses such as atmospheric pollution caused by the combustion of high sulphur coal.

The consumption tax was introduced to China's tax system during the 1994 tax reform, which purported to constrain consumption of certain goods as well as modify behavior and at the same time raise tax revenues. The Provisional Regulations on Consumption Tax promulgated by the State Council in 1993 were amended at the end of 2008. The tax is imposed on fourteen types of consumer goods. Taxable items related to the environment include petrol, diesel, aviation kerosene, automobile tires, motorcycles, cars, yachts, disposable wooden chopsticks, and tobacco, wine and liquor. Since energy consumption and vehicle use are closely related to air pollution, the most serious environmental problem in China, I will return to review the consumption tax on fuel and vehicles in detail in Section 3.

The vehicle tax is composed of the vehicle acquisition tax and the vehicle (and vessel) tax. The vehicle acquisition tax applies to vehicles purchased that are specified as taxable vehicles according to the Provisional Regulations on Vehicle Acquisition Tax.[14] This tax is administered by the State Administration of Taxation (SAT, see Figure 2.2 in the Appendix

---

[13]   The Provisional Regulations on Resource Tax were promulgated by the State Council on December 25, 1993 and effective on January 1, 1994.

[14]   The Provisional Regulations on Vehicle Acquisition Tax were issued by the State Council on October 22, 2000 and effective January 1, 2001.

to this chapter) and, accordingly, the tax revenue belongs to the central government, being used specifically for traffic construction work. Motor cars, motorcycles, trams, trailers, and transportation vehicles for farm use constitute taxable vehicles. The tax is payable by the acquirer upon acquisition. Acquisition occurs when taxpayers obtain vehicles through purchase, importation, self-production, or as a gift. The applicable tax rate is 10 per cent of the vehicle value and the tax is paid in one lump sum. The tax should be paid to the relevant tax authorities at the location where the vehicle is registered. Where vehicles need not be registered (for example, where a vehicle is being used only on a farm and there is no need to apply for a vehicle license plate),[15] taxpayers should report and pay the tax to the relevant tax authorities at the location where the taxpayer is situated. It is required that taxpayers pay tax upon acquisition before registering their vehicles with the vehicle administration division of the public security department.

The vehicle (and vessel) tax is applied to specific types of vehicles and it is administered by local tax bureaus (see Figure 2.2 in the Appendix to this chapter). The main purpose of this tax is to provide funds for local governments to upgrade local public roads and maintain the infrastructure. The Provisional Regulations on Vehicle and Vessel Tax replaced the old regulations on vehicle and vessel usage tax, as well as the vehicle and vessel usage license tax.[16] In general, the tax is levied on motor vehicles (and vessels), and the tax rate is calculated either according to the number of taxable vehicles, or according to the net-weight capacity of the taxable vehicles. Passenger vehicles and motorcycles are taxed per item. The annual tax payment for the former is from RMB 60 to 660 depending on the specific size of the vehicle and for the latter it is from RMB 36 to 180. Cargo vehicles and motor-tricycles are taxed according to per ton of net load capacity. The annual tax payment for the former is from RMB 16 to 120, and for the latter is from RMB 24 to 120.

The urban construction and maintenance tax has been applied since 1 January 1985. It is a local tax, which is levied for the purpose of expanding

---

[15] Rules on Motor Vehicles Registration, Article 5. The Rules were issued by the Ministry of Public Security of the People's Republic of China (PRC), amended on April 21, 2008 and effective on October 1, 2008.

[16] The Regulations were issued by the State Council on December 29, 2006, which came into effect from January 1, 2007. Accordingly, the Provisional Regulations on Vehicle and Vessel Usage License Tax promulgated in 1951 and the Provisional Regulations on Vehicle and Vessel Usage Tax promulgated in 1986 ceased to have effect. It should be noted that the 2007 Regulations will soon be replaced by the Law on Vehicle and Vessel Tax passed by the National People's Congress Standing Committee (NPCSC) from January 1, 2012.

and stabilizing the source of funds for urban infrastructure such as housing, road and bridge maintenance, flood prevention structures, water supply and drainage, afforestation and environmental sanitation. Those who are obliged to pay value-added tax (VAT), consumption tax and business tax are subject to the tax. Tax payable is calculated on the basis of the actual amount of VAT, consumption tax and business tax paid by the taxpayers. Rates vary depending on whether the taxpayers are located in cities (7 per cent), counties and towns (5 per cent), or other areas (1 per cent). The tax is a kind of "green" tax because revenues from the tax have become an important source for investment in environmental protection, in particular in the improvement of urban air and water quality undertaken by local authorities.

The land-use tax includes the city and township land use tax and farm land occupation tax. The city and township land use tax, imposed according to the Provisional Regulations on City and Township Land Use Tax,[17] is aimed at promoting effective use of urban land resources and to adjust differential rents of urban land. The taxpayers are the enterprises and individuals who use land in cities, counties, towns, and dedicated industrial and mining areas. Revenues from the tax belong to local government. This tax has generated less than 1 per cent of overall tax revenue since its imposition. Not surprisingly, this tax has had little effect on protecting urban land resources and promoting efficiency in land use. It is in fact a small tax type that supplements the funds for local governments. The farm land occupation tax was introduced in April 1987, and it underwent reform in December 2007.[18] The amount of tax levied varies across provincial regions according to the local average occupation of farm land and the level of economic development. Although tax revenues account for a small portion in the total revenues, the tax has proved effective in controlling, to a degree, arbitrary occupations and misuse of farm land.

Apart from the above taxes, a nation-wide pollution charge system has been applied for over two decades in China (as noted earlier). The charge system was reformed in 2003. The pollution charge can be considered a quasi-tax on the basis of the "polluter pays" principle. It is applied to waste water, waste gas, solid waste, and noise pollution. The current system is not based only on the amount of emissions that exceed the

---

[17]   The Provisional Regulations on City and Township Land Use Tax were promulgated by the State Council on September 27, 1988, and were amended on December 30, 2006 and effective January 1, 2007.

[18]   The Provisional Regulations on Farm Land Occupation Tax were promulgated by the State Council on April 1, 1987, and were reformed on December 1, 2007 and effective January 1, 2008.

relevant national or local pollution discharge standard, but also the total amount of pollution discharged. The charge rates have been increased so as to move from a low-cost system for polluters to one making up the pollution abatement cost for the environmental agency. Paying pollution charges does not exempt the polluters from all liabilities for preventing and abating pollution, compensating for the pollution damages, nor for other liabilities provided for by the administrative regulations. Environmental protection agencies above the county level are responsible for the collection of charges. All pollution charges should be remitted to the State Treasury, incorporated into the general fiscal budget, and listed as special funds for environmental protection. These funds should be mainly used for financing the following projects: prevention of major pollutant sources, regional pollution prevention, popularization and application of new technologies and techniques on pollution prevention, and other pollution prevention projects decided by the State Council.[19] Despite these improvements, the pollution charge system is still problematic. For instance, the rate schedules applied to major pollutants are still too low to fully make up the pollution abatement cost (thereby resulting in a low cost of violation for the polluters), and some local governments remove or hoard funds from the pollution charges for purpose other than environmental protection.[20]

2.3 Environmental Problems in China

2.3.1 An overview
China has been experiencing rapid economic development since the "open door" policy was introduced in the late 1970s. With the acceleration of urbanization and industrialization, China's environmental and ecological problems have become increasingly critical. The remarkable economic growth has given rise to grave environmental consequences.

---

[19] *See* Regulations on the Collection and Use of Pollution Charges (promulgated by the State Council on January 2, 2003 and effective July 1, 2003), Method on Administration of Pollution Charges Collection Standard (promulgated by the State Development Planning Committee, Ministry of Finance (MOF), State Environmental Protection Administration (SEPA, elevated to the Ministry of Environmental Protection (MEP) from 2008), and National Economic and Trade Committee on February 28, 2003 and effective July 1, 2003), and Method on the Collection and Use of the Funds of Pollution Charges (promulgated by the MOF and SEPA on March 20, 2003 and effective July 1, 2003).

[20] The National Development and Reform Commission of the PRC (NDRC), "China's Pollution Charge System" (in Chinese), http://www1.ndrc.gov.cn/jggl/jgqk/t20070404_126543.htm, May 13, 2010.

First, the domestic environment has deteriorated rapidly. According to the Annual Report on the State of the Environment in China, acute pollution problems and ecological destruction continued until 1996. Improvements in the environment were made in some areas in 1997. From 1999 onwards, environmental pollution problems have come under greater control by government. Ecological destruction has still remained a great concern, however. As far as the atmospheric environment is concerned, China is the world's largest pollutant emitter with SO_2 emissions around 20 million tons a year since 2003.[21] About 66 per cent of the urban population, or about 360 million people, were exposed to certain forms of air pollution that were in excess of the permissible standard according to the relevant data in 2004. Acid rain has polluted more than one-third of Chinese territories.[22] As for water pollution, about 70 per cent of the seven major water systems in China are heavily polluted,[23] over 400 cities are short of water, and about 320 million out of the 800 million farmers in the rural China do not have access to safe drinking water, threatening the health of rural residents, the lives of animals and crop production. Land degradation is another severe problem in addition to land scarcity. The main forms of land degradation include wind and water-induced soil erosion, desertification, salinization, and soil contamination. Among them, desertification has been experiencing fast growth. Between the late 1950s and 1975, the average annual rate of increase in desertification was about 1560 km², but by 1987 it had increased by 35 per cent to 2100 km² per annum and by 2000, it had increased by another 71 per cent to 3600 km² per annum. Around 27 per cent of the total land area of China, or 2.6 million km², had already turned into deserts by

---

[21] *See* Li, Z. D., "Energy and Environmental Problems behind China's High Economic Growth: A Comprehensive Study of Medium and Long-term Problems, Measures and International Cooperation" (2003), http://eneken.ieej.or.jp/en/data/pdf/188.pdf, April 24, 2011; *see also* the MEP, "Annual Reports on the National Environmental Statistics from 1999 to 2008" (in Chinese).

[22] From 1995 to 2010, China's coal consumption is expected to rise by up to 0.5 billion tons, resulting in a large increase in SO_2 emissions. SO_2 is the main source of acid rain and urban air pollution. The economic loss from SO_2 pollution includes damage to human health, decrease in crop yield and quality of produce, reduction in water quality and corrosion of materials and buildings. These pollutions have become an important factor limiting the social and economic development in some areas. *See* Dong, C., Yang, J. T. and Ge, C. Z., "SO_2 Charge and Tax Policies in China: Experiment and Reform" in the OECD, *op. cit.*, pages 233–5, 254.

[23] The water systems in China include the Yangtze, Yellow, Pearl, Songhua, Huai, Hai, and Liao rivers.

the end of 2004. This is estimated to have adversely affected the lives of almost 400 million people and resulted in a direct economic loss of RMB 54 billion per year.[24]

Second, cross-border pollution, in particular acid rain and sandstorms, have reached the Korean Peninsula and Japan. According to the United Nations Environment Programme (UNEP) Global Environment Outlook (GEO) Year Book 2004/5, sandstorms originating in the dry regions of northern China and Mongolia have blown across the Korean Peninsula and Japan. They have caused considerable hardship through disruption of communications, respiratory problems and related deaths, loss of livestock and crops over large areas, and associated loss of income.[25] Freshwater resources were also under cross-border threat. The UNEP warned that Lake Balkhash in Kazakhstan could dry up, producing another major environmental crisis in the region. Apart from Kazakhstan's own heavy use of water, industrial pollution and high usage of the river by China contributed greatly to the problem.[26]

In the context of certain global environmental problems, China has become the world's largest CO_2 producer over the course of the last three decades. China has also changed from a major oil-exporter in the 1980s to a major net importer since 1993, with an increase in rank from the seventh to the second among world oil importers. The era of energy self-sufficiency and net export that lasted for nearly three decades has gone. Energy security has become a serious problem in the country (a problem hidden, to a degree, by its high economic growth) which potentially has huge implications for the international community.[27]

2.3.2 Air pollution
The most notable environmental problem in China may be seriously falling air quality. Although urban air quality significantly improved during the 10th Five Year Plan (FYP) period (2001 to 2005), the situation yet remains very serious.[28] From the available data between 1999 and

---

[24] Asian Development Bank (ADB) (2007), *Country Environmental Analysis for the People's Republic of China,* http://www.adb.org/Documents/Produced-Under-TA/39079/39079-PRC-DPTA.pdf, May 13, 2010, pp.36–38.

[25] UNEP (2005), *GEO Year Book 2004/5: An Overview of Our Changing Environment,* http://www.unep.org/geo/yearbook/yb2004/, May 13, 2010.

[26] *Ibid.*, page 19.

[27] China's energy outlook in the next 20 years is dominated by coal and oil. According to the International Energy Agency, even with pro-energy efficiency and pro-renewable energy policies, coal will remain dominant in China's energy mix in 2030. *See* the ADB, *op. cit.*, page 32.

[28] *See* the ADB, *op.cit.*, page 44.

2008,[29] emissions of air pollutants from domestic sources stabilized, but emissions from industrial sources increased remarkably due to the rapid increase in industrial output and continued low efficiency of energy use in the industrial sector. Seven of the ten most air-polluted cities in the world are in China. Of 500 monitored cities in the country, less than 1 per cent meets the relevant World Health Organization's air quality standards.

Moreover, in many large cities, vehicular emissions have overtaken industrial and domestic sources as the number one air pollution source for urban areas, owing to the rapid increase in vehicular ownership. The resulting nitrogen oxide pollution has become a serious urban air quality problem. Rapid economic growth allows people to earn more money and thus to enhance their living standards. Rapidly rising incomes are concomitant with a fast developing culture of consumerism. There were almost no private cars in China in the 1980s. By the end of 2005, however, there were over 43 million. The annual growth rate of car ownership by 2005 was 20.6 per cent. Based on this sort of a trend, it is expected that there will be 150 million cars in China by 2015.[30] In addition, urbanization has also experienced a rapid increase. By the end of 2005, the official urban-rural division ratio was 43:57, but, as the government expects, with around a 1 per cent urbanization rate per annum for the next 15 years, the ratio will be roughly 55:45 by 2020.[31] It can be inferred that with increased urban populations, demand for private cars as well as public transportation will increase strikingly. Accordingly, consumption of oil for fuel will continue to grow. The already grave air pollution problems including CO_2 and The Suspended Particulate (TSP) are likely to become still worse without efficient control measures.

In China, transport fuels are not clean. Within a global context, the transport sector contributes up to 25 per cent of worldwide greenhouse gas emissions. Transport-related pollutants of greatest concern in a developing country like China are health-threatening emissions of fine particles and lead from the combustion of leaded gasoline, according to a World Bank report.[32] Transportation is very important in the national economy and will continue to remain so, both domestically and internationally. For the Chinese government, therefore, future emissions reduction strategies

---

[29] MEP Reports, *op. cit.*
[30] *See* the ADB, *op. cit.*, page 6.
[31] *See* the ADB, *op. cit.*, page 7.
[32] Gwilliam, K. et al., "Transport Fuel Taxes and Urban Air Quality", *Pollution Management in Focus*, (World Bank, Discussion Note 11), 2001, http://www.thepep.org/ClearingHouse/docfiles/transport_fuel%20taxes.pdf, May 13, 2010.

must take into account the need to persuade users, by means of incentives, compulsory taxes or penalties, to change their behavior with respect to transportation.

3. APPLYING A FUEL TAX IN CHINA

3.1 Current Taxes and Charges on Fuel Consumption and Vehicle Usage

As mentioned above, there is a close relationship between air pollution and energy consumption as well as vehicle use. Under China's current tax system, the consumption tax applies to petrol and diesel and vehicles in addition to VAT. The major reason underpinning the double taxation is that transport fuel, like petrol and diesel, is a non-renewable resource and therefore it is necessary to constrain consumption to conserve energy resources and to protect the environment. The VAT has become the largest revenue source for the government since its imposition in 1994 and the consumption tax also has seen a steady increase as a revenue source in recent years. The VAT and consumption tax systems were reformed in December 2008. The new systems began to be effective from 1 January 2009.[33] The main purpose of the reforms was to make the systems more equal, transparent, and efficient than before.

3.1.1 Vehicles

Before the 2008 reform, vehicles were subject to VAT either at the standard rate of 17 per cent or at the rate of 4 per cent, depending on whether the seller is a general VAT payer or a small-scale VAT payer engaging in commercial activities. Apart from this, vehicles (motor cars) were liable to consumption tax according to the automobile engine displacement (capacity).[34] The applicable tax rates for cars with different capacity are provided in Table 2.1 below (before reform), which were adjusted

---

[33] Provisional Regulations on Value Added Tax and Provisional Regulations on Consumption Tax were issued by the State Council on December 13, 1993, amended on November 5, 2008 and effective January 1, 2009 according to the State Council Order No. 538 and No. 539, respectively.

[34] Briefly, engine displacement is the volume swept by all the pistons of an engine in a single movement from top dead centre to bottom dead centre. It can be specified in cubic centimeters, liters, or cubic inches. Power output of a combustion engine is directly proportional to the engine displacement. Alternatively, displacement must sometimes be defined as the total volume of air/fuel mixture an engine draws in during one complete engine cycle, howsoever defined and subject to further interpretation by taxation authorities. *See* KnowledgeRush.

Table 2.1　Consumption tax on vehicles

Before reform		Tax rate	After adjustment in 2006		Tax rate	After reform in 2008		Tax rate
Taxable item (capacity)			Taxable item (capacity)			Taxable item (capacity)		
Motor cars	less than 1 liter	3%	Motor cars	less than 1.5 liters	3%	Motor cars	less than 1 liter	1%
	1 liter to less than 2.2 liters	5%					1 liter to 1.5 liters	3%
				1.5 liters to 2 liters	5%		1.5 liters to 2 liters	5%
	2.2 liters or more	8%		2 liters to 2.5 liters	9%		2 liters to 2.5 liters	9%
				2.5 liters to 3 liters	12%		2.5 liters to 3 liters	12%
Cross-country vehicles (four wheel drive)	less than 2.4 liters	3%		3 liters to 4 liters	15%		3 liters to 4 liters	25%
	2.4 liters or more	5%		more than 4 liters	20%		More than 4 liters	40%
Mini-buses and vans	less than 2 liters	3%	Mini-buses and vans		5%	Mini-buses and vans		5%
	2 liters or more	5%						

once, with more detailed brackets, in 2006 (after adjustment).[35] The 2008 reform in VAT and consumption tax have changed these tax rates to varying degrees. While the standard VAT rate of 17 per cent remained unaltered, the rate for small-scale payers was reduced to 3 per cent. The consumption tax rates on vehicles with a much higher capacity have been increased dramatically. Table 2.1 (after reform) shows the changed tax rates.

It is obvious that the reformed consumption tax rate schedule encourages the purchase and use of cars with a capacity of less than 1 liter, but discriminates against those cars with a capacity of 3 liters to 4 liters or more than 4 liters. The tax rate for the former has been decreased by 2 per cent, while in sharp contrast the rate for the latter has been increased by 10 or 20 per cent, respectively. This change illustrates that the Chinese government

---

com, "Engine Displacement", http://www.knowledgerush.com/kr/encyclopedia/ Engine_displacement/, April 24, 2011.
[35]　Circular of Adjusting and Improving the Policy on Consumption Tax issued by the MOF and the SAT on March 20, 2006.

intends to try and employ economic instruments, in particular taxation, to address emerging concerns related to environmental protection and energy conservation – but without creating too much impact on the economy. The new rate schedule is more environmentally friendly than before, and it may exert a positive influence on improving air quality in the country.

It should be noted that there are two other taxes applying to vehicles. As discussed above, one is the vehicle (and vessel) tax, and the other is the vehicle acquisition tax.[36] The former is charged annually and the tax rate is based on the net-weight capacity or the number of the taxable vehicles. It is clear that there is no direct relationship between vehicle tax and the actual intensity of vehicle use, such as the number of kilometers driven or the amount of petrol consumed. The vehicle (and vessels) tax only forms a small part of the cost of using vehicles, which means that the tax had little effect in terms of adjusting the behavior of vehicle owners. In reality it is other control measures, like limiting the issuance of new vehicle licenses and applying an "even and odd license number" system, that play a more significant role in mitigating traffic congestion and air pollution problems.

The vehicle acquisition tax seems to have had little impact on slowing down the rapid growth of car ownership, also. At the beginning of 2009, the government decided to reduce the tax on cars with capacity of less than 1.6 liters to 5 per cent during the period from 20 January 2009 to 31 December 2009,[37] in order to offset the adverse effects of the global financial crisis on the domestic economy. The government has been aware of the importance of relying on domestic consumption instead of exports to boost

---

[36] In China, no vehicle is allowed to be driven on a road unless it is registered and licensed. The vehicle acquisition tax (along with VAT and consumption tax) applies at the time of registration of a vehicle in a one-off manner. This is much like the first registration tax on the first registration of a motor vehicle in Hong Kong. The vehicle (and vessel) tax is then charged annually in China, which is like licensing of a vehicle annually in Hong Kong. Vehicle owners in China, like those in Hong Kong or elsewhere, are required to renew their vehicle licence each year. This conveys the right for a vehicle to be driven on a road. Apart from the above taxes, a mandatory insurance applies to the first issue or renewal of a vehicle licence according to the Law of Road Transport Security of the PRC. The insurance is similar in essence as the contribution to the Traffic Accident Victims Assistance Scheme applied to the first issue or renewal of a vehicle licence in Hong Kong. For detailed information on registration and licensing of a vehicle in Hong Kong, *see* the website of Transport Department of the Hong Kong Government, http://www.td.gov.hk/en/public_services/licences_and_permits/vehicle_and_driving_licences/index.html, May 13, 2010.

[37] This reduction was extended to the year of 2010, with a tax rate of 7.5 per cent, according to the MOF and the SAT Notice No. 154, 2009. The tax reduction policy has ceased no effect since January 1, 2011.

the economy.[38] This policy, though mainly for the economic purposes, applied conditionally to cars of less-pollution capacity. This tax preference reflects that, although the government encourages production and ownership of cars, it now equally emphasizes the "resource-efficient and environmentally-friendly" idea as put forward in the government's 11th Five Year National Economic and Social Development Plan (2006–2010).

3.1.2 Petrol and diesel

With the imposition of VAT and consumption tax in 1994, the tax burden on petrol and diesel has increased substantially. The VAT rate for general VAT payers remained the same after the VAT reform in 2008. The tax payable is based on the sales value of petrol and diesel, on which the applicable rate is levied. Under the VAT, crude oil including natural crude oil and artificial oil attracts the standard rate of 17 per cent. The 2008 consumption tax reform has changed the tax rate structure slightly. Before the reform, petrol was taxed at RMB 0.2 per liter without differentiating whether it is leaded or non-leaded. Since the reform, leaded petrol is taxed at RMB 0.28 per liter, but non-leaded petrol remains taxed at RMB 0.2 per liter.

Although the consumption tax rate has not changed too much, new taxable items have been added to the category of taxable oil products. These items are: aviation kerosene, fuel oil, naphtha, solvents and lubricant oil, of which the former two are taxed at RMB 0.1 per liter, and the latter three at RMB 0.2 per liter.

Soon after the VAT and consumption tax reform, the government decided to increase the fuel consumption tax by seven-to-eight-fold starting from 1 January 2009 as part of a reform on fuel taxation and pricing approved by the State Council.[39] According to the Notice announced on 18 December 2008, the tax on petrol, naphtha, solvents and lubricants was raised to RMB 1 per liter from RMB 0.2 and the levy on diesel, aviation kerosene and fuel oil was raised to RMB 0.8 a liter from RMB 0.1. The tax bracket for leaded petrol climbed to RMB 1.4 per liter from RMB 0.28, higher than the rate for unleaded petrol. Consumption tax on imported naphtha has been reinstalled, while taxation of aviation kerosene has been temporarily postponed. (Table 2.2 below illustrates the changes in tax rates with the recent two reforms). The fuel consumption tax is collected at the production or import stage, and therefore refiners and importers of oil products are the taxpayers.

---

[38]   The MOF and the SAT, Fiscal and Taxation Document No. 12, 2009.
[39]   The State Council Notice of Implementing the Reform on Fuel Taxation and Pricing, No. 37, 2008 (henceforth "SC Notice"); and MOF and SAT Notice of Increasing the Consumption Tax Rates on Fuel Products, No. 167, 2008 (henceforth "MS Notice").

Table 2.2   Consumption tax on fuel

Before reform		After consumption tax reform in 2008		After fuel taxation and pricing reform in 2009	
Taxable item	Tax rate (yuan/ liter)	Taxable item	Tax rate (yuan/ liter)	Taxable item	Tax rate (yuan/ liter)
Petrol	0.2	Petrol Lead	0.28	Petrol Lead	1.4
		Non-lead	0.2	Non-lead	1
		Aviation Kerosene	0.1	Aviation Kerosene	0.8
		Naphtha	0.2	Naphtha	1
		Solvents	0.2	Solvents	1
		Lubricants	0.2	Lubricants	1
		Fuel Oil	0.1	Fuel Oil	0.8
Diesel	0.1	Diesel	0.1	Diesel	0.8

The tax revenues belong to the central government, but are to be distributed to local governments through formal procedures of government transfer.[40]

The fuel consumption tax increase was introduced against the background that crude oil in the global market plunged 75 per cent in value from the record prices of July, 2008 (more than US$147 per barrel), which eased the import costs and provided China with room to implement energy tax reforms first proposed about ten years ago.[41] As the world's second-biggest oil user, the reform in fuel taxation and pricing has the potential to have a significant influence on the country's economy and environment. As shown in the Notice, the government aims to spur energy saving, cut pollution in cities and reduce oil imports. The adjustment of consumption taxes on oil products is also aimed at playing a role in promoting economic restructuring, standardizing imposition of administrative charges, and ensuring equal sharing of tax burdens among users.

Concomitant with the increase of the tax rate on oil products, it was argued that reform in the road charge system was needed. According to the Notice, six types of government charges were waived, that is, road maintenance fee, channel maintenance fee, administration fee of highway transportation, highway transportation surcharges, administration fee of water transportation, and water transportation surcharges. In addition,

---

[40]   SC Notice, Section 2, Article 1(4), (6).
[41]   Crooks, E., "Oil Groups Face up to Lower Prices", *Financial Times*, July 27, 2009, page 14.

the governmental debt-repaying secondary road fees were to be abolished gradually.[42] The central government subsidizes (with the increased income from fuel consumption tax) the losses of local governments due to the abolition of certain road tolls. It is argued that this will help streamline the transport and taxation departments of government, making clear the delineation of their responsibilities as well.[43]

To offset the effect of tax increases, government subsidies are provided for grain-producing peasants, urban public transportation, country road passenger transportation, forestry, and fishery industries as well as taxis following the changes of oil prices.

In addition to the lift in tax rates, the fuel pricing mechanism was changed. The pricing of domestic refined oil has begun to be linked with global prices under the control of government. This approach can help reflect fluctuations of international oil prices and production costs, and help balance domestic oil supply and demand.

It is hoped that the newly reformed "more consumption (of fuel), more payment" mechanism could enhance the role of taxation in fostering energy efficiency and pollution abatement.

3.2   Environmental Impact of the Current Tax System

Before the fuel consumption tax and pricing reform, many experts believed that the current limited use of economic instruments in China including taxes and charges was not sufficient to encourage polluters to mitigate their pollution because it made more economic sense to pay charges and fines than to control pollution. It was argued that China needed to develop economic instruments to prompt polluters to adopt pollution-control practices and technologies.[44]

---

[42]   The road charges were collected by local governments who received loans from banks to build highways and relied on toll revenues to pay back their debts. There were a great number of toll stations and a large number of people that were employed for the collection of the charges. Qin, T. B., "Energy Tax: How Far is It from Idea to Practice? Lessons Learned from The Experience in China", in J. Cottrell et al. (eds.), *Critical Issues in Environmental Taxation*, (Vol. VI), Oxford University Press, 2009, page 867.

[43]   Before the reform, the Ministry of Transport (MOT) was in charge of all types of charge related to construction, maintenance, and management of highways. The imposition of tax on oil products and vehicles by the SAT might overlap or even conflict with the collection of charges by the MOT. The fuel consumption tax reform, combined with abolition of highway-related charges, is helpful to redefine the relationship between the two departments.

[44]   ADB, *op. cit.*, page 120.

Despite the fact that several taxes have applied to the production and ownership of vehicles since 1994, the number of motor vehicles privately owned has increased very quickly. Taxation (at least at the rate applying) has had little effect on restraining car ownership. One of major reasons was that the government's policy encourages vehicle production and use. Since the ninth FYP (1996–2000), the automobile industry has been listed as a pillar industry. However, from an environmental point of view, limitation of vehicle usage can have a direct impact on alleviating air pollution problems. As mentioned before, the number one emitter of air pollutants in many large cities in China has become motor vehicles. In 2006, China overtook the US as the biggest emitter of CO_2, the chief greenhouse gas blamed for the bulk of global warming.[45] Although fuel taxation is not efficient in reducing externalities from emission, fuel consumption does have a direct linkage with emissions of CO_2. In the case of CO_2, the correlation between emissions and gasoline quantity consumed is very strong, regardless of the age or type of motor vehicle.[46]

Energy efficiency and safety are further serious problems. Efficiency in energy use has seen a significant deterioration over the last 20 years. The combined tax burden of current VAT and consumption taxes on transport fuel in China is only around 23 per cent, lower than comparable rates applying in many other countries.[47] This low level of taxation has to some extent led to low energy prices in China for a relatively long time, which has contributed significantly to the waste of energy and inefficient utilization. The lack of efficiency has more than environmental consequences; it is of strategic significance also. With regard to petroleum, some reports estimated that the remaining exploitable reserves in China are only 2.4 billion tons of coal equivalent (tce) which, at current rates of extraction, will only last about 14 years. Dependence on external sources for petroleum increased from 45 per cent in 2006 to around 52 per cent in 2009.[48]

---

[45] "China Overtakes U.S. in Greenhouse Gas Emissions", *New York Times*, June 20, 2007, http://www.nytimes.com/2007/06/20/business/worldbusiness/20iht-emit.1.6227564.html?_r=1, May 13, 2010.

[46] Hsu, S. L., "Psychological Barriers to Gasoline Taxation", in Cottrell, *op. cit.*, pages 337–8.

[47] For instance in the third quarter of 2010, the fuel tax in Norway was 63% of its fuel price. In Netherlands, 64.3% of the total price of petrol was taken for taxes. By comparison, the tax share in the petrol price in the U.S. was only 18.2%. *See* the International Energy Agency (IEA), *Energy Prices and Taxes: Quarterly Statistics Fourth Quarter 2010* (2010), http://www.oecd-ilibrary.org/docserver/download/fulltext/6210041e.pdf?expires=1303638181&id=id&accname=ocid194359&checksum=5E618C3BAAF0CB98B52394886C902C5, April 24, 2011, page xxxii.

[48] Wang, Q., "Oil Imports Hit Alarming Level in China", *China Daily*, January

The latest report from the International Energy Agency estimates that a continuation of "business as usual" in China will increase import dependency to 75 per cent by 2020.[49]

The recent reforms in fuel taxation and pricing have certainly helped to promote environmental protection compared to the previous regime. They have helped to standardize the fiscal system by gradually reducing the road charge system and enhancing the role of taxation as well as formalizing inter-governmental transfers. Nevertheless, the reformed system does not constitute an independent fuel taxation system. Unlike other taxes, fuel tax has its own special characteristics, and connects closely with energy consumption and environmental quality. Many countries have imposed fuel taxes, such as the UK and Japan, mainly for the purpose of energy conservation and efficiency, and pollution reduction (as well as revenue raising). It is worth thinking if it is feasible to introduce, formally, a consolidated fuel tax system to China so as to help achieve the aim of sustainable development.

3.3   A Consolidated Fuel Tax?

According to some official statements from China, creation of a fuel tax may not be necessary because of the recent reforms in the fuel consumption tax and pricing. It is argued that the reforms have "hit the targets" that a fuel tax would need to hit, such as eliminating arbitrary road charges, addressing the problem of overloading of freight, easing the financial pressure caused by the abolition of the highway charges, and improving energy efficiency and air quality.[50]

In a sense, this argument holds water. The old consumption tax failed to play a role in restricting unreasonable consumption of petrol and to help reduce air pollution because the tax rates (and prices) of fuel have remained very low since the implementation of the fuel consumption tax in 1994. During the 10th FYP period, the swelling demand for oil, driven in large part by the speedy growth of automobile ownership, was

---

14, 2010, http://www.chinadaily.com.cn/bizchina/2010-01/14/content_9317926. htm, April 24, 2011.

[49]   ADB, *op. cit.*, page 9.

[50]   "Reform in Fuel Taxation and Charge Systems" (in Chinese), *People's Daily*, January 8, 2009, http://finance.people.com.cn/GB/8641285.html, May 13, 2010; and Chaohu Municipal Office of the SAT, "An Introduction to the Reform in Provisions and Implementation Methods on Consumption Tax and the Reform in Fuel Taxation and Charge Systems" (in Chinese), http://www.ch365.com.cn/ad/guoshui2009/index-1.html, May 13, 2010.

accompanied by a compounding urban air pollution problem, which boosted carbon dioxide emissions.[51] Increasing the fuel consumption tax rates and linking the domestic oil price to the international market price have had effects on domestic oil supply and demand.

Nonetheless, a specific, focused fuel tax is still needed, which may be a forerunner for the introduction of a whole set of environmental taxes in China in the future. From a constitutional perspective, the recent reforms in fuel taxation and pricing do not meet the principle of "no taxation without law". The reform scheme was drafted and released jointly by the National Development and Reform Commission (NDRC), the Ministry of Finance (MOF), and the SAT at the end of 2008, and the final result was announced and issued by the State Council. The reform increased the tax rate and changed imposition methods, which had a direct impact on the tax burden of taxpayers. In a modern constitutional polity, such a change should be imposed through a legislative procedure since only by law should taxpayers' rights and interests be altered.[52]

From an environmental viewpoint, the reform plays no more than a very limited role in enhancing public awareness of the need to save energy and reduce pollution. Consumers would not feel pressed to restrict their consumption due to the fact that the reform only slightly changed the final fuel prices. Currently the tax applies a fixed rate on the basis of quantity, that is, sales volume of oil. Although this method follows international practice, the effect of taxation is meager since the reformed tax rate is still too low compared with the rates that apply in many other countries. The tax in China is an indirect subsidy to all transport fuel consumption. When the production price and cost are increased across the world, if China's consumers still enjoy comparatively lower fuel prices, it would amount to the waste of scarce resources. When the (international) price decreases, huge profits would go to the monopolist fuel producers and, again, this does not help to control producers' pollution.[53] Collection of fuel consumption tax currently at the production stage may be ineffective in inducing producers to control pollution and wastage of energy, even if the full amount of tax is collected. It is strongly argued that levying the tax

---

[51] ADB, *op. cit.*, page 31.
[52] This means that law is the basic source for taxation. No other government regulations and rules are allowed to create new taxes, alter tax rates, or change the imposition method since taxes have a direct or indirect relationship with taxpayers' private property and other related civil and political rights.
[53] In China, there are three big state-owned oil companies. They are China National Petroleum Corporation (CNPC), China Petroleum & Chemical Corporation (SINOPEC), and China National Offshore Oil Company (CNOOC).

at the consumption stage would be more effective both to adjust the price to world prices and to control pollution.

From an economic perspective, the existence of negative externalities, like pollution and waste of energy, and the failure of the market to adequately deal with them have serious implications for the achievement of true allocative efficiency within the economy. This is precisely so in today's China. Vehicular emissions and road congestion, along with other related environmental problems, will impede sustainable development in the Chinese economy. China's government has resolved to shift the balance of growth from exports towards domestic spending. It has taken bolder action to boost consumption – a host of incentives have been applied to encourage households to consume over recent months. Rural residents got subsidies for buying vehicles and other goods like refrigerators and computers; urban residents got a subsidy if they traded in cars and home appliances for new goods; and tax rates on low-emission cars were cut. The government also has taken several measures to improve the social safety net, which should, in the long-run, encourage people to save less and spend more. All these signal a very likely increase in fuel consumption in the near–medium future. It is necessary to use taxation in a more advanced way, to combat negative externalities. Ideally, we need taxes which impose tax upon each unit of pollution in an amount equal to the marginal damage it inflicts upon society at the efficient level of output.

In fact, China has pushed for fuel tax reform for many years. The idea of a fuel tax was raised as early as 1994. The key goal set up by the 12th FYP (2011–2015) – creation of a "circular economy" – is to achieve certain environmental objectives, particularly a 16 per cent reduction in energy intensity and a 17 per cent reduction in CO_2 emissions per unit GDP by 2015.[54] The use of economic instruments proposed for the 11th FYP period including environmental taxes, environmental funds, and ecological compensation funds is continuing to be applied in the 12th FYP period. The Ministry of Environmental Protection of the PRC (MEP) has been working with the SAT to design environmental levies on polluting products, and the imposition of environmental taxes, according to a recent survey, is likely to be supported by the public if the individual income tax burdens on low and middle income people are to be decreased. It appears that introduction of a formal fuel tax (and gradually a whole-set of environmental taxes) to China is politically, psychologically, and financially feasible.

---

[54] *See* the Outline of the Twelfth Five Year Plan for National Economic and Social Development of the PRC (2011), approved by the National People's Congress on March 14, 2011.

4. HOW TO IMPOSE A CONSOLIDATED FUEL TAX IN CHINA

4.1 Examples from Abroad

Modern fuel taxes of one sort or another have been introduced in many countries. Tax rates on automotive fuels vary markedly from country to country, ranging from heavy subsidies for all fuels in Nigeria and Iran (negative taxation) to high positive tax rates in Europe. Imposition of a (sensible) fuel tax usually aims to meet multiple objectives including raising government revenues for general expenditure purposes, efficiently allocating resources to and within the transport sector, financing road provision and maintenance, reducing road congestion, reducing the environmental externalities of road transport, and redistributing income. Since it is difficult to achieve all these objectives simultaneously through fuel tax policies alone, most countries use other policy instruments as supplements of fuel taxation, particularly to correct for externalities. The difficulty of meeting the various aims is especially demanding in low-income countries where fewer policy instruments are available (often due to demands to address dire unmet basic needs).

The UK was the first country to introduce a fuel tax. Today it imposes a significantly high rate of fuel tax among OECD countries.[55] The "Motor Spirit Duty" was applied in the UK in 1909, at the rate of £0.013 per UK gallon[56] and later on the Hydrocarbon Oil Duties Act 1979 was enacted to govern the imposition of fuel taxation. This is an excise duty levied on oils (mainly road vehicle fuels), which is added to the price of motor fuel per unit of volume. Since the introduction of the Fuel Price Escalator (FPE) by the Conservative government in 1993, a significant rise in the cost of fuel persisted until the cancellation of the FPE in 1999.[57] It is worth nothing

---

[55] *See* the IEA, *op. cit.*

[56] One UK gallon equals to 4.546 liters.

[57] The FPE was an automatic increase in hydrocarbon oil duty ahead of inflation in the UK from 1993 to 1999. It forced the UK fuel prices up from one of the lowest in Europe to one of the most expensive. When it was first added, it was set at an annual increase of 3 per cent above inflation, and therefore fuel prices rose by 3 pence a liter and tax contributed to 72.8 per cent of the total cost. In 1997, the increase rate was raised by the Labour government to 6 per cent per year, which added 11.1 pence to the cost of unleaded petrol and was at 75 per cent of the total cost. The FPE was a way of the UK government making money and also to help protect the environment by discouraging people from using their cars. Despite it being abandoned in 1999, fuel prices did continue to rise rapidly. The increase in fuel duty for 2009 was above inflation and the tax is planned to increase further "on

that the government introduced a duty differential to petrol in 1996 and to diesel in 1997 based on the sulphur and aromatics content of the fuel. The lower the content, the lower are the taxes. From April 2008, the fuel duty rate structure was simplified to a single rate for diesel and two rates for petrol (leaded and unleaded). The tax rate for unleaded petrol and diesel after 23 March 2011 and before 1 January 2012 is £0.5795 per liter, and for leaded petrol and other light oils £0.6767.[58] In addition to the duty, VAT is applied as a percentage of the combined total (20 per cent at present). The share of fuel prices accounted for by fuel duty was 64.2 per cent for petrol and 63.2 per cent for diesel in the 3rd quarter of 2010.[59] There is a fuel duty rebate available for local bus transport operators. Aviation fuel is exempt from fuel duty and VAT because of the Convention on International Civil Aviation.[60] The revenue generated from fuel duty is used for general purposes including but not confined to environmental protection. The UK government is committed to meeting its required 34 per cent cut in emissions by 2020 through domestic action (such as taxation).

The situation with fuel tax in the US serves as a sharp contrast with that in the UK. A report released by the Organization of Petroleum Exporting Countries (OPEC) shows that within the G7 countries[61] the UK enforces the highest tax on consumption of oil products, at a rate five times higher than that levied in the US. The high tax rates in the UK have pushed fuel prices to double those in the US.[62] In the US, gasoline and diesel fuel are taxed by federal and state governments. State taxes have been applied for a long time. Oregon introduced the first US state tax on fuel at 1 cent per US gallon in 1919.[63] All other states applied such a tax in the following decades. The federal gasoline tax at 1 cent per US gallon was applied in

---

1 April from 2010 to 2013 by 1 ppl above indexation in each year", according to the 2009 Budget of the government. *See* HM Revenue & Customs, "Hydrocarbon Oils Duty rates", http://www.hmrc.gov.uk/budget2009/bn66.pdf, May 14, 2010.

[58]   HM Revenue & Customs, "Fuel Duty Rates", http://www.hmrc.gov.uk/budget2011/tiin6330.pdf, April 24, 2011.

[59]   *See* the IEA, *op. cit.*

[60]   The Convention is also known as the Chicago Convention, which established the International Civil Aviation Organization. It came into effect in 1947. It exempts air fuel from tax for international air travel.

[61]   G7 countries are France, Germany, Italy, Japan, United Kingdom, United States, and Canada.

[62]   OPEC (2010), "Who Gets What from Imported Oil?", http://www.opec_web/static_files_project/media/downloads/publications/Whogetswhat2010.pdf, April 24, 2011.

[63]   One US gallon equals 3.785 liters.

1932 through the enactment of the Revenue Act of 1932.[64] As of January 2011, the nationwide average tax on gasoline was 48.1 cents per US gallon and on diesel 53.1 cents per US gallon. The federal tax on gasoline was 18.4 cents and on diesel 24.4 cents per US gallon. At the state level, the tax rates vary. On average, the state gasoline excise tax was 20.6 cents per US gallon, while the state diesel excise tax was 19.2 cents. Other state and local taxes on gasoline and diesel, including applicable sales taxes, gross receipts taxes, oil inspection fees, county and local taxes, underground storage tank fees and other miscellaneous environmental fees, averaged 9.0 cents and 9.5 cents per US gallon, respectively.[65] Revenues from federal and state fuel taxation are primarily used for highway and bridge construction, though other tax revenues are also used in transportation-related programs.[66] The fuel taxes are deemed as user taxes in America. Because money is required for road construction and maintenance, the idea is that drivers who use state highways should pay for them through taxes. Certain groups are exempted from paying tax on fuel consumption, such as volunteer fire companies and governmental units. Fuel taxes are often refunded to farmers for gasoline used in their farming operations.

The tax burden of fuel consumption in the US is indeed quite low when looked at in a global context. According to US official statistics released in February 2011, taxes on both gasoline and diesel accounted for 13 per cent of the fuel price, and taxes on diesel 16 per cent.[67] This is one very likely reason for the decline in air quality in the US over the post-WWII period, especially.[68] Although China overtook the US as the biggest CO_2 emission producer, the US emits more, per head, than any other country. Many economists and policy analysts argue that Americans drive too much in

---

[64]   Revenue Act of 1932, Public Law 154, 72d Congress, approved June 6, 1932.

[65]   American Petroleum Institute (API), "Motor Fuel Taxes Summary Report", http://www.api.org/statistics/fueltaxes/upload/January_2010_gasoline_and_diesel_summary_pages.pdf, May 14, 2010.

[66]   The Highway Revenue Act of 1956 of the US established the Highway Trust Fund, which was primarily to ensure a dependable source of financing various highway programs. Federal Highway Administration Office of Policy Development, "Highway Trust Fund Primer", http://www.fhwa.dot.gov/policy/primer98.pdf, May 14, 2010; *see also* March, J., United States Department of Transportation, "The Future of Highway Financing", in *Public Roads,* 69(3), 2005, http://www.fhwa.dot.gov/publications/publicroads/05nov/02.cfm, April 24, 2011.

[67]   The Energy Information Administration, "Gasoline and Diesel Fuel Update", http://www.eia.doe.gov/oog/info/gdu/gasdiesel.asp, April 24, 2011.

[68]   The US Environmental Protection Agency, "Nonattainment Areas Map – Criteria Air Pollutants", http://www.epa.gov/air/data/nonat.html?us~usa~United%20States, April 24, 2011.

motor vehicles that consume too much gasoline, and that a gasoline tax is called for to reduce both of these amounts. Advocates like Gregory Mankiw and Paul Krugman[69] have been arguing for an increased gasoline tax. It is demonstrably true that taxing undesirable behavior is generally more effective than subsidizing desirable behavior.

Though not as severe as the tax regime which applies in the UK, Hong Kong has a significant fuel taxation system. According to the Environment Bureau of the Hong Kong Government (ENB), the retail prices of vehicular fuel in Hong Kong are determined by oil companies, having regard to international oil prices, commercial practices and their operating costs. At the retail station, the price of fuel comprises the product cost, government excise duties and taxes, land cost,[70] operating costs including distribution, marketing, salaries and utilities at service stations, and so on, and net margin. The duty for unleaded petrol is HK$ 6.06 per liter, which accounts for 30 to 40 per cent of the fuel list price.[71] This is lower than the tax rate that applies in some developed countries

---

[69]   Both Mankiw and Krugman are American economists. Mankiw has advocated for the implementation of Pigouvian taxes, and to this end he founded the informal Pigou Club. Krugman won the Nobel Memorial Prize in Economics in 2008.

[70]   Land cost is one of fixed costs for fuel service stations in Hong Kong. In respect to land cost, there is a special lease and rental system for service stations in Hong Kong. Since June 2003, the Hong Kong Government has adopted new measures regarding the tender arrangements for service stations, which include putting up existing stations for tender upon the expiry of their leases instead of having the tenancy renewed automatically, and putting up stations for tender in batches, and allowing tenderers to submit a single bid for all the stations in a tender, with a view to facilitating new market players in acquiring a commercially viable number of stations to achieve scale merit. Depending on the availability of the stations in the year including those existing stations of which the leases would expire within that year, the available stations are arranged in batches of three to four months apart for sale. Each batch contains two to five stations. Recently, the Lands Department of Hong Kong Government announced that the tender for two service stations had been awarded on a 21-year land grant at a total premium of HK$ 228.191 million. The two stations were awarded to ExxonMobil Hong Kong Limited at HK$ 59.509 million and HK$ 168.682 million respectively. *See* "Tendering Arrangements for Petrol Filling Station Sites" in Legislative Council Meeting May 21, 2008, http://www.legco.gov.hk/yr07-08/chinese/counmtg/floor/cm0521-confirm-ec.pdf, May 14, 2010; *see also* Hong Kong Information Service Department, "Press Releases: Tender Awarded for Petrol Filling Stations", http://www.info.gov.hk/gia/general/200904/29/P200904290257.htm, May 14, 2010.

[71]   Customs and Duties of the Government of the Hong Kong Special Administrative Region, "Types and Duty Rates", http://www.customs.gov.hk/en/trade_facilitation/dutiable/types/index.html, April 24, 2011.

like the UK and Japan.[72] For diesel, while ultra low sulphur diesel is taxed at HK\$ 2.89, the duty on Euro V diesel is zero, since the Hong Kong government has aimed at making Euro V diesel (an ultra low sulphur diesel) the statutory standard in Hong Kong to encourage the market to switch to this more environmentally friendly fuel.[73] Petrol is used by private cars. (Diesel powered and liquefied petroleum gas (LPG) vehicles cannot normally be registered for private use in Hong Kong.) Private cars are primarily not a necessity in Hong Kong, thus the government tends to be notably reluctant in considering any proposals to reduce the duty rate for petrol. Vehicle ownership has increased at an acceptable rate in recent years in Hong Kong, with an average annual growth rate of 1.5 per cent in the past 10 years.[74] The duty differential on diesel and petrol reflects the government's policy on fuel consumption, that is, encouraging public transport while controlling private cars so as to help abate air pollution problems. Since the statutory Euro V diesel is clean, and it is substantially consumed by the public transport sector (and for commercial goods transportation), a low rate is conducive to the livelihood of those people relying on public transportation, and to the improvement in air quality as well.

From the above examples, it can be seen that, for efficient protection of the environment, the instrument of taxation should be employed efficiently. Government tax policy should promote efficient consumption of fuel and encourage switching to new, more fuel-efficient vehicles. This will save drivers money and also help to tackle climate change factors. Some research has argued that improving the fuel efficiency of new cars could make the single biggest contribution to tackling the climate change emissions from road transport. Second, government should introduce fuel duty increases as part of a tax shift, transferring the burden of taxation from people and jobs onto pollution. If government could match the rise in taxes on fuel and other pollutants by cuts in taxes on jobs and income, it would be politically popular. Third, government should seek ways to provide better public transport and make cycling and walking safer and easier to encourage less use of private cars.

---

[72] *See* the IEA, *op. cit.*

[73] The ENB (2009), "Air Pollution Control Strategies", http://www.epd.gov. hk/epd/english/environmentinhk/air/prob_solutions/strategies_apc.html, May 14, 2010.

[74] *See* Press Release, Hong Kong Information Service Department, "Retail Prices of and Duty Rates for Vehicular Fuel", November 14, 2007, http://www. info.gov.hk/gia/general/200711/14/P200711140101.htm, April 24, 2011.

4.2   A Proposal for China

In designing a consolidated fuel tax in China, we must bear in mind that adding any new tax to the existing tax system would be likely to trigger mass suspicion that government would waste the tax proceeds, or at least spend them in a way that is inconsistent with the stated purposes. This is primarily because China lacks a sound, efficient, and transparent budgeting and accounting system to safeguard public money. It is therefore necessary for the state's legislative body to fully consider every issue of fuel taxation, soliciting public opinion as widely as possible, before such new measures can be passed as a law. It is also necessary for policy makers to be innovative in their thinking about how to structure an advanced fuel tax over the medium–long term and how to enable revenues raised to be spent in smart ways.

A well-elaborated proposal is needed, covering matters of imposition principle, tax base, rate schedule, collection method, and use of the revenues. In making fuel tax policy, the Chinese government needs to take into account such serious environmental problems as the increasingly poor air quality in the country, the unsafe dependence on imported oil and the inefficiency of fuel utilization, as well as the impact of the fuel tax structure on economic activities and on the poor.

What makes good tax policy? From a fiscal point of view, a "good" tax is one that produces maximum revenue with efficiency, stability, simplicity, and equality. For revenue-raising purposes, goods for which demand is least sensitive to price increases should tend to bear the highest tax rates; goods that are close substitutes should be taxed at similar rates to prevent demand from switching from the higher-to-lower-taxed good (and hence reducing government revenue). Where equity is an important concern, goods accounting for a larger share of budgets for the rich than for the poor should be taxed more heavily; goods that produce large negative externalities, such as emissions from automotive fuels or congestion from excessive road use, should be taxed at high rates, also, in order to discourage their consumption and reduce social harm.

In the case of fuel tax, this configuration may turn out to be complex or even paradoxical. Emissions from diesel fuel are more harmful than those from gasoline, for instance, but encouraging the use of diesel-powered public transport may be desirable as a way of relieving congestion (and lowering overall pollution levels). Since China is so vast a state and so large a portion of the population has to rely on mass transit, diesel may not be well suited to the imposition of a high tax rate because of low demand elasticity. On the other hand, if a tax differential applies to gasoline and diesel, consumers would switch to lower-taxed diesel for private use, which is not, overall, environmentally favorable. To avoid this diversion and perverse inter-fuel substitution, it may be better to keep the tax rates on (unleaded) petrol and diesel the same (like the UK) or within a small range of difference. A tax differential, however, can be applied to leaded and unleaded petrol to modify consumer behavior (which has proved effective in OECD countries). In the meantime, the government should provide incentives for the use of "clean diesel" technology to lower emissions of the greenhouse gas carbon dioxide, like promoting the use of Euro V diesel in Hong Kong. Compressed natural gas (CNG) and LPG are two of the cleanest fuels, which currently are taxed at 13 per cent of the sales value according to the VAT law in China.[75] For the purpose of controlling air pollution, if these fuels can be provided at lower prices than other fuels, vehicles using them will be more economically viable.

Secondly, setting a tax rate appropriately is an important yet difficult task. By comparison, in Europe and Asia, most countries have resorted to higher taxation to mitigate pressures on their oil insufficiency. Germany for example, as the largest European economy, has adopted a very high tax rate, only slightly lower than the UK, on fuel consumption.[76] Such a high tax has contributed much to the development of energy-efficiency technologies and the popularity of lower-emission vehicles. In sharp contrast, as the world's largest economy, the US has adopted very low tax rates on fuel. The ratio of the country's high-emission car ownership has long been higher than in other countries. In China, some domestic energy experts have claimed that the new tax level, RMB 1 per liter on unleaded petrol and RMB 0.8 on diesel, would not play an important role in promoting energy conservation and emission reduction unless it is raised to RMB 3 or more per liter.[77] Indeed, levy standards should make resource prices reflect resource dependence and over-use and the costs of pollution abatement. Future reform will need to consider this view.

Currently, China allows retail fuel prices to fluctuate around a state-set benchmark.[78] When operating this oil-pricing mechanism, the calculation

---

[75] Provisional Regulations on Value Added Tax, Article 2(2).

[76] *See* the IEA, *op. cit.*

[77] *See* Ma Hongman, "Fuel Tax Reform Needs More Transparency", *China Daily*, December 15, 2008, http://www.chinadaily.com.cn/bizchina/2008-12/15/content_7306264.htm, April 24, 2011.

[78] China's transport fuel pricing is now measurably more sensible than before, though the application of the pricing and taxation system is less clear. *See* "Driving

methods for the final pricing should be improved and the external price references for oil products need to be readjusted in order to flexibly reflect supply, demand and price conditions on domestic and foreign markets and to help crack down on domestic oil speculation. To improve the pricing mechanism and for the long-term efficiency of fuel taxation, subsidies in fuel production and consumption (for private transportation) should be abolished. Some studies argue that environmental externalities should be corrected for by taxing polluting goods, not by subsidizing nonpolluting alternatives (in the private sphere).[79] Subsidies in transport and fuel in China have been found to exert negative effects on resources and the environment.[80] The recent reform in fuel consumption taxation and pricing still provided subsidies for specific sectors and groups. Some subsidies in the transitional period may be needed but some may not be needed. If subsidies are necessary in the short-term, they should be addressed within a coherent policy for reducing distortions in fuel and transport markets.

Energy and resource taxation policy needs to adjust to improve taxation standards to guarantee the reasonable earnings of the state as resource owners and to avoid the excessive shift of social income to some enterprises.

Third, how fuel tax revenues should be used must be clearly provided for by law, which has not only fiscal, but also environmental implications.

---

in the Right Direction", *Economist*, September 19, 2009.

[79]   In the G20 meeting of 2009 in Pittsburgh, world leaders announced they would phase out fossil fuel subsidies in the medium term. The G20 account for 80 per cent of greenhouse-gas emissions. China, as a non-OECD country, spent more than US$ 25 billion a year on subsidies for fuel in 2007. The International Energy Agency and OECD calculate that eliminating fossil fuel subsidies would result in a 10 per cent reduction in global greenhouse-gas emissions by 2050. If China concentrates on better taxing (transport) fuel, it could have a major impact on the environment. *See* "Energy Subsidies in Non-OECD Countries", *Economist*, October 3, 2009.

[80]   *See* Ge, C. Z. and others, "Subsidy Policy and the Environment in China" in the OECD, *op. cit.*, pages 109–159; *see* also "The Key of Fuel Taxation is the Oil Pricing Mechanism", *Xinhua News Online*, November 27, 2007, http://news.xin-huanet.com/comments/2008-11/27/content_10419397.htm, May 14, 2010. Prices of oil products in China have been state-controlled for many years. Each time adjusting price was accompanied by governmental subsidies. In the past, subsidies were mainly provided for the urban transport sectors, such as taxis and buses. Government also subsidized oil companies when production costs and international crude oil prices rose, which however wasted taxpayers' money and resulted in energy inefficiency. Some study argued that domestic oil pricing should be referred to the international oil markets. Otherwise, a tax based on distorted prices would be doomed to fail. Any discussions of whether tax burden is high or low would be meaningless.

There are two main categories where the use of fuel tax is concerned. The first way such tax revenue can be used consists in paying it into the general government budget in accordance with common fiscal principles. Secondly, the tax revenue can be allocated to specific purposes, some of which may be environmental, especially by setting up funds or mechanisms for reallocating the revenue to environmental protection programs (for example, cleaning contaminated water). But allocation entails serious drawbacks. Fixing the use of revenues of a tax in advance, without evaluating its economic and environmental rationale beforehand, may lead to economic wastage. For instance, allocating fuel tax to road infrastructure may lead to over-investment in that sector. Programs may last longer than their optimal period as a result of habits, administrative slowness, situation returns or other "acquired rights". Notwithstanding these problems, allocating revenues does have its advantages. Thus, the political acceptability of taxes and charges can be enhanced because of transparency of use, where certain tax revenues are clearly dedicated to the popular cause of environmental protection.[81] In China, income from the fuel taxes may be earmarked for specific purposes associated with environmental protection, given its urgent need and public acceptance. However, the revenue must be used in a transparent way, providing legal channels for individual taxpayers to supervise expenditure, in addition to the general budget control from the state's legislative supervision body.

Another possible mechanism to control the spending of earmarked fuel taxes revenue is a "sunset clause".[82] A sunset clause or provision is part of a law or statute that repeals the law or parts of it at a specified time period. If the earmarked revenue is set up under existing legislation or decrees, there should be a sunset clause for a discussion to determine when it should be regularized by passing basic legislation or closed down. Earmarked taxes are sometimes introduced to meet a temporary expendi-

---

[81]   *See* Barde, J. P., "Environmental Taxes in OECD Countries: An Overview" in the OECD, *op. cit.*, pages 30–1.

[82]   For more detailed discussions on the use of a sunset clause in tax laws, *see* Kysar, R. M., "Sun also Rises: The Political Economy of Sunset Provisions in the Tax Code", *Georgia Law Review*, Volume 40, Number 2, 2006, pages 335–406; and Viswanathan, M., "Sunset Provisions in the Tax Code: A Critical Evaluation and Prescriptions for the Future", *New York University Law Review*, Volume 82, Number 2, 2007, pages 656–88. The most famous use of a sunset clause in the PRC is to guarantee that the previous capitalist system and way of life in the Hong Kong Special Administrative Region (HKSAR) remain unchanged for 50 years in the Basic Law of the HKSAR.

ture need and thus they are made subject to a sunset clause.[83] This may help to improve initial estimates of their effects on revenue and to ensure systematic *ex post* evaluation so that waste or inefficiency of earmarked fuel taxes, if any, can be reduced.

Last, it is important to note that urban air emissions have a greater impact on human health than do the same emissions in rural areas. This is so because people are often exposed to such pollution in cities and, second, the concentration of pollutants in the air is higher in urban areas, and the impact often rises more than proportionately to the concentration of emissions. As a result, in urban areas transport demand has to be carefully managed to avoid detriment to the environment, quality of life, and public finance. Adequate access to opportunities for work, housing, shopping, entertainment, and so on, is fundamental to economic growth and social welfare. Motorized transport can significantly expand these opportunities but an optimal mix of non-motorized, public and private transport can result in much better performance than unmanaged growth of private transport. With the rapid urbanization and strong increase in private car ownership, a well-planned public transport system is a necessity to help relieve air pollution problems and at the same time to facilitate market operation. In regulating public transport systems including the national railways, the key to controlling finance is transparency.

Another concern with regard to the road usage efficiency is to think about a tolling system as supplemental to fuel taxation in China. The current fuel consumption taxation and pricing reforms were, in part, aimed at eliminating highway tolls. The government has provided a plan to solve the resulting debt payment and unemployment problems. This tax policy has been used to control the previous arbitrary road charges that applied in many local areas. Although this policy is commendable to some extent, it does not necessarily increase the efficiency in utilization of roads. If all highway tolls are to be eliminated, users will have no incentive to take

---

[83]   Tax earmarking in its purest form means that all revenue from a particular tax is kept separate from general revenue, can only be used for a specific government expenditure program and fully funds that program. A soft version of earmarking involves the earmarked tax funding only part of a specific expenditure program, with the remainder funded from general revenue. This arguably represents a major departure from pure earmarking since segregation of the earmarked tax becomes meaningless when it is mixed with general revenue to fund a program. *See* Carling, R., "Tax Earmarking: Is it Good Practice?", (The Center for Independent Studies (CIS) Perspectives on Tax Reform 12, Monograph 75), 2007, https://www.cis.org.au/images/stories/policy-monographs/pm-75.pdf, November 13, 2010.

care how often they use (and abuse) the roads. Problems such as overloading or traffic congestion are notably more likely to occur. Therefore, a new tolling system may be needed to enhance road efficiency and reduce consumption of fuel as well. The tolling system should be based on a national electronic charging system with appropriate allocation of toll stations. The charge should not be collected on a lump sum that applied before, but on the basis of the number of kilometers driven or the amount of fuel consumption so as to actually reflect road usage as well as cars' emissions. By this way, a more just, transparent and efficient fuel taxation system may be achieved with fewer unintended consequences.[84]

In general but particularly for an emerging market economy like China, the design of a fuel tax should be guided primarily by practical considerations of simplicity, uniformity and transparency. As the European Conference of Ministers of Transport (ECMT) concluded, in the short-term a fuel tax is the main fiscal approach to internalize negative externalities in view of the simplicities and relatively low cost of application.[85] The fact that CO_2 emissions are directly related to fuel consumption makes an advanced fuel tax an ideal instrument to respond to climate change concerns.[86]

5. CONCLUSION

Various economic instruments have their own niches; they can be used effectively in combination, however. Although fuel taxes can strongly affect fuel consumption patterns, they have other significant welfare impacts. To address externalities from air pollution we need not just the

---

[84] Collection of the road charge automatically via credit cards or debit cards is of great use to avoid tax evasion and inefficiency in charge administration. Payment and collection through a national uniform banking system will not only enhance the overall efficiency and transparency of fuel tax and charge system, but more importantly, facilitate the environmental protection purpose.

[85] Pollution, as a typical example of negative externalities, is problematic because the agents who own and use an asset do not pay for the indirect costs arising due to their usage. These indirect costs become "social costs" since they are borne by the society to a larger extent rather than by the polluters. The inclusion of these indirect costs to polluters will reduce externalities – such an inclusive process is known as the process of internalization and it promotes cooperation. *See* Brandenburger, A.M., and Nalebuff, B.J., *Co-operation: A Revolution Mindset that Combines Competition and Cooperation*, New York, Doubleday, 1996.

[86] Perkins, S., "Environmental Taxation of Transport" in the OECD, *op. cit.*, page 324.

single instrument of fuel taxes but a combination of instruments including environmental regulations. For instance, fuel quality standards and vehicle emission standards constitute an effective internalization instrument to reduce air pollution from road traffic. They make vehicle owners and fuel users pay for their cleaner fuels and vehicles, and reduce the environmental damage caused to others.

In China, a stream of environmental protection policies has been issued by government in recent years as a response to the rapidly growing awareness of the damage caused by natural disasters and environmental pollution.[87] In addition, security of petroleum supplies in China has been a frequent worry especially after oil imports spiked by 17 per cent in 2004 (above the trend growth rate of 6–7 per cent). As a result, strong pollution abatement and energy conservation goals have been enshrined in the government's 11th FYP and the new 12th FYP. These are frequently referred to together as "energy efficiency and pollution abatement" (*Jie Neng Jie Pai*). In order to fulfill the country's ambitious emission target,[88] China is expected to adopt various efficient instruments, among which taxation occupies a high rank. Fuel taxation in many developed countries has proved comparatively effective in protecting the environment, saving energy, and enhancing economic efficiency. A consumption tax on fuel has been implemented in China for over two decades, but it is inefficient in addressing the severe air pollution problems. Though the recent reforms have made some progress in lifting the role of taxation in environmental protection, a more comprehensive fuel tax system is needed for the long-term sustainable development in the country.

Fuel taxation is not a panacea. The right place for it (and other environmental taxes) is most likely to be found in a "mixed" system combining a selection of instruments like regulation, standard, and tradable permits. The challenge is to deal with environmental problems, bearing in mind the relevant policy objectives: steady progress in reducing risks, cost-effectiveness, encouragement of technological innovation, fairness, and administrative simplicity.

---

[87] *See* the ADB, *op. cit.*, pages 53–6.
[88] The Chinese central government set up a new emission target on November 26, 2009. It aims to reduce its "carbon intensity of the economy" by 40–45 per cent by the year 2020, compared with 2005 levels. *See* "China's Emission Reduction Targets" (in Chinese), *The Xinhua News Agency*, November 27, 2009, http://news. xinhuanet.com/world/2009-11/27/content_12552374.htm, May 14, 2010; *see* also "China Unveils Emissions Targets ahead of Copenhagen", *BBC World News,* November 26, 2009, http://news.bbc.co.uk/2/hi/8380106.stm, May 14, 2010.

APPENDIX

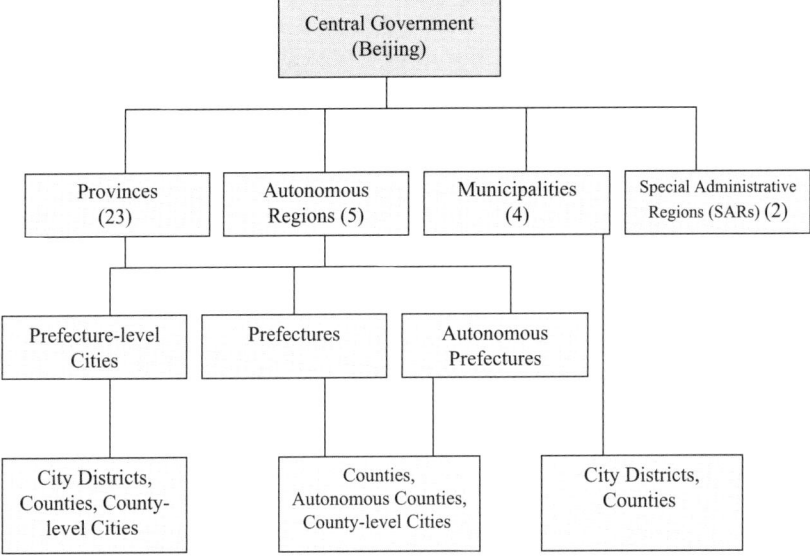

Notes:
1. There are 23 provinces in China, one of which is claimed province, known as Taiwan. Taiwan is controlled by the Republic of China (ROC), not the PRC.
2. The five autonomous regions are: Guangxi, Inner Mongolia, Tibet, Ningxia, and Xinjiang.
3. The four municipalities are Beijing, Tianjin, Shanghai, and Chongqing.
4. The two SARs are Hong Kong and Macau.

Figure 2.1   Administrative division system of China

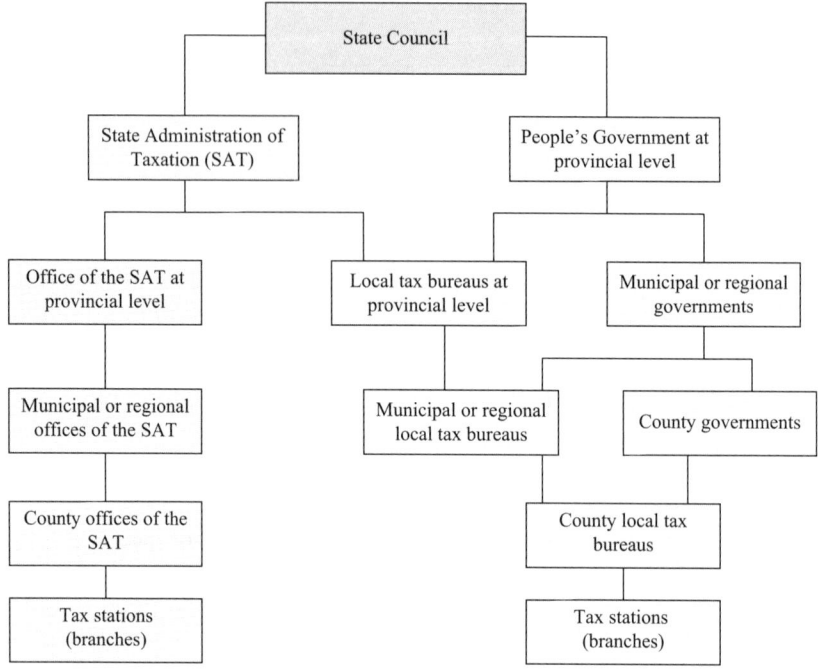

Notes:
1.   The headquarters of the SAT exercise vertical leadership over its offices across China, and assists People's Governments at the provincial level through dual leadership over local tax bureaus.
2.   Local tax bureaus at the provincial level are department-level administrative organs of the People's Governments at the provincial level. They are under the dual leadership of the provincial governments and the headquarters of the SAT, with the former having predominant control. Local tax bureaus below the provincial level are under the dual leadership of the higher local tax bureaus and the People's Governments at the same level, with the former being the predominant one.

Figure 2.2   Tax administration structure of China

Table 2.3   Tax-sharing structure of China

	Post-1994 tax regime
Central taxes	Consumption Tax
	Vehicle Acquisition tax
	Customs Duties/Tariffs
	VAT collected by Customs on behalf of the tax administration
Local taxes	Business Tax
	City and Township Land Use Tax
	House Property Tax
	Tobacco Leaf Tax
	Farm Land Occupation Tax
	Land Appreciation Tax
	Vehicle and Vessel Tax
	Deed Tax
Shared taxes	Domestic VAT
	Enterprise Income Tax
	Individual Income Tax
	Resource Tax
	Urban Construction and Maintenance Tax
	Stamp Tax

Notes:
1. For domestic VAT, revenue collected is shared at the ratio of 75: 25 between the central and local governments.
2. For Business Tax, revenue collected from the following entities is assigned to the central government: (1) the railway department; (2) the headquarters of various banks; and (3) the headquarters of various insurance companies. All other revenues collected from this tax belong to the local governments.
3. For Enterprise Income Tax, except for the revenue from the following sectors and enterprises that is assigned to the central government, all other revenues collected from this tax is shared at 60: 40 between the central and local governments: (1) railway transportation and state postal services; (2) the Industrial and Commercial Bank of China, the Agricultural Bank of China, the Bank of China, the Construction Bank of China, the State Development Bank, the Agricultural Development Bank of China, and the Import & Export Bank of China; (3) China Oil and Natural Gas Company Limited, China Petroleum & Chemical Corporation, and offshore oil and natural gas enterprises.
4. Revenue from the Individual Income Tax is shared at 60: 40 between the Central and local governments.
5. Revenue of Resource Tax collected from the offshore oil enterprises is assigned to the central government. All other revenue collected from this tag belongs to the local governments.
6. Revenue from the Urban Construction and Maintenance Tax paid on a consolidated basis by the following entities is assigned to the central government: (1) the railway department; (2) the headquarters of various banks; and (3) the headquarters of various insurance companies. All other revenue collected from this tax belongs to the local governments.
7. Stamp Tax revenue from securities transactions is shared at the ratio of 97: 3 between the central and local governments. All other tax revenues belong to the local governments.

Table 2.4   Environmentally-related taxes and charges in China

		Taxable item
Resource tax		Mineral resources (crude oil, natural gas, coal, other non-metal ores, ferrous metal ores, and non-ferrous metal ores)
		Salt (solid salt and liquid salt)
Consumption tax		Petrol, diesel, aviation kerosene, automobile tires, motorcycles, cars, yachts, disposable wooden chopsticks, and tobacco, wine and liquor
Vehicle tax	Vehicle acquisition tax	Motor cars, motorcycles, trams, trailers, and transportation vehicles for farm use
	Vehicle and vessel tax	Passenger vehicles, cargo vehicles, motor-tricycles, and motorcycles
Urban construction and maintenance tax		Items that are subject to value added tax (VAT), consumption tax and/or business tax
Land use tax	City and township land use tax	Land owned by the State or land owned collectively in areas prescribed by the effective regulations
	Farm land occupation tax	Land for planting crops including grain and economic crops, land for vegetables, garden plots, and newly cultivated wasteland, idle land, crop rotation land, and grass rotation plant land
Pollution charges		Waste water, waste gas, solid waste, and noise pollution

3. Green tax measures for Hong Kong: a policy proposal

Jefferson VanderWolk

1. INTRODUCTION

In this chapter, I will discuss green taxation[1] in Hong Kong from a policy perspective. After surveying the relevant legal and tax landscape, I will turn to policy proposals for the immediate future. Specifically, I will argue that the Hong Kong government should consider introducing well-designed tax measures related to the use of fossil fuels in the energy and transport sectors, and to the use of water. The benefits of these measures could be significant, including the broadening of Hong Kong's tax base, a reduction of taxes on desirable economic activity, enhancement of Hong Kong's competitive position in the region, and improvement of the environment.

2. GLOBAL TRENDS

The use of tax measures to help address climate change and other environmental factors is increasing worldwide. Carbon taxes have been enacted in several European countries including Ireland and all of the Scandinavian countries, and also in Quebec and British Columbia.[2] In 2009, carbon

---

[1]   The phrase "green taxation" in this chapter includes not only Pigouvian taxes on negative externalities but all types of tax rules related either directly or indirectly to environmental factors such as emissions from the burning of fossil fuels, waste disposal, the use of water and other natural resources, traffic congestion, aircraft noise, and so on.

[2]   Pakistan enacted a carbon tax in June 2009 but its implementation has been suspended by the country's Supreme Court. The UK has a tax called the Climate Change Levy which is imposed on energy use rather than by reference to any measure or approximation of carbon emissions. Regarding British Columbia's carbon tax, *see* the provincial government's publication on the Carbon Tax Act and regulations, B.C. Ministry of Finance, "British Columbia Carbon Tax Update",

tax proposals were introduced in France and Taiwan.[3] Policy bodies in a number of other countries, including China and the United States, have advocated the adoption of carbon taxes and other green tax measures in their countries.[4]

Many economists believe that market-based instruments are likely to be more effective than direct regulation in establishing a price for carbon and thereby mitigating harmful emissions.[5] Between the two most commonly cited market-based instruments – a carbon tax and an emissions trading system – a carbon tax is more often said to be the preferred option from an economic perspective, although the two can co-exist. For the purposes of this chapter, it is not necessary to set out the arguments regarding the pros and cons of the options. It is sufficient to note that a tax on importing fossil fuels that will be consumed in the taxing jurisdiction, with the additional features of the carbon duty described later in this chapter, is consistent with current thinking on the optimal design for a carbon tax.[6]

More generally, green taxation appears to be a valid policy option. A paper published by the Organisation for Economic Co-operation and Development (OECD) concludes that "using taxes to achieve

---

Tax Notice 2008-23, January 2010, http://www.sbr.gov.bc.ca/documents_library/ notices/BC_Carbon_Tax_Update.pdf, November 13, 2010. Regarding Quebec, *see* Chalifour, N., "Carbon Taxes and the Constitution", October 18, 2008, pages 10, 12–13, www.queensu.ca/iigr/conf/EnviroConference2008/Materials/ NathalieChalifour.ppt, November 13, 2010. Regarding the Scandinavian countries, *see* Daugbjerg, Carsten, and Pedersen, A. B., "New Policy Ideas and Old Policy Networks: Implementing Green Taxation in Scandinavia," *Journal of Public Policy*, Volume 24, 2004, pages 219–49. Regarding Ireland, *see* Finance Bill 2010, Sections 60–83, http://www.revenue.ie/en/practitioner/law/finance-bill-2010/ index.html, November 13, 2010.

3   Regarding Taiwan, *see*, e.g., "Taiwan Panel OKs Energy, CO_2 Taxes; May Start In 2011", *Wall Street Journal*, October 19, 2009. The French proposal was shelved by the Sarkozy administration at the start of 2010 in favour of an attempt to reach agreement on a pan-EU carbon tax. *See*, e.g., Saltmarsh, M., "France Abandons Plan for Carbon Tax," *New York Times*, March 23, 2010.

4   Regarding China, *see* text at note 11, below; regarding the United States, *see*, e.g., The Congress of the United States, Congressional Budget Office, "Policy Options for Reducing CO_2 Emissions," February 2008, http://www.cbo.gov/ ftpdocs/89xx/doc8934/02-12-Carbon.pdf, November 13, 2010.

5   *See*, e.g., Avi-Yonah, R. and Uhlmann, D., "Combating Global Climate Change: Why a Carbon Tax is a Better Response to Global Warming than Cap and Trade," *Stanford Environmental Law Journal,* Volume 28, 2009, page 3 and economic studies cited therein.

6   *See*, e.g., Metcalf, G. and Weisbach, D., "The Design of a Carbon Tax," *Harvard Environmental Law Review*, Volume 33, 2009, page 499.

environmental objectives is clearly efficient for the economy as a whole".[7] The paper notes that in the OECD countries, environment-related taxes currently raise revenues of between 2 per cent and 2.5 per cent of gross domestic product. The paper also observes that such taxes can be designed to have low administrative costs: "For example, taxes on petroleum products are usually levied on a limited number of petroleum refineries and depots, and are hence relatively simple to administer and enforce."

The OECD goes on to say, "Applying the new taxes to broad-based tax bases, and introducing them as part of broader fiscal reform, can also make it easier to win political acceptance, and thus make the tax easier to implement." The paper stresses the importance of public awareness of the relevant environmental problem and of the likelihood that the tax will reduce the problem. Involving all stakeholders in policy formulation is also recommended.

Acknowledging the regressiveness of broad-based consumption taxes, including those linked to negative environmental factors, the OECD paper recommends using "direct compensation measures to address concerns for low-income households, e.g. through the social security or tax systems . . . For individuals whose income is so low that they pay little or no tax, it can be preferable to provide cash transfers." The paper highlights the importance of addressing regressivity concerns early in the policy-making process, so as to ensure that the public perceives the taxes to be fair.

The 2009 report of the Irish Commission on Taxation notes that "environmental taxes give effect to the polluter-pays principle," which is enshrined in Article 174 of the European Union Treaty.[8] The report also notes:

> Environmental fiscal measures may be seen as serving a dual purpose. They provide economic incentives to protect the environment, and in addition a source of revenue to alleviate actual or future tax burdens in other parts of the tax system. The aim of an environmental tax may be to improve economic efficiency or contribute to economic growth for example, by funding cuts in social insurance payments. Alternatively, they could be used to address social issues – funding tax cuts or social welfare increases for lower income households and/or to subsidise further action on emissions reduction . . . Tax-shifting policies, under which environmental tax revenues have been used to reduce other taxes, have been used in a number of countries.[9]

---

[7] "The Political Economy of Environmentally Related Taxes," *OECD Observer*, February 2007, http://www.oecd.org/dataoecd/26/39/38046899.pdf, November 15, 2010.

[8] Irish Commission on Taxation, "Report 2009", page 329, http://www. commissionontaxation.ie/downloads/Commission%20on%20Taxation%20Report%202009.pdf, November 13, 2010.

[9] *Ibid.*, pages 330–31.

The Irish Commission on Taxation concluded by recommending the introduction of a carbon tax on fossil fuels, as well as new taxes on motor fuel and road usage.[10]

In China, a government research institute within the Ministry of Finance has recently issued a report on carbon tax reform, advocating the adoption of a tax on the use of coal, natural gas, and petrol. The report suggests using the revenue raised by the tax for reductions in other taxes and the funding of research and development of alternative energy sources and energy-efficiency technologies.[11]

Against this background, let us consider the position of Hong Kong and how it might benefit from implementing green tax measures.

3. HONG KONG: THE CURRENT POSITION

Hong Kong is an unusual jurisdiction. It is an autonomous city-state within a large nation.[12] It has seven million inhabitants, virtually all of whom live in densely packed urban areas. Its economy consists almost entirely of trade and services, since most manufacturing operations were moved across the border to Guangdong province in the 1980s and 1990s. It has no natural resources. Its government provides certain welfare benefits to a large percentage of the populace, but its tax system is extremely limited and taxes are imposed at low rates. Its economic *raison d'être* is in doubt due to the rise of Shanghai and other Chinese cities as international business centers. Yet Hong Kong has continued to attract international business and to thrive economically.

The picture is not all rosy, however. One problem is environmental degradation, with air pollution being a particular concern. Hong Kong's

---

[10] These recommendations are in line with the European Parliament resolution of 24 April 2008 on the European Commission's "Green Paper on market-based instruments for environment and related policy purposes" (April 2008), *Official Journal of the European Union*, 29 October 2009, page C259E/86.

[11] M. Su, Z. Fu, W. Xu, Z. Wang, X. Li, and Q. Liang, "Carbon Tax Reform," Research Institute of Fiscal Science, Ministry of Finance, People's Republic of China, September 2009. *See also* "Institute Warms to Carbon Tax by 2013," *China Daily*, October 9, 2009, page 39, http://www.chinadaily.com.cn/china/2009summerdavos/2009-09/10/content_8675126.htm, November 13, 2010.

[12] Formally, Hong Kong is a "special administrative region" of the People's Republic of China. Under the Basic Law of the Hong Kong Special Administrative Region (SAR), the legal system prevailing in Hong Kong at the time of China's resumption of sovereignty on 1 July 1997 is to be maintained until 30 June 2047 at a minimum.

roads and waterways are congested with vehicles and vessels that run on fossil fuels. Coal-burning power plants, and thousands of factories in nearby Guangdong, add their emissions to the air above Hong Kong. The air pollution has become a factor that deters some people from moving to Hong Kong and prompts others to leave. For those who live in the city, breathing is sometimes a health hazard.

Hong Kong has other kinds of environmental problems as well. Management of the disposal of waste, both solid and liquid, is not as good in Hong Kong as it is in many other countries. And Hong Kong needs to reduce its emissions of carbon dioxide as part of the global effort to mitigate climate change.

The Hong Kong government also faces a number of economic and fiscal challenges. Hong Kong's formerly dominant position as a regional center for international business has been eroded, not only by Shanghai and other Chinese cities but also by Singapore, which has profited from offering tax incentives to multinationals and other types of international investors. Hong Kong's population is aging and increasingly in need of subsidized health care, while the tax base of individual salary earners is gradually shrinking.

Moreover, the overall tax base is already very narrow. Hong Kong's income tax system is schedular: tax is charged separately on business profits, employment income, and rental income from property. No tax is imposed on investment income such as capital gains, dividends, or interest (unless the taxpayer is a bank, in the case of interest). In addition, the tax system is territorial in nature. The law provides that profits and salaries arising outside Hong Kong are not taxable, even when the profits are remitted to Hong Kong.[13] Only a portion of the compensation paid to Hong Kong-based employees is taxed, due to generous exemptions.[14]

---

[13] The territorial limitation on taxation of employment income has been interpreted by the Hong Kong courts in a manner that, in most cases, permits the government to tax Hong Kong residents on employment income earned outside Hong Kong, subject to the possibility of a foreign tax credit. In contrast, the territorial limitation on profits tax has been enforced by the courts, but a great deal of uncertainty remains in many cases as to how to determine whether the taxpayer's profits arose in Hong Kong or offshore.

[14] The basic exemption for a single individual is HK$108,000 (about US$13,850) per year; for a married individual it is HK$216,000 (US$27,700) per year, as of 2009–10. Various additional allowances in respect of dependent family members can bring an individual's total exemption up to several hundred thousand dollars for a given year. In 2007–08, nearly half of the total revenue from salaries tax was collected from only 36,706 individuals – a mere 1.7 percent of the 2,173,000 salaries taxpayers in that year. Considering that the working population

There is no value-added tax, or goods and services tax, or retail sales tax. Transaction taxes are limited to stamp duty on transactions in real property and listed shares; betting duty on horse racing, football and lotteries; a tax on the first registration of cars; a miniscule tax on plastic shopping bags, and excise duties on liquor, tobacco, and motor fuel.

The Hong Kong government touts its "low and simple taxes" and "rule of law" in promoting itself to the international business community as a base for regional operations.[15] However, in reality the application of Hong Kong's territorial taxes on business profits and employee salaries is often far from clear, which detracts from Hong Kong's attractiveness to multinationals' finance managers, who want to be able to predict tax costs with as much certainty as possible. In the profits tax area, the primary area of uncertainty is how to determine whether profits are considered to be sourced in Hong Kong. The Court of Final Appeal has indicated that the inquiry should be limited to the operations that are the direct and proximate cause of the profits in question, with the acts of agents and contractors outside Hong Kong being taken into account.[16] However, the Inland Revenue Department has continued to raise assessments on the basis of operations in Hong Kong that are several steps removed from the realization of the profits, often disregarding the acts of agents or contractors outside Hong Kong who acted on behalf of the taxpayer. Moreover, such assessments have been upheld by the Inland Revenue Board of Review and the lower courts despite the Court of Final Appeal's guidance.[17] In the salaries tax area, the law has long been applied in a

---

in Hong Kong is at least 3,500,000 people, it appears that about half of all salaries tax was paid by about one percent of the working population in 2007–08, and perhaps 35–40 percent of the working population paid no salaries tax at all. Special salaries tax concessions in 2008–09 and 2009–10 have undoubtedly further increased the share of the total salaries tax revenue paid by the top one percent of the working population.

15   *See*, e.g., "Hong Kong. Right Place. Right Time," advertisement by InvestHK in *Financial Times*, November 3, 2009, page 11. *See also* the website of InvestHK, the government department for promoting foreign direct investment, www.investhk.gov.hk.

16   *ING Baring Securities (Hong Kong) Ltd v CIR* [2008] 1 HKLRD 412. The Court of Final Appeal specified that profits should not be considered to arise at the place where the taxpayer negotiated and entered into the contracts under which the profits were earned, but rather should be considered to arise where the operations for which the taxpayer was paid were performed, whether by the taxpayer itself or by its contractor or agent.

17   *See*, e.g., *D16/08* (2008) 23 IRBRD, in which profits from the supply of building materials in Mainland China were held to arise in Hong Kong on the basis that the relevant contracts were negotiated and signed by the taxpayer in

manner that both defies common sense and is difficult to apply in practice to individuals hired from abroad to perform a regional role.[18] Such people include senior managers of the multinational businesses that Hong Kong is seeking to attract. Taxing them on income that they perceive as having been earned outside Hong Kong is not the best way to sell Hong Kong's territorial tax regime to them.

Because of the narrow tax base, the public revenue may decline dramatically when a downturn in the business cycle results in reduced business profits and payrolls. Recognizing this, the government commissioned a study on base-broadening which led to the publication, in July 2006, of a Consultation Document on Tax Reform.[19] In that document the government advocated the adoption of a goods and services tax (GST). The government said that a GST would stabilize public finances by broadening Hong Kong's narrow tax base, and would comply with the "capacity to pay" principle (since it would be based on consumption) without damaging Hong Kong's competitiveness or its low-tax business environment.

Various organizations and individual members of the community expressed strong opposition to the GST proposal, on a number of different grounds. Some were concerned that a GST would complicate tax compliance, making Hong Kong a more expensive and less

---

Hong Kong. *See also CIR v Datatronic Ltd* [2009] 4 HKLRD 675 and *CIR v C G Lighting Ltd*, CACV 119/2010 (7 March 2011), in which manufacturing operations performed by a controlled subsidiary outside Hong Kong on a cost-recovery basis were held to be irrelevant to the derivation of the taxpayer's profits. For a discussion of additional case law and administrative practice, *see* Willoughby, P. and Halkyard, A., *Encyclopaedia of Hong Kong Taxation*, (Vol. 3, Issue 19), 2009, at II [5900] – [6841.3].

[18] Under Section 8 of the Inland Revenue Ordinance, the salaries tax charge is limited to "income arising in or derived from Hong Kong from . . . any office or employment . . ." The Hong Kong courts, the Inland Revenue Board of Review, and the Inland Revenue Department all take the view that the place where the employee actually worked is irrelevant in determining as a threshold matter whether his or her employment income arose in Hong Kong. Rather, they consider it necessary to look at all other facts and circumstances in order to determine whether the taxpayer's *contract* of employment should be treated as located in Hong Kong. This approach has no statutory basis. In practice, it is rare for a Hong Kong-based employee to succeed in claiming that his or her income from work done outside Hong Kong should be treated as arising outside Hong Kong for salaries tax purposes. For a discussion of the case law and administrative practice, *see*, e.g., Willoughby and Halkyard, *op. cit.,* at II [2522] – [2655].

[19] "Broadening The Tax Base, Ensuring Our Future Prosperity: What's the Best Option for Hong Kong?", http://www.taxreform.gov.hk/eng/document.htm, November 13, 2010.

business-friendly place. Others stressed that a GST would increase the cost of consumer goods and services, reducing Hong Kong's attractiveness to Asian visitors as a "shopper's paradise". Still others argued that a GST would be regressive, having a more burdensome effect on lower-income people than on the wealthy.

In December 2006, the government published an Interim Report[20] on tax reform, in which it acknowledged that, as a practical matter, a GST could not be enacted in the immediate future due to the community's general opposition to the proposal. The government noted, however, that a majority of commentators had recognized the need to broaden Hong Kong's tax base.

The Financial Secretary (FS) mentioned the tax reform consultation exercise in his 2007–2008 Budget speech on 28 February 2007. He reiterated the government's intention to introduce base-broadening measures after giving due consideration to all suggestions received. In the 2008–09 Budget Speech, the FS again alluded to the consultation on base broadening, but in noncommittal terms.[21] In both the 2009–10 Budget Speech and the 2010–2011 Budget Speech, base-broadening was not mentioned at all.[22]

A broader tax base continues to be desirable, simply as a matter of good policy in public finance. The financial crisis and economic recession of 2008–09 serve as reminders that the good times do not always roll. The taxable profits of Hong Kong businesses have been greatly reduced, and the salaries tax base has also diminished. However, the government seems to have stopped thinking about taking steps to broaden the tax base. And, not surprisingly, there is no pressure from public interest groups to revive the base-broadening initiative.

---

[20] "Interim Report of Public Consultation on Tax Reform," http://www.tax reform.gov.hk/eng/interim.htm, November 13, 2010.

[21] "We should adopt a pragmatic approach to the problem of the narrow tax base of Hong Kong. In July 2006, the Government launched a public consultation on reforming Hong Kong's tax system to broaden our tax base. According to consultation findings, the community recognises that there is a need for the government to broaden the tax base. However, there is no clear consensus or inclination on how to achieve this objective."

"We will continue to study options on broadening the tax base. I hope to provide opportunities for the community to discuss the tax reform options that are equitable and conform to the 'ability-to-pay' principle, can generate stable revenue, offer certainty and are predictable." (paragraphs 59–60)

[22] In the 2010–2011 Budget Speech, the increasingly narrow tax base was mentioned in paragraph 42, but the Financial Secretary did not suggest that base broadening was required; rather, he asserted a need to increase fiscal reserves, clearly implying that cost cutting was the way to achieve this.

In contrast, the government has been under pressure to take action on environmental protection. Consequently it has adopted, or announced its intention to adopt, a number of environmental initiatives. For example, green tax incentives have been offered in the form of accelerated deductions for capital expenditure on "environment-friendly" machinery and equipment; reduced taxes on Euro V diesel fuel; and exemption from First Registration Tax on electric vehicles. Separately, in July 2009 the government launched a public consultation on proposals aimed at reducing air pollution.[23] In a recent Policy Address,[24] the Chief Executive, Donald Tsang, included a section called "Low Carbon Economy". It highlights a number of environmental measures that are being undertaken or considered, including:

• Reduction of the energy intensity of Hong Kong by at least 25 percent by 2030, compared with 2005 levels.
• Increased use of nuclear and natural-gas-fired sources of electricity supply.
• Subsidizing improvements in energy efficiency in buildings and homes.
• A tax on plastic bags (which was implemented in July 2009).

Environmental watchdogs are skeptical about whether the government is doing enough to address the issues. It is beyond the scope of this chapter to discuss non-tax measures that the government has taken or might take in regard to environmental protection. As for the "green" tax measures that have been implemented in recent years, they have mainly consisted of incentives in the form of tax relief for environmentally friendly expenditure – which further narrows the tax base.

4. GREEN TAXATION IN HONG KONG: EXISTING MEASURES

As noted, current law in Hong Kong contains a number of tax measures that fall under the rubric of green taxation. They include import duties on certain hydrocarbon oils, as follows:

---

[23] The consultation document and related materials are available at http://www.epd.gov.hk/epd/english/environmentinhk/air/air_quality_objectives/air_quality_objectives.html.
[24] "The 2009–2010 Policy Address: Breaking New Ground Together", http://www.policyaddress.gov.hk/09-10/eng/docs/policy.pdf, November 13, 2010.

(a) aircraft spirit   – HK$6.51 per litre
(b) light diesel oil   – HK$2.89 per litre
(c) motor spirit (leaded petrol)   – HK$6.82 per litre
(d) motor spirit (unleaded petrol)   – HK$6.06 per litre
(e) ultra low sulphur diesel   – HK$2.89 per litre.

The duty on light diesel oil is waived for franchised bus service operators.[25] An exemption from duty applies to Euro V diesel oil.

Another green tax in Hong Kong is the newly implemented plastic bag levy, which applies at the rate of HK$0.50 per bag supplied to customers by the large supermarket chains. This tax is the first measure to be introduced under the Product Eco-Responsibility Ordinance, which was enacted in 2008.[26] According to the Environmental Protection Department:

> The Ordinance is a piece of "framework" legislation that provides a legal basis for implementing producer responsibility schemes in Hong Kong. The environmental levy scheme on plastic shopping bags is the first scheme to be implemented under the Ordinance, with the objective of reducing the indiscriminate use of plastic shopping bags.[27]

In the first three months after the levy began to be charged, there was a drop of more than 80 percent in the use of new plastic bags for purchases at covered retailers.[28]

Certain green tax incentives also exist under the current profits tax legislation. These are:

* a full and immediate write-off of capital expenditure on "environmental protection machinery", which includes specified plant and machinery related to air pollution control, waste treatment, wastewater treatment, and low-noise construction; and

---

[25] Duty on diesel oil used by franchised bus companies is refunded to those companies, effectively giving them an exemption from the duty. The total refund for 2005 has been estimated as exceeding HK$1 billion. The net revenue to the government from duties on hydrocarbon oils in 2005 was approximately HK$3.3 billion.

[26] Chapter 603, Laws of Hong Kong.

[27] Environmental Protection Department, "Legislative Council Brief: Product Eco-Responsibility Ordinance: Product Eco-Responsibility (Plastic Shopping Bags) Regulation", December 2008, http://www.epd.gov.hk, November 13, 2010.

[28] "Shoppers Pay for 6m Plastic Bags", *South China Morning Post*, October 29, 2009, page C3.

- a 5-year write-off of capital expenditure on an "environmental protection installation", which is defined as any installation that forms all or part of a commercial or industrial building or structure and is related to any of the following:
  - solar water heating
  - solar voltaic cells
  - wind turbines
  - offshore wind farms
  - landfill gas utilization
  - anaerobic digestion
  - thermal waste treatment
  - wave power
  - hydroelectric power
  - bio-fuels
  - biomass combined-heat-and-power
  - geothermal power
  - energy-efficient buildings (subject to registration under the scheme administered by the Electrical and Mechanical Services Department)

Finally, as noted earlier, the government recently implemented an exemption from First Registration Tax for electric vehicles.

Taken together, the existing green tax measures in Hong Kong do not amount to more than a very small part of the overall tax regime. Given the need both to broaden the tax base and to take further action against environmental degradation, it appears that there is scope to do a great deal more in the area of green taxation in Hong Kong.

5. BASE-BROADENING AND GREEN TAXATION

In 2002, the Financial Secretary received the Final Report of the Advisory Committee on New Broad-Based Taxes.[29] The Advisory Committee had met regularly for two years to consider the best options for broadening the tax base. Eight widely accepted principles of good taxes were used in evaluating different possibilities: neutrality, fairness, effectiveness, efficiency, certainty and simplicity, flexibility, international competitive effect, and

---

[29] "Final Report to the Financial Secretary by the Advisory Committee on New Broad-Based Taxes," http://www.fstb.gov.hk/tb/acnbt/english/finalrpt/btfinal-report.htm, November 13, 2010.

stable revenue yield. The Advisory Committee concluded that, of all the options that it had surveyed, a general consumption tax was the only one that satisfied the main goals of being broad-based and effective in producing a significant amount of revenue even when imposed at a low rate. In addition, a general consumption tax scores well on most of the other criteria for evaluating the design of a tax.

After considering the Advisory Committee's report, the government concluded that a GST should be introduced following a period of public consultation, which began in July 2006. As noted above, the public was generally hostile to the GST proposal, and the government shelved it in December 2006. The government solicited further public comments on other base-broadening possibilities. A list of 10 possible measures (other than a GST) was published on the government's tax reform website. One of the listed possibilities was green taxes on goods or activities that harm the environment.

On the question of green taxes, the Advisory Committee had decided not to decide. The committee had excluded from its deliberations all green tax proposals related to the consumption of goods that have a harmful environmental effect, choosing to refer them to the government for further study. In its Final Report, the Advisory Committee said:

> A specific "green tax" may yield meaningful revenue and have a broad tax base. That said, the Advisory Committee is concerned that it does not possess the expertise to advise whether it will hamper or help the environmental protection objective, or whether a non-tax measure could achieve a superior result. The Advisory Committee considers it appropriate to leave to the Government and its relevant advisory bodies to deliberate on what "green taxes" would be most useful in furthering the environmental protection cause and how each initiative should be prioritized and targeted. The Advisory Committee has therefore not discussed "green taxes" as a tax-base-broadening proposal.[30]

Thus it appears that the Advisory Committee was focused on the environmental-protection aspect of green taxes, rather than considering the revenue-raising and base-broadening potential of particular proposals.

The narrowness of Hong Kong's tax base has been accentuated by the Court of Final Appeal's decision in the *ING Baring* case, as the court's guidance on how to determine the source of profits for tax purposes should make it easier for many taxpayers to treat at least part of their profits as tax-free offshore profits. The reluctance of the Inland Revenue Department to accept that the principles articulated in *ING Baring* have

---

[30] *Ibid.*, paragraph 40.

general application is undoubtedly due to concerns about potential revenue loss. Similarly, the fact that the government has not implemented proposals to clarify the salaries tax rules, by determining the source of employment income on the basis of where the employee worked rather than where the contract of employment is thought to be located, is presumably due to concerns that such a change would result in a loss of revenue.

The goal, now, should be to achieve the base-broadening benefits of a GST without the detrimental effects of a GST. A broad-based consumption tax such as GST has a number of favorable elements, including effectiveness (significant, stable revenue yield), fairness (vertical equity), and neutrality (horizontal equity). Hong Kong's current tax system, with its narrow tax base and mainly income-based taxes, is not at all certain to achieve the systemic goals of effectiveness, fairness and neutrality in any given year. There is widespread agreement, therefore, that Hong Kong's tax base should be broadened, provided that the new taxes are fair and neutral.

At the same time, the people of Hong Kong made it clear in 2006 that they are not keen to live with the negative aspects of a full-fledged GST. Hong Kong's prosperity is due, at least in part, to the ease of doing business in the city and the relative lack of government intrusion in the private sector. Taxes have always been low and tax compliance has always been very simple: for those who are taxable, an annual tax return must be filed, after which an assessment is received and the tax due is paid. In addition, Hong Kong has been free of most import duties and has never had a general sales tax. Compared to most other jurisdictions, Hong Kong is wonderfully free of red tape and tax-related paperwork and cost. This is a competitive advantage that the government should strive to maintain.

Consequently, the government needs to consider alternative base-broadening taxes that would not have the problematic aspects of the GST proposal, namely, substantial new paperwork requirements and compliance costs, and would not involve the imposition of a general sales tax on retail goods and services.

This raises the question of whether the public would support the introduction of green taxes that would affect a broad base of consumers. One indicator is a public opinion survey published by the *South China Morning Post* (SCMP) on January 3, 2007 entitled "Tax Reform, Fiscal Health and the Proposed Goods and Services Tax."[31] A two-thirds majority felt that Hong Kong's tax base is too narrow and that tax reform is needed, but a

---

[31] The survey obtained responses from 690 people described as "opinion leaders and business decision-makers" aged 25 or above with monthly household income of at least HK$40,000. Only 32 percent were readers of the SCMP.

majority said that a GST was not a good idea. Of 15 tax options presented, only two were supported by at least a two-thirds majority: a "tax on luxury goods" (82 percent), and a "green tax such as plastic bag tariff and additional surcharge on waste disposal" (73 per cent). More than 60 percent of those surveyed felt that new taxes would be acceptable even if the reduction in their salaries tax and profits tax liability was only 5 percent or less.

After the shelving of the GST proposal, a public commentator observed:

> One of the options that seems to have gained increasing support from lawmakers and civic leaders is the introduction of an environment-related "green" tax. This appears to be the most sensible choice because Hongkongers can be counted on to chip in for the improvement of the environment, which has been a major concern not only to environmentalists but also to the general public.[32]

The existence of groups such as the Business Coalition on the Environment (Project Clean Air) and the Business Environment Council's Business-Led Initiative on Air Pollution in Hong Kong and the Pearl River Delta indicates that the business community is seriously concerned about air pollution in Hong Kong. In a December 2005 report, "Living Under Blue Skies Paper No. 4: Clean Energy for the PRD", the following conclusions were stated by the Business Environment Council:

> [T]he current deterioration in environmental quality is a result of burning fossil fuels . . . The main regional sources of air pollution are power and transport. For any improvement measures to be effective, general policy mechanisms must be in place . . . Both fuel technologies and pollution controls require financing. Novel ways to do so should be explored . . .

Thus there are grounds for optimism that the Hong Kong community would accept the introduction of green tax measures if they did not have the objectionable features of a GST.

6.   GREEN TAXATION IN HONG KONG: PROPOSALS

In light of the need to address both base-broadening and environmental issues, the Hong Kong government should consider introducing the following tax measures:

---

[32]   Liang, H., "Green Tax the Most Sensible for Hongkongers", *China Daily*, December 19, 2006.

6.1 Carbon Duty

Currently, only motor fuels such as petrol, light diesel, aircraft spirit, and ultra low sulphur diesel are dutiable. It would be advisable to impose duty on the importation, for use in Hong Kong, of fossil fuels such as coal, fuel oil, naphtha, and natural gas. This carbon duty should be payable by the importer at the time of importation.

Carbon duty should be determined on the basis of a fixed charge per ton of carbon dioxide emitted when the fuel is consumed. For example, if burning a ton of a particular type of coal results in the emission of 2.86 tons of carbon dioxide into the atmosphere,[33] and if carbon duty were calculated on the basis of a fixed charge of HK$200 per ton of carbon dioxide emissions, then the amount of carbon duty payable on the importation of a ton of that type of coal would be HK$572. The duty payable in respect of a less carbon-intensive commodity would be lower. For example, the duty payable with respect to a quantity of natural gas that, when burned, would produce the same amount of energy as a ton of coal of the type mentioned above would be about 40 percent less than the duty payable on the ton of coal – that is, about HK$345 rather than HK$572 – because the burning of natural gas emits about 40 per cent less carbon dioxide per unit of energy than the burning of coal.

It is likely that the only significant importers of fossil fuels, other than motor fuels, into Hong Kong are the main suppliers of electricity and gas, namely China Light and Power (CLP), Hong Kong Electric (HKE), and Hong Kong and China Gas (Towngas) which supplies over 1.6 million customers with natural gas. As a result, most of the carbon duty revenue would be collected from only three companies. Under revised Scheme of Control agreements between the Government and the utility companies, part of their carbon duty costs could be passed on to their customers – that is, essentially every household in Hong Kong as well as non-residential users.[34]

---

[33] *See*, e.g., Hong, B. and Slatick, E., "Carbon Dioxide Emission Factors for Coal", *Quarterly Coal Report, January–April 1994*, DOE/EIA-0121(94/Q1), Washington D.C., August 1994, pages 1–8.

[34] Metcalf and Weisbach identify two principles that enable a tax on fossil fuel emissions to be collected efficiently. First, because the amount of carbon emissions from burning a particular type of fuel is known in advance, the fuel, rather than the emissions, can be taxed. Second, because the incidence of a tax is unrelated to the initial collection of the tax, the tax can be collected from upstream producers to minimize collection and enforcement costs and maximize the base of people on whom the incidence of the tax will fall (i.e., downstream consumers). Metcalf and Weisbach, *op. cit.*, page 24.

The remainder of the carbon duty cost would fall on the utilities. To encourage them to shift to cleaner technologies, they should be permitted to pass on all of the costs involved in producing energy from renewable sources.

Thus, the carbon duty would be likely to:

- discourage the burning of fossil fuels by the utilities;
- encourage the development of renewable energy sources;
- encourage conservation of energy by consumers; and
- broaden Hong Kong's tax base.

For low-income households, some form of relief from increased electricity and gas costs would need to be provided. One possibility might be the provision of cash subsidies directly to low-income households through the social security assistance program.

6.2   Motor Fuel Duties Enhancement

Hong Kong already collects duties on motor fuels such as petrol (gasoline) and diesel fuels. However, the rates and scope of these duties can and should be increased.

In particular, the franchised bus companies should be required to pay full rates of fuel duty. Hong Kong can rightly take pride in its public transportation system, but the franchised bus services could be greatly improved from an environmental perspective. Even a casual visitor to Hong Kong is likely to notice the large number of double-decker buses with very few passengers aboard, clogging the main roads and belching exhaust smoke as they lumber slowly up the steep hills. Leaving aside the question of whether the bus companies should be required to replace their existing fleets with smaller, lighter vehicles, there can be little doubt that eliminating their exemption from duty on motor fuel would encourage them to use fuel more efficiently.

In addition, liquefied petroleum gas (LPG), which is used by a broad base of over 700,000 customers, should be dutiable as well, although at an appropriately low rate. Euro V diesel, which is currently exempt from duty, should perhaps continue to be exempt for a period of time in order to encourage investment in new vehicles that use such fuel. At some point in the future, however, the exemption should be removed.

As in the case of carbon duty, the cost of these increased duties on motor fuels would ultimately be borne by the public at large through increased prices for public transportation and for privately purchased motor fuels, thus broadening Hong Kong's revenue base. At the same time, energy efficiency would be encouraged, as the more efficient commercial users of motor fuels would have a competitive advantage over less efficient competitors. Relief for low-income individuals from the burden of increased public transport costs would need to be provided, perhaps together with the relief provided for increased utility costs mentioned above.

6.3 Water and Sewage Charges Enhancement

The Hong Kong government provides subsidized water and sewage services to 99.9 percent of Hong Kong's population through the Water Supplies Department (WSD) and the Drainage Services Department (DSD). These services are provided at a loss, in that the revenue from water charges and sewage charges is far less than the operating costs of the WSD and DSD respectively.[35] These charges should be substantially increased, so that the cost of the services is borne by their users in proportion to their level of use. This would help broaden the base of Hong Kong's public finances.

In 2008–09, the WSD collected approximately HK$2.43 billion of water charge revenue from 2.73 million accounts (2.45 million of which were households). In 2005–06, approximately 45 percent of households paid no more than HK$25 per month in water charges, and only 21 percent paid HK$75 or more per month. The operating costs of the WSD for 2008–09 were approximately HK$6.68 billion (of which HK$2.58 billion was the cost of purchasing water from Guangdong). The government subsidy for the year was nearly HK$4 billion.

The DSD collected sewage charges from 2.49 million accounts in 2007–08, raising approximately HK$700 million. Its operating costs for the year were approximately HK$1.86 billion, resulting in an operating deficit of more than HK$1.15 billion.

The international trend is for governments to set water and sewage charges at a level that will cover costs. The OECD has noted that, in member countries, "pricing structures for municipal and industrial water services increasingly reflect the full costs of providing the services . . . OECD countries are working towards more complete recovery of infrastructure and operating costs from users."[36]

Relief for any low-income households in Hong Kong affected by the increased water and sewage charges could be provided, together with the

---

[35] Financial information can be found at the websites of the WSD (www.wsd. gov.hk) and the DSD (www.dsd.gov.hk).

[36] "Pricing Water", *OECD Observer*, March 2003.

relief relating to utility and public transport costs. Also, beneficial uses of water could be encouraged through refunds of water charges imposed on the relevant use. For example, a refund mechanism could be instituted for water used in water-cooled air conditioning systems, which are far less energy-intensive than air-cooled systems. The refund could be for a portion (or even all) of the water charge payable in respect of the water used for the beneficial purpose.

7. ISSUES FOR CONSIDERATION

7.1 Benefits

The proposed green tax measures could produce multiple benefits. First, they could have a significant base-broadening effect, producing a stable flow of revenue fairly and efficiently, without requiring undue start-up costs or substantial ongoing administrative costs. The existing administrative arrangements relating to import duties on motor fuels could form the basis of the necessary arrangements for collection of carbon duty. As noted earlier, the number of payers of carbon duty would be very small.

Second, the proposed green tax measures would shift the tax burden toward negative externalities, allowing for reduced tax revenue from beneficial productive activity such as business and labor, thereby producing a more business-friendly economic environment. Specifically, the revenue obtained from the green tax measures could make up for revenue lost as a result of a change of policy in respect of the determination of income arising outside Hong Kong from both offshore business activity and offshore services by Hong Kong-based employees. Allowing taxpayers' claims for tax-free treatment of offshore income, under clear and sensible source rules, would help Hong Kong to compete successfully with Singapore and other regional competitors for multinationals' regional headquarters.

Third, the proposed green tax measures would encourage the adoption of cleaner and more efficient methods of producing and using energy and water, and would help to alleviate Hong Kong's air pollution problem and the long-term negative public health consequences associated with it. This benefit would be the single most powerful factor in persuading the public that the new tax measures should be enacted.

Thus, the proposed tax measures could be beneficial from a public finance perspective (broadening the tax base), a public health perspective (reducing air pollution), and a business perspective (increasing Hong Kong's attractiveness as a place to visit, or as a place in which to live and work).

7.2 Political Acceptability

Green tax measures such as those proposed in this chapter stand a reasonably good chance of being acceptable to the community, provided that the public is fully informed of the benefits as well as the costs. It is widely recognized that Hong Kong's standing as an international business center is being harmed by its air pollution problem, and that more needs to be done to discourage emissions and encourage clean energy and energy conservation. The proposed tax measures would conform to the "polluter pays" principle, falling more heavily on those who consume more products and services associated with negative externalities.

The proposed tax measures would also be relatively simple to administer. The vast majority of the broad base of consumers who would share the cost would not be required to file any forms or pay any new bills. Moreover, the charges would be invisible to international visitors, who would continue to enjoy shopping in Hong Kong with no sales tax on retail goods.

Appropriate relief could and should be provided to low-income households, helping to ensure that the new measures were perceived as fair. Finally, the government could use the revenue from the increased charges for a "green shift" of the overall tax burden, reducing taxes on beneficial economic factors such as employment.

Moreover, it is highly likely that the Chinese government would approve of base-broadening tax measures in Hong Kong that were in line with national Chinese tax policy initiatives aimed at reducing carbon emissions. China appears eager to be perceived as actively addressing climate change issues. For example, at the U.N. Summit on Climate Change in September 2009, President Hu Jintao spoke to the General Assembly and affirmed that China's goal is to reduce carbon dioxide emissions per unit of GDP "by a notable margin" from the 2005 level by 2020.

Public acceptance of noticeable increases in the cost of electricity, gas, public transportation and petrol would depend in large part on the government's ability to communicate that Hong Kong's continuing prosperity requires both that the revenue base be broadened (with appropriate relief for low-income households) and that more be done to improve the environment.

8. CONCLUSION

The Hong Kong government's "Brief of Other Options for Broadening the Tax Base" stresses three widely accepted principles for evaluating the strength of a proposed tax: (1) fairness, which depends on adherence to the "user pays" and "capacity to pay" principles; (2) stable and significant revenue yield, regardless of economic conditions or demographic structure; and (3) maintenance of international competitiveness, which in the case of Hong Kong means simplicity, lack of paperwork and compliance costs, and a low overall tax burden.[37] In addition, the need to broaden Hong Kong's tax base means that base-broadening potential is a key criterion for any new tax proposal.

For the reasons discussed above, all of these criteria are met by the green tax measures proposed in this chapter. They would be fair, assuming that appropriate relief was provided to low-income households. They would yield a significant amount of revenue regardless of economic conditions or demographic changes, as they would be based mainly on consumption of essential utilities. They would raise the revenue from an extremely broad base, that is, every household and business in Hong Kong. And they would maintain, and even enhance, Hong Kong's international competitiveness, because they would not require any significant new administrative or compliance requirements; the revenue derived from them would permit clarification of the profits tax and salaries tax rules regarding offshore activities in a manner conducive to attracting and retaining cross-border business; and they would contribute to the reduction of air pollution, which is currently threatening Hong Kong's reputation as a desirable base for international business activities.

The proposed green tax measures should be politically acceptable, assuming the government would clearly explain their benefits and include all stakeholders in the process of designing the final form of the taxes. The most effective message to the community might be "This package of green tax measures will improve our public finances by broadening the tax base, but will not involve the features of a GST that were considered objectionable; and, in addition, the green tax measures will help to improve the environment, reduce other taxes, and preserve our attractiveness as an international business center."

---

[37] "Brief of Other Options for Broadening the Tax Base", http://www.tax reform.gov.hk/eng/pdf/Other_options.pdf, November 13, 2010.

4. Land transportation in Singapore: tax and regulatory policies to promote sustainable development

Stephen L.H. Phua

1. INTRODUCTION

With sustained economic growth, the demand for private transportation becomes an aspiration for those with increased disposable income. This poses a huge urban planning challenge for major cities as the trend towards urbanization continues unabated. Today, half of the world's population lives in urban areas. Based on current trend projections, the world will become primarily urbanized by 2050 with the main source of population growth emanating from urban areas.[1]

In Singapore, the land transportation sector accounts for about 19 per cent of total greenhouse gas emissions, 13 per cent of our overall energy consumption and 50 per cent of the fine particulate matter (specifically PM2.5) in the air.[2] Land Transport Authority (LTA), the statutory board charged with the key responsibility of managing land transportation, has identified several major targets for reducing energy consumption and pollution by 2030. The main strategies to be adopted are: (a) control vehicle population and discourage usage; (b) promote the use of public transport;[3] (c) improve fuel economy; (d) promote the use of green vehicles; [4] and (e) facilitate the use of alternative transport modes.

---

[1] UN-HABITAT, *State of the World's Cities Report 2010/2011 Bridging the Urban Divide*, Earthscan, 2010, page IX.

[2] Inter-Ministerial Committee on Sustainable Development, "A Lively and Liveable Singapore: Strategies for Sustainable Growth", Ministry of Environment and Water Resources and Ministry of National Development, 2009, page 56.

[3] Yam Ah Mee, Chief Executive Officer, Land Transport Authority (LTA), speech made during the inaugural World Urban Transport Leaders Summit, November 11, 2008.

[4] Ministry of Environment and Water Resources, "Mitigation of Greenhouse

In this chapter, the author will describe and evaluate the effectiveness of the major tax and non-tax initiatives that have been, or are being, put in place to address the long-term sustainability of Singapore's land transportation sector. A critical analysis of some of the schemes with suggestions for improvements will also be attempted. This chapter is divided into three main parts. The first relates to the management of private vehicle ownership and usage. The second relates to the incentives available for the promotion of environmentally-friendly vehicles. The last part evaluates the measures that are in place to promote the use of public transport.

2.   MANAGING VEHICLE OWNERSHIP AND USAGE

2.1   Introduction

Although Singapore's primary goal is to prevent or minimize traffic congestion, the approach and mechanisms adopted recognize the "Polluter Pays Principle". In other words, "the cost of these measures should be reflected in the cost of goods and services which cause pollution in production and/or consumption".[5] The system imposes charges as Pigouvian tools to reflect the marginal external costs created by private transport.[6]

This policy is evident in various pricing measures on private car ownership and usage. The imposition of taxes, duties and fees at import, and the requirement to secure certificates at a public auction have significantly increased the cost of acquisition of vehicles in Singapore relative to many other countries.[7]

The ownership control measures are complemented by a road pricing

---

Gas   Emissions",   http://app.mewr.gov.sg/data/ImgUpd/NCCS_Chapter_3_-_ Mitigation.pdf, May 15, 2010.

[5]   Organisation for Economic Co-operation and Development (OECD), "Recommendation of the Council on the Implementation of the Polluter-Pays Principle", adopted on November 14, 1974, C (74)223.

[6]   Resource Renewal Institute, "Green Plans in Action: Singapore: Management Strategies", http://www.rri.org/singapore_strategies.html, May 15, 2010.

[7]   Lye, L. H., "Environmental Taxation in the Regulation of Traffic and the Control of Vehicular Pollution in Singapore", in Milne, J. et al., (eds.), *Critical Issues in Environmental Taxation*, (Vol. I), Oxford University Press, 2003, page 387.

scheme. Notwithstanding the policy shift from an ownership-based system to a more usage-based one,[8] it remains clear that the twin pillars of controlling car ownership and usage will continue to be crucial to Singapore's strategy of managing private vehicle transport. This strategy not only avoids an undue reliance on one system over the other but also decouples the relationship between car ownership and usage.[9] A broad measure of success from this twin-policy shift is evident in the slower rate of growth in car journeys relative to the growth in the car population during the period between 1997 and 2004 as compared with the period between 2004 and 2008.[10]

2.2 Measures Directed at Private Vehicle Ownership

The aspiration to own a car is consistent with urban agglomeration and the correlation between the prosperity of cities and urbanization.[11] These measures thus culminated in the high cost of vehicle ownership in Singapore. A multi-tier taxation and fee structure is designed to create a strong disincentive to own private vehicles.[12]

Currently, a person who intends to purchase a vehicle has to pay a registration fee of S$140, an additional registration fee (ARF) calculated at 100 per cent of the open market value (OMV), an excise duty at 20 per cent of the OMV and a Goods and Services Tax of 7 per cent is further imposed on the OMV plus other taxes and duties. The OMV is assessed by the Singapore Customs, based on the price actually paid or payable for the vehicle.[13]

---

[8] Prime Minister Mr Lee Hsien Loong, "National Day Rally 2008", NUS University Cultural Centre, August 17, 2008.

[9] "Report of the Vehicle Quota System Review Committee", March 1999; review by the Government Parliamentary Committee (Communications) of the Vehicle Quota System (VQS), following the implementation of the Electronic Road Pricing (ERP) system and new vehicle tax structure.

[10] From 1997 to 2004, a 10 per cent increase in the car population triggered a corresponding 23 per cent increase in car journeys, whereas from 2004 to 2008, a 32 per cent increase in the car population resulted in a proportionately lower increase of 31 per cent in car journeys over the same period. *See* LTA, "More Journeys are Made on both Private and Public Transport", http://app.lta.gov.sg/corp_press_content.asp?start=hgsaeh28887x80v8eyw74vjf02tnhy0xnv36xqcuc87g8r9qk4, May 15, 2010.

[11] UN-HABITAT, *op. cit.*, page 18.

[12] Prime Minister Lee Hsien Loong, *op. cit.*

[13] The price is based on the cost, insurance and freight charges. *See* LTA, "Vehicle Ownership: OMV", http://app.lta.gov.sg/motoring_vo_omv.asp, May 15, 2010.

In order to register the car, a purchaser has to bid for a Certificate of Entitlement (COE) under the Vehicle Quota System (VQS). The final COE price payable is dependent on the engine capacity based on the successful bid price submitted in each fortnightly bidding exercise. The system is an open-bidding system with real time information available to each bidder to enable a competitive and transparent basis for the placement of bids.

2.2.1 Vehicle quota system

The VQS was implemented in response to the unintended circumstances of the 1980s that had eroded the effectiveness of car-ownership policies. Implemented on 1 May 1990, the quota system for vehicle ownership seeks to fix a limit to the number of vehicles allowed for registration in a given period of time. The Select Committee on Land Transportation was of the view that since the demand for cars was much more income elastic than price elastic, the taxation system on ownership alone was becoming less effective in controlling the growth in the car population during periods of rapidly rising incomes. Therefore, it recommended the adoption of a quota system to control car ownership.[14]

The car quota system achieved the planners' intention of achieving absolute certainty in the numbers of cars registered in Singapore. Central to the VQS is the outcome of capping the growth rate of the vehicle population at 3 per cent per annum, compared with an average of 6.8 per cent per annum in the three years prior to the implementation of the VQS[15] (see Figure 4.1 below).

It was suggested that the VQS had averted the certainty of traffic congestion and pollution reaching levels that would have become detrimental to the economic development and quality of life in Singapore.[16] With the VQS in place, the trend of growth in the population of private vehicles was curbed and in its place a more moderate pace of growth is permitted if the infrastructure and other variables permit (see Figure 4.2 below).

2.2.2 Conclusion

As a measure to regulate the general vehicle population, the VQS was thoroughly successful. During periods that coincided with rapid economic

---

[14]   Select Committee on Land Transportation, 1990, page 6.
[15]   As of May 2009, the LTA has lowered this growth rate from 3 per cent to 1.5 per cent per annum.
[16]   Omar, M. and Rahman, A., "Certificates of Entitlement (COEs)", *Singapore Infopedia*, National Library Singapore, April 7, 2006, http://infopedia.nl.sg/articles/SIP_1005_2006-04-07.html, May 15, 2010.

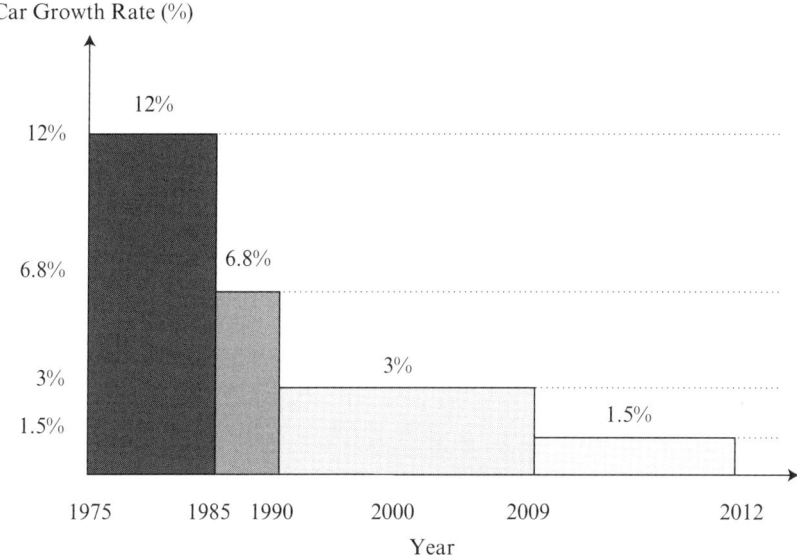

Car Growth Rate (%)

Source: Report of the Vehicle Quota System Review Committee, 1999

Figure 4.1   Growth rate of cars[17]

prosperity, the growth rate of private vehicles was kept constant throughout. In the absence of a quota system, vehicle growth rate would have exploded especially during periods of prosperity when the premium paid for the COEs rose about the average historical amounts (see Figure 4.3 below).

Notwithstanding this, it was apparent that the high cost of private vehicles ownership had an unintended effect. On the simple basis of fixed-cost amortization, the cost of each kilometre travelled is inversely proportional to the distance travelled by each vehicle. Thus, it was felt that unless something was done to curb marginal travel demand, the "sunk cost" of vehicle ownership may incentivize rather than curtail vehicle usage.[18]

---

[17] Mr Raymond Lim, "On Land Transport at the Committee of Supply Debate" (Speech by Minister for Transport and Second Minister for Foreign Affairs), March 6, 2008 [unpublished].
[18] According to the theory of "sunk cost", there is a tendency to continue with an activity once an investment of time, money or energy has been made. *See* Arkes, H. R. and Blumer, C., "The Psychology of Sunk Cost", *Organizational Behaviour and Human Decision Processes*, Volume 35, Issue 1, 1985, page 124.

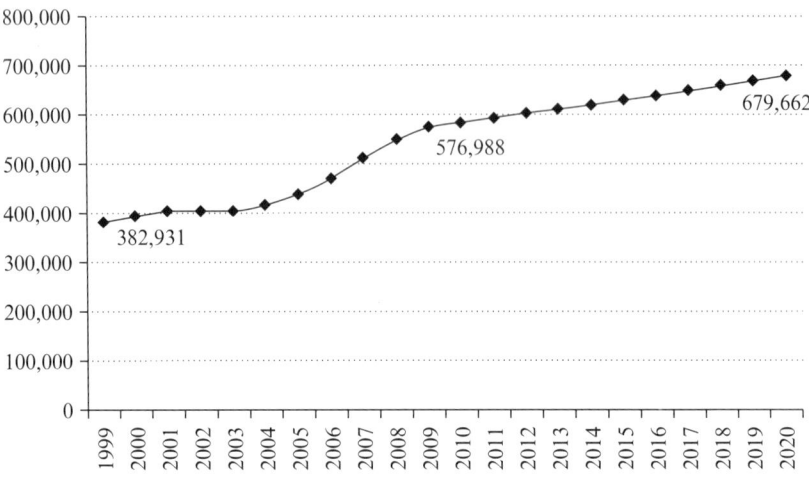

Source: *Annual Vehicle Statistics*, 2009, LTA

Figure 4.2   Car population growth

2.3   Measures Directed at Private Vehicle Usage

Adopting the recommendations of the Economic Review Committee, the Singapore government shifted its transport management strategy from ownership-based to usage-based. The primary rationale for the introduction of a usage-based payment system was that the continued prosperity of the country had created a situation in which an "increasing numbers of Singaporeans view the ownership of cars as an integral part of middle class aspirations." [19] In order to cater to the rising demand for vehicle ownership from a larger spectrum of the population, more COEs were issued and the charges and taxes on vehicle ownership were reduced. As a result of the major policy shift, more households can afford to own cars.[20] The number of car-owning households increased by about one-third, from 320,000 in 2000 to 430,000 in 2008. (See Figures 4.4 and 4.5 below)

---

[19]   The 1990 Report of the Select Committee cautioned that the "situation acquires social and political dimensions." It also warned that the problem will worsen as incomes rise to levels comparable to Japan and the other advanced economies.

[20]   Prime Minister Mr Lee Hsien Loong, *op. cit*. An example cited by the Prime Minister was that of a 1.6L Toyota Corolla: in year 2000, a buyer would have had to pay S$110,000 whereas the same model would cost S$64,000 in 2008 even though the Open Market Value has remained roughly unchanged.

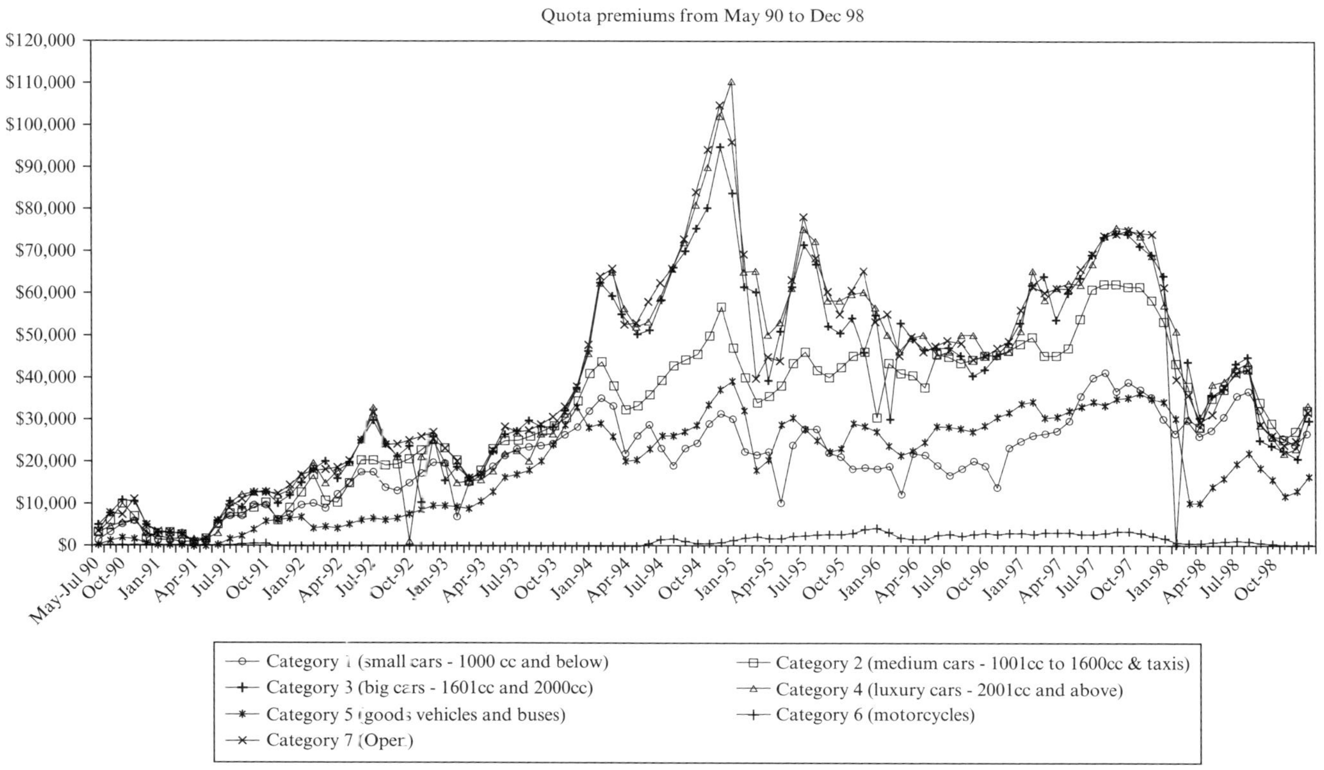
Quota premiums from May 90 to Dec 98
$120,000
$110,000
$100,000
$90,000
$80,000
$70,000
$60,000
$50,000
$40,000
$30,000
$20,000
$10,000
$0
May-Jul 90
Oct-90
Jan-91
Apr-91
Jul-91
Oct-91
Jan-92
Apr-92
Jul-92
Oct-92
Jan-93
Apr-93
Jul-93
Oct-93
Jan-94
Apr-94
Jul-94
Oct-94
Jan-95
Apr-95
Jul-95
Oct-95
Jan-96
Apr-96
Jul-96
Oct-96
Jan-97
Apr-97
Jul-97
Oct-97
Jan-98
Apr-98
Jul-98
Oct-98
Category 1 (small cars - 1000 cc and below)
Category 2 (medium cars - 1001cc to 1600cc & taxis)
Category 3 (big cars - 1601cc and 2000cc)
Category 4 (luxury cars - 2001cc and above)
Category 5 (goods vehicles and buses)
Category 6 (motorcycles)
Category 7 (Open)

Figure 4.3 Premiums paid for COEs

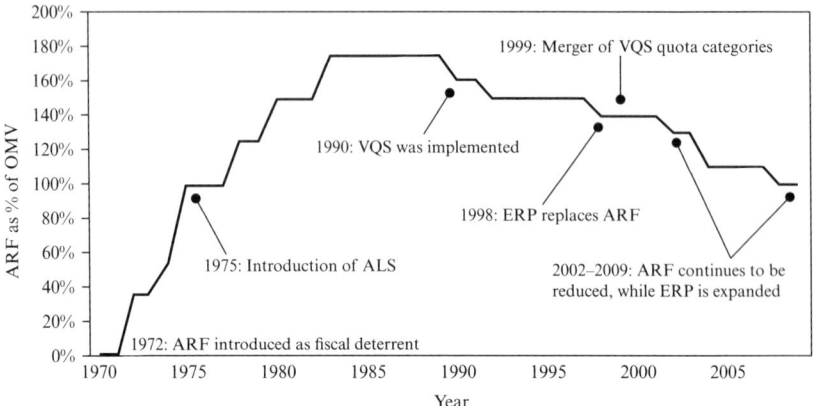

Source: Lew Der and Leong Wai Yan: *Managing Congestion in Singapore – A Behavioural Economics Perspective*, 2009

Figure 4.4   Reduction in the taxes and charges of ownership

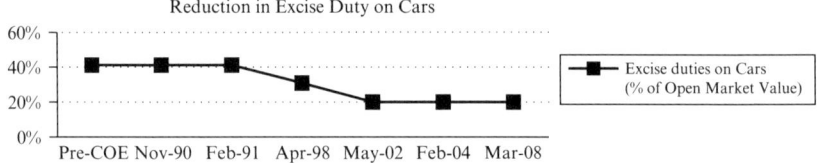

Figure 4.5   Reduction in excise duties

Initiatives implemented to curb private vehicle usage may be subdivided into three broad categories: (1) tax measures; (2) tax incentives; and (3) non-tax measures.

2.3.1   Tax measures

It is reasonably foreseeable that owners who have invested heavily in a private vehicle are unlikely to refrain from using it so long as the marginal cost of driving per kilometre remains low relative to the cost of the vehicle.[21] Based on the demographic trends and vehicle population growth rate, it has been projected that the demand for vehicular trips would continue to soar (see Figure 4.6 below).

---

[21]   LTA, "A World Class Land Transport System: White Paper" (Cmd. 1 of 1996), Presented to Parliament by command of the President of the Republic of Singapore, page 33 (henceforth "White Paper").

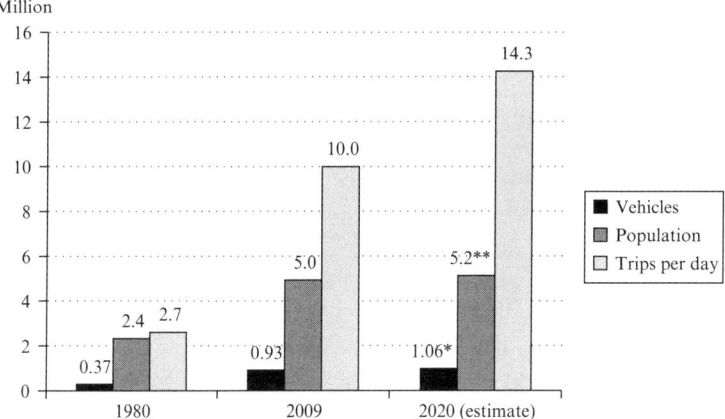

Notes:
*   Based on 1.5% growth per year.
** Based on *World Population Prospects: The 2008 Revision*, Population Division of the Department of Economic and Social Affairs of the United Nations Secretariat.

Source: CEO, LTA, Yam Ah Mee, *Developing a Sustainable, People-centred Land Transport System in Singapore – Principles of Governance*, 2008, World Urban Transport Leader Summit

Figure 4.6   Growing travel demand

The current duties and taxes that relate to usage comprise mainly road tax[22] and excise duty levied on petroleum. The rate of excise duty payable on petrol has remained unchanged since 2003. (See Table 4.1 below)

2.3.2   Road pricing charges: ERP

An annual road tax based solely on engine displacement capacity and a flat rate of excise duty on petroleum are blunt instruments for controlling congestion.[23] With the increase in the car population, one of the solutions was to increase the capacity of the infrastructure. However, there is a clear physical limit to the amount of land that could be set aside for road infra-structure. Furthermore, the Singapore land use policy has earmarked only one-fifth of the available land for total infrastructural use. As Figure 4.7 below shows, there is a real limit to the extent to which congestion can be alleviated by means of infrastructural growth.

---

[22] LTA, "Vehicle Ownership", http://www.lta.gov.sg/motoring_matters/motoring_vo_tax_pte.htm, May 15, 2010.
[23] White Paper, *op. cit.*, page 33.

Table 4.1   Excise duty on petroleum

Commodity	Before 1998	25-Nov-98	13-Oct-01	4-May-02	28-Feb-03
Premium, leaded	46% + S$0.078 per litre or S$0.71 per litre	No change	No change	No change	S$0.71 per litre
Premium, unleaded	46% or S$0.57 per litre	40% or S$0.50 per litre	35% or S$0.44 per litre	No change	S$0.44 per litre
Regular, leaded	46% + S$0.078 per litre or S$0.63 per litre	No change	No change	No change	S$0.63 per litre
Regular, unleaded	46% or S$0.49 per litre	40% or S$0.42 per litre	35% or S$0.37 per litre	No change	S$0.37 per litre
Other, leaded	46% + S$0.078 per litre or S$0.68 per litre	No change	No change	No change	S$0.68 per litre
Other, unleaded	46% or S$0.54 per litre	40% or S$0.47 per litre	35% or 0.41 per litre	No change	S$0.41 per litre
High Speed Diesel	S$0.074 per litre	No change	No change	No change	No change

As a result, the introduction of road-pricing was inevitable. The main purpose of congestion management is to curb marginal usage as a means to offset the larger population of vehicles.[24] The ERP system was implemented in April 1998 as a key measure to control vehicle usage. The primary objective is to charge drivers for the use of certain roads and highways based on location and usage during different times of the day. This seeks to moderate travel demand during peak periods and to encourage the use of alternative routes. As described by the Minister for Transport, Mr Raymond Lim, "[the] ERP is a congestion measure, to help ensure that we have a liveable city. So that, even as the economy and population grow, we need the ERP to ensure that we are in a city in a garden and not a city in a car park."[25]

ERP rates are calibrated to achieve a certain average traffic speed at specific periods of time and location. The rates may be adjusted freely to

[24]   Prime Minister Lee Hsien Loong, *op. cit.*
[25]   Popatlal, A., "More ERP Gantries, Higher ERP Rates but Motorists to Get Road Tax Cuts", *Straits Times*, January 30, 2008.

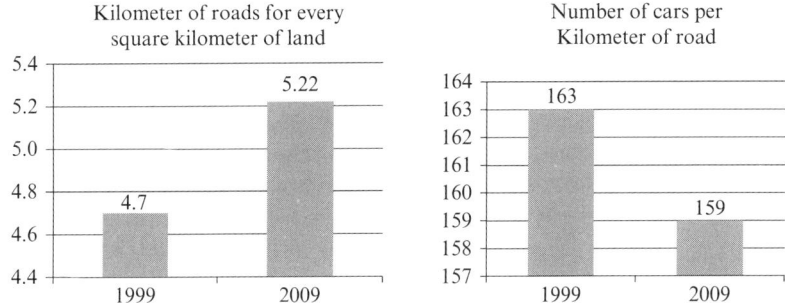

Source: Report of the Vehicle Quota System Review Committee, 1999

Figure 4.7   Road density in 1999 and 2009

respond to changing travel demand and patterns. Currently, ERP rates are reviewed every quarter to maintain optimal travelling speed ranges of 45 to 65 kilometre per hour and 20 to 30 kilometre per hour for expressways and arterial roads respectively. [26]

Figures 4.8 and 4.9 below show the average speeds that are maintained throughout Singapore during the peak hours and the maximum ERP rate that is imposed to achieve this outcome. Figure 4.10 shows that the speeds achieved in the central business district during morning peak hours in Singapore compare favourably with those in some major cities in the world. Figure 4.11 shows the result of a one-off study by LTA to gauge the overall effectiveness of the ERP and Area Licensing Scheme (predecessor to ERP) in maintaining the volume of traffic in the central business district during the morning peak hours.

Enforcement of ERP violations   It is important to highlight that the success of the ERP is also made possible by a robust enforcement mechanism. Vehicles that pass through an operational ERP gantry without an in-vehicle unit (IU) that facilitates instantaneous deduction via an inserted cash card or fails to ensure sufficient balance in the cash card would have the rear vehicle registration plate details captured through high-resolution cameras mounted on all ERP gantries. The penalties and

---

[26]   LTA, "Land Transport Master Plan: A People-Centred Land Transport System", http://www.lta.gov.sg/ltmp/pdf/LTMP_Report.pdf, page 52, May 15, 2010 (henceforth "LTMP").

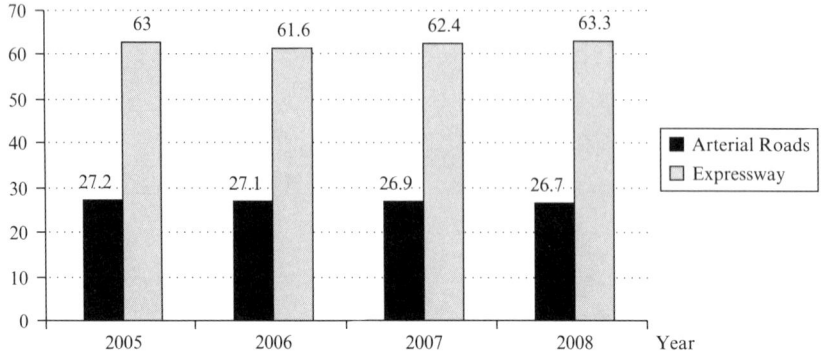

Figure 4.8   Average speed during peak hours in Singapore

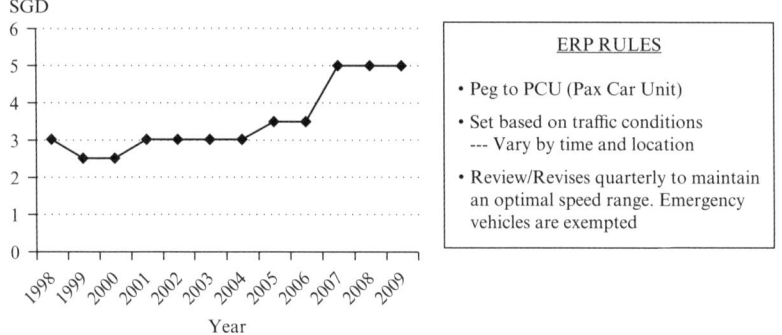

Notes:
1.   These rates do not apply to every gantry in each particular year. (percentage of gantries with these rates is less than 10%).
2.   The rates on the graph do not take into account periodic rate revisions within a given year in question.

Source: Raw Data from LTA

Figure 4.9   Max ERP rates, 1998–2009, elasticity

fines for composition range from S$10 to S$70 depending on the nature of the offence.

2.3.3   Tax incentives for weekend car/off-peak car schemes
Besides the pay per use ERP scheme, there is another scheme that is equally effective in limiting the usage of cars that contribute directly to congestion during peak hours. The government introduced a tax rebate for private vehicles registered for only weekend or off-peak use. The weekend car

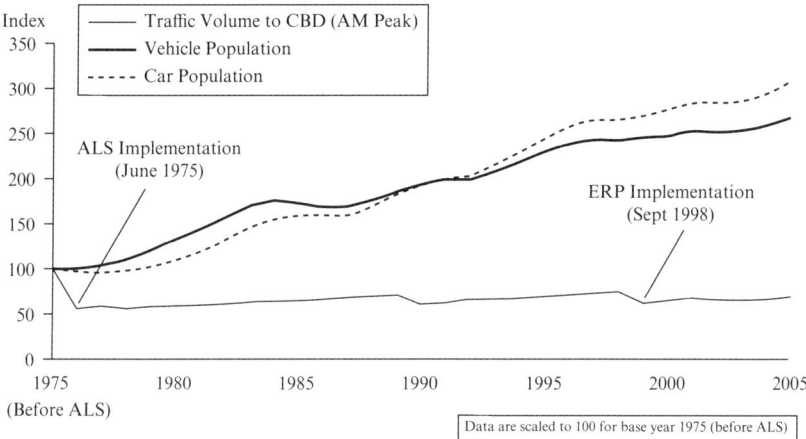

Figure 4.10   Result of a special study of traffic volume in the central business district (AM)

Smooth Flowing Roads

>95% of expressways and major arterial roads during peaks are congestion-free.

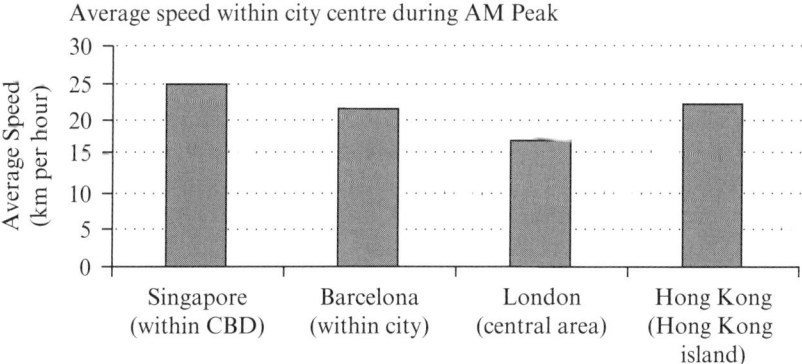

Source: World Cities Research, 2005

Figure 4.11   A comparison of selected cities

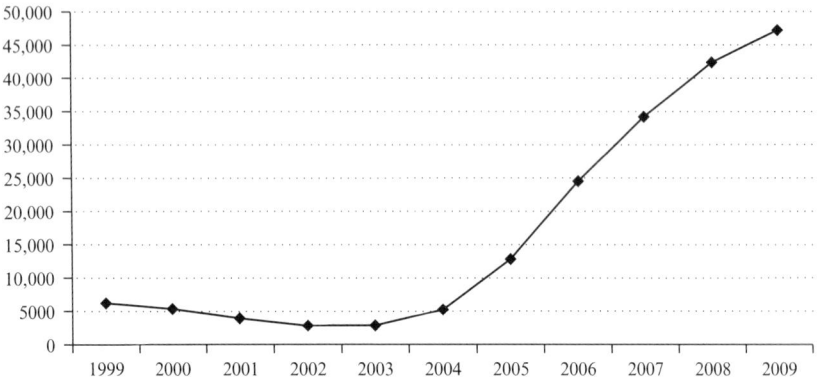

Source: Data from *Annual Vehicle Statistics*, 2009

Figure 4.12   Population of weekend and off-peak cars

scheme was implemented in May 1991.[27] In consideration for accepting a restricted right to use the vehicle only on weekends and during off-peak hours, owners are eligible for rebates against the ARF, excise duty and COE premium subject to a maximum of S$15,000 per vehicle. Owners of these vehicles also enjoy significant reductions in the annual road tax.

Subsequently, the weekend car scheme was tweaked and replaced with the Off-Peak Car (OPC) scheme in October 1994. Under the OPC, the eligibility and quantum of incentive rebates were applied regardless of engine capacity. A buyer of any OPC is entitled to a fixed rebate of S$17,000 at the time of registration, together with a flat S$800 discount on the annual road tax.

The schemes have proved to be very successful and the number of OPCs has risen steadily over the years (see Figure 4.12 below).

In August 2009, the LTA announced that it would implement three initiatives progressively to make the OPC scheme more attractive. First, the e-Day Licence would replace the current paper licence. This would offer greater flexibility to owners who wish to pay the daily S$20 supplementary licence fee for the use of the OPC outside of the regulated hours. Second, the OPC scheme was revised to allow unrestricted usage on Saturdays and on the eve of five public holidays, with effect from January 2010. Last, cash rebates are now available for owners of existing non-OPC cars to

---

convert their cars to OPCs. Owners may claim up to S$1100 for every six months' registration as an OPC.[28]

Hopefully, the details of the OPC scheme will continue to be refined and the supplementary fees reviewed to better reflect the true cost of vehicular usage. With the present global positioning technology, the option of computing rebates on a daily basis for any owner who elects to forgo the right to use the car is now available. Such a scheme would provide an added visibility factor in pricing the direct opportunity costs of taking the car onto the roads.

2.3.4 Non-tax measures

There are two main schemes that offer alternative transport solutions without aggravating the congestion problem on the roads. Basically, these schemes further promote the utilization of vehicles without the need to own a vehicle or to use the vehicle in the central business district. They are the Car Cooperatives and the Park and Ride Scheme.

(a) Car Cooperatives Car-sharing cooperatives were implemented in May 1997, with the objective of allowing more people to share the use of a car without having to own one.[29] Most were modeled after those found in some European cities, and four schemes took off.[30] They were NTUC Car Coop, DCitySpeed, Honda DIRect AcCCESS (DiraCC) and WhizzCar.

In March 2006, there were approximately 432 vehicles and 12,200 users. Recently, the viability of the scheme appears to be in doubt. DCitySpeed closed down in 2007. Honda ceased its DiraCC in 2008. Most recently, NTUC Car Coop also ceased business in 2010. The current operators are much smaller and appear to be trying to find the right balance between meeting service quality benchmarks and profitability.[31]

Without a critical mass of users and convenient locations for car ports, it is going to be a real challenge to keep the current operators in business to serve about 4000 plus users. Several reasons have been tendered for the outcome but two common reasons have been cited. They are (1) the

---

[28] LTA, "Vehicle Ownership", http://www.lta.gov.sg/motoring_matters/motoring_vo_policynschemes_offpeak.htm#new, May 15, 2010.

[29] "Members Pay to Drive When They Need A Car – Car-sharing Co-op to Start at Two Estates", *Straits Times*, February 10, 1997.

[30] Barth, M. and Shaheen, S., "Carsharing and Station Cars in Asia: An Overview of Japan and Singapore", *Journal of the Transportation Research Board*, 2006, page 9.

[31] Lee, D. H., "Honda Car-sharing Scheme to End", *Straits Times,* March 1, 2008.

sustained fall in the car prices in the last few years has eroded the potential savings from car-sharing and (2) the schemes on offer do not appear to offer meaningful advantages over the traditional daily car rental option.[32]

(b) Park & Ride Scheme   The Park & Ride scheme was first introduced in 1975 but abandoned several months later as the take-up rate was too low. The main drawback was that it was a bus-centered system that proved to be cumbersome and inconvenient.[33] In 1990, the scheme was re-introduced with significant improvements.

Currently, the Park & Ride Scheme is in operation at several public car parks located near Mass Rapid Transit (MRT) stations and major bus interchanges. The main purpose of the scheme is to encourage motorists to park their vehicles at these designated car parks. Vehicle owners pay discounted monthly parking rates.[34] The scheme is much more attractive, with the parking rates priced at, or less than, the applicable ERP charges to drive into the central business district.[35]

Nevertheless, the scheme has yet to realize its full potential. The take up rate is lower than the total supply available.[36] Some of the locations are not popular due to the relatively long distance between the parking lots and the MRT stations or bus interchanges. The LTA has studied the scheme and it is likely to announce details on improvement soon.[37] Several challenges or obstacles have been cited. I name but two.[38] There is clearly an infrastructural limitation to the provision of car parks near key public transport nodes. The other is that ERP charges and parking rates in the central business district must attain prohibitive levels for vehicle owners to consider the inconvenience of the arrangement an attractive trade-off.

2.3.5   Conclusion

It is submitted that efforts to price and charge for usage would not be entirely effective without making adjustments to price car parking

---

32   *Ibid.*
33   Foo, T. T., *"*Experiences from Singapore's Park-and-Ride Scheme (1975–1996)", *Habitat International,* Volume 21, Number 4, 1997, page 429.
34   Public Transport @ SG, "Park and Ride Information", http://www.pub lictransport.sg/publish/ptp/en/park_ride/parknride_information.html,   May   15, 2010.
35   Foo, *op. cit.*, page 441.
36   Minister for Transport, Mr Raymond Lim Siang Keat, "Parliamentary Debates", Volume 86, February 22, 2010, at paragraph 8, http://www.parliament. gov.sg/reports/public/hansard/full/20100222/20100222_HR.html.
37   *Ibid.*
38   Foo, *op. cit.*, page 442.

provision as a private good that reflects more accurately the market value of the use of land. In the second global survey of car park rates in 145 cities in the world, Colliers International released its findings in June 2010.[39] Singapore scored with the lowest monthly parking rate among the top 10 global financial centres. The comparable rate in Singapore is about one-fifth of that payable in the city of London, which topped the most expensive at US$932 per month.

Another possible area of improvement is the use of satellite or global positioning system (GPS) technology in lieu of the current gantry system applied in electronic road-pricing.[40] This will empower motorists to chart the most desirable alternative routes. The authorities will also be able to roll out a more responsive and comprehensive system of charging for road use.[41] This improvement appears to be on track for implementation. In a speech to the World Urban Transport Leaders Summit 2010, the Minister for Transport highlighted the practical problem of installing more physical gantries in the long term as congestion becomes more widespread.[42] The LTA has then identified a key potential technology application to the second-generation ERP system, namely, the Global Navigation Satellite System (GNSS). This system makes use of satellites to determine the position of a vehicle. The development and testing of the new ERP technologies is expected to take some years before the system could be launched and implemented.

3. PROMOTING THE USE OF ENVIRONMENTALLY-FRIENDLY VEHICLES

3.1 Tax Incentives for Upgrading from pre-Euro IV Diesel-driven Cars

With effect from 15 February 2007, a new section 19A(9) of the Income Tax Act[43] was enacted to grant to a taxpayer a capital allowance of 100

---

[39] Colliers International, "Parking Rate Survey 2010", http://www.colliers.com/content/globalcolliersparkingratesurvey2010.pdf, May 15, 2010.

[40] White Paper, *op. cit.*, page 36.

[41] *Ibid.*

[42] A Speech by Mr Raymond Lim, Minister for Transport, at the World Urban Transport Leaders Summit 2010, June 30, 2010, http://app.mot.gov.sg/News_Centre/Latest_News.aspx?NewsID=5753&Source =%2fNews_Centre%2fLatest_News_List.aspx&isSearch=true, May 15, 2010.

[43] Rev Ed 2008, Chapter 134.

per cent in respect of capital expenditure incurred for the purposes of a trade or profession in the purchase of a new vehicle to replace an existing vehicle. The effect of this new section is to encourage the deregistration of old diesel-driven vehicles registered before 1991.

The same subsection further provides a similar allowance in respect of the capital expenditure incurred in purchasing a new vehicle during the period from 15 February 2007 to 14 February 2012 to replace an existing vehicle. This incentive effectively promotes the replacement of existing diesel-driven vehicles with those that comply with the Euro IV standards.

3.2   Green Vehicle Rebate Scheme[44]

The Green Vehicle Rebate (GVR) scheme is an inter-agency effort by various Government agencies, namely, the Ministry of Finance, Ministry of the Environment and Water Resources, Ministry of Transport, Land Transport Authority and the National Environment Agency. It offers incentives to promote the adoption of green vehicles which are more fuel-efficient and emit less air pollutants than their conventional petrol or diesel equivalents. The scheme was first introduced in January 2001 for the registration and use of electric and hybrid cars to encourage the use of green vehicles. It was later extended to Compressed Natural Gas (CNG) vehicles in October 2001.

The scheme aims to narrow the existing cost differential between green vehicles and conventional vehicles. Under the current GVR scheme, owners of green vehicles (electric, hybrid and CNG vehicles) can enjoy rebates equivalent to: (i) 40 per cent of the vehicle's OMV for electric, hybrid and CNG passenger cars, (ii) 5 per cent of the vehicle's OMV for electric, hybrid and CNG buses and commercial vehicles, and (iii) 10 per cent of the vehicle's OMV for electric motorcycles. The rebate can be used to offset the ARF payable.

Other tax incentives enjoyed by green vehicles are: (a) CNG cars enjoy a special tax exemption until 31 December 2011;[45] (b) Hybrid, electric and CNG buses and commercial vehicles are eligible for a special concession in road tax. The road tax is pegged to that of petrol equivalents, which is 20 per cent lower than their diesel equivalents.

The scheme has enjoyed relative success. Figure 4.13 below shows

---

[44]   National Environment Agency, "Green Vehicle Rebate", http://app2.nea. gov.sg/topics_gvr.aspx, May 15, 2010.
[45]   With effect from January 1, 2012, CNG cars will no longer be subject to the special tax. Instead, a CNG duty will be phased in at S$0.20 per kg.

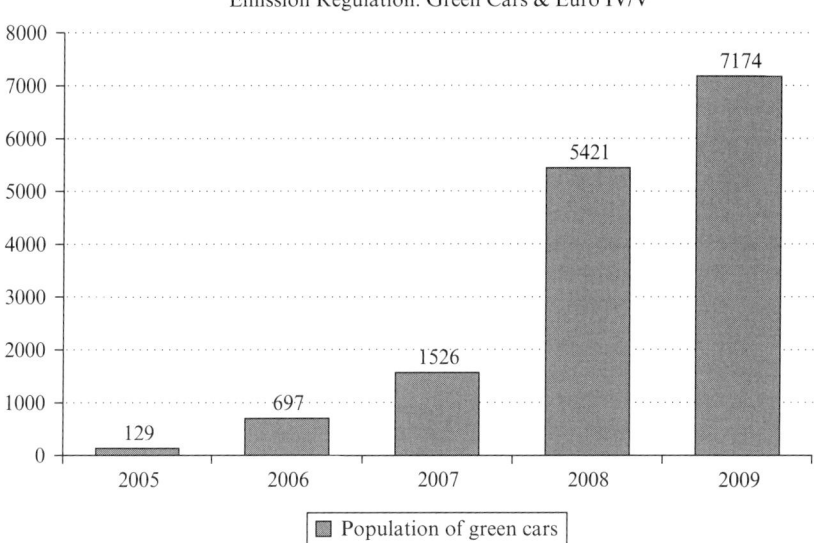

Source: *Annual Vehicle Statistics*, 2009, LTA

Figure 4.13   Population of green vehicles

the steady growth in the population of vehicles over the last couple of years. However, the adoption rate would ultimately be contingent upon further technological advancements, the cost premium over traditional vehicles and the availability of infrastructure. It is important to continue to monitor the market developments to maintain the subsidies for green vehicles at desired levels to incentivize the adoption of green vehicles until the cost differentials narrow sufficiently.[46]

3.3   Improving Fuel Economy and Reducing Pollution

As of April 2009, the National Environment Agency (NEA) has implemented the mandatory Fuel Economy Labeling Scheme (FELS) which provides buyers of passenger cars and light goods vehicles with fuel

---

[46]   Lye, L. H., "Environmental Taxation in the Management of Traffic in Singapore", in Milne, J. et al. (eds.), *Critical Issues in Environmental Taxation*, (Vol. VII), Oxford University Press, 2009, page 217.

economy information at the point of sale.[47] This allows potential car owners to make more informed choices on fuel-efficient vehicle purchases. Non-compliance with the labeling requirement attracts criminal liability.

Imposing high fuel and gasoline tax may have an influence on the vehicle fleet composition by favoring vehicles that use different fuel types, attain greater fuel efficiency, built with other environment-friendly features. As stated above, Singapore has been imposing petrol duty at S$0.44 per litre since 2003.[48] On the other hand, diesel duty was lifted as of 1998.[49] No duty is levied on diesel because a special tax is payable in addition to the road tax for diesel cars. For a diesel car that does not comply with the Euro IV[50] or Euro V emission standard, the current special tax is 6 times that of the road tax of an equivalent petrol-driven vehicle. However, this special tax is reduced to 4 times for a diesel car that meets the Euro IV or Euro V emission standards.

The Environmental Protection and Management Act (EPMA)[51] confers on the Ministry of Environment and Water Resources (MEWR) the authority to prescribe emission standards from any source of air pollution "including motor vehicles".[52] Vehicular emission standards are established in Singapore by the Pollution Control Department (PCD) of MEWR. The regulatory standards are differentiated according to the different categories of vehicles: (i) Light-Duty Highway Vehicles (includes motorcycles, petrol-driven and diesel-driven vehicles), (ii) Heavy-Duty Highway Vehicles, and (iii) Off-Road Engines.[53]

---

[47] Under Section 40C of the Environment Protection Management Act (Chapter 94A of 2002 Rev. Ed. Sing.), the supply of registrable goods is prohibited unless the goods are registered and labeled in the prescribed manner. The list of registrable goods can be found in Part III of the Environmental Protection and Management (Registrable Goods) Order. *See also* Environmental Protection and Management (Energy Conservation) Regulations and Environmental Protection and Management (Composition of Offences) Regulations.

[48] *See* Rev Ed 2009, Chapter 27, First Schedule, Customs (Duties) Order.

[49] Prior to 1998, diesel tax was levied at S$0.08 per litre.

[50] Note that it is mandatory for vehicles registered on or after October 1, 2006 to meet the Euro IV standards. *See* Part II, Second Schedule of the Environmental Protection (Vehicular Emission) Regulations.

[51] 2002 Rev. Ed. Sing., Chapter 94A.

[52] EPMA, Paragraph 4, Third Schedule. *See also* EPM (Vehicular Emissions) Regulations.

[53] For the latest vehicle and engine regulations, refer to website: "New Vehicle and Engine Regulations", Emission Standards Singapore, http://www.dieselnet.com/standards/sg/, May 15, 2010.

In addition, all vehicles are subject to mandatory periodic inspections.[54] During such inspections, vehicle emissions are tested to ensure that they comply with the prescribed standards.[55] To reduce emissions from vehicles, the PCD also takes stringent enforcement actions against smoky vehicles on the roads. It is an offence for any person to use or permit the use of any smoky vehicle on the road.[56] Video cameras are used to capture vehicles that emit visible smoke.[57] Since September 2000, smoke tests have also been carried out on chassis dynamometers of vehicles.[58]

4. IMPROVING AND PROMOTING THE USE OF PUBLIC TRANSPORT

Another key strategy to achieve greater energy efficiency in the transport sector is the improvement of public transport as an alternative to cars.[59] As Singapore is able to allocate only a limited amount of land to infrastructure, the expected increase in travel demand must therefore be met largely by public transport.[60] Public transport is a more efficient mode of transport in terms of energy use. According to the Sustainable Singapore Blueprint, a private car carrying only the driver uses nine times the energy

---

[54] *See* Section 90 of the Road Traffic Act and Road Traffic (Motor Vehicles (Compulsory Inspection)) Rules. The frequency of inspection ranges from 6 monthly periods for taxis, omnibus and motor cars more than 10 years old to biennial periods for motor cars aged 4 to 10. The exact period depends on the age and type of vehicle.

[55] In 2009, the average pass rate at the first inspection for all classes of vehicles was 91.2 per cent. Generally, vehicles that are older than 10 years achieved a first inspection pass rate of about 10 per cent less than those that are less than 5 years old. *See* http://www.lta.gov.sg/corp_info/doc/MVP06-1%20(Veh%20Insp).pdf, May 15, 2010. Due to structural tax incentives designed to encourage the scrapping of vehicles that hit the statutory 10 year life span, the average age of the vehicular fleet in Singapore is relatively young, *see* http://www.lta.gov.sg/corp_info/doc/MVP06-1%20(Veh%20Insp).pdf, May 15, 2010.

[56] Section 19 of the Environmental Protection and Management (Vehicular Emissions) Regulations.

[57] 50 HSU (Hartridge Smoke Unit).

[58] Chua, Y. P., "Towards Environmentally Sustainable Transportation Singapore", National Environment Agency, http://www.uncrd.or.jp/env/2nd-regional-est-forum/presentations/Singapore.pdf, May 15, 2010.

[59] Prime Minister Lee Hsien Loong, *op. cit.*

[60] Mr Yam Ah Mee, *op. cit.*

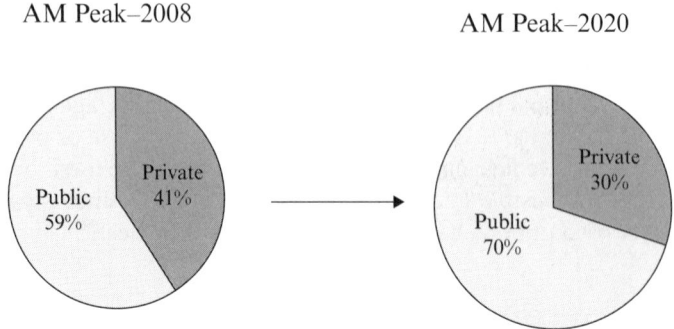

AM Peak–2008   AM Peak–2020

Sources:
Yam Ah Mee, *Developing a Sustainable, People-Centred Land Transport System in Singapore – Principles of Governance*, 2008, World Urban Transport Leader Summit
Raymond Lim, *Welcome Address*, 2009, the 2nd World Roads Conference

Figure 4.14   High transport mode share

used by a bus and 12 times that used by a train on a per passenger-kilometer travelled basis.[61]

The Singapore government aims to achieve a modal share of 70 per cent of public transport journeys made during morning peak hours by 2020,[62] an increase from the 59 per cent in 2008.[63] To achieve this, more than S\$40 billion has been set aside to improve the public transport system to make it more convenient and accessible to commuters.[64] See Figure 4.14.

4.1   Expanding the Rail Transport Network

The LTA will double Singapore's rail network from the current 142 km to 278 km, by adding new lines and extensions to enhance direct rail access throughout the country. These new lines include the Circle Line, Downtown Line, the North-South Line Extension, the Tuas Extension, the Thomson Line, and the Eastern Region Line.

---

[61]   Inter-Ministerial Committee on Sustainable Development, "A Lively and Liveable Singapore: Strategies for Sustainable Growth", *op. cit.*, page 56.

[62]   *Ibid.*, page 57.

[63]   Ministry of Environment and Water Resources, *op. cit.*, page 12.

[64]   Inter-Ministerial Committee on Sustainable Development, "A Lively and Liveable Singapore: Strategies for Sustainable Growth", *op. cit.*, pages 56–7.

4.2   Greater Priority for Buses on the Roads

The LTA is also charged to take over the role of central bus planning, in order to develop a more integrated and seamless connections between Singapore's bus and rail services. New measures will be introduced to further enhance priority of buses over other traffic during peak periods. They include the expansion of the bus lane scheme and the Mandatory Give-Way to Buses scheme at selected bus stops island wide,[65] and a traffic signal priority for buses at some major heavy traffic junctions.

The improvement of the bus service forms an important part of the integrated transport policy of Singapore.[66] However, buses are often subject to delays like other vehicles, especially during peak hours. To increase the travelling speeds of buses, 112 km of road lanes have been designated as bus lanes since 1974.[67] The lanes operate for a period of around two-and-a-half hours during the morning and evening peak hours respectively. Furthermore, full-day exclusive bus lane schemes have been implemented in the city to further increase the attractiveness of bus transport. The implementation of such bus lanes has increased bus speeds by up to 16 per cent.[68]

The scheme is also rendered effective by a ban on roadside parking on the left lane. Loading and unloading activities by goods vehicles are permitted only during non-bus lane operating hours. Hefty fines are levied on the violation of the bus lane rules during peak hours.[69] While bus lanes are effective, the increased use would entail a reduction in road capacity for the other vehicles during the peak hours. Bus lanes are only designated after detailed studies are done and they usually meet predetermined parameters such as a requirement that at least 50 buses use that section of the road every hour during the peak hours.[70]

Under the Land Transport Master Plan, the average bus speeds for feeder and trunk services would have achieved 20–25 kilometres per hour in 2009.[71] Among the various measures taken, the aggregate distance of

---

[65]   LTA, "More Journeys are Made on Both Private and Public Transport", http://app.lta.gov.sg/corp_press_content.asp?start=hgsaeh28887x80v8eyw74vjf02 tnhy0xnv36xqcuc87g8r9qk4, May 15, 2010.

[66]   LTMP, *op. cit.,* page 74.

[67]   Menon, G. and Kuang, L.C., "Lessons from Bus Operations", LTA, paragraph 16.1, http://www.lta.gov.sg/corp_info/doc/Lessons%20from%20Bus%20 Operations%20REV5.pdf, May 15, 2010.

[68]   LTMP, *op. cit.,* page 32.

[69]   LTA, "Lessons from Bus Operations", *op. cit.,* paragraph 16.2.

[70]   *Ibid.,* paragraph 16.2.

[71]   LTMP, *op. cit.,* page 6. The previous speed range in 2006 was 16 to 29 kilometres per hour.

bus lanes was increased. In 2000, the total distance of bus lanes stood at 120 km. Normal bus lanes increased to 155 km in 2009 and full-day exclusive bus lanes also increased from 8 km in 2007 to 23 km in 2009.[72]

Last, the LTA discovered after a detailed study that "9 per cent of journey time was spent by buses trying to exit bus bays."[73] A pilot "Mandatory Give-Way to Buses" Scheme was implemented at 22 bus bays in December 2008 to reduce the total journey time. The scheme requires motorists to give way to buses that exit designated bus stops.[74] The result of the pilot study showed that buses were able to exit the bus bays faster by up to 73 per cent. Consequently, the total journey time for these bus services was reduced by up to 7 per cent. The LTA intends to extend that scheme to an estimated 180 bus bays.[75]

4.3   More Choices for Public Transport Users

To cater for different segments of commuters and their different needs, differentiated services are being introduced to provide more choices for commuters. These include the premium bus service scheme that caters for commuters who are prepared to pay a higher fare for a higher level of bus service, innovative basic bus services such as the Fast Forward bus service, and liberalization of the taxi industry (that is, deregulation of fares or supply of taxis) for commuters who wish to have a personalized door-to-door service that is similar to using private cars.[76]

As a further measure to help commuters conveniently plan their travel routes and reduce overall journey times on public transport, the LTA is in the process of implementing online and mobile platforms that will provide real-time and multi-modal public transport travel information.[77]

4.4   Bicycles

Increasingly, bicycles are being regarded as a viable form of transportation despite the inclement weather, tropical temperatures and absence of infrastructure. Currently, the use of bicycles in Singapore as a commuting

---

[72]   LTA, "Annual Report 2009", page 26, http://www.lta.gov.sg/corp_info/corp_pub.htm, May 15, 2010.

[73]   LTMP, *op. cit.*, page 32.

[74]   *Ibid.*

[75]   LTA, "Annual Report 2009", *op. cit.*, page 26.

[76]   LTMP, *op. cit.*, pages 36–8.

[77]   Inter-Ministerial Committee on Sustainable Development, "A Lively and Liveable Singapore: Strategies for Sustainable Growth", *op. cit.*, page 57.

tool is limited.[78] Under the Land Transport Master Plan, the LTA intends to develop cycling as a non-motorized transport option to link homes and transport nodes.[79]

To achieve this, LTA has set out to provide more bicycle parking facilities around housing estates and MRT stations. Portable bicycles that comply with specific dimensions are also allowed on MRT trains. LTA also plans to utilize the Park Connector Networks already in place to link cyclists to nearby transport hubs.[80]

In 2007, a feasibility study on the use of pedestrian footpaths in the Tampines town region was conducted as part of a 2-year trial.[81] As a general rule, cycling on the pedestrian pathways is prohibited.[82] Cycling on pedestrian walkways for the Tampines Town Region is now fully legalized. The success has led to the adoption of similar schemes in the other major towns. The trial validates the value of promoting cycling as a mode of transport.[83] It is affordable and environmentally friendly. The use of bicycles should be further encouraged especially for short distances within high density areas with public amenities. The infrastructure should be further improved to strike a good balance between cyclists and other road users.[84]

5. CONCLUSION

It is clear from the above survey that the policies designed to enhance the energy-efficiency of personal transportation in Singapore have enjoyed a good measure of success. The key to Singapore's approach has been a high degree of inter-government agency co-operation in the conceptualization

---

[78] Barter, P. A., "The Status of Bicycles in Singapore", in Tiwari, G. A. and Jain, H. (eds.), *Bicycling in Asia*, Interface for Cycling Expertise (I-CE), Utrecht, 2008, pages 49–66.

[79] LTA, LTMP, *op. cit.*, page 74.

[80] *Ibid.*

[81] News release by Tripartite Committee comprising LTA, Singapore Traffic Police and Tampines Grassroot Organisation, "The Cycling On Footways Study In Tampines Town From 27 May 2007 To 30 May 2008", May15, 2007, http://app.lta.gov.sg/corp_press_content.asp?start=1774, May 15, 2010.

[82] Road Traffic Rules, Rev.Ed. 1999, Rule 28.

[83] LTA, "Background on 'Cycling on Footways' Study in Tampines Town (May 2007 to May 2008 & August 2008 to January 2009)", http://www.lta.gov.sg/images/Annex%20A%20-%20Background%20on%20Cycling.pdf, May 15, 2010.

[84] Road Traffic (Bicycles) (Exemption) Order 2010. *See also* Town Council of Tampines (Common Property and Open Spaces) By-laws (S 72/2010).

and implementation of policies. The strategy is best described as eclectic and pragmatic. Taxes and tax expenditures are used in combination with user-based charges to price and influence the behaviour of land transport consumers.

Notwithstanding the positive outcomes, Singapore must continue to invest in its public infrastructure to reduce the carbon footprint of the transport industry. It is no longer sufficient to focus on congestion avoidance as a goal. Energy security and costs have a long-term impact on the survival and prosperity of nations. The adoption of sustainable development policies such as conservation, enhancing energy-efficiency and abatement are becoming increasingly critical. Education of the public is the best long-term strategy but there must also be the political will to take short-term measures to enforce the reduction of each person's carbon footprint.

Last, the incorporation of sustainable development into a nation's policy goal is not necessarily a zero sum game. By participating in the development of green energy technologies, nations stand to reap long-term benefits. Technology acquisition and transfer would typically entail a transfer of skills to the domestic labour market. The discovery of new technologies through investments in research and development would eventually enable some nations to export green goods and services to the rest of the world.

5. Environmental taxation in the United States: retrospective and prospective

Janet E. Milne*

The fight against pollution . . . is not a search for villains. For the most part, the damage done to our environment has not been the work of evil men, nor has it been the inevitable by-product either of advancing technology or of growing population. It results not so much from choices made, as from choices neglected; not from malign intention, but from failure to take into account the full consequences of our actions. Quite inadvertently, by ignoring environmental costs we have given an economic advantage to the careless polluter over his more conscientious rival.

President Richard M. Nixon, 1970[1]

1. INTRODUCTION

In 1920, A. C. Pigou quietly launched the effort to use tax systems to address environmental problems with his statement that it is "possible for the State, if it so chooses, to remove the divergence in any field [between trade and social net product] by 'extraordinary encouragements' or 'extraordinary restraints' upon investments in that field,"[2] citing taxes as an example.[3] Although not confined to environmental problems, his concept has become synonymous with the principle of internalizing environmental externalities. Taxes that increase the cost of environmentally damaging activities can serve as "extraordinary restraints" that bring the external environmental

---

* The author expresses her appreciation to Richard Cullen for organizing the conference that generated this chapter. A modified version of this chapter was published in Lewis & Clark Law Review, Volume 15, Issue 2, 2011.

[1] President Richard Nixon, *Special Message to the Congress on Environmental Quality*, February 10, 1970 (henceforth "President Nixon Message").

[2] Pigou, A.C., *The Economics of Welfare*, Macmillan and Co., Limited, 1920, page 168.

[3] *Ibid.*

costs back into the private sector's calculations. They can also reflect the polluter-pays principle[4] and the concept of least-cost abatement that evolved later in the 20th century.[5] On the other side of Pigou's coin, environmental tax expenditures can serve as "extraordinary encouragements" for environmentally positive activities that otherwise might not occur, allowing society as the beneficiary to assume some of the cost.[6]

The federal government in the United States has a long history of exploring the imposition of environmental taxes on environmentally damaging activities. In the early 1970s President Nixon proposed taxes on lead additives to gasoline and sulfur dioxide emissions[7] and, although unsuccessful, his efforts represented one of the early attempts to try to harness tax systems for environmental protection. Later measures were more successful. For example, in the wake of the Oil Embargo, Congress enacted a tax on gas guzzling cars in 1978[8] and two years later a tax on chemicals to finance the Superfund, a fund dedicated to cleaning up hazardous waste sites.[9] Following the negotiation of the Montreal Protocol in the late 1980s, Congress imposed a tax on ozone-depleting chemicals,[10] and the idea of a broad-based energy tax was quietly but seriously discussed during negotiations over deficit reduction between Congress and the administration of President George Herbert Walker Bush in 1990. In 1993, discussions went public when President Clinton proposed a broad-based energy tax,[11] which generated intense national debate but ultimately failed to gather sufficient support for passage.

Since 1993, Congress has not seriously debated any significant new

---

[4]   European Environment Agency, *Using the Market for Cost-effective Environmental Policy: Market-based Instruments in Europe*, European Environment Agency, 2006, page 13; Organisation for Economic Co-operation and Development (OECD), *Polluter-Pays Principle*, OECD, 1975, page 6.

[5]   Surrey, S., *Pathways to Tax Reform*, Harvard University Press, 1973, pages 156–60. For discussions of the theory of environmental taxes and how they affect the design of environmental taxes, *see* Milne, J.E., "Environmental Taxation: Why Theory Matters," in J. Milne et al. (eds.), *Critical Issues in Environmental Taxation* (Vol. I), Richmond Law & Tax, 2003, pages 3–26.

[6]   When describing extraordinary encouragements, Pigou referred to "bounties", which took the form of a variety of government support programs. Pigou, *op. cit.*, page 169. The same concept would seem to apply to tax expenditures.

[7]   *See* Surrey, *op. cit.*, page 164.

[8]   26 U.S.C. § 4064 (enacted as part of the Energy Tax Act of 1978).

[9]   *Ibid.* §§ 4661, 4662.

[10]   *Ibid.* §§ 4681, 4682.

[11]   *See* Department of Treasury, Office of Tax Policy, "Specifications of the Administration's Modified Btu Energy Tax Proposal," United States Government, 1993 (henceforth "Office of Tax Policy Specifications").

environmental taxes. Attention has turned instead to tax expenditures that reduce the cost of environmentally positive choices, building on a history of using environmental tax expenditures that started in the late 1960s. Recently, the question of repealing tax expenditures for the oil and gas industry has been placed on the table.

While this chapter cannot provide a comprehensive inventory of environmental tax measures in the United States, it selects examples that illustrate lessons one might learn from the U.S. experience. It focuses primarily on federal measures and explores the use of both environmental taxes and environmental tax expenditures. After considering institutional questions that can influence the use of environmental taxation instruments (Section 2), the chapter highlights lessons one can learn from the U.S. experience about the design features of environmental taxes – the choice of the tax base and tax rate (Section 3) and the use of the tax revenue (Section 4). It then turns to the tax expenditure side of the equation, reviewing the extent to which the U.S. has used tax expenditures and their budgetary context (Section 5). It concludes with thoughts about the future use of environmental tax measures in the United States (Section 6) and themes that may be relevant to other countries as they consider the role of environmental taxation in their environmental portfolio (Section 7). The discussion below refers to environmental tax increases as environmental taxes[12] and environmental tax benefits as environmental tax expenditures, and it uses the term environmental taxation to apply to both.

2.   INSTITUTIONAL CONSIDERATIONS

2.1   The Structure of the Tax System

The use of environmental taxation instruments in the United States is inevitably shaped by the nature of tax systems at different levels of government. The federal government relies on income taxes, excise taxes, estate taxes and social security taxes, the first three of which are adaptable vehicles for environmental taxation instruments.[13] As a general but

---

[12]   The OECD uses the term "environmentally related taxes" in recognition of the fact that some taxes may have environmental features without being classic environmental taxes. For the sake of simplicity this chapter has reduced the term to environmental taxes. OECD, *The Political Economy of Environmentally Related Taxes*, OECD, 2006, page 26.

[13]   In 2008, individual income taxes generated US$1.146 trillion, corporate income taxes US$304 billion, social security taxes US$900 billion, excise taxes

not absolute rule, environmental tax expenditures tend to lie within the income tax regime, pollution taxes often take the form of excise taxes, and tax expenditures for inheritances of conservation-related lands lie within the estate tax. Most states also impose income taxes, excise or sales taxes, and estate or inheritance taxes, which can provide similar opportunities for environmental measures. Where states use the federal income tax principles to define state tax liability, environmental features of the federal tax code are silently wrapped into the state tax system.

At the state and local levels, the property tax – an annual tax on the value of real property – enters the picture. Not used by the federal government, it plays a significant role in generating revenue for municipal governments. Under state policies that apply to the municipalities, the property tax frequently serves as a vehicle for tax expenditures for undeveloped land, taking the form of reduced property tax assessments for agricultural or forest land or protected conservation land.[14] With limited independent taxing authority,[15] municipalities may have less freedom to design and implement environmental taxes, but exceptions prove that this is not a flat rule. For example, Boulder, Colorado, has enacted a tax on electricity that funds the city's climate action program.[16]

This allocation of taxing systems among the different levels of government means that the environmental tax message is not consistent nationwide. While the federal measures are broadly applicable, states will decide which goals they will pursue through their tax policies. In addition, the variation in tax regimes from state to state (for example, some with income taxes and some without) naturally leads to deviations. The U.S. tax regime reflects the principle of federalism on which the country was founded: federal unity but retained state powers, which inevitably means a lack of uniformity. Thus, environmental tax instruments reflect the characteristics of the tax regimes to which they are harnessed, and each instrument should not be analyzed in isolation but rather in light of the interactions with policies at the different levels of government. The fact that the discussion below focuses on federal environmental tax measures is not intended to suggest that states have not enacted measures that would affect an analysis of the role of tax policy in achieving environmental protection. It

US$67 billion, and estate and gift taxes US$29 billion. United States Office of Management and Budget, *Analytical Perspectives: Budget of the U.S. Government, Fiscal Year 2010*, United States Government, 2009, pages 277–8.

[14]   *See* generally Malme, J., *Preferential Property Tax Treatment of Land*, Lincoln Institute of Land Policy, 1993.

[15]   Some cities, such as New York, have the authority to impose income taxes.

[16]   Boulder Rev. Code §§ 3-12-1, 3-12-2.

merely reflects a practical limitation on the scope of coverage possible in this analysis.

2.2   The Implications of Jurisdictional Turf

Jurisdictional divides within one level of government have significant implications for environmental taxation in the United States. In the legislative branch of the federal government, environmental committees within Congress have jurisdiction over environmental matters, while tax-writing committees have jurisdiction over "revenue measures," placing tax writers in the position of controlling environmental policies executed through the tax code. Although the House of Representatives and Senate must vote on measures, committees shape the proposals that are presented for vote. Using the term "fee" rather than "tax" to describe a measure will not necessarily circumvent the tax-writing committees. For example, although the Superfund taxes started as fees in the infancy of their legislative history, the tax-writing committees nonetheless obtained jurisdiction over the measures.[17]

A parallel separation of power occurs at the executive level, where the Environmental Protection Agency, Department of Energy and other agencies have regulatory authority over environmentally related programs, while the Department of Treasury is responsible for tax matters. Because environmental taxation instruments fall within the Department of Treasury, it is the Treasury rather than the agencies of substantive environmental expertise that becomes the agent for administering the environmental taxation programs.

These jurisdictional divides yield several lessons. First, and very fundamentally, one should understand at the start who has the authority over design and implementation. Intuitions about the relevant players may not always be correct.

Second, the fragmentation of authority among different legislative committees and executive agencies may call for a higher level of coordination than normal institutional procedures may require. Tax-writers should understand the environmental committees' agendas for environmental regulation and vice versa so that each considers how different policies might interrelate. Similarly, environmental and tax agencies should cooperate to maximize the benefit of the environmental taxation programs. They should avoid the risk that environmental taxation measures might

---

17   *See* Milne, J.E., "New Instruments on Old Turf: The Institutional Challenges of Environmental Taxation," in N. Chalifour et al. (eds.), *Critical Issues in Environmental Taxation* (Vol. V), Oxford University Press, 2008, pages 146–7.

become the fiscal equivalent of children who do not realize their full potential because they live with the tax parent, not the environmental parent or both. In the last several years, the environmental agencies have increasingly been integrating environmental tax expenditures into their publications and webpages, which is a positive step forward that still respects Treasury's ultimate responsibility. Interagency task forces can also help cross the boundaries of agencies' expertise.

Third, drafting techniques can import the knowledge of environmental experts into the tax arena, where tax-writers and administrators may be less conversant with environmental technicalities. For example, Congress on occasion has statutorily required Treasury and the agencies of environmental expertise to work together in designing the implementing details of environmental tax instruments, allowing Treasury to benefit from the other agencies' expertise and encouraging the integration of tax instruments into the environmental agencies' agendas.[18]

The jurisdictional divides may be different in other countries. Where fragmentation of authority occurs, however, policymakers, administrators and interested parties should consider how best to ensure that environmental taxation – a hybrid instrument – is sufficiently integrated into both the environmental and tax spheres during creation and administration.

2.3   The Implicit Influence of Historical Preferences

Institutional traditions may create an implicit preference for one type of environmental instrument over another that affects the use of environmental tax instruments. Although President Nixon wanted to pursue environmental taxes, environmental protection in the United States has been firmly rooted in a major command-and-control regulatory regime, which started with the passage of the federal National Environmental Policy Act and the Clean Water Act and the creation of the Environmental Protection Agency in 1970 and grew from there.[19] The regulatory emphasis has not precluded the use of environmental tax instruments, but its historical dominance, which has generated institutional stakeholders,

---

[18]   *See*, e.g., 26 U.S.C. § 48A (requiring the Department of Energy to review proposals for the allocation of tax credits for carbon capture and sequestration before the Department of Treasury awards the credits); *ibid.* § 45L (requiring Treasury to consult with Energy about certification procedures for new energy efficient homes that qualify for tax credit).

[19]   Lazarus, R.J., *The Making of Environmental Law*, University of Chicago Press, 2004, page 67.

momentum and entrenched environmental advocates, may have implicitly influenced views of environmental taxation.

The relationship between command-and-control regulation and market-based approaches has shifted somewhat in recent years. The U.S. government has become familiar with trading regimes, and it has relied heavily on federal tax expenditures designed to reduce reliance on fossil fuels. Market-based instruments increasingly are recognized as an alternative or complement to regulation, but trading regimes still seem to have the upper hand over environmental taxes, perhaps in part because they carry more regulatory characteristics. A country starting with a relatively clean policy slate at this point in time might assess the merits and role of environmental taxation differently than a country with a longstanding regulatory tradition; policymakers and stakeholders, including environmental NGOs, might be more receptive to environmental taxes.

3.   DESIGN FEATURES OF ENVIRONMENTAL TAXES – THE TAX BASE AND TAX RATE

The basic design components of environmental taxes are quite simple and are common to most taxes:

$$\text{Tax Base} \times \text{Tax Rate} = \text{Tax Revenue}$$

The *raison d'être* of environmental taxes lies in their environmental goal, and the choice of the tax base and tax rate reflect that goal, as can the use of the revenue. Like other taxes, however, the design details of environmental taxes are also shaped by traditional tax policy considerations, such as their economic impact, equity and administrative feasibility, and by calculations of political feasibility. The design features of two U.S. environmental taxes and President Clinton's proposed energy tax illustrate how policy and political considerations affect the choice of the tax base and tax rate. Section 4 below considers the question of how to use the revenue from environmental taxes.

3.1   The Ozone-Depleting Chemicals Tax – A Useful Model

The federal excise tax on ozone-depleting chemicals[20] offers a positive example of design features of an environmental tax. It was enacted

---

[20]   26 U.S.C. §§ 4681, 4682. *See* Barthold, T.A., "Issues in the Design of

to help address the problem of emissions of ozone-depleting chemicals that erode the stratospheric ozone layer and leave the earth more vulnerable to ultraviolet radiation. Under the international Montreal Protocol, countries agreed to phase out the use of key ozone-depleting chemicals, and the U.S. tax supplements U.S. obligations under the Protocol.

The tax neatly correlates the tax base and the tax rate to the environmental problem. The tax base consists of 20 chemicals known to have ozone-depleting characteristics. By the same token, the tax base rightly excludes chemicals that will be entirely consumed in the manufacture of another chemical (feedstocks) and therefore will never be released into the atmosphere.[21] The tax rate varies according to the ozone-depleting potential of each chemical. An annual increasing base tax rate[22] is multiplied by the ozone-depleting factor for each chemical, using factors established in the international Montreal Protocol. For example, CFC-11 has an ozone-depleting factor of 1.0 whereas Halon-1301 has a factor of 10.0, causing the tax on the more potent Halon-1301 to be ten times greater. Thus, the tax base and the tax rate link directly with the chemicals' potential to damage the environment.

From an administrative feasibility perspective, the tax was logically imposed on the manufacturers, producers and importers of the chemicals at the time of their sale or use. This upstream taxable event facilitates the collection of the tax and yet is consistent with the environmental assumption that most non-feedstock ozone-depleting chemicals ultimately will be released into the atmosphere at some point in the life of the final products. Placing the collection point at the more environmentally precise point of emission would not have been administratively feasible. In a finessing detail, the annual increases in the tax rate apply to chemicals that have already passed the collection point but are still being held for the manufacture of future products (a tax on floor stocks).

The tax's design was also shaped by economic considerations, in particular the effect on competitiveness of U.S. industries. As indicated

---

Environmental Excise Taxes," *Journal of Economic Perspectives*, Volume 8, Number 1, 1994, pages 136–7.

[21] 26 U.S.C. § 4682 (d) (2). Chemicals that are "recovered in the United States as part of a recycling process" are also exempt. *Ibid.* § 4682 (d) (1).

[22] The base amount was adjusted by statute from the original amount of US$1.37 per pound in 1990 to US$5.35 for years after 1995, and the base amount automatically increases 45 cents per year. 26 U.S.C. § 4681 (b) (1) (B). The base amount was US$11.65 per pound in 2009.

above, the tax base includes imported chemicals, and it also extends to imported products that contain or were made using ozone-depleting chemicals, thereby imposing a border tax adjustment that puts U.S.-manufactured chemicals and products on equal economic footing with imports. According to one study, the tax on imported products represented about $80 million dollars, or 11 per cent of the revenue, in 1993,[23] indicating that the border tax adjustment on products containing the chemicals was a significant feature of the tax. Regulations implementing the tax on imported chemicals and products offer a very useful example of how to address the details of a border tax adjustment, such as how to account for subsequent uses that are exempt and how to determine the amount of ozone-depleting chemicals associated with imported products.[24] This border tax adjustment is consistent with the tax's environmental rationale, although the same cannot be said of the partial exemption for exports of U.S.-manufactured ozone-depleting chemicals.[25]

The tax has generated an interesting, undesired, but perhaps not unforeseeable consequence relevant to the administrative feasibility of the tax and its border tax adjustment. The combination of the substantial tax and the Montreal Protocol's phase-out requirements created an incentive to smuggle ozone-depleting chemicals into the United States from countries subject to more liberal phase-out rules and no tax. As a result, the government has brought charges based in part on multi-million tax evasions.[26] Thus, the question of administrative feasibility can extend beyond the normal auditing procedures, which may be inevitable when dealing with high tax rates and non-harmonized international markets.

---

[23] Boroshok, S.P., "Environmental Taxes, Focusing on Ozone-Depleting Chemicals, 1993," *Statistics of Income Bulletin*, Winter 1995–1996, Internal Revenue Service, page 16.

[24] 26 C.F.R. §§ 52.4681-0–52.4682.-4.

[25] 26 U.S.C. § 4682 (d) (3).

[26] *See 1996 Annual Report of the Attorney General of the United States*, United States Department of Justice, undated, page 50 (noting joint enforcement efforts by the Environmental Protection Agency, Internal Revenue Service, and Customs Service); Press Release, United States Department of Justice, "Miami Federal Grand Jury Indicts Four in Multi-million Dollar 'Freon' Excise Tax Fraud Scheme," September 5, 1996 (discussing failure to pay US$22 million in excise taxes on CFC-12 (freon)); Daley, B. and Barry, E., "Five Indicted in Coolant Smuggling Scheme," *Boston Globe*, August 1, 2001 (describing US$20 million tax evasion and black market in freon).

3.2   The Gas Guzzler Tax – the Need to Update to Preserve the Environmental Effect

The federal excise tax on gas guzzling vehicles[27] similarly employs an environmentally logical tax base and tax rate, but it contains design features that reduce its environmental effectiveness and serve as warnings to future tax writers. Although the tax was enacted in 1978 in response to concerns about reliance on imported oil following the Oil Embargo, its existence today is directly relevant to the environmental problems caused by carbon dioxide and other emissions from motor vehicles' combustion of gasoline, including climate change.

The tax applies to automobiles based on their fuel economy, which is a significant factor contributing to the level of emissions,[28] and the tax rate appropriately increases as fuel economy decreases. The tax rate starts at US$1000 for vehicles with fuel economy less than 22.5 but more than 21.5 miles per gallon, and it rises with each one-mile decrease in fuel economy until it reaches US$7700 for vehicles with fuel economy less than 12.5 miles per gallon. In terms of administrative feasibility, the tax is imposed on the manufacturer at time of sale, but to preserve the environmental awareness and behavioral impact of the tax, dealers must place a notice about the tax on the sticker price for the car.[29]

The environmental effectiveness of the tax, however, has been eroded significantly by the fact that it does not apply to "non-passenger vehicles," a term that now encompasses sport utility vehicles (SUVs). Part of the original 1978 law, this exemption was created long before SUVs were contemplated as a common choice for everyday travel, but the failure to amend the law to adjust to new circumstances has significantly undercut its force as an environmental instrument. In addition, the tax rates have not been increased since 1990, nor have the fuel economy thresholds been changed since 1978. If an environmental tax is intended to serve a long-term environmental purpose, the tax rate should be indexed for inflation or adjusted periodically to preserve its incentive effect and policymakers should consider adjustments to the definitions and thresholds that determine the tax base.

---

[27]   26 U.S.C. § 4064.

[28]   Other factors, such as the distance driven per year, will also affect an automobile's emissions profile, so fuel economy is a convenient but not necessarily the precisely perfect tax base for a tax on vehicles' emissions.

[29]   40 C.F.R. § 600.306-86. Manufacturers have passed the tax cost on to purchasers. Conner, Jr., J.Y., "Revisiting CAFE: Market Incentives to Greater Automotive Efficiency," *Virginia Environmental Law Journal*, Volume 16, 1997, page 435.

3.3   The Btu Tax Proposal – the Influence of Politics and Policy

President Clinton's proposal to enact a broad-based energy tax illustrates how politics and policy can temper the choice of the tax base and the tax rate.[30] When President Clinton assumed office in 1993, he was determined to reduce the federal deficit. His team immediately started considering energy taxes – a gas tax increase, a carbon tax, or an energy tax based on the energy content of fuels measured by British thermal units (Btus).[31]

To some extent, the choice among these alternatives was influenced by political happenstance. A significant increase in the gas tax could have been politically problematic, given Clinton's opposition to a proposal to raise the gas tax by 50 cents per gallon during the presidential campaign,[32] as well as the perception that gas tax increases were politically volatile.[33] The environmentally preferable carbon tax would have had the most significant impact on coal, an industry lying in the constituency of the legendarily powerful Senator Robert Byrd from West Virginia.[34] The choice also involved the relative regional impacts of each alternative, a consideration carrying political, economic and equity implications. A gas tax would have greater impact on regions where people must drive longer distances without public transit options, and a carbon tax would hit hardest the regions dependent on the coal economy or coal-fired energy sources.[35] Given these political and policy challenges, President Clinton settled on a tax based on the Btu content of energy (the

---

[30]   For a discussion of the Btu tax, *see* Milne, J.E., "Carbon Taxes in the United States: The Context for the Future," *Vermont Journal of Environmental Law*, Volume 10, 2008, pages 1–16.

[31]   *See*, e.g., Staff Reporter, "Gore Says an Energy Tax Is Under Consideration," *Wall Street Journal*, January 18, 1993, page A12; Wessel, D. and Wartzman, R., "Clinton's Options: Tax Increases Seem Inevitable, Including Some on Middle Class," *Wall Street Journal*, January 22, 1993, page A1; Wessel, D., "Bentsen Sees Higher Taxes on Consuming," *Wall Street Journal*, January 25, 1993, page A2; Wald, M.L., "Pondering an Energy Tax That Can't Please All the People," *New York Times*, January 31, 1993, page 10.

[32]   Noah, T., "Clinton Aides Seek Gasoline Tax Boost, New Carbon Levy," *Wall Street Journal*, December 9, 1992, page A2.

[33]   Wessel and Wartzman, *op. cit.*, page A1.

[34]   Ehrlandson, D., "The Btu Tax Experience: What Happened and Why It Happened," *Pace Environmental Law Review*, Volume 12, 1994, pages 175–6.

[35]   *See* 139 *Congressional Record* H674, H678 (1993) (State of the Union Address by President Clinton); *Administration's Energy Tax Proposals: Hearings Before the Committee on Finance, 103d Cong.,* Government Printing Office, 1993, page 7 (statement of Hon. Lloyd Bentsen, Secretary, Department of Treasury).

Btu tax). Covering fossil fuels, nuclear power and hydropower,[36] it would have affected regions of the country relatively equally. According to the Administration's estimates, the tax would vary by region from 0.54 per cent to 0.67 per cent of taxpayers' disposable personal income, at most a 0.13 per cent range.[37]

The Btu tax rate was relatively modest, translating for example into US$3.24 per barrel of oil.[38] It was not the product of a refined notion of the internalization of external costs but rather seems to have been driven more by the extent to which the tax needed to contribute to the deficit-reduction goal (as discussed in Section 4), as well as presumably concerns about the financial impact on individuals and industry. Even so, the tax was projected to provide a real, but modest reduction in energy consumption, reducing anticipated growth by 7 per cent.[39]

The Btu tax proposal also was accompanied by measures designed to address equity concerns. The tax was part of a larger budget bill that included spending and tax provisions to help low-income households that might otherwise suffer from the burden of the Btu tax.[40] The Administration was keenly aware of the need to consider those interests, both as a matter of policy and politics.

Even with these tempered design choices, the Btu tax did not survive. Louis XIV's financial minister has been quoted as saying, "The art of taxation consists in so plucking the goose as to obtain the largest possible amount of feathers with the smallest possible amount of hissing."[41] The Clinton Administration encountered too much hissing. After a narrow victory in the House of Representatives, the tax failed to garner sufficient

---

[36]   Office of Tax Policy, Department of Treasury, "Description of Modified Btu Tax," United States Government, 1993, page 1.

[37]   *Energy Tax Hearings, op. cit.,* page 120 (prepared statement of Hon. Lloyd Bentsen, Secretary, Department of Treasury).

[38]   When fully phased in, the basic tax rate would have been 25.7 cents per million Btus, with a supplemental tax rate of 34.2 cents per million Btus for refined petroleum products. These rates translate into US$5.57 per short ton of coal, US$2.66 per thousand kilowatt hours of electricity, and US$3.24 per barrel of refined petroleum products. Office of Tax Policy Specifications, *op. cit.,* page 1.

[39]   Office of Tax Policy, Department of Treasury, "The Administration's Modified Btu Energy Tax Proposal," United States Government, 1993, page 1.

[40]   Office of Tax Policy, Department of Treasury, "Frequently Asked Questions Regarding the Administration's Proposed Modified Btu Tax," United States Government, 1993, pages 10–11.

[41]   Durning, A.T., and Bauman, Y., *Tax Shift,* Northwest Environment Watch, 1998, page 13 (Jean Baptiste Colbert as quoted by John Steele Gordon, "American Taxation," *American Heritage,* May/June 1996).

support for passage in the Senate,[42] defeated by Senators from oil-and-gas producing states and an opposition emboldened by the Administration's concessions.[43] The deficit-reduction package passed, but the Btu tax was replaced by a modest 4.3-cent increase in the gas tax[44] and other measures.

In sum, the tax on ozone-depleting chemicals provides a very useful example of design features that accommodate the environmental, economic and administrative concerns. The gas guzzler tax has strong environmental features, but the passage of time and circumstances have diminished its environmental role, highlighting the need to ensure that environmental taxes are adjusted over time to preserve the environmental impact. The Btu tax proposal illustrates how the compromises of policies and politics can generate a tax design with more muted environmental credentials but which would still have been a defensible policy step in the right direction.

4.   THE REVENUE ISSUE

The revenue-raising function of taxes is axiomatic. Taxes exist to provide government with the revenue it needs to provide its government services. Environmental taxes will raise revenue, but policymakers must decide whether the environmental features of the tax primarily lie in the tax base and tax rate, freeing some or all of the revenues for non-environmental purposes, or whether the environmental character of the tax arises in whole or part from the way in which its revenues are used. The decision about how to use the revenue from an environmental tax can be reduced to three basic choices or some combination thereof:

- dedicating the revenue to the environmental problem;
- using the revenues for some other governmental purpose, such as deficit reduction or increased spending (including the possibility of using revenue to address the equity and economic impacts of the tax); or
- using the revenues to reduce other tax burdens to achieve significant tax reform, often on a revenue-neutral basis.

---

[42]   For a discussion of the policies and politics of the tax proposal, *see* Milne, J.E., "Carbon Taxes in the United States: The Context for the Future," *Vermont Journal of Environmental Law*, Volume 10, 2008, pages 6–18.

[43]   *Ibid.*, pages 12–13.

[44]   Staff of Joint Committee on Taxation, "Description of Chairman's Mark on Revenue Reconciliation Proposals Scheduled for Markup by the Senate Committee on Finance," Joint Committee on Taxation, 1993.

To date, the United States has chosen the first two options but Congressional proposals illustrate how the third might be designed.

4.1   Revenue Dedication

Three Superfund taxes[45] serve as leading examples of taxes that generate their environmental impact primarily through the use of their revenues. The tax base for each is somewhat associated with the environmental problem, but absent dedication of the revenue, it would be more difficult to classify the Superfund taxes as strong environmental taxes. Note, however, that dedication of revenue to the environmental problem need not necessarily suggest that a tax is not an independently strong environmental tax. In some instances, policymakers may choose to devote the revenues to the environmental problem to achieve enhanced or accelerated results.[46]

The Superfund taxes were created to provide financing for the Superfund, a federal trust fund.[47] Part of a regulatory liability regime that requires operators or owners to be responsible for remediation of hazardous waste sites, the Superfund provides the federal government with funds to clean up abandoned sites.[48] One Superfund tax imposed an excise tax on 42 chemicals sold by manufacturers or imported into the United States, with tax rates varying by chemical from US$0.22 to US$4.87 per ton,[49] and a

---

[45]   26 U.S.C. §§ 59A, 4611, 4661, 4671.

[46]   In fact, some controversy exists over the question whether the Pigouvian theory of environmental taxation requires dedication of the revenue. Pigou's discussion suggests that revenues should be used to repair the damage caused by the activity on which the tax is paid. Pigou, *op. cit.*, page 168, footnote 2. *See* Andersen, M.S., *Governance by Green Taxes: Making Pollution Prevention Pay*, Manchester University Press, 1994, pages 36–7; Milne, J. E., "Environmental Taxation: Why Theory Matters", *op. cit.*, page 19. Some commentators, however, argue that it is not efficient to dedicate the revenues to the environmental problem. *See* Baumol, W. J. and Oates, W. E., *The Theory of Environmental Policy*, Cambridge University Press, 1998, pages 23–4; OECD, "Discussion Paper for Conference of Environmental Fiscal Reform," OECD, 2002, pages 4–5.

[47]   26 U.S.C. § 9507.

[48]   The Superfund was created by the Comprehensive Environmental Response, Compensation, and Liability Act of 1980, codified in 42 U.S.C. §§ 9601-9675. While the law creates a liability regime for owners and operators of hazardous waste sites, the Superfund allows government to proceed with remediation in the absence of private action, but the government can seek recovery from responsible parties. *See* generally United States Government Accountability Office, *Superfund: Funding and Reported Costs of Enforcement and Administration Activities*, United States Government, 2008.

[49]   26 U.S.C. §§ 4661-4662.

border tax adjustment for imported taxable substances.[50] The second tax applied to crude oil and imported petroleum products at the rate US$0.097 per barrel.[51] The third took a different approach, taxing corporations at a rate of 0.12 per cent of their modified alternative minimum taxable income over US$2 million.[52] By statute, the taxes expired at the end of 1995,[53] and efforts to reinstate them have been intertwined with difficult negotiations over the associated, ongoing liability regime for hazardous waste sites.[54]

The design of the Superfund taxes does not provide the tight correlation between the tax base and the resulting pollution evident in the tax on ozone-depleting chemicals. The taxed chemicals and products and the taxable income cannot be traced directly to specific hazardous waste sites but rather served as a rough "guilt by association" proxy. In addition, the relatively low levels of tax were unlikely to significantly influence behavior. The stronger environmental identity of the taxes instead derived from the dedication of their US$19 billion cumulative revenue stream to cleaning up contaminated sites.[55] Supplemented by recoveries from responsible parties, the taxes generated approximately two-thirds of the Superfund's revenue through 1995.[56] Thus, the dedication of the revenue to environmental purposes gave heft to their environmental nature.[57]

Since 1995, governmental appropriations have served as a partial replacement, but the level of revenue flowing into the fund has fallen

---

[50] *Ibid.* §§ 4671-4672.

[51] *Ibid.* §§ 4611-4612.

[52] *Ibid.* § 59A.

[53] *Ibid.* §§ 59A, 4611 (e), 4661 (c).

[54] *See* generally Cartwright, M. E., "Superfund: It's No Longer Super and It Isn't Much of a Fund," *Tulane Environmental Law Journal*, Volume 18, 2005, page 299; Rhoades, T. A., and Shogren, J. F., "Current Issues in Superfund Amendment and Reauthorization: How is the Clinton Administration Handling Hazardous Waste?" *Duke Environmental Law and Policy Forum*, Volume 8, 1998, page 245; National Commission on Superfund, *Final Consensus Report of the National Commission on Superfund*, joint project of the Keystone Center and Environmental Law Center of Vermont Law School, 1994; Cushman, Jr., J. H., "Congress Foregoes Its Bid to Hasten Cleanup of Dumps," *New York Times*, October 6, 1994.

[55] United States Government Accountability Office, *op. cit.*, page 8.

[56] *Ibid.*, page 7.

[57] The federal gasoline tax provides another example of revenue dedication. 26 U.S.C. § 4081 (a) (2). Its tax rate of 18.4 cents per gallon is not high enough to significantly shape behavior, but small portions of its revenue are dedicated to environmental purposes. *Ibid.* § 9508 (Leaking Underground Storage Tank Trust Fund): § 9503 (e) (Mass Transit Account within the Highway Trust Fund).

significantly in the absence of taxes.[58] With almost 1600 hazardous waste sites on the National Priorities List, a prerequisite for Superfund assistance, and more than 47,000 sites potentially qualifying,[59] the need for revenue remains strong. President Barack Obama has called for reinstatement of the Superfund taxes,[60] but Congress has not yet accepted his invitation to act.

4.2   Revenue for Other Governmental Objectives

If dedication of the revenue is not an essential part of the environmental role of the tax, government can use the revenue for other purposes. Those purposes can provide independent and often important opportunities and momentum for environmental taxes, as illustrated by U.S. efforts to reduce the deficit in the late 1980s and early 1990s.

The tax on ozone-depleting chemicals was first enacted in 1989 as part of a comprehensive budget bill, designed to reduce the deficit by US\$14 billion,[61] and the tax on ozone-depleting chemicals contributed US\$4.3 billion toward that goal.[62] An amendment to the tax enacted the next year, which added three more chemicals to the tax base, was part of a nearly US\$500 billion deficit-reduction package.[63] The environmental demand for action on the ozone problem, industry's acquiescence to phasing out

---

[58]   Government Accountability Office, *op. cit.*, pages 7–8.

[59]   *Ibid.*, page 1.

[60]   United States Office of Management and Budget, *Analytical Perspectives: Budget of the U.S. Government Fiscal Year 2011*, Office of Management and Budget, 2010, page 175; United States Office of Management and Budget, *Analytical Perspectives: Budget of the U.S. Government Fiscal Year 2010*, Office of Management and Budget, 2009, pages 267–8.

[61]   President George Herbert Walker Bush, *Statement on Signing the Omnibus Budget Reconciliation Act of 1989*, December 19, 1989 (estimating five-year budget impact).

[62]   Joint Committee on Taxation, "Estimated Revenue Effects of Conference Agreement on Revenue Provisions of H.R. 3299, the Omnibus Budget Reconciliation Act of 1989," Joint Committee on Taxation, 1989 (estimating five-year revenue impact). The 1989 budget bill also contained revenue-losing tax expenditures, so one could argue that the same portion of the new revenues was used to fund those expenditures. Nevertheless, the tax on ozone-depleting chemicals was the second largest revenue raiser in the tax portion of the budget bill, which generated almost US\$25 billion in net revenues, so it was a significant contributor to the revenue stream. *Ibid.*

[63]   President George Herbert Walker Bush, *Statement on Signing the Omnibus Budget Reconciliation Act of 1990*, November 5, 1990 (estimating five-year budget impact). The amendment for ozone-depleting chemicals was estimated to generate US\$485 million. Joint Committee on Taxation, "Budget Reconciliation (H.R.

ozone-depleting chemicals,[64] and the call for deficit reduction coalesced to provide support for the tax.

In the largest experiment to date in using environmental taxes to reduce the deficit, President Bill Clinton presented his Btu tax proposal as a way to reduce emissions while also reducing the deficit.[65] The Btu tax would have contributed US$70 billion toward the US$500 billion goal.[66] Although the tax failed to pass, it illustrates how the demand for new, undedicated revenue can provide the opportunity and initial momentum for an environmentally related tax.

Environmental taxes, of course, can generate funding for other policy objectives as well. For example, a US$1 billion expansion of the tax on ozone-depleting chemicals in 1992, for example, helped fund US$1.3 billion in unrelated tax expenditures for energy conservation and alternative energy.[67]

4.3 Tax Reform

Another alternative is to use the revenue to fund offsetting tax relief on a largely revenue-neutral basis, sometimes referred to as environmental tax reform. The United States has not yet engaged in any major revenue-neutral tax shifts, but the concept is present in pending carbon tax proposals. Following the example of some European tax reforms that have shifted tax burdens from payroll taxes to environmental taxes,[68]

5835) Revenue Measures as Reported by the Conferees," Joint Committee on Taxation, 1990 (estimating five-year revenue impact).

[64] Benedick, R. E., *Ozone Diplomacy*, Harvard University Press, 1991, pages 134–6

[65] State of the Union Address by President Bill Clinton, 139 *Congressional Record* II674, H678, 1993 (projecting five-year budget impact).

[66] *Ibid.; Administration's Energy Tax Proposals: Hearings Before the Committee on Finance, 103d Cong.,* Government Printing Office, 1993, pages 6–7 (statement of Hon. Lloyd Bentsen, Secretary, Department of Treasury). The deficit-reduction feature also allowed the Clinton Administration to address concerns about the impact of the tax on the economy and households. The Administration argued that reducing the deficit would strengthen the economy by lowering interest rates, which would reduce the cost of capital for business and mortgages for individuals. Those lower costs in turn would soften the economic impact of the Btu tax. Milne, "Carbon Taxes in the United States," *op. cit.*, pages 15–16.

[67] Joint Committee on Taxation, "Estimated Budget Effects of Conference Agreement for Revenue-related Provisions of H.R. 776," Joint Committee on Taxation, 1992.

[68] *See* Andersen, M. S., "Environmental and Economic Implications of Taxing and Trading Carbon: Some European Experiences," *Vermont Journal of*

two carbon tax bills introduced in Congress in 2009 called for using the revenue from carbon taxes to reduce Social Security taxes[69] in order to provide economic benefits and address equity concerns. While the Congressional focus remained on cap-and-trade proposals for greenhouse gas emissions, these tax proposals lay fallow, but they serve as models for revenue-neutral, or near-revenue-neutral, tax reform.

Thus, a strong environmental tax should achieve its environmental purpose through the design of its tax base and tax rate, leaving policymakers to decide how the revenue can best serve the government's purposes. The government may use some portion of the revenue to address the economic impact or equity of the tax; it may use the revenue for policy goals unrelated to the tax, including other environmental goals; it may engage in structural tax reform; or it may choose some combination. The government may find itself in a position where the revenue side of the equation – the demand for new revenues – is the force driving enactment of the tax. When the tax itself is not sufficiently strong to deliver the desired environmental benefits, however, dedication of some or all of the revenue to the environmental goal is necessary or advisable to maintain the environmental nature of the tax.

5. ENVIRONMENTAL TAX EXPENDITURES

Following the defeat of the Btu tax, the federal government has not enacted any new or significantly increased environmental taxes. The politics implicitly have shifted toward environmental tax expenditures, in particular tax expenditures designed to reduce reliance on fossil fuels. Whether or not the timing was coincidental, tax expenditures are often the politically easier route – and a route well traveled in the first decade of the 21st century.

Environmental tax expenditures have resided in the federal tax code for decades. For example, legislation in 1969 provided deductions for pollution-control facilities.[70] The Energy Tax Act of 1978[71] contained incentives for renewable energy, as did the Energy Policy Act of 1992,[72]

Environmental Law, Volume 10, 2008, page 61.
  [69]   America's Energy Security Trust Fund Act of 2009, H.R. 1337; Raise Wages, Cut Carbon Act of 2009, H.R. 2380. H.R. 1337 is not quite revenue neutral. It would allocate a small portion of the revenues to a tax credit for clean energy technology and for transition assistance for industry.
  [70]   Tax Reform Act of 1969, P.L. 91-172, § 704 (a).
  [71]   Energy Tax Act of 1978, P.L. 95-618.
  [72]   Energy Policy Act of 1992, P.L. 102–486.

which introduced tax incentives for alternative fuel vehicles and the production tax credit for electricity produced from renewable sources, then primarily wind. The use of tax expenditures escalated substantially under the Administration of President George W. Bush, which was not interested in tax increases and saw tax incentives as a way to achieve energy goals, including reduced reliance on fossil fuels.[73] Comprehensive energy legislation in 2005[74] provided tax benefits for clean coal, energy efficient buildings and appliances and alternative motor vehicles and motor fuels. The economic stimulus legislation in late 2008 under President Bush[75] and early 2009 under President Obama[76] included almost US$40 billion for tax incentives for renewable energy, energy conservation, and low-carbon technologies.[77]

Tax expenditures now address a wide range of environmental issues, only briefly and partially identified in the following list:

- A tax deduction for environmental remediation of brownfields;[78]
- A tax deduction for donations of conservation easements that permanently restrict development rights on land that serves a conservation purpose;[79]
- Tax credits for energy efficient new homes, improvements to existing homes and the manufacture of energy efficient appliances, as well as a tax deduction for energy efficient commercial buildings;[80]
- A tax credit for the production of electricity for resale from wind, biomass, geothermal or solar energy, municipal solid waste and other sources;[81]

---

[73] *See* Office of the President of the United States, *National Energy Policy: Report of the National Energy Policy Development Group*, United States Government, 2001.

[74] Energy Tax Incentives Act of 2005, P.L. 105–58.

[75] Emergency Economic Stabilization Act of 2008, P.L. 110–343.

[76] American Recovery and Reinvestment Act of 2009, P.L. 111–5.

[77] Joint Committee on Taxation, "Estimated Budget Effects of the Revenue Provisions Contained in the Conference Agreement on H.R. 1, The American Recovery and Reinvestment Act of 2009," Joint Committee on Taxation, 2009; Joint Committee on Taxation, "Estimated Budget Effects of the Tax Provisions Contained in an Amendment in the Nature of a Substitute to H.R. 1424, Scheduled for Consideration on the Senate Floor on Oct. 1, 2008," Joint Committee on Taxation, 2008. These estimates are based on a 10-year period.

[78] 26 USC § 198.

[79] *Ibid.* § 170.

[80] *Ibid.* §§ 25C, 25D, 45M, 179D.

[81] *Ibid.* § 45.

- A tax credit for businesses that use fuel cells, wind, solar or geothermal energy to meet their on-premises needs;[82]
- Tax credits for the purchasers of bonds issued for certain forestry conservation, renewable energy or energy conservation projects;[83]
- Tax credits for purchases of alternative fuel vehicles and for the installation of refueling infrastructure;[84]
- Exclusions from income for employer-provided mass transit, van pool and bicycle benefits;[85]
- Tax credits for the production of biodiesel, renewable diesel,[86] and ethanol, including cellulosic ethanol;[87]
- Tax credits for carbon capture and sequestration;[88]
- A tax credit for manufacturers' capital investments in manufacturing processes for a wide range of low-carbon technologies;[89]
- A tax credit for the production of low sulfur diesel fuel and a deduction for refiners' capital costs incurred to comply with low sulfur regulations.[90]

Although an extensive critique of these tax expenditures from a policy perspective lies beyond the scope of this analysis,[91] several trends warrant highlighting. First, the federal government's budget rules directly influence the political ease with which tax expenditures are enacted. During the deficit-reduction years of the 1990s, federal budget procedures required revenue neutrality under a rule known as "pay-as-you-go."[92] Tax reductions, including tax expenditures, generally had to be offset by tax increases, which created an institutional restraint on the natural appetite for tax expenditures. For example, tax expenditures in the Energy Policy Act of 1992 had to be offset by revenue increases.[93] When the statutory

---

[82]   *Ibid.* § 48.
[83]   *Ibid.* §§ 54B, 54C, 54D.
[84]   *Ibid.* §§ 30, 30B, 30C, 30D, 179A.
[85]   *Ibid.* § 132.
[86]   *Ibid.* § 40A.
[87]   *Ibid.* § 40.
[88]   *Ibid.* §§ 45Q, 48A, 48B.
[89]   *Ibid.* §48C.
[90]   *Ibid.* §§ 45H, 179B.
[91]   The use of tax expenditures rather than direct spending programs to achieve non-tax policy objectives has been the source of a longstanding debate. *See,* e.g., Surrey, *op. cit.,* pages 126–74.
[92]   *See* generally Keith, R., "Pay-As-You-Go Procedures for Budget Enforcement," Congressional Research Service, 2008.
[93]   Joint Committee on Taxation, "Estimated Budget Effects of Conference

pay-as-you-go budget rule lapsed in 2002, the Republican Congress and the President enacted significant tax cuts without finding offsetting revenues. These tax cuts included US$14 billion in energy-related tax expenditures in the Energy Policy Act of 2005, some environmentally positive and some not.[94] Internal House and Senate procedures in effect in 2008 and early 2009[95] allowed Congress to enact an unprecedented US$40 billion in carbon-reducing tax expenditures as part of its deficit-financed, economic stimulus legislation on declaration that the situation was an emergency.[96] Without deficit financing, the political prospects for success for these tax expenditures might have been very different.

Thus, tax expenditures cannot be divorced from their fiscal consequences. Their feasibility will depend on internal rules and the political willingness of the government to find new revenue or spending cuts to pay for them or to engage in deficit financing. Tax expenditures may be more politically popular than tax increases, but budget discipline may limit their use.

Second, from a design level, tax incentives increasingly are taking the form of tax credits rather than tax deductions. Tax credits offer the benefit of avoiding the fluctuating value of deductions, which depend on the taxpayers' marginal tax rate. U.S. environmental tax expenditures, however, are not refundable so their value may still be limited for some taxpayers.[97] Third, a number of recent environmental tax expenditures contain caps limiting the aggregate dollar amount of tax credits available, which can

---

Agreement for Revenue-related Provisions of H.R. 776," Joint Committee on Taxation, 1992.

[94] Joint Committee on Taxation, "Estimated Revenue Effects of the Conference Agreement for Title XIII of H.R. 6, The Energy Tax Incentives Act of 2005, Joint Committee on Taxation, 2005.

[95] S. Cong. Res. 21, § 204 (110th Cong); House of Representatives Rules, Rule XXI, Clause 10 (110th Cong.); H. Res. 5, § 2(j) (111th Cong.) (amending the House rules). Congress reinstated a statutory pay-as-you-go rule in 2010. H.J. Res. 45, P.L. No. 111–139, 124 Stat. 8.

[96] Emergency Economic Stabilization Act of 2008, § 204, P.L. No. 110-43, 122 Stat. 3814; Joint Explanatory Statement of the Committee of Conference, H.R. Rep. No. 116-16 (Conf. Rep.) (2009). The cost of the energy tax incentives in the Emergency Act was offset by tax increases in part on the oil and gas industry, Emergency Economic Stabilization Act, *op. cit.*, §§ 401–402, but their inclusion in a larger, deficit-financed package provided the political momentum for their passage.

[97] A refundable tax credit provides the full benefit to taxpayers even if they do not have enough tax liability to offset the tax credit. The government directly pays the taxpayer for the amount by which the tax credit exceeds the taxpayer's tax liability.

both protect the government from open-ended exposure and allow it to exercise discretion in awarding the tax credits to the projects that seem to have the most merit.[98] With this capped feature, however, the tax credits operate more like grant programs, underscoring the question of whether these benefits instead should be delivered through traditional spending programs rather than through the tax code. Judgments about policy and political expediency can influence the choice. Finally, from an environmental perspective, it is often difficult to determine the success of the tax expenditures. The federal government, unfortunately, has not engaged in systematic analysis of their behavioral impact.

6.   PATHS FORWARD IN THE U.S.

Over the past two decades, the concept of using tax regimes to send environmentally positive messages has become increasingly accepted as a matter of practice in the United States, particularly with the growing reliance on tax expenditures. The arenas of tax policy and environmental policy are merging. In addition, the rationales for using tax instruments to address energy issues have evolved. The Oil Embargo in the 1970s triggered interest in energy-related tax provisions to increase energy independence. When climate change emerged as an environmental issue in the 1990s, it provided a second policy rationale that continues to increase in significance. At the end of the first decade of the new century, climate change has joined with the need to build a stronger post-recession economy, resulting in calls for a new, green economy. This troika of converging goals – energy security, climate change and economic growth through a green economy – may provide a broader base of support for using tax instruments.

Although market-based instruments have become part of common policy parlance, a key question for the future is whether the United States will favor cap-and-trade regimes over carbon taxes if it seeks to place a price on carbon. The environmental and fiscal magnitude of an enacted carbon tax would represent a seismic step in the endorsement and implementation of environmental tax policy in the United States.[99] Congress to date has focused almost exclusively on cap-and-trade regimes for

---

[98]   *See,* e.g., 26 U.S.C. §§ 48A, 48B, 54C.
[99]   Note that the two choices – cap-and-trade or carbon tax – are not necessarily mutually exclusive. A trading regime could apply to one just sector, as in the European Union's Emissions Trading Scheme, and there is an argument that a carbon tax could operate with a cap-and-trade system if the emissions allowances are not auctioned.

greenhouse gas emissions, but their history has been fraught with peril. In 2008, a cap-and-trade proposal was defeated in the Senate.[100] In July 2009, a somewhat different proposal narrowly passed in the House of Representatives,[101] but momentum languished in the Senate in the waning months of 2009.[102] It remains to be seen whether the political gap between a trading regime and a carbon tax has narrowed sufficiently to swing the pendulum toward a carbon tax, the preferred outcome in the eyes of this author.[103] Even in the absence of a carbon tax, however, new environmental taxes have the potential to play an important policy role.

The future appetite for tax expenditures will depend largely on the question of whether or how to pay for the resulting lost revenue. Environmental tax expenditures have built momentum and supportive constituencies, so their use would be likely to continue if they could be fiscally justified. With mounting concern over the record federal deficit and debt, however, deficit financing will be increasingly difficult, particularly if Congress applies pay-as-you-go rules with stringent procedural restraints. It is likely that proponents will need to find new revenue to offset the cost. A carbon tax or a cap-and-trade program that auctions emissions allowances could generate new revenue, some of which might be allocated to climate-related tax expenditures. Alternatively, Congress could repeal existing tax expenditures.

The repeal of environmentally damaging tax expenditures represents the third and sometimes neglected facet of environmental tax policy. Often overshadowed by environmental taxes and environmental tax expenditures, the repeal of perverse incentives can certainly help correct price signals for polluting activities. A recent study found, for example, that the federal government provided US$47 billion in tax expenditures for fossil fuels over a seven-year period.[104] Attention to this issue is increasing

---

[100]   Lieberman-Warner Climate Security Act, S. 3036.

[101]   American Clean Energy and Security Act of 2009, H.R. 2454.

[102]   Clean Energy Jobs and American Power Act, S. 1733. The bill was reported out by the Senate Environment and Public Works Committee with a partisan vote but had not been brought to the Senate floor for debate as of May 2010.

[103]   An analysis of the relative merits of carbon taxes and trading regimes lies beyond the scope of this chapter, but the author is particularly concerned about the lack of a stable price signal and the complexities of an enormous, new trading market, especially given the role of derivatives. *See* Milne, J.E., "Carbon Taxes Versus Cap-and-Trade: The Relative Burdens and Risks of Market-Based Administration," in L. Lye et al. (eds.), *Critical Issues in Environmental Taxation* (Vol. VII), Oxford University Press, 2009, pages 445–62.

[104]   Environmental Law Institute, *Estimating U.S. Government Subsidies to Energy Sources: 2002–2008*, Environmental Law Institute, 2009, pages 7–9.

nationally and internationally. The economic stimulus legislation in late 2008 included US$7 billion in cutbacks in tax expenditures for the oil and gas industry.[105] President Obama's budget for the fiscal year 2011 called for eliminating a number of tax benefits for fossil fuel production, totaling US$39 billion over ten years,[106] a suggestion Congress has not yet accepted. On the international front, the G-20 agreed at its meeting in Pittsburgh in September 2009:

> To phase out and rationalize over the medium term inefficient fossil fuel subsidies . . . Inefficient fossil fuel subsidies encourage wasteful consumption, reduce our energy security, impede investment in clean energy sources and undermine efforts to deal with the threat of climate change.[107]

These events suggest that the United States might look seriously at subsidy repeal in the coming years, aided by the quest for new revenue to support other endeavors.

Thus, revenue issues could drive the greenness of the tax code in the future. If government needs new sources of revenues to reduce the deficit or to invest in the economy or the environment, it has the opportunity to turn to environmental taxes or the repeal of existing, environmentally damaging incentives. If it cannot find the revenues, it may need to curb its use of environmental tax expenditures. As reporters Woodward and Bernstein did during the Watergate investigation, we may follow the money.

A final factor is the question of the role of regulation in the future – whether the federal government will return to its 1970s roots and look more to regulation than market-based instruments. The Environmental Protection Agency has started using its authority under the Clean Air Act

---

During the same period, tax expenditures for renewable energy totaled US$18 billion. *Ibid.*, page 21.

[105]   Joint Committee on Taxation, "Estimated Budget Effects of the Tax Provisions Contained in an Amendment in the Nature of a Substitute to H.R. 1424, Scheduled for Consideration on the Senate Floor on October 1, 2008," Joint Committee on Taxation, 2008 (estimating 10-year revenue impact).

[106]   Office of Budget and Management, *Analytical Perspectives: Budget of the U.S. Government, Fiscal Year 2011*, Office of Management and Budget, 2010, pages 177, 186. *See also* United States Office of Budget and Management, *Analytical Perspectives: Budget of the U.S. Government, Fiscal Year 2010*, United States Office of Management and Budget, 2009, pages 269 and 274 (proposing US$31 billion in repeal of tax expenditures for oil and gas companies).

[107]   "Leaders Statement, The Pittsburgh Summit," September 24–25, 2009, page 3, http://www.pittsburghsummit.gov/mediacenter/129639.htm, November 15, 2009 (emphasis in original omitted).

to regulate greenhouse gas emissions.[108] If resistance to a cap-and-trade regime or carbon tax continues in Congress, the Obama Administration could use its regulatory authority to gain leverage for legislative action or to proceed in the absence of Congressional action. A dominantly regulatory approach could diminish the role of market-based instruments at least with respect to climate change, one of the most significant environmental issues of the early 21st century. One suspects, however, that the increasing national and global recognition of the importance of price signals will support the use of market-based instruments, particularly taxes or auctioned permits, for a range of environmental problems.

7. CONCLUDING OBSERVATIONS ABOUT ENVIRONMENTAL TAXATION

As President Nixon said in 1970, "by ignoring environmental costs we have given an economic advantage to the careless polluter over his more conscientious rival."[109] There are multiple ways to correct the economic imbalance – through Pigou's extraordinary restraints or extraordinary encouragements, regulations that impose costs and obligations, and other means.

The United States experience shows that the design of environmental taxes is technically feasible. As demonstrated by the ozone-depleting chemicals tax and the gas guzzler tax, one often can find an appropriate tax base that bears a sound correlation to the environmental problem. Even good designs, however, may require updating, such as expansions of the tax base when circumstances change, or adjustments in the tax rate over time.

The end result often is not an idealized Pigouvian tax but instead what one might consider a pragmatic Pigouvian approach, tempered by equity, economic impact, administrative feasibility, and political considerations. These considerations are an inherent and proper part of the analysis of a tax, but they may place taxes at a perceived disadvantage relative to regulatory approaches. Regulatory instruments tend to disguise the non-environmental impacts or at least lower their visibility to voters and consumers. Government should be concerned with the same issues because the impacts are no less real, and proponents of environmental taxes may

---

[108] E.g., Prevention of Significant Deterioration and Title V, Greenhouse Gas Tailoring Rule, 40 CFR Parts 51, 52, 70 and 71 (approved May 13, 2010).

[109] President Nixon Message, *op. cit.*

need to ensure that both types of instruments are judged by the same standards.

A pragmatic approach is justifiable. Environmental taxes can take significant steps toward implementing and accentuating the polluter-pays principle and the internalization of externalities. By adjusting prices, they can influence behavior and send significant educational messages. Pragmatism may carry less cause for concern when the tax is designed to achieve long-term structural shifts. In that case, the government is not designing the tax rate to try to achieve shifts to known technologies on a least-cost-abatement basis, where precision may be important to cost-effectiveness. Instead it is sending a blunter signal for change in potentially unpredictable ways. In addition, tolerance may be higher where the revenues are allocated in part or whole to the environmental problem, buttressing the environmental impact of the tax itself.

It is also important to place environmental taxes in their broader regulatory context. For example, the tax on ozone-depleting chemicals operates alongside the Montreal Protocol's mandates for phasing out the chemicals. While the environmentally positive results are not solely attributable to the injection of a tax into the private sector's decision-making process, studies of the ozone-depleting chemicals tax suggest that it did help accelerate the use of substitute chemicals.[110] In the environmental arena, where problems and solutions are often multi-faceted, problems frequently may require multiple instruments.

The presence of some degree of pragmatism and the presence of multi-faceted solutions enhance the need for *ex post* analyses to determine the effectiveness of the taxes standing alone, in relation to the use of their revenue, and in relation to any surrounding environmental regulations.[111] Environmental taxes should not retain their environmental credentials merely by virtue of having environmentally oriented design

---

[110]   *See* Hoerner, J. A., "Tax Tools for Protecting the Atmosphere: The U.S. Ozone-depleting Chemicals Tax," in R. Gale et al. (eds.), *Green Budget Reform*, Earthscan Publication Ltd., 1995, pages 191–3; Boroshok, S. P., "Environmental Excise Taxes, 1994–1995," *Statistics of Income Bulletin*, Spring 1996, page 103. The tax also helped capture for government the windfall from the regulatory phase-out that presumably would otherwise have gone to the industry. Similarly, the gas-guzzler tax applies to vehicles that are also subject to federal fuel-economy standards for manufacturers' fleets of vehicles, 49 U.S.C. §§ 32901–32919, and other regulatory and tax measures that influence behavior. *See* generally Milne, J.E., "The American Love Affair with Cars: The Mixed Beats of Taxation's Background Music," in A. Cavaliere et al. (eds.), *Critical Issues in Environmental Taxation* (Vol. III), Richmond Law & Tax, 2006, pages 85–111.

[111]   For an example of *ex post* analysis of carbon and energy taxes in Europe,

features; they should prove their worth, just as environmental regulations must be enforced to have merit. Environmental protection is not well served by paper tigers. *Ex post* studies of the effectiveness of tax signals are challenging, because one must isolate the tax factors from other factors that contributed to decisions, but they are a frequently neglected essential in the United States. *Ex post* studies also could evaluate institutional aspects, such as the effectiveness with which the government has overcome the jurisdictional barriers between tax and environmental authorities.

As a matter of policy, environmental taxes generally seem preferable to environmental tax expenditures. Although sometimes politically more challenging, they place the cost on the polluters. They also avoid the problem of government picking winners and losers, which inevitably happens when choosing among technologies or practices that will qualify for tax expenditures. Tax expenditures nevertheless may serve a role, such as when government needs to further accelerate the deployment of technologies that are known but not yet assimilated into everyday commerce. Their use should be closely monitored, however, to ensure that they are serving as incentives, not rewards for activities that would occur in any event. They may be politically popular because they reduce tax burdens, but their real fiscal consequences in forgone revenues should carry a high burden for showing necessity. Again, the lack of systematic *ex post* accountability of their environmental effectiveness and fiscal impact is a glaring omission in the United States.

In the end, environmental taxation offers interesting opportunities. The two sides to its identity – the environmental side and the tax side – place it in a position of strength. Environmental taxation can harness the tax regime, a potent delivery system, to send a broad spectrum of negative or positive price signals, and the price signals it sends can penetrate into the corners of private decision-making. The motivation for enactment may come from the environmental goal or from the fiscal side – the desire for new revenues or the desire to deliver financial benefits – or both.[112] Environmental regulation is more rigid and monochromatic in nature, and it must rely primarily on the environmental motivation for enactment.

Environmental taxation faces its largest global test of policy and politics in the coming decade. As countries around the world consider policies

---

see *Carbon Energy Taxation: Lessons from Europe*, Edited by M. S. Andersen and P. Ekins, Oxford University Press, 2009.
[112]   By the same token, as noted above, the lost revenues from environmental tax expenditures can limit their use in times of fiscal restraint.

for reducing greenhouse gas emissions, they will decide how to use environmental tax policy to address climate change. Given the multi-sectoral, multi-faceted nature of the issues, one suspects that taxation will play a notable role among the range of policy instruments, although the size and nature of that role remain to be seen. Environmental taxation's versatility will allow it to continue to play a role in other spheres as well. The need for extraordinary restraints and encouragements will continue.

6. Optimal climate change tax policy for small open economies

Arthur J. Cockfield*

1. INTRODUCTION

What are the best climate change tax policies for governments with relatively small open economies such as the Canadian one? This chapter assesses recent Canadian government climate change tax policy initiatives, discusses the merits of carbon taxes versus cap-and-trade solutions and then considers the constraints imposed on optimal climate change (or global warming) tax policy by increasing regional and global economic interdependence.

The perhaps obvious conclusion is that governments with small open economies should seek collective action solutions to confront climate change challenges: the suggested approach is to develop consensus surrounding the imposition of a global carbon tax with, at least initially, a low rate. Yet Canada and certain other countries resist the adoption of a carbon tax, and probably serve as a barrier to effective international efforts to curtail global warming emissions. Because perceived national welfare concerns (for example, the need to exploit carbon-based natural resources) continue to trump international welfare concerns, a comprehensive global environmental tax policy solution appears unlikely in the near term.

The analysis also highlights the need to continue to scrutinize international tax policy developments on a regional – and not global – basis, despite the ill fit between these regional developments and their ability to address global environmental concerns. International reform efforts need to address different national/regional cap-and-trade approaches to

* An earlier draft was presented at the 'Green Taxation in East Asia: Problems and Prospects' conference at the University of Hong Kong Faculty of Law on January 29, 2010, and the author would like to thank the participants for their many helpful comments. The author is grateful for the research assistance provided by Matthew Urback.

reducing emissions by focusing on the ways that these approaches increase the price of carbon, which could eventually be incorporated into a global carbon tax solution.

Part 2 overviews Canadian federal and provincial government global warming tax policy responses, including the British Columbia (B.C.) and Quebec carbon taxes; along with Canada's inability to lower overall carbon emissions over the past two decades. Part 3 briefly discusses the merits, identified in the literature, of carbon taxes versus cap-and-trade programs. In particular, carbon taxes have the virtue of transparency and consistency that responds to concerns set out in the optimal tax and compliance theory literature and to law and technology writings concerning incentivizing innovation. Part 4 describes how Canada's economic ties to the U.S. economy makes it difficult to unilaterally impose certain policies such as a carbon tax, which enhances the likelihood of a regional cap-and-trade solution in North America. It concludes by describing how an international agreement that focuses on the price of carbon can, in the beginning stages, incorporate regional cap-and-trade (or other) programs with the aim of ultimately evolving into a global carbon tax. Part 4 also considers the development of a global carbon income tax with withholding taxes imposed on non-participating countries to ensure that participating nations do not violate their World Trade Organization non-discrimination obligations with respect to the cross-border consumption taxation of goods and services.

2. CANADIAN TAX POLICIES DIRECTED AT CONSTRAINING GLOBAL WARMING

The Canadian government as well as certain provincial governments accept that climate change is provoking, or will provoke, adverse outcomes such as falling crop yields, rising sea levels, damage to ecosystems, and the risk of abrupt and major irreversible climate changes.[1] After briefly

---

[1] The most authoritative perspective on climate change is typically traced to the Intergovernmental Panel on Climate Change (IPCC). *See* IPCC, *Climate Change 2007: Synthesis Report. Contribution of Working Groups I, II and III to the Fourth Assessment Report of the Intergovernmental Panel on Climate Change* in Pachauri, R. K. and Reisinger, A. (Core Writing Team) (eds), 2007, IPCC, Geneva, Switzerland. Of particular concern to policymakers is the potential for "runaway feedback" scenarios that lead to rapid and large-scale shifts in the climate system. For instance, the release of methane from deep oceans 250 million years ago may have led to the Permian extinction that wiped out virtually all species. *See* Ryskin, G., "Methane Driven Oceanic Eruptions and Mass Extinctions", *Geology*, Volume 31, 2003, page 737.

reviewing certain environmental tax policies proposed or implemented by the Canadian federal government or one of the provincial governments, this Part discusses why many Canadians appear to be content with policies that have had a negligible impact on reducing overall global warming emissions from Canadian sources.

2.1 Federal Tax Policies

Under the Kyoto Protocol, Canada pledged to bring down total greenhouse gas emissions to 6 per cent below emission levels in 1990. To assist with this goal, Canada has legislated certain taxes to incentivize firms to adopt environmentally friendly energy sources that, it was hoped, would reduce global warming emissions.[2] Since 1996, for example, Canada offers preferential expense treatment for certain expenses called Canadian Renewable Conservation Expenses (CRCEs).[3] To be eligible for the preferential treatment, CRCEs must be incurred in the development of a project such that at least 50 per cent of the cost of any depreciable property should fall within stipulated asset classes. These classes generally cover property used to generate energy from "greener" sources such as wood waste, bio-oil, solar energy or wind equipment.[4]

To the extent that the taxpayer deploys even more energy efficient methods (determined by measuring the BTUs per KWH) then it is permitted to depreciate equipment at an even faster rate. This tax policy is intended to encourage firms to purchase more energy-efficient assets.[5] Importantly, Canadian tax laws also provide faster depreciation for expenses incurred in the process of locating and developing non-renewable energy sources.

To encourage individuals to use public transportation (thereby reducing car emissions), Canada provides a transit pass tax credit to individuals who buy these passes.[6] In addition, Canada imposes special excise taxes

---

[2] Technical Committee on Business Taxation, *Taxes as User Charges: Environment Taxes*, Department of Finance, 1997, page 9.1.

[3] *See* Income Tax Act, Sections 66 and 66.1 and Regulation 1219, R.S.C. 1985, c.1, 5th Supp (Income Tax Act).

[4] Wach, T. and Flaherty, N., "New Tax Incentives for Wind Energy Investment in Canada", Note, *International Business Lawyer*, Volume 31, 2003, page 3.

[5] Dueck, R., "Generating a Green Tax Policy for Renewable Electricity in Canada," *Appeal*, Volume 12, 2007, page 90.

[6] *See* Income Tax Act, Section 118.02, *op. cit. See also* Di Domenico, A., "Employer-Provided Benefits and the Environment: Transit Passes," *Canadian Tax Journal*, Volume 54, Number 1, 2006, page 115.

(as do the provinces) on the consumption of gasoline.[7] These excise taxes are significantly lower than ones imposed by most European governments, in part due to the apparent desire of North American consumers for cheap fuel for their cars (although gasoline taxes along with fuel prices remain higher in Canada than they are within the United States).[8]

There are additional federal tax policies that try to encourage behavior that protect the environment, including special tax breaks for contributions to Qualified Environmental Trusts (QETs),[9] ecological gifts,[10] and to encourage the use of recyclable materials such as returnable containers.

The Canadian government has also implemented a number of non-tax policies to try to reduce global warming emissions. Between March 20, 2007, and December 31, 2008, Canadians who purchased or leased fuel-efficient vehicles (for example, hybrid vehicles that use gas and electricity) were eligible to receive rebates ranging from C$1000 to C$2000. This rebate program proved to be popular and the government issued over 169,800 rebates totaling C$191.2 million.[11] Certain Canadian provinces provided additional rebate incentives for the purchase of fuel-efficient vehicles.

2.2   Provincial Tax Policies

Canada is a federal country with specified powers allocated to provincial governments, including the power to tax and regulate environmental matters.[12] In the last few years, two provinces – British Columbia and Quebec

---

[7]   Ngo Anh-Thu, Halley, P. and Calkins, P., "Bio-fuels in Canada: Normative Framework, Existing Regulations, and Politics of Intervention," *McGill J.S.D.L.P.*, Volume 4, 2008, page 19. The Technical Committee on Business Taxation suggested reformulating and/or replacing the fuel excise tax to address pollutants from a wider variety of sources, such as energy use and industrial emissions (since they correctly point out that petroleum from transportation is far from the only source of environmental degradation). *See* Technical Committee on Business Taxation, *op. cit.*, page 9.1.

[8]   Turner, G. S., "Gasoline Taxes as Environmental Policy – Time for a Common Canada-U.S. Approach", *Tax Notes International*, Volume 39, 2005, page 711.

[9]   *See* Income Tax Act, Paragraphs 20 (1) (ss) and (tt), *op. cit. See also* Frankovic, J., "The Case for 'Reverse Depreciation' of Reclamation Costs," *Canadian Tax Journal*, Volume 52, Number 1, 2004, page 38.

[10]   *See* Income Tax Act, Sections 38 (a.2), 110.1 (i) (d) and 118.1, *op. cit.*

[11]   *See* Transport Canada, "ecoAUTO rebate program", http://www.tc.gc.ca/programs/environment/ecotransport/ecoauto.htm, October 27, 2010.

[12]   *See* Chalifour, M. N., "Making Federalism Work for Climate Change: Canada's Division of Powers over Carbon Taxes", *National Journal of*

– have legislated carbon taxes, which could serve as possible models for subsequent national or even international developments.

Perhaps the most interesting global warming tax policy development in Canada is the new carbon tax developed by the Canadian province of British Columbia. Beginning on July 1, 2008, British Columbia implemented a carbon tax of C$10 per tonne of carbon dioxide equivalent emissions (2.41 cents per litre on gasoline).[13] More technically, the government lists nineteen fossil (carbon-based) fuels sold within the province and assigns a tax rate for each fossil fuel that approximates C$10 per tonne of carbon dioxide. The tax is designed to apply to a broad tax base that captures nearly all emissions from fossil fuel combustion with narrow exemptions that are required to integrate the B.C. carbon tax with other climate action policies. The tax will increase each year after until 2012, reaching a final price of C$30 per tonne (an increase of 7.24 cents per litre at the gas pumps), hence promoting price certainty for the first five years of the plan.[14]

The B.C. carbon tax is an indirect (consumption) tax paid by the consumer, whether it is an individual or business, of the carbon-based good or service at the retail level. For example, the carbon tax is collected for automobile fuel at the pump and is added to existing federal and provincial excise taxes on fuel. Other retailers such as gas companies must collect the carbon tax from their consumers. The carbon tax is imposed on a destination basis so that exports leave the province tax free.

There are other important aspects of the B.C. carbon tax. Legislation was passed to keep the carbon tax revenue neutral by reducing corporate and income taxes at an equivalent rate. In other words, the carbon tax revenues will be recycled through tax reductions. To address concerns surrounding regressivity, a Low Income Climate Action Tax Credit provides tax refunds to low income individuals and households. Finally, the carbon tax is designed to be integrated with other green measures, including a planned cap-and-trade system. Hence the carbon tax is considered by the B.C. provincial government to be an important, but not exclusive, element of its climate action plan.

In addition, Quebec enacted a low rate carbon tax on large emitters and distributors in 2007, making it the first jurisdiction in North America

---

Constitutional Law, Volume 22, Number 2, 2008, page 119 (discussing constitutional concerns at both the national and provincial level with respect to carbon taxes).

[13]   *See* Government of British Columbia, *Climate Action Plan*, 2008, pages 14–20.

[14]   *See* Ministry of Small Business and Revenue, *Notice, British Columbia Carbon Tax*, 2008, page 4.

to implement a carbon tax. Quebec's carbon tax covers a broad-base of carbon resources from coal to heating oil. The amount of the carbon tax varies according to the amount of carbon dioxide each fuel produces: for gasoline, the tax is 0.8 cents per litre. "Fuel distributors" who must pay the carbon tax include firms within the mining, steel, or aluminum industries, cement manufacturing plants, and others large emitters. Quebec intends to recycle the collected revenues into programs to promote sustainable development.

Other Canadian provinces have proposed or implemented different approaches to tackling carbon emissions. Alberta implemented a (weak) cap-and-trade system in 2007, the first North American jurisdiction to do so. In addition, certain Canadian provinces, including British Columbia, Manitoba, Ontario and Quebec, have joined a California-sponsored Western Climate Initiative (at this writing, seven US states have signed on) that envisions a cap-and-trade system designed to reduce carbon and other greenhouse gas emissions. Certain provinces have also passed legislation to phase-out coal-fired generation plants.

Consistent with perspectives in public choice theory, providing jurisdictions with the power to develop their own tax policies enables innovation and experimentation that may ultimately yield the best approach to tackling climate change challenges.[15] Under one view, this "competition" among provincial governments could lead to the development of the most effective solution that inhibits global warming at the lowest cost.[16] On the other hand and as discussed elsewhere, current provincial environmental

---

[15] Early work in the field is often traced back to Charles Tiebout's ground-breaking article in 1956 on "A Pure Theory of Local Expenditure" that theorized competition among U.S. municipal governments for workers would tend to promote beneficent outcomes, namely an optimal level and mix of taxes and spending as workers "voted with their feet" by moving to the city that best reflected their tax preferences. One of the first shots fired hence supported the view that government competition would lead to a "race to the top". Later tax theorists such as Wallace Oates deflated the earlier and more optimistic view by asserting that government competition for mobile factors such as capital might in fact lead to a "race to the bottom" as each government responded by lowering its taxes to such a point that they would be unable to fund needed government services. *See* Tiebout, C., "A Pure Theory of Local Expenditures," *Journal of Political Economy*, Volume 64, 1956, page 416; Oates, W. E., *Fiscal Federalism*, Harcourt, Brace, Jovanovich, Inc., 1972.

[16] For discussion, *see* Olewiler, N., "Environmental Policy in Canada: Harmonized at the Bottom?," in Harrison, K., *Racing to the Bottom? Provincial Interdependence in the Canadian Federation*, University of British Columbia, 2006, page 113 (concluding that the evidence does not show that Canadian provinces have competed with each other via environmental policy).

tax policies are dictated by the specific socio-economic interests and needs of each province.[17] A worry exists that these differing interests will set some provinces against others. In addition, ongoing political conflicts between the federal and provincial governments with each side at times blaming the other for a lack of progress has arguably inhibited effective tax policy responses. Accordingly, an optimal outcome may not result through this regulatory competition among provinces, in the absence of strong coordinated action at the federal level.

2.3 Summary: Failing Grades on Curbing Emissions

The previously described federal and provincial tax policies appear to thus far have had no material impact on curbing carbon emissions that are considered to be harmful to the environment. In fact, the Canadian record in this regard is less than impressive:

(a) total carbon dioxide emissions have risen from 432 million tonnes of carbon dioxide in 1990 to 573 million tonnes of carbon dioxide in 2007, representing an increase of 32 per cent (while the population grew by 19.1 per cent during this time);[18] and

(b) carbon dioxide emissions per capita increased from 15.6 tonnes of carbon dioxide per capita in 1990 to 17.4 tonnes of carbon dioxide per capita in 2007, representing an increase of 11.3 per cent.[19]

As a result of this last figure, Canada was placed 10th out of 210 countries surveyed with respect to per capita carbon dioxide emissions.

A number of plausible factors could explain Canada's poor record, at least when compared to certain similarly situated countries in Europe and elsewhere. First, Canada is the second largest country (by total area) in the world with a relatively small population of roughly thirty million people. Global warming concerns may be perceived by many Canadians to be less of a problem, given the amount of habitable space available to the current and forecast population.

Second, Canada is a northern country and the fear of "global warming" may not appear too troublesome to many Canadians (who may not be familiar with the view that global warming science also emphasizes

---

[17] Anh-Thu et al., *op. cit.*, page 19.
[18] *See* International Energy Agency, *CO$_2$ Emissions from Fuel Combustion*, Paris: OECD/IEA, 2009, pages 44, 77.
[19] *Ibid.*, page 89.

significant swings in the weather). If global climate change was labeled "global cooling" – as it was under a scientific theory from the 1970s – then Canadians might be searching for more effective tax policies. Anecdotally, most Canadians might even welcome an overall warmer climate and may not be overly concerned with the plight of individuals living in foreign countries who are expected to be worse off. Nevertheless, certain public opinion polls suggest that a majority of Canadians worry their government has not done enough to reduce overall carbon emissions.[20]

Third, resource exploitation plays an important part in provincial and national economic development, creating jobs and bringing in government tax revenues. The trade-off from projects such as the Albertan oil sands is that emissions almost invariably rise. So far the trade-off appears politically acceptable to most Canadians: in the 2006 federal election, the opposition Liberal party lost in part due to its support for a carbon tax.

Finally, the alleged uncertain science of global warming may be playing a role in reducing political support for effective tax policy solutions.

3.   WHAT IS OPTIMAL TAX POLICY FOR CLIMATE CHANGE?

An extensive literature in law, politics, economics, and other fields has examined the merits of different tax policy approaches that strive to address global warming.[21] This part will not canvass this literature in

---

[20]   *See*, e.g., Spencer, C., *Planet in Peril: Poll*, Toronto Sun, 2010 (discussing how more than half of Canadians surveyed believe greenhouse gases produced by human activity are a key factor spurring climate change and that significant policy action is required to confront the challenge).

[21]   An authoritative report, although controversial, is the Stern Review. *See* Stern, N., *The Economics of Climate Change: The Stern Review*, Cambridge University Press, 2007. *See also* Congressional Budget Office, *Policy Options for Reducing CO_2 Emissions*, 2008, page viii (claiming that a carbon tax would be the most efficient option for reducing emissions); Waggoner, M., "How and Why to Tax Carbon," *Colorado Journal of International Environmental Law and Policy,* Volume 20, 2009; Metcalf, G. and Weisbach, D., "The Design of a Carbon Tax", (University of Chicago Law School John Olin Law and Economics Working Paper, No. 447), 2009; Mintz, J. and Olewiler, N., "A Simple Approach for Bettering the Environment and the Economy: Restructuring the Federal Fuel Excise Tax" (Sustainable Prosperity Initiative, University of Ottawa, 2008); Avi-Yonah, R. S. and Uhlmann, D. M., "Combating Global Climate Change: Why a Carbon Tax is a Better Response to Global Warming than Cap and Trade", (University of Michigan Law School Public Law and Legal Theory Working Paper No. 117, 2008); Duff, D. G., "Tax Policy and Global Warming", *Canadian*

detail but rather will only highlight the main arguments in favor or against the use of the two most discussed policy approaches: carbon taxes and cap-and-trade taxes. A discussion of the usage or expansion of other government policies that seek to reduce global warming, including regulatory standards, government subsidies, "command and control" policies that mandate emissions reductions to stipulated levels (for example, the Kyoto Protocol), or other government programs (such as carbon sequestration) is beyond the scope of this chapter.

3.1 Carbon Taxes

One of the main challenges for policymakers who wish to restrict global warming emissions is that polluters can generate these emissions in such a way without paying for the environmental costs associated with them. The polluters pass their costs onto third parties who are not directly involved with the purchase of the polluter's goods and services. These outcomes are considered to be market failures because firms and consumers do not pay for the current and future costs of their global warming emissions. To address this type of market failure Alfred Pigou proposed imposing taxes on certain activities so that the price of the activities would accurately reflect the costs associated with the activities.[22] In theory, the tax should equal the marginal cost, which is often referred to as the social cost of carbon (that is, the value of the damage to nations caused by climate change).

Carbon taxes are sometimes portrayed as one way to more accurately reflect the price of engaging in emission activities. The tax collected on the sale or production of carbon (and other global warming chemicals) would serve three main purposes. First, it would correct the market failure noted-above and lead to a more efficient allocation of resources throughout the

---

Tax Journal, Volume 51, Number 6, 2003, page 2063 (concluding that a broad-based carbon tax, along with other environmental policies, could promote energy efficiency).

[22] *See* Pigou, A.C., *The Economics of Welfare*, (4th ed.), Macmillan and Company, 1932. As discussed by Janet Milne, there are different theories that try to evaluate the efficacy of environmental taxes. The "Polluter Pays Principle" tries to hold those who pollute financially responsible for the pollution. Under the "Least Cost Abatement" theory, a tax is seen as the least economically costly method for dealing with environmental problems. The "Double Dividend" theory states that revenues generated by environmental taxes can be used to reduce taxes on other sources. *See* Milne, J. E., "Environmental Taxation: Why Theory Matters" in J. Milne et al. (eds.), *Critical Issues In Environmental Taxation*, (Vol. I), Richmond Law & Tax, 2003.

economy. Second, it would raise the price of emissions thereby incentivizing firms or other taxpayers to engage in more environmentally friendly activities by, for example, adopting "greener" fuels (see also Section 3.3). Third, it would raise revenues to pay for the costs associated with global warming (such as flooding of coastal regions) as well as the adaptation costs to prevent harm (such as building dykes in coastal regions).

Carbon taxes can be structured as either consumption or income taxes. A consumption carbon tax does not typically tax the activities of the emitters themselves. Rather, the tax is applied to a good or service whose production included the use of global warming emissions. As such, a carbon tax such as the British Columbia one described above is an indirect tax that is typically imposed on consumers. Certain observers advocate an "upstream" or "production" carbon tax, such as the Quebec one, that would be imposed on the emitters themselves.[23]

Critics maintain that carbon taxes are not the most effective or cost-efficient way to reduce global emissions. First, it is difficult to identify the marginal social costs associated with these emissions. A variety of empirical studies have tried to estimate the social cost of carbon and these estimates, at times, are based on contentious premises. Policy makers in Canada, for instance, sometimes argue the social cost of carbon is smaller for this large northern country.

Second, public choice theory, touched on in Section 2.2, suggests that firms may migrate from jurisdictions that impose carbon taxes to more leniently taxed jurisdictions. In other words, tax leakage could result from the fact that countries without carbon taxes may attract businesses (and tax revenues) by decreasing the costs of doing business in their jurisdictions. One way to address this problem would be to levy an import tax on goods and services imported, or withholding taxes on cross-border income, from a carbon tax-free country (see Section 4.3).

Third, while a carbon tax might encourage price certainty, there would remain uncertainty with respect to the quantity of emissions. Consumers may not reduce the purchase of carbon-intensive goods even if these goods were subjected to a high carbon tax because consumer response depends on the elasticity of the demand for the goods and services in question: a low rate carbon tax on automobile fuel may not appreciably alter consumer behavior, and thus may not materially reduce carbon emissions from driving cars.

Fourth, carbon taxes – especially indirect taxes imposed on consumers – can be regressive. Canada's national value-added tax, the Goods and

---

23   *See* Metcalf and Weisbach, *op. cit.*; Avi-Yonah and Uhlmann, *op. cit.*

Services Tax, strives to address regressivity by offering quarterly rebates to low-income households and by exempting certain goods and services that are considered to be necessities (for example, food). Similar tax relief such as the British Columbian Low Income Climate Action Tax Credit touched on previously may need to be offered under a carbon tax.

3.2 Cap-and-trade Taxes

Cap-and-trade is a regulatory scheme that strives to reduce global warming emissions by providing financial incentives to emitters to reduce their emissions. A government (or, potentially, a global authority) sets a "cap" or maximum amount of emissions for taxpayers. Firms and other emitters are issued permits that provide them with the right to emit up to the cap. Firms that wish to emit beyond the allotted amount must buy emission permits from others who remain below their own specified cap: this is the "trade" component of the scheme. In theory, firms that can reduce emissions most efficiently will do so (and sell their permits to others who cannot), thus achieving the most cost-efficient approach to reducing overall emissions. Under some approaches, the cap is also reduced over time to further inhibit emissions.

Critics suggest that cap-and-trade programs are inferior to carbon taxes for a number of reasons.[24] First, cap-and-trade programs may not promote price certainty. Without a certain (and higher) price for carbon, firms may not invest in less carbon-intensive energies. Businesses engage in new ventures to earn expected returns on their investments. As long as the price of carbon remains volatile these firms may be unwilling to risk their resources to exploit alternative fuels (as their competitors may not do so and, if the price of carbon comes down, then these competitors may find themselves with a competitive advantage). In particular, if a cap-and-trade system includes a so-called "safety valve" provision that permits auctioning additional carbon allowances if the price of allowances exceeds stipulated levels, then carbon prices will remain volatile. Existing cap-and-trade programs, such as the U.S. one to limit acid rain or the E.U. cap-and-trade program for carbon, demonstrate a high degree of price volatility for the tradeable permits.

Second, a carbon tax could arguably be implemented much more quickly than a complex cap-and-trade system. Existing and proposed

---

[24] *See*, e.g., Nordhaus, W., *A Question of Balance: Weighing the Options on Global Warming Policies*, Yale University Press, 2008, pages 148–62; Metcalf and Weisbach, *op. cit.*; Avi-Yonah and Uhlmann, *op. cit.*

cap-and-trade programs appear inherently complex. Issues that must be resolved include the level of the cap, implementation timing issues, allowance allocations, certification processes, penalties, and processes for exceptions by affected parties. Analysis of the proposed Australian cap-and-trade program suggests there are a host of tax issues that need to be addressed, including how acquisition costs of permits should be deducted, valuation of permits held at year end, timing issues surrounding the auction of the permit and any subsequent trades, as well as compliance issues.[25] In contrast, existing national carbon tax programs, such as ones adopted by Finland in 1990 and Sweden in 1991, appear to have been implemented without much difficulty and without too many transitional challenges.[26]

Third, cap-and-trade systems do not generally generate any revenues that can be redistributed by governments to those who have been more directly and adversely affected by global warming (for example, to pay for adaptation strategies such as building levies and dykes). In addition, revenues could be used to support government projects that seek to reduce emissions such as carbon sequestration programs and mass transit. On the other hand, governments can charge for emission permits, which would raise revenues under a cap-and-trade scheme (although it may be politically difficult to do so).

Fourth, there is little experience with international cap-and-trade systems. The most notable example is the European Union's emissions trading scheme (ETS) that was established in 2005 so that EU nations could meet their Kyoto Protocol target of reducing greenhouse gas emissions by 8 per cent in 2012 from their baseline emissions in 1990. To date, the ETS has failed to materially reduce greenhouse gas emissions from EU countries.

Fifth, the existence of permit trading requires financial intermediaries to develop mechanisms (and charge fees) to enable firms to price and trade in permits. This development could impose significant transaction costs on cap-and-trade programs.

Finally, cap-and-trade programs may be exploited or manipulated by certain taxpayers who will divert resources to reduce the impact of these programs. The inherent complexity of any cap-and-trade system also provides avenues for exploitation as firms devote resources to seek exemptions

[25]   *See* Black, C., "Climate Change and Tax Law: Tax Policy and Emissions Trading", (Sydney Law School Legal Studies Research Paper No. 09/09, 2009).
[26]   *See*, e.g., Johansson, B., *Economic Instruments in Practice: Carbon Tax in Sweden*, OECD: Paris, 2000.

or cutbacks to shield themselves from the full costs of such a system. As subsequently discussed, these final points make a cap-and-trade program particularly unappealing from a policy perspective.

3.3   Global Carbon Tax, Compliance Theory, and Green Innovation

The previous analysis briefly set out perceived merits and detriments of carbon taxes and cap-and-trade taxes, which are the two most frequently discussed approaches by academics and policy makers as potential mechanisms to constrain global warming. Due to the voluminous nature of writings on this topic, a tentative conclusion at best can be drawn from this review. Cap-and-trade solutions have the virtue of political feasibility and, from an international relations perspective, could be justified as the best possible reform, given existing political constraints. Nevertheless, there appears to be an emerging consensus, at least among legal commentators, that a global carbon tax instead of cap-and-trade solution appears to be better suited to address global warming concerns.[27]

While in-depth analysis is beyond the scope of this chapter, this view appears to be supported by insights and perspectives set out in the optimal tax and compliance theory literature.[28] Taxpayers deploy resources for tax planning with the goal of reducing or eliminating their taxes. These tax planning activities are generally considered to be wasteful from a social welfare perspective as they do not contribute to productive activities: the tax planning is a form of rent-seeking by attempting to extract value from others without adding "real" value to economic activities. Because resources are devoted to planning, it results in an inefficient (or suboptimal) allocation of all economic resources, which in turn is thought to reduce overall economic growth and standards of living that would otherwise be enjoyed by citizens and residents.[29]

---

[27] *See also* Sandmo, A., "Efficient Environmental Policy with Imperfect Compliance," *Environmental and Resource Economics,* Volume 23, 2002, page 85 (describing how both carbon taxes and cap-and-trade systems may be evaded by polluters).

[28] *See*, e.g., Mankiw, N. G., Weinzierl, M., and Danny Yagan, "Optimal Taxation in Theory and Practice" (Harvard Institute of Economic Research Discussion Paper No. 2176, 2009); Curry, P. A., Hill, C., and Parisi, F., "Creating Failures in the Market for Tax Planning," *Virginia Tax Review*, Volume 26, 2007, page 943; Boadway, R. and Keen, M., "Public Goods, Self-Selection and Optimal Income Taxation", *International Economic Review*, Volume 34, 1993, page 463.

[29] *See* generally Cockfield, A .J., *NAFTA Tax Law and Policy: Resolving the Clash between Economic and Sovereignty Interests*, University of Toronto Press, 2005, pages 15–17 (henceforth "NAFTA Tax Law and Policy").

In other words, firms under a cap-and-trade system may devote resources toward lobbying the government for relief or exemptions instead of, say, trying to build a better mouse trap. Firms and other taxpayers subjected to a cap-and-trade system may also have greater flexibility to "game" the system and continue to emit without fear that their actions will be constrained by taxation: cap-and-trade may not reduce the after-tax cost of emitting for many taxpayers as long as their emissions remain below the cap. Finally, the complexity inherent in a cap-and-trade system provides opportunities for more loopholes that can be exploited through planning that seeks to comply with technical tax rules while maintaining current and expected emissions levels.

Carbon taxes will also not be immune to manipulation as well as rent-seeking: industries will still seek exemptions from the tax for reasons that include the need to promote global competitiveness. As discussed in Section 4.3, a global carbon tax may curtail these exemptions as industries from all participating governments will be subject to the same carbon price and non-participating governments will face border tax adjustments that negate competitive advantages associated with lower carbon prices. The uniform taxation of the final consumption of all carbon-based goods and services would also be consistent with optimal tax theory that generally indicates production efficiency is enhanced when factors inputs (that is, intermediate goods) remain untaxed so that they can be allocated as efficiently as possible. Value-added taxes seem to follow this prescription because they call for rebates or credits so that only final goods and services are taxed.[30]

For this reason, a "carbon-added tax", proposed by Thomas Courchene and John Allan, may reflect optimal taxation of carbon-based goods and services.[31] Under this proposal, a tax is applied to carbon emissions added at each stage of production. The taxes levied in previous stages are rebated as the product moves through the production chain so that only the carbon added at each stage is taxed at that stage. When the product reaches the final stage, the tax is on the cumulative value of carbon emission, that is, on the sum of the amounts of carbon added at each stage. The approach promotes compliance as taxpayers must charge the tax to receive the tax rebate: governments now have decades of positive experiences with a similar mechanism with VATs and GSTs.

A complicating issue surrounds measuring the amount of carbon

---

[30]   Mankiw et. al., *op. cit.*, page 19.
[31]   *See* Courchene, T. J. and Allan, J. R., "Climate Change: The Case for a Carbon Tariff Tax", *Policy Options*, 2008, pages 59, 62–4.

added at each stage of the production. If this problem could be effectively addressed (through carbon auditing or some other process) then the carbon-added tax, like other VATs, would be relatively simple to implement and fairly difficult for taxpayers to dodge.[32] The analysis, however, assumes an idealized carbon-added tax imposed on a broad tax base of goods and services and to the extent the tax departs from this idealized vision it will encourage efficiency losses.

Another important issue surrounds the ability of a carbon tax versus a cap-and-trade program to incentivize the development of green sources of energy. A fairly extensive literature examines the interaction between technology developments and tax policy, mainly in the context of the taxation of e-commerce.[33] Certain writings examine how tax laws can provoke technology change to indirectly obtain a desired policy outcome by influencing the behavior of individuals and firms (in this case, to affect the behavior of producers and consumers of carbon-based goods and services).[34] A broad-base carbon tax would encourage the most efficient allocation of resources by reducing distortions that would otherwise be associated with a cap-and-trade system that applies unevenly, or not at all, to different taxpayers.[35] Firms whose emissions are currently below the specified cap will not seek alternative energy sources as there is no sanction for doing so: under a carbon tax, in contrast, a firm will continue to pay the tax as long as it emits carbon or another greenhouse gas; hence there will always be an incentive to reduce carbon dependence.

As oft-noted, a broad-base carbon tax should more evenly and more transparently raise the price of carbon: this price change should send a signal to markets that alternative, and more reasonably priced sources of energy, are needed. The price change does not select potential winners as can occur through government subsidies, but lets markets innovate a host of potential green solutions that may one day become viable. As long as one accepts that markets, and not governments, are best-suited

---

[32] *Ibid.*, at page 62 (discussing the need for international agreement on the measurement of the carbon footprints of goods).

[33] *See*, e.g., Doernberg, R. L., Hinnekens, L., Hellerstein, W. and Li, J. Y., *Electronic Commerce and Multijurisdictional Taxation*, Kluwer Law International/International Fiscal Association, 2001.

[34] Cockfield, A. J., "Towards a Law and Technology Theory," *Manitoba Law Journal*, Volume 30, 2004, pages 383, 391–5 (discussing the relationship between tax policy and technology change).

[35] This insight that a broad tax base reduces economic distortions is sometimes traced to Mirrlees, J. A., "An Exploration in the Theory of Optimal Taxation", *Review of Economic Studies*, Volume 38, 1971, page 175.

to generate innovative responses then a properly designed carbon tax should better address the future development and diffusion of low-carbon or carbon-free energy sources.[36] Most importantly, these greener energy sources must eventually become less costly than their carbon-based counterparts so that firms will adopt them to gain competitive advantage.

The analysis suggests that small open economies that wish to effectively address global warming should seek collective action solutions that would impose binding obligations on small and large economies. These countries should adopt a global carbon tax that, in its ideal form, would broadly apply on a value-added basis to all carbon-based goods and services, and at a rate that would equal the marginal social cost of carbon.[37] Part 4 shows how constraints imposed by globalization influence the potential design of this global carbon tax.

4.   FROM REGIONAL TO GLOBAL CLIMATE CHANGE POLICIES

4.1   Specific North American Issues

The North American context serves as one example of the ways that regional economic integration can drive international tax policy and environment developments. Canada, Mexico and the United States are tied together through the North American Free Trade Agreement (NAFTA). Within North America, the United States constitutes the bulk of gross domestic product. NAFTA can thus be portrayed as a three-player game in which the tax policy of one big player exerts a disproportionate economic impact on the two relatively smaller players.[38] In this environment, the two smaller players, Canada and Mexico, pursue a policy of tax and regulatory emulation by amending their tax laws to follow U.S. tax developments with respect to taxes on highly mobile cross-border factors of production like capital. In particular, Canada sometimes tries to ensure

---

[36]   For a discussion of the relationship between law and technological diffusion, *see* Bernstein, G., "The Role of Diffusion Characteristics in Formulating a General Theory of Law and Technology," *Minnesota Journal of Law, Science and Technology*, Volume 8, 2007, page 623.
[37]   For an earlier call for a global carbon tax, *see* Cnossen, S. and Vollebergh, H., "Toward a Global Excise on Carbon," *National Tax Journal*, Volume 45, 1992, page 23.
[38]   NAFTA Tax Law and Policy, *op. cit.*, pages 164–74.

it maintains a favorable tax climate for inward investment vis à vis the Americans.[39]

In the context of global warming tax policy, one big player may dictate North American policy. Even if the Canadian or Mexican government believes that a carbon tax will promote superior national and international policy outcomes there are powerful economic incentives to adopt the proposed U.S. approach. For example, major trade and investment partners could have paid a significant price if they departed from an earlier U.S. cap-and-trade approach that proposed, starting in 2020, to impose border adjustments on imports from countries that have not taken comparable action. It is not surprising that the Canadian government appeared to be following the regulatory approach under the proposed U.S. cap-and-trade program.[40]

In any event, neither the current Canadian government nor, at least arguably, the Canadian public currently appears to support a carbon tax that would impose significant costs on emissions activities (see Section 2.3). Indeed, the U.S. cap-and-trade approach provided political cover to the Canadian government as it could argue that it must adopt a similar cap-and-trade regime, otherwise overall cross-border trade and investment between the two countries will be harmed, reducing Canadian welfare. Because similar incentives exist for the Mexican government, a possible outcome is a North American regional solution that follows the proposed U.S. cap-and-trade approach.[41] The next two sections discuss

---

[39] This voluntary change to tax legislation creates a situation of de facto harmonization in certain circumstances. Regulatory emulation, along with tax coordination via bilateral tax treaties, permits the NAFTA governments to control their tax destinies to the greatest extent possible. In addition, this environment permits Canada and Mexico to make up for the sovereignty sacrifice by choosing tax policies that reduce tax burdens on capital in comparison to the ones imposed by the United States, hence engaging in limited tax competition without fear of retaliation by the bigger player, which is indifferent to the moves by the smaller players (largely because capital outflows, if any, from this competition do not likely represent a significant portion of overall U.S. flows). *Ibid.*

[40] *See* McCarthy, S., "Canada to Match U.S. Climate Rules", *The Globe and Mail*, July 1, 2009, at B3. Importantly, however, the Canadian government proposed a cap-and-trade program in a very rough form prior to the U.S. proposals, which ultimately failed to be enacted.

[41] In 2009 the leaders of each NAFTA nation pledged to cooperate on plans to fulfill their shared "vision for a low-carbon North America," including cooperation on the development of their respective cap-and-trade programs. *See North American Leaders' Declaration on Climate Change and Clean Energy*, Guadalajara, Mexico, August 10, 2009.

how regional cap-and-trade (or other) programs could evolve over time into a global carbon tax.

4.2   Tax Sovereignty and Regional Environmental Competition

International tax policy analysis often attempts to address international developments with an emphasis on maximizing global economic welfare. The roots and pre-occupation with global efficiency concerns can be traced back to post-World War I developments, where a group of tax economists were commissioned by the League of Nations to come up with appropriate tax treaty responses to overcome problems associated with international double taxation and, to a lesser extent, fiscal evasion to promote international trade and investment.[42] Yet it is equally clear that actual international tax developments are driven by more mundane concerns such as the desire by governments to maintain tax sovereignty and to maximize national – not global – welfare.[43] As such, the study of international tax law differs (or ought to differ) from the study of international trade or investment where sovereignty concerns are significant but, at least in the last half century, less prominent.[44] In fact, because governments have ceded political control over areas such as international trade by entering into binding multilateral agreements and processes such as the World Trade Organization, they may have become even more reluctant to cede control over aspects of their tax systems.

For these reasons, analysts sometimes scrutinize international tax developments within a regional context where countries are witnessing higher degrees of economic, social, technological and other forms of integration.[45] Similarly, environmental policies, including climate change

---

[42]   See Professors Bruins, Enaudi, Seligman and Sir Josiah Stamp, *Report on Double Taxation Submitted to the Financial Committee,* League of Nations, 1923.

[43]   *See* Cockfield, A. J., "Purism and Contextualism within International Tax Law Analysis: How Traditional Analysis Fails Developing Countries", *eJournal of Tax Research*, Volume 5, 2007, page 199.

[44]   Certain writers focus on the political and institutional processes that shape international tax policy. *See*, e.g., Ring, D., "Democracy, Sovereignty and Tax Competition: The Role of Tax Sovereignty in Shaping Tax Cooperation", *Florida Tax Review*, Volume 9, 2009, page 555; Christians, A., "Hard Law and Soft Law in International Taxation," *Wisconsin Journal of International Law*, Volume 25, 2007, page 325; and Ault, H.J., "Reflections on the Role of the OECD in Developing International Tax Norms", *Brooklyn Journal of International Law*, Volume 34, 2008–2009, page 770.

[45]   In particular, observers have analyzed tax developments within regional European integration. *See,* e.g., Easson, A. J., *Tax Law and Policy in the EEC,*

policies, are, at times, studied on a regional basis. To confront global warming, for instance, the European Union developed in 2005 its own cap-and-trade program called an Emissions Trading Scheme (ETS). To strengthen the ETS, in 2008 the European Commission proposed to centralize the allocation of emission permits, auction more permits instead of granting them for free, and expand coverage over other greenhouse gases. Similarly, regional environmental policy solutions have been discussed in Asia and elsewhere.[46]

A regional cap-and-trade system may not effectively reduce overall emissions, but it does have the one advantage of political feasibility in part because the system does not appear to impose any binding tax policies on participating governments. These regional cap-and-trade solutions are likely to be a superior policy alternative than a no-coordinated approach.

There may also be a benefit to regional approaches. As previously touched on in Section 2.2, certain public choice theoretical perspectives assert that optimal outcomes are promoted by tax or regulatory competition among jurisdictions (although some observers note that the necessary premises to provoke optimal outcomes may exist at the local or subnational level, but may not occur at the international level). With respect to international tax competition, there is increasing recognition that formal or informal harmonization of business taxes at the regional level can promote efficiencies that enable firms based in regional blocs to compete more effectively with firms outside of the blocs.[47] Similarly, regions that develop coordinated climate change policies (via cap-and-trade, a carbon tax or some other policy mix) may promote cost efficiencies for firms originating or operating within the regions.

In theory, the region that adopts the best global warming policy will

---

London: Sweet and Maxwell, 1980. Provoked initially by the Treaty of Rome in 1957, European governments have been struggling with policies responses to problems caused by the interaction of differential national tax systems. While there has been an effective response to cross-border consumption tax issues via VAT harmonization in 1993, the progress with respect to cross-border income tax has been more uneven.

[46] *See*, e.g., Asian Development Bank, *Climate Change: Strengthening Adaptation and Mitigation in Asia and the Pacific* (2009). For a discussion of soft law approaches to assist with environmental matters in parts of Asia, *see* Chung, Suh-Yong, "Is the Mediterranean Regional Cooperation Model Applicable to Northeast Asia?," *Georgetown International Environmental Law Review*, Volume 11, 1999, pages 363, 395.

[47] *See* Commission of the European Communities, *Company Taxation in the Internal Market*, Luxembourg: Office for Official Publications of the European Communities, 2002.

curtail emissions to the greatest extent at the least possible cost, develop green industries that promote heightened levels of economic growth, and maintain low compliance costs for taxpayers and low enforcement costs for tax authorities. The new "green competition" may thus occur among competing regions. Over time, those regions that have adopted the most effective policies will be able to demonstrate the "value" (for example, reduced emissions without corresponding reductions in economic growth, employment, and so on) such that other nations and/or regions will adopt these policies.

4.3   Broadening Regional Solutions to a Low Rate Global Carbon Tax

4.3.1   Transitioning from regional to global solutions by focusing on the price of carbon

In the medium term, the possible regional cap-and-trade systems may ultimately make room for progress at the international level, which would meet the collective action needs of the relatively small economic players that wish to address global warming challenges. Cap-and-trade programs, if they work as hoped, will drive up the price of carbon (only in a much less transparent fashion when compared to carbon taxes). Governments should hence develop consensus on a price of carbon (that is, the price per tonne of carbon dioxide equivalent emissions) that reflects the expected price increase under their cap-and-trade programs as well as under other government taxes and programs (such as fuel taxes and mandated automobile emissions standards). The expected price should reflect the impact of the different environmental approaches and thus should presumably be a small increase on the prevailing price of carbon. In other words, the initial agreement would not force most governments to take any steps that they are not already taking. In addition, the agreement could include exemptions for small firms.

Governments could fulfill their obligations by meeting the targeted price of carbon through their cap-and-trade (or other programs) or they could more meet the price through an international carbon tax. A global agreement on a cap-and-trade system would require agreement on the extent of emissions reductions; in this context, the voices of countries with large economies may drown out the smaller players who may be forced to agree on emissions reduction targets that will not be politically viable. In contrast, a global carbon tax would simply force participating nations to set a domestic carbon price that would be at least the level of the internationally agreed price. In addition, a chief justification for a global carbon tax is that it would help to equalize among all polluters the marginal cost of pollution cutbacks, hence satisfying the demand for global production efficiency.[48]

Moreover, as discussed in Section 3.3, it is likely that carbon taxes would provide a more predictable price for carbon and would be easier to enforce by the national tax authorities. For this reason, a global carbon tax may become a more attractive option for governments to meet the newly established carbon price. Due to the reluctance of nations to be bound at the supranational level, any agreement on a carbon tax would, at least initially, have to be at a low rate; hence the corresponding increase in the price of carbon would also be low.[49]

The "carrot" to enter into the agreement will include the hoped-for political upside for governments to appear to be doing something to address global warming. In addition, participating countries will agree on a fixed price for carbon, which, as discussed in Section 3.3, should act as a signal for industry to develop more environmentally friendly sources of energy to promote cost savings. To the extent that green innovation is encouraged by a global carbon tax then participating governments will enjoy an advantage in the development of goods and services through sustainable energy policies, as well as a comparative advantage over other competitor nations whose industries lag behind in generating green innovation.

4.3.2 Consumption border tax adjustments for non-participating countries
Once an agreed carbon price was reached (via cap-and-trade, other policies or the global carbon tax agreement), the corollary will be that border tax adjustments will be imposed on any non-participating countries: imports from non-participating nations will be subject to an additional carbon tax.[50] This will act as a "stick" to encourage participation in the international agreement. It would forestall leakage that could occur as firms shift their operations to more leniently regulated countries (see Section 3.1). In some senses, the international agreement will serve as protectionism

---

[48]   *See* Sandmo, A., *The Scale and Scope of Environmental Taxation*, (NHH Discussion Paper, Oct. 2009), page 22 (henceforth "Sandmo, Scale and Scope of Environmental Taxation").

[49]   As Michael Waggoner notes, "[A] carbon tax should be phased in over several years, with low initial rates that slowly but substantially increase, to allow both consumers and producers to adjust gradually to the new system." Waggoner, *op. cit.*, Section II.C.

[50]   For an elaboration of this view, *see* Cnossen and Vollebergh, *op. cit.*, pages 32–3; Couchene and Allan, *op. cit.*, page 60; Gilbert and Metcalf, *op. cit.*, pages 40–50.

for governments who adopt a carbon tax: this sort of "green" protection-ism will appeal to governments who feel they are losing out to low-cost competitors based in foreign countries with fewer environmental taxes or regulations.

In particular, a global agreement would address what is perhaps the main deficiency of existing national carbon taxes – the exemptions for industries due to concerns about global competitiveness.[51] Exemptions to promote international competitiveness would, at least in theory, be reduced because participating nations would be subject to the same tax and non-participating nations would be sanctioned by import taxes.

The meshing of such an agreement with other international agreements such as the WTO's GATT and GATS would be complex, and may result in prohibited discrimination against WTO members.[52] Accordingly, the WTO itself may be the most suitable forum for the development of a global carbon tax agreement because it could seek, if necessary, an exemption from non-discrimination and national treatment provisions for nations that participate in the global carbon tax agreement. If progress within the WTO is not obtainable, the OECD, which currently acts as the main inter-national organization to promote reform for international income and, increasingly, consumption taxes could act as a suitable forum.[53]

In any event, a carbon tax and corresponding border tax adjustment should not be portrayed as a prohibited tariff or subsidy: the tax simply seeks to capture the marginal costs associated with production involv-ing carbon. Moreover, a unified carbon tax could stave off even greater protectionist problems associated with the proposed "green" tariffs such as the ones envisioned under the European Union's ETS. An earlier U.S. cap-and-trade proposed program, as discussed, appeared to be infused with protectionism by indirectly forcing certain trade partners such as Canada to adopt the U.S. approach or, beginning in 2020, face significant barriers to cross-border trade.

4.3.3   Income border tax adjustments for non-participating countries

Nevertheless, the specter of a trade war triggered by green protectionism may inhibit the development of a global carbon tax. Instead of deploying

---

[51]   *See* Stern Review, *op. cit.*, page 386.

[52]   *See,* e.g., Veel, P., "Carbon Tariffs and the World Trade Organization: An Evaluation of Feasible Policies," *Journal of International Economic Law*, Volume 12, Issue 3, 2009, page 749.

[53]   *See* Cockfield, A. J., "The Rise of the OECD as Informal 'World Tax Authority' through National Responses to E-commerce Taxation", *Yale Journal of Law and Technology*, Volume 8, 2006, page 136.

a destination-based carbon consumption tax, countries could consider coming to an agreement on a carbon income tax that applies a special income tax on large carbon emitters (the income tax rate could vary depending on the level of carbon dioxide equivalent emissions from the emitter). If the tax is structured as an income tax then participating countries will not have to fear they have violated their national treatment and most favored nation treatment obligations under WTO trade rules (or obligations set out within regional free trade agreements such as NAFTA or customs unions such as the EU). Income taxes are generally carved-out of trade agreements to permit governments to continue to develop their own distinct income tax policies.[54]

An income tax could extend over domestic emitters as well as, under tax treaty law, fixed places of business maintained by non-resident emitters. More technically, through a general principle in the over 2000 bilateral tax treaties throughout the world, resident countries can impose their income taxes over the attributable profits of "permanent establishments" (defined to include "fixed places of business" under tax treaties) maintained by non-residents. If non-residents do not maintain a permanent establishment within a source country then a creditable withholding tax can be applied on payments for goods and services provided by the non-residents (the gross withholding tax is applied in lieu of the income tax obligation): this withholding tax will not extend to payments made to businesses based in participating countries (because they already levy a carbon income tax and would be able to receive foreign tax credits for the withholding tax).[55] Tax treaties, however, generally only restrict a nation's taxing power and do not create any additional taxes. Each participating country would therefore have to enact a "carbon withholding tax" into its domestic tax laws to achieve the desired outcome.

---

[54] While certain trade agreements such as NAFTA have general "carve-out provisions" for income tax measures, the GATT does not have one but has nevertheless been generally interpreted to apply only to consumption (indirect) taxes on products, and not to income (or direct) taxes. Certain WTO agreements such as the Agreement on Subsidies and Countervailing Measures prohibit income taxes that provide exemptions on subsidies for goods, but they do not apply to the proposed income tax for carbon emitters. *See* Cockfield, A. J. and Arnold, B. J., "What Can Trade Teach Tax?: Examining Reform Options for Article 24 (Non-Discrimination) of the OECD Model Tax Treaty", *World Tax Journal*, Volume 2, 2010, page 139.

[55] For a discussion on how this withholding tax could work, *see* Doernberg, R., "Electronic Commerce and International Tax Sharing", Tax Notes International, Volume 16, 1998, page 1013; Cockfield, A. J., "Transforming the Internet into a Taxable Forum: A Case Study in E-Commerce Taxation," *Minnesota Law Review*, Volume 85, 2001, pages 1171, 1240–4.

The end result of such an international agreement will be to, effectively, impose taxes on non-participating countries that will then have a powerful incentive to sign on to the agreement (otherwise their tax payments will go to foreign governments instead of generating revenues for the exporting non-participating country). While the proposed scheme is meant to dodge the anticipated trade litigation under a global carbon consumption tax, non-participating countries may still complain the plan is unfair and choose to retaliate in some fashion, again potentially triggering a trade war.

4.3.4 Reaction by group of two?

Moving briefly from smaller to larger economies, a globally coordinated plan will be unworkable unless the world's two largest carbon emitters, China and the United States, agree to participate. The U.S. government may eventually sign on to such an agreement in part as a way to address its massive trade imbalance with countries such as China. China itself may be agreeable to this proposal because it does not export significant amounts of carbon-intensive goods such as steel, aluminum, chemicals, paper and cement, to the United States: as noted elsewhere, Canada, as of 2007, was the dominant exporter of these goods to the U.S.[56]

In addition, while global warming problems via carbon emissions may seem distant or theoretical to many Canadians and Americans, the Chinese people are currently experiencing more direct results from emissions in terms of air pollution within major urban centers. This air pollution may eventually lead to lower economic growth rates to the extent that associated health concerns make Chinese and foreign workers more reluctant to reside in cities. A global carbon tax could help to address these air quality issues by incentivizing the usage of low-carbon energy sources. Moreover, international income tax laws in China have been amended in recent years in part to make them more consistent with international norms with respect to taxing cross-border investments, and a carbon tax could be portrayed as consistent with this approach.[57] Hong Kong and other parts of China that have traditionally imposed low taxes, however, might resist the new taxes.[58]

---

[56] *See* Metcalf and Weisbach, *op. cit.*, page 42 (citing Houser et al. (2008)).

[57] For a discussion of the evolution of Chinese income tax laws, *see* Halkyard, A. and Ren, L. H., "China's Tax Incentive Regime for Foreign Direct Investment: An Eassionian Perspective", in Arthur J. Cockfield (ed.), *Globalization and its Tax Discontents: Tax Policy and International Investments*, University of Toronto Press, 2010, page 35.

[58] A complicating factor is that China has distinct regions or jurisdictions (such as Hong Kong) that depart from the general Chinese income tax approach.

It may be necessary to provide concessions to China or other countries to incentivize them to adopt a global carbon tax. Agnar Sandmo discusses two possible approaches: (a) provide a lower rate for countries with fewer resources; or (b) develop an international scheme of redistribution whereby wealthier nations make transfers of income in return for agreement to adopt a global carbon tax (or at least meet the specified price of carbon through other policies).[59] He notes that the latter approach would ensure global production efficiency to a greater extent.

A global carbon tax accepts the need for firms and other taxpayers to internalize the true (or at least truer) costs of their actions. A global carbon tax with a low rate and emissions exemptions would arguably do little to inhibit overall carbon emissions, in part because it would not significantly increase the price of carbon. In any event, an optimal carbon tax – where the tax would price a tonne of carbon at a level equal to the marginal social cost of emitting a tonne of carbon – will be likely to remain elusive in the near term, in part because of the ongoing uncertainty surrounding the actual costs associated with global warming. As the partners to the international agreement learned to trust the new approach (as well as its implementation) they may be willing to gradually increase the rate over time. In addition, as countries with transitional economies become wealthier then the tax rates for these countries could be increased to meet the global norm and/or redistributive policies could be curtailed.

5. CONCLUSION

Canada, like many other small open economies, is struggling with the appropriate tax policy response to reduce global warming emissions. But Canada, also like many other countries, fears that a significant curtailment of emissions by, say, a carbon tax will reduce economic growth and employment. Moreover, there are reasons fairly unique to the Canadian situation that may help to explain Canadian reluctance to enact a broad-base carbon tax. For example, Canada is a northern country and the

---

See Cullen, R. and Wong, A., "Globalization and the Hong Kong Revenue Law System" in Arthur J. Cockfield (ed.), *Globalization and Its Tax Discontents: Tax Policy and International Investments*, University of Toronto Press, 2010, page 171. For comparative analysis of Hong Kong's tax system with the tax systems of ten other countries, *see* Cockfield, A. J., *Examining Policy Options for the Taxation of Outbound Direct Investment*, Ottawa: Advisory Panel on Canada's System of International Taxation, 2008, pages 22–34.

[59] Sandmo, Scale and Scope of Environmental Taxation, *op. cit.*, pages 22–3.

second largest country in the world with significant exploitable carbon resources. As a result, despite the growing academic and policy views that carbon taxes are best suited to reducing these emissions, the Canadian government is currently supporting a cap-and-trade system that will be likely to permit certain firms to maintain high emissions for some time.

Also of critical importance is that the Canadian economy is so closely tied to the largest economy in the world: the U.S. economy. It is not economically feasible for Canada to develop a policy solution that differs in any significant way from a possible cap-and-trade system in the United States otherwise cross-border trade and investment flows would be unduly inhibited, lowering Canadian economic growth. For this reason, North American regulatory policy, at times, follows the regulatory emulation (or "follow the leader") approach whereby Canada and Mexico pursue policies that are closely aligned with U.S. policies in areas that could harm the economies of the two smaller free trade partners.

A North American cap-and-trade system, however, may not effectively reduce global emissions. It nevertheless has the virtue of being the only apparent politically feasible solution, and may start the NAFTA partners on the road toward addressing global warming concerns in a more effective manner. The analysis highlights how regional developments, and not international developments, continue to play an important role in driving international environmental tax policy developments. Unless and until the sky appears to be actually falling (or burning), Canada and many other small open economies will be likely to pursue tax and regulatory policies that satisfy perceived socio-economic internal needs without having a material impact on reducing global warming emissions.

For those governments that actually wish to constrain global warming, a global carbon tax that would bind participating countries is the most effective route. This perspective appears to be supported by the literature on optimal tax and compliance theory because a carbon tax will be more difficult for taxpayers to dodge through tax planning efforts. In addition, a carbon tax will more transparently raise the price of carbon and incentivize firms to use low or nil carbon-based energy sources. In the medium term, an international agreement that focused on the price of carbon could incorporate existing national and regional cap-and-trade programs as well as other programs targeted at reducing carbon emissions, with a view toward evolving into a global carbon tax.

7. Not enough room for optimal choices? The European legal framework for green taxes

Mattias Derlén and Johan Lindholm

1. INTRODUCTION

There are several regulatory solutions capable of protecting and enhancing the environment, one of these being (green) taxation. In selecting which regulatory option to use it is rational to seek for an "optimal policy", meaning the regulatory solution that most effectively achieves the intended aim with the least amount of undesired side-effects. For example, several contributions in this volume discuss whether taxation or emission trading (a cap-and-trade system) is the better regulatory solution for the purpose of reducing CO_2 emissions.[1]

The task of formulating an optimal environmental policy is a difficult one.[2] Within the European Union, this is aggravated by a complex constitutional framework that largely places tax measures outside the scope of EU law. This chapter focuses on this constitutional framework and its effects on the use of green taxes and other environmental measures in the EU.

To achieve this aim, we will make two important distinctions. First,

---

[1]   *See* contributions by Cockfield, A.; Milne, J.; Gumley, W., and Stoianoff, N.; Griffiths, S.

[2]   Much scholarly work in this area apply law and economics theory to approach this task. *See, e.g.*, Albrecht, J., "The Use of Consumption Taxes to Re-Launch Green Tax Reforms," *International Review of Law and Economics*, Volume 26, 2006, page 88; Andersen, M.S., "Environmental and Economic Implications of Taxing and Trading Carbon: Some European Experiences," *Vermont Journal of Environmental Law*, Volume 10, 2008, page 61; Faure, M. and Johnston, J., "The Law and Economics of Environmental Federalism: Europe and the United States Compared," *Virginia Environmental Law Journal*, Volume 27, 2009, page 205; Revesz, R., "Environmental Regulation in Federal Systems," in *Yearbook of European Environmental Law*, Volume 1, Oxford University Press, 2000, page 1.

it is necessary to distinguish between when actions are taken by the European Union and when they are undertaken by a Member State. With regard to actions undertaken by the European Union, the central issue is whether the Treaties creating the Union confer upon it the necessary powers. With regard to Member States' actions it is central to consider whether national regulation violates fundamental EU law principles, most importantly the ban on discriminatory and protective taxes or other aspects of the internal market. Second, a distinction will be made between green taxes and other types of legal measures intending to protect the environment. This distinction is of central importance to the extent of the EU's and the Member States' regulatory power under the legal framework. Based upon these concepts, we recognize four regulatory options available when seeking to protect the environment: (A) EU green taxes, (B) other EU measures, (C) national green taxes and (D) other national measures.

As will be explained more fully below, the possibility to regulate under EU law differs between these regulatory options. Part 2 describes under what conditions the European Union may establish green taxes and other, similar measures. Part 3 similarly describes when and how EU law may impact green taxes established by the Member States and similar, national measures.

The findings of Parts 2 and 3 are that the constitutional framework affects regulatory options differently and, briefly summarized, (A) that it is difficult for the European Union to establish green taxes unless the tax created primarily intends to support the establishment and functioning of the internal market; (B) that the European Union has significantly greater power to protect the environment measures other than green taxes; (C) that although the Member States' use of green taxes is limited by EU law, they still enjoy significant discretion to take such actions; (D) and that other types of national measures than green taxes can more frequently be challenged using EU law even if they seek to achieve the same aim.

Based upon those findings, it is concluded in Part 4 that the legal framework steers the EU away from green taxes and towards other measures (for example, emission trading over carbon taxes) whereas the reverse is true for the Member States. We argue that this is problematic as it detracts from finding optimal regulatory options.[3]

---

[3] The reader should however be aware that this chapter does not make claims regarding the advantages and disadvantages of different regulatory options.

2. FRAMEWORK GOVERNING ACTIONS BY THE EUROPEAN UNION

2.1 EU's Power Generally

The powers of the European Union are limited. According to the principle of conferral, the Union may only undertake an act if it seeks to achieve an objective entrusted to it by the Member States under the Treaty on European Union (TEU) or the Treaty on the Functioning of the European Union (TFEU).[4] In this regard, the principle of conferral constitutes an important part of the legal framework within the European Union. The principle of conferral means, among other things, that the European Union can only take action if it can show that it has power to do so under a specific Treaty provision.

These power-conferring Treaty provisions differ with regard to the extent of the EU's competence in different areas vis-à-vis the Member States. In this regard, the TFEU divides the competence of the EU into three categories. First, in some areas the European Union enjoys exclusive competence, which means that the Member States may not regulate these matters even in the absence of EU legislation.[5] Second, the EU and the Member States more commonly share competence to act for the purpose of achieving the aims identified in the Treaty.[6] Third and finally, in some areas the European Union may only support, coordinate and supplement actions undertaken by the Member States.[7]

It is important to remember that different Treaty Articles prescribe different legislative procedures. Some Articles provide that the Council must be unanimous to enact legislative acts.[8] Other Articles prescribe the use of the ordinary legislative procedure that, simplified, only requires support by a qualified majority of the Council and a majority of the European Parliament.[9]

As the extent of the EU's regulatory power differs depending on which Treaty provision is used, the choice of legal basis may be important. According to the case law of the European Court of Justice, the

---

[4] Treaty on the Functioning of the European Union (TFEU), Article 5.
[5] TFEU, Articles 2.1 and 3.
[6] TFEU, Articles 2.2 and 4.
[7] TFEU, Articles 2.5 and 6.
[8] *See, e.g.*, TFEU, Articles 113, 115, 192 (2) and 352 discussed further below.
[9] *See, e.g.*, TFEU, Articles 91, 114 and 192 (1) discussed further below. The ordinary legislative procedure is laid out in TFEU, Article 294.

determination of the correct legal basis is based on objective and verifiable factors, most importantly the aim and content of the act in question.[10] This means that the correct basis for a measure that *inter alia* intends to protect the environment is not necessarily a Treaty provision specifically dealing with the environment.[11] There are two possible outcomes if a legislative act could be based on more than one provision. If possible, the requirements of all provisions should be applied. If this is not possible, the EU should apply the legal ground that correlates with the "principal" objective of the act and disregard any objective that is a mere "accessory".[12]

As will be demonstrated below, actions undertaken by the European Union for the purpose of protecting the environment have frequently been based upon Treaty provisions that provide that the competence to act is shared between the European Union and the Member States.[13] In light of this, the general legal conditions that govern the powers of the EU and the Member States in areas of shared competence shall be explored briefly.

First, even when the European Union has been granted shared competence to regulate a certain area, its power to act is subject to two important limitations: the principles of subsidiarity and proportionality. The principle of subsidiarity provides that Union actions should be reserved to situations when the aims of the measure could not be achieved through national action.[14] The principle of proportionality requires the European Union to limit the scope of its measure to what is necessary to achieve the underlying aim.[15]

---

[10]   *See, e.g.*, Case 45/86, *Commission v Council* [1987] ECR 1493, para. 11; Case 62/88, *Greece v Council* [1990] ECR 1527, para. 13; Case C-295/90, *Parliament v Council* [1992] ECR I-4193, para. 13.

[11]   *See, e.g.*, *Greece v Council* [1990], paras. 17–19.

[12]   Lenaerts, K., "The Principle of Subsidiarity and the Environment in the European Union: Keeping the Balance of Federalism," *Fordham International Law Journal*, Volume 17, 1994, page 846, at pages 872–3. For example, in *Commission v Council*, the Court was asked to determine whether a directive on waste management should be based on a Treaty provision intending to achieve the internal market (Article 36 TFEU) or on a provision intending to protect the environment (Article 192 TFEU). The ECJ concluded that although the directive could affect the internal market, Article 192 was the correct basis as the act had as its primary aim to implement the "polluter pays" principle by ensuring that waste is disposed near the place where it is produced. Case C-155/91, *Commission v Council* [1993] ECR I-939.

[13]   TFEU, Article 4 (2) (e).

[14]   TFEU, Article 5 (3).

[15]   TFEU, Article 5 (4).

Second, when the EU and the Member States share competence they are allowed to regulate in the same area and it is then possible that national and EU regulation conflict with each other. Such conflicts are resolved by the principle of supremacy according to which EU law takes precedence over national law, regardless of form or time of enactment.[16]

Third and finally, how the EU regulation is framed determines the extent of its preemptive effect on the Member States. This partially depends on policy decisions made throughout the legislative process,[17] but the room to make such choices may also be subject to limitations in the Treaty text. A limitation of practical importance is the distinction between, on one hand, Treaty provisions which allow the EU to introduce terms which the Member States may exceed but not fall under (minimum harmonization)[18] and, on the other, Articles that permit terms from which the Member States may not in any way deviate (maximum harmonization).[19] It is, of course, possible for the EU to enact minimum harmonization acts even if the Treaty provision serving as the basis for its legislative power allows maximum harmonization. Such restraint may be attributed to the reluctance of the Member States to support maximum harmonization, the principles of subsidiarity or the principle of proportionality. It may, however, also be due to requirements posed in the different Treaty articles, as will be exemplified below.

---

[16] *See, e.g.,* Case 6/64, *Costa v ENEL* [1964] ECR 585; Case 11/70, *Internationale Handelsgesellschaft mbH v Einfuhr- und Vorratstelle für Getreide und Futtermittel* [1970] ECR 1125. The application of the principle of supremacy is relatively straightforward. It may, however, sometimes be difficult to determine if national law actually is contrary to EU law, in other words, the extent of EU legislation. This matter is resolved by the broader and more illusive principle of preemption. *See, generally,* Chalmers, D. et al., *European Union Law,* Cambridge University Press, 2006, pages 188–93; Cross, E., "Pre-emption of Member States Law in the European Economic Community: A Framework for Analysis," *Common Market Law Review,* Volume 29, 1992, page 447; Schültze, R., *From Dual to Cooperative Federalism,* Oxford University Press, 2009, pages 190–214; Waelbroeck, M., "The Emergent Doctrine of Community Pre-emption – Consent and Re-delegation," in T. Sandlow and E. Steiners, *Courts and Free Markets: Perspectives from the United States and Europe,* (Vol. 2), Clarendon Press, 1982, page 548; Weatherill, S., "Beyond Preemption? Shared Competence and Constitutional Change in the European Community," in D. O'Keefe and P. Twomey, *Legal Issues of the Maastricht Treaty,* Wiley Chancery Inn, 1994, page 13.

[17] For some examples of this, *see* the legislative EU acts discussed *further below* Part 2.3.

[18] *See, e.g.,* Articles 191–193 discussed further below.

[19] *See, e.g.,* Articles 91 and 113 discussed further below.

2.2   EU's Power to Protect the Environment

When enacted in 1957, the Treaty establishing the European Economic Community (EEC) provided the thereby created Community with very limited competence to enact environmental legislation.[20] In fact, the original text of the EEC Treaty did not contain the word "environment". Subsequent revisions of the basic Treaties have gradually extended the competence of the EU in the field of the environment. It is important to note that even before such Treaty revisions, EU measures intended, among other things, to protect the environment were nevertheless enacted on the basis of Treaty provisions providing the EU with regulatory competence for the purpose of achieving aims not directly related to the environment. Still today, after the European Union has been granted independent competence with regard to the environment, such measures are prominent. As will be discussed here below, this type of regulation has an especially important role to fill with regard to green taxes.[21]

Commentators identify three phases in the development of EU environmental law. The first phase covers the period of 1957–1972 during which environmental protection played a relatively marginal role. The second phase begins with the Paris Summit of 1972 that served as the starting point for a process in which environmental issues became a central part of the Union's work. The most important result of this process, which marks the end of the second phase and the beginning of the third phase, is the Single European Act that entered into force in 1987.[22]

The Single European Act was the first of several Treaty revisions that strengthened the position of environmental issues in the EU. The most important contribution of the Single European Act was the introduction of what can here be referred to as the "Environmental Title" in what is now the TFEU.[23] The Maastricht Treaty and the Amsterdam Treaty

---

[20]   *See* Brus, M. et al., "Balancing National and European Competence in Environmental Law," *Connecticut Journal of International Law*, Volume 9, 1994, page 633, at pages 635–6; van Calster, G., "Public Environmental Law in the European Union," in R. Seerden et al., *Public Environmental Law in the European Union and the United States – A Comparative Analysis*, Kluwer Law International, 2002, page 465, at page 472.

[21]   *See* further the discussion below Part 2.3.

[22]   van Calster, *op. cit.*, pages 472–3; Jans, J., "The Development of EC Environmental Law," in G. Winter, *European Environmental Law – A Comparative Perspective*, Dartmouth Publishing Co., 1996, page 271 (additionally recognizes a fourth phase beginning with the adoption of the Treaty of Maastricht).

[23]   Single European Act, OJ L 169/1, 29.06.1987, introduced what is now TFEU, Part Three, Title XXII.

introduced protection and improvement of the quality of the environment and sustainable development as aims of the Union and moved regulation in the field of environmental law from unanimity to what is now the ordinary legislative procedure.[24] The most recent revisions through the Lisbon Treaty *inter alia* made the above-mentioned aims relevant for the entire EU,[25] extended the EU's power to act internationally in the field of environmental law,[26] and awarded the principle of the protection and improvement of the environment status as a fundamental right defined in a Treaty.[27]

The EU's power to initiate environmental measures is now (in the post-Lisbon version of the Treaties) quite significant. The extension of the EU's competence amounts to legislative power in the field of environmental law being transferred from the individual Member States to the European Union. This transfer of power does not carry any immediate effects. As previously mentioned, the Union's power to enact environmental regulation is largely shared with the Member States and the Member States may continue to regulate as long as it does not conflict with any enacted EU acts.[28]

In addition, Article 11 TFEU requires that "environmental protection requirements must be integrated into the definition and implementation of Union policies . . ." This provision, commonly referred to as the

---

[24]   Treaty on European Union (TEU), OJ C 191/1, 29.07.1992 and Treaty of Amsterdam, OJ C 340/1, 10.11.1997 introduced provisions now found in TEU, Article 3 and TFEU, Article 192.

[25]   These aims were previously found in the Treaty on the European Community and thus applied only to actions by the European Community (EC). However, with the abolition of the EC, these aims (now found in the TEU) also extend to actions previously considered to fall within the larger concept of the EU but outside the narrower concept of the EC.

[26]   *See, e.g.*, Article 191 (1) TFEU.

[27]   More specifically, Article 6 (1) TEU provides that the Charter of Fundamental Rights of the European Union "shall have the same legal value as the Treaties," including Article 37 of the Charter on Environmental Protection. Three caveats are, however, in order. First, the practical importance of this status change remains uncertain. *See* Dougan, M., "The Treaty of Lisbon 2007: Winning Minds, Not Hearts," *Common Market Law Review*, Volume 45, 2008, page 617, at pages 661–72. Second, this change is not intended to extend the competences of the EU. TFEU, Article 6 (1). Third, Article 37 of the Charter is marginally broader than TFEU, Article 11 (discussed further below) and since the use of the former is limited to certain circumstances it is questionable how often it would be valuable to resort to the former.

[28]   *See* above Part 2.1. It is important to remember that an enlargement of the EU's competence constitutes an equally large restriction of the Member States' competence.

integration principle, seeks to introduce environmental considerations into the other policy areas outside the environmental title. Thus, it is not only possible for the EU to take environmental interest into account when formulating policy, it is under a general duty to do so in all policy areas.

Having said all this, we shall now address the individual Treaty provisions capable of supporting green taxes and similar EU measures. These are presented below along with some examples of EU legislation created based upon the various provisions.

2.3   EU's Power to Introduce Green Taxes

2.3.1   Indirect taxation and the internal market

The arguably most important green tax measure introduced by the EU is the Energy Products Directive which imposes a duty on Member States to impose minimum rates of taxation for motor fuel, fuels for industrial or commercial use, heating fuel and electricity.[29] While the Member States may impose higher levels of taxation, they may not impose less tax than the minimum rates set in the Energy Products Directive.[30] It follows from the Directive that it serves two main purposes. First, by imposing minimum rates of taxation, the Energy Products Directive seeks to reduce existing national differences in taxation that threatens a well-functioning internal market.[31] Second, in framing the Act the European Union has, in accordance with Article 11 TFEU, also taken environmental protection into consideration as it seeks, *inter alia*, to encourage more efficient use of energy and to reduce greenhouse gas emissions.[32] This is, for example, evident in that it allows Member States to reduce the tax rate on energy products that are environmentally friendly or used for public transportation.[33]

A similar line of reasoning can be found in the proposed Car Tax Directive.[34] Currently, each Member State has its own taxation system for passenger cars, many of which are designed with the intent to reduce CO_2 emissions from cars. Such taxes may be levied on sale, registration,

---

[29]   Council Directive 2003/96/EC of 27 October 2003 restructuring the Community framework for the taxation of energy products and electricity, OJ L 283/51, 31.10.2003 (henceforth "Energy Product Directive").

[30]   *Ibid.*, article 4.

[31]   *Ibid.*, paras. 2–5 of the preamble.

[32]   *Ibid.*, paras. 6–7 of the preamble.

[33]   Energy Product Directive, article 15.

[34]   Commission, Proposal for a Council Directive on passenger car related taxes, COM(2005) 261 final, 5.7.2005 (henceforth "Car Tax Proposal").

or continuously as long as the car is in use. As previously mentioned,[35] Member States retain regulatory competence in the absence of harmonizing EU legislation, albeit subject to certain limitations.[36] The existence of parallel tax systems does, however, in the opinion of the Commission, hinder the proper functioning of the internal market. According to the Commission, the difference in taxation of passenger cars in the Member States distorts and fragments the passenger car market, causing inefficiencies and thereby preventing industries from exploiting economies of scale. Moreover, national taxation may hinder individuals from exercising their right to free movement. Finally, the harmonized car tax is framed so that it contributes to the reduction of CO_2 emissions from passenger cars.[37] The proposed Car Tax Directive would eliminate registration taxes[38] and introduce in all Member States an "annual circulation tax" on all registered cars that contains a differentiated part (constituting at least 25 per cent) based on the car's CO_2 emission.[39]

That protection of the environment is secondary in relation to the aim of improving the internal market is hardly surprising given that both the Energy Product Directive and the Car Tax Directive are based on Article 113 TFEU. This provision is one of the few in the Treaties that explicitly provide the EU with the power to introduce, which allows the EU to harmonize taxes, more precisely indirect taxes. However, such measures may only be taken when "necessary to ensure the establishment and the functioning of the internal market and to avoid distortion of competition." To do so requires unanimity in the Council and may include Acts that completely harmonize the regulated matter.

The Energy Products Directive and the Car Tax Directive illustrate how the EU can use Article 113 TFEU to introduce green taxes. It is important to note that the primary aim of the measure must be to ensure the functioning of the internal market. Indeed, it follows explicitly from the Treaty that the measure must be "necessary" for the functioning of the internal market. However, when introducing an indirect tax the EU must, in accordance with Article 11 TFEU, take environmental protection into consideration. This may, for example, be done by imposing higher tax rates on regulated objects that are environmentally harmful. It may also be achieved on a national level. Although Article 113 TFEU is capable of supporting maximum harmonization, such measures are rare and the EU

---

[35] *See* note 16 above and accompanying text.
[36] Discussed *further* below Part 3.
[37] Car Tax Proposal, pages 2–3.
[38] *Ibid.*, articles 7–8.
[39] *Ibid.*, articles 3–5.

measures are commonly supplemented by actions by the Member States, not least for the purpose of protecting the environment.

As previously mentioned, Article 113 TFEU covers only indirect taxes but it is supplemented by Article 115 TFEU.[40] As Article 113 governs the adoption of indirect taxes, only direct taxes come under the ambit of Article 115 TFEU. The EU has in fact used Article 115 to regulate some aspects of direct taxation.[41] Article 115 has, however, not yet been used to introduce green taxes. One can only speculate as to the cause of the absence of legislation but plausible explanations include that green tax solutions have traditionally been aimed at indirect taxation and that harmonization of direct taxes is a politically sensitive matter. It is in this context sufficient to note that there are, for the purposes of this examination, few relevant differences between Articles 113 and 115: both require a unanimous Council and only allow regulation when the regulated issues "directly affect the establishment or functioning of the internal market."

2.3.2 Transport policy

While Article 113 explicitly authorizes the EU to enact indirect taxation measures, including green taxes such as those previously mentioned, it is not the only provision capable of supporting such measures. One provision that has been used by the Union to introduce green tax measures is Article 91 TFEU. Although structured differently,[42] Article 91 functions much in the same way as Article 113 in that it can support measures introducing taxes and other charges that have as a secondary purpose to protect the environment. The primary purpose of a measure enacted under Article 91 must, however, be to implement the common transport policy which, in turn, shall seek to achieve the objectives of the Treaties.[43]

The so-called Eurovignette Directive illustrates how Article 91 TFEU can be used as the basis for environmental measures.[44] The Directive

---

[40]   TFEU, Article 114 cannot support the enactment of fiscal provisions which *e contrario*, means that such measures can only be enacted under TFEU, Article 115. TFEU, Article 114 (2).

[41]   The EU has also regulated direct taxes on the basis of Article 115. *See, e.g.,* Council Directive 2003/49/EC of 3 June 2003 on a common system of taxation applicable to interest and royalty payments made between associated companies of different Member States, OJ L 157/49, 26.6.2003.

[42]   Most importantly, Article 91 lacks an explicit reference to taxation such as the one in Article 113.

[43]   TFEU, Article 90.

[44]   Directive 1999/62/EC of the European Parliament and of the Council of 17 June 1999 on the charging of heavy goods vehicles for the use of certain infrastructures, OJ L 187/42, 20.7.1999 (henceforth "Eurovignette Directive").

allows Member States to maintain or introduce tolls or user charges for heavy road vehicles (defined as those exceeding 12 tons).[45] In addition, the Eurovignette Directive introduces minimum harmonization of registration taxes for heavy road vehicles by requiring the Member State to charge a tax upon registration that may exceed but not be less than that specified in the Directive.[46] It is clear that the primary aim of the Directive is to eliminate competition distortion and to internalize infrastructure, congestion and accident costs of transportation in accordance with the principle of "user pays".[47] These charges can, however, also improve the environment by constituting incentives against pollution following the "polluter pays" principle.[48] In this regard, tolls and user charges on heavy goods traffic supports sound economic growth, the proper functioning of the internal market, and the environment.[49]

Much like the aforementioned Energy Products Directive and the Car Tax Directive, the Eurovignette Directive takes into account both internal market and environmental interests and, much like those, this follows from the Treaty. While the improvement of the internal market and the environment are both objectives that the EU shall pursue, environmental considerations are frequently only relevant when they do not detract from a well-functioning internal market. For example, while the harmonized registration tax introduced in the Eurovignette Directive is intended to improve both the internal market and the environment, it allows Member States to lower or exempt taxes or charges on vehicles when doing so does not affect the internal market. Environmental impact, by comparison, is not a directly relevant factor in determining if such deviation is allowed.[50]

Article 91 offers a distinct advantage over Articles 113 and 115 in that the ordinary legislative procedure applies when acting under Article 91. Thus, Article 91 allows for the enactment of measures without complete unanimity in the Council. The main deficits of Article 91 are that it is narrow in scope (adopted measures must implement the common

---

[45] *Ibid.*, article 7.
[46] *Ibid.*, articles 5–6. In this regard, the Eurovignette Directive resembles the Car Tax Directive discussed above.
[47] *Ibid.*, preamble, para. 1; *see also* Directive 2006/38/EC of the European Parliament and of the Council of 17 May 2006 amending Directive 1999/62/EC on the charging of heavy goods vehicles for the use of certain infrastructures (henceforth "2006 Eurovignette Amendment"), preamble, paras. 1–2.
[48] Eurovignette Directive, preamble, paras. 7, 18; 2006 Eurovignette Amendment, preamble, para. 2.
[49] Eurovignette Directive, preamble, articles 1–2.
[50] *Ibid.*, article 6 (2).

transport policy) and can only support measures which primarily serve the internal market.

2.3.3 Environmental protection

For the purpose of protecting the environment it is a significant limitation that Articles 91, 113 and 115 TFEU make any environmental interest secondary to the interest of supporting the internal market. This will reasonably weaken the effectiveness of any green measure introduced under these articles. One would expect that the solution to this problem would be found in the increasingly stronger Environmental Title of the TFEU.

Articles 191 and 192 TFEU make up the core part of the Treaty that gives the European Union independent regulatory power in the field of the environment: Article 191 defines the objectives of the Union's policy on the environment and Article 192 provides under what conditions the EU may enact legislative acts for the purpose of achieving these aims. Since the objectives are broadly formulated, so is the range of measures capable of being enacted under Articles 191 and 192.

The EU's power to introduce taxation rules under the Environmental Title is, however, subject to an important limitation. From the broad range of measures intended to protect the environment (Article 192 (1)), Article 192 (2) singles out "provisions primarily of a fiscal nature" and provides that these may only be enacted by a unanimous Council.[51] Thus, in effect, any Member State may veto a green tax introduced under the Environmental Title. Moreover, EU measures enacted under these provisions may only include minimum harmonization.[52]

Article 192 (2) is more powerful than Articles 91, 113 and 115 in that the EU can use it as the basis for regulating direct or indirect taxation for the purpose of protecting the environment without having to show that the measure is necessary for the functioning of the internal market. In theory, Article 192 (2) can support a green tax that interferes with the function of the internal market. However, Article 192 (2) does not allow for maximum harmonization and, more importantly, require unanimous support among the (currently) twenty-seven Member States. It can be difficult to achieve unanimity, especially when the suggested measure may have far-reaching economic implications. As a consequence, any measure enacted under Article (2) is likely to be the result of extensive compromises. Perhaps this

---

[51] TFEU, Article 192 (2) (a).
[52] TFEU, Article 193. The reason for this provision is that some Member States were worried that the standard that the Member States could commonly agree upon would be lower than existing national standards. Brus et al., *op. cit.*, page 640.

is the reason why the EU has yet to introduce a green tax based on this provision. Even recent initiatives that are reasonably capable of being supported by Article 192 (2), such as the Car Tax Directive, use Article 113 as their suggested basis.[53]

2.4 EU's Power to Introduce Non-Tax Measures

Prior to the Single European Act entering into force,[54] Articles 114 and 115 TFEU on the approximation of national law for the purpose of establishing a well-functioning internal market served as the primary basis for environmental EU regulation.[55] Article 114 TFEU cannot support green taxes[56] and Article 115 TFEU can, as previously discussed, only support direct taxation measures and only when supported by all Member States. While these Treaty Articles serve as a poor basis for the introduction of green EU tax measures, they are capable of supporting non-tax measures aiming to protect the environment.[57] Article 115 served as the basis of many EU measures aiming to protect the environment prior to the creation of the special environmental title in 1987,[58] sometimes in combination with Article 352 TFEU which gives the EU broad regulatory powers to achieve the aims of the Union, including environmental protection.[59]

As the powers of the European Union under the Environmental Title has grown stronger with each Treaty revision,[60] Articles 114 and 115 have become less important as Articles 191 and 192 provide the EU with broad

---

[53] Discussed above Part 2.3.1.
[54] *See* the discussion above Part 2.2.
[55] Brus et al., *op. cit.*, page 638; van Claster, *op. cit.*, page 472.
[56] TFEU, Article 114 (2).
[57] In this regard, Article 114 is the more commonly used ground as it uses the ordinary legislative procedure.
[58] *E.g.* Council Directive 67/548/EEC of 27 June 1967 on the approximation of laws, regulations and administrative provisions relating to the classification, packaging and labelling of dangerous substances, OJ 196/1, 16.8.1967; Council Directive 70/220/EEC of 20 March 1970 on the approximation of the laws of the Member States relating to measures to be taken against air pollution by gases from positive-ignition engines of motor vehicles, OJ L 76/1, 6.4.1970; Council Directive 73/404/EEC of 22 November 1973 on the approximation of the laws of the Member States relating to detergents, OJ L 347/51, 17.12.1973; Council Directive 75/716/EEC of 24 November 1975 on the approximation of the laws of the Member States relating to the sulphur content of certain liquid fuels, OJ L 307/22, 27.11.1975; Council Directive 85/203/EEC of 7 March 1985 on air quality standards for nitrogen dioxide, OJ L 87/1, 27.3.1985.
[59] Jans, *op. cit.*, pages 273–5.
[60] *See* the discussion above Parts 2.2 and 2.3.3.

regulatory powers for the purpose of protecting and enhancing the environment.[61] Article 191(1) TFEU allows the EU to enact a wide range of environmental, non-tax measures using the ordinary legislative procedure, including Acts leading to minimum harmonization. For example, the EU has exercised this power to ensure that environmental considerations are integrated in plans and programmes,[62] to impose civil and criminal liability on certain environmentally harmful actions,[63] and to promote the purchase of environmentally friendly goods through non-fiscal means.[64] These are but a few examples of the broad range of environmental measures that can be enacted by the EU under Article 191 (1).

While Article 191 (1) cannot support the introduction of green taxes,[65] the European Union can use it to enact other market-based measures. The most famous example of such a measure is the Emission Trading Directive which established the European Union Emission Trading System (EU ETS) also discussed elsewhere in this volume.[66] The EU ETS is a cap-and-

---

[61]   TFEU, Articles 114 and 115 are, however, still sometimes used as the basis for legislation which that in addition to environmental protection also intend to achieve a well-functioning internal market *See, e.g.*, Directive 2006/66/EC of the European Parliament and of the Council of 6 September 2006 on batteries and accumulators and waste batteries and accumulators and repealing Directive 91/157/EEC; Commission, Proposal for a Regulation of the European Parliament and of the Council setting emission performance standards for new passenger cars as part of the Community's integrated approach to reduce CO_2 emissions from light-duty vehicles, COM(2007) 856 final, 19.12.2007, page 8. *See also* the discussion above Part 2.1 regarding choosing the correct legal basis for EU measures.

[62]   Directive 2001/42/EC of the European Parliament and of the Council of 27 June 2001 on the assessment of the effects of certain plans and programmes on the environment, OJ L 197/30, 21.7.2001.

[63]   Directive 2004/35/EC of the European Parliament and of the Council of 21 April 2004 on environmental liability with regard to the prevention and remedying of environmental damage, OJ L 143/56, 30.4.2004; Directive 2008/99/EC of the European Parliament and of the Council of 19 November 2008 on the protection of the environment through criminal law, OJ L 328/28, 6.12.2008.

[64]   *E.g.* Directive 2009/33/EC of the European Parliament and of the Council of 23 April 2009 on the promotion of clean and energy-efficient road transport vehicles, OJ L 120/5, 15.5.2009; Regulation 1980/2000/EC of the European Parliament and of the Council of 17 July 2000 on a revised Community eco-label award scheme, OJ L 237/1, 21.9.2000; Directive 2003/30/EC of the European Parliament and of the Council of 8 May 2003 on the promotion of the use of biofuels or other renewable fuels for transport, OJ L 123/42, 17.5.2003.

[65]   *See* note 51 above and accompanying text.

[66]   Directive 2003/87/EC of the European Parliament and of the Council of 13 October 2003 establishing a scheme for greenhouse gas emission allowance trading within the Community and amending Council Directive 96/61/EC, OJ L 275/32, 25.10.2003 (henceforth "Emission Trading Directive").

trade system that constitutes a cornerstone of the EU's climate change strategy.[67] In short, the system provides that Member States are to initially grant operators permits in accordance with an allocation plan (cap) that allow them to emit a specified amount of greenhouse gases. If the amount of gas emitted by the operator exceeds the initial grant, additional permits must be obtained from other operators who have not released their allotted quota or at Member State operated auctions (trade). The idea is that this creates economic incentives for producing less emission, for example, by investing in energy-efficient technologies. In addition, it allows for the measurement and gradual reduction of greenhouse gases.[68]

2.5 Summary and Conclusions

It follows from the discussion above that the Treaties make an important distinction between tax and non-tax measures. Whereas the Treaties allow the EU to enact green taxes, its powers are circumscribed in three regards: such measures must primarily serve the internal market (Articles 113, 115 and 91), require unanimous support by the Member States (Articles 113, 115 and 192 (2)), or may only include minimum harmonization (Article 192 (2)). The power of the EU to enact environmental non-tax measures is not subject to such limitations. Whereas environmental non-tax measures traditionally had to primarily serve the internal market (Article 114), the Environmental Title now provides the EU with broad regulatory powers for the purpose of protecting the environment (Article 192 (1)).[69]

One can thus conclude that the ability of the EU to enact environmental non-tax measures is significantly greater than its ability to introduce green taxes. Most importantly, Article 192 (1) allows the EU to enact non-tax measures using the ordinary legislative procedure (unanimity not required) even if the measure does not support the internal market.

In comparison with other Treaty Articles discussed here, the only limitation to Article 192 (1) is that it only allows for minimum harmonization of national law and not maximum harmonization. The importance of that limitation should, however, not be overstated. First, even if a Treaty provision allows for maximum harmonization, this may be prevented by the principles of subsidiarity and proportionality.[70] Second, the Member

---

[67] *Questions and Answers on the Commission's proposal to revise the EU Emissions Trading System*, MEMO/08/35 Brussels, 23.1.2008.

[68] Emission Trading Directive, preamble.

[69] *See* below Table 7.1.

[70] *See* the discussion above Part 2.1.

Table 7.1   Simplified overview of Treaty Articles

Article	Type of measure	Objective	Procedure	Harmonization
113	Indirect taxes	Internal market	Unanimity	Maximum
115	Direct taxes	Internal market	Unanimity	Maximum
91	Direct/indirect taxes	Internal market	Ordinary	Maximum
192 (2)	Direct/indirect taxes	Environment	Unanimity	Minimum
114	Non-taxes	Internal market	Ordinary	Maximum
192 (1)	Non-taxes	Environment	Ordinary	Minimum

States may be reluctant to support maximum harmonization. The skeptical attitude of Member States towards EU harmonization in the environmental area was evident in the development of the Environmental Title.[71] In fact, while some Treaty Articles are capable of supporting maximum harmonization, the measures discussed herein have allowed the Member States to impose more stringent standards.[72]

3.   MEMBER STATE ACTIONS UNDER REVIEW

3.1   Member State Residual Regulatory Powers

As demonstrated in Part 2 above, the European Union has limited competence when it comes to environmental measures in general and environmental taxation in particular. In the absence of harmonization it is up to the Member States to adopt such measures. Even if environmental measures have been adopted pursuant to Article 192 TFEU the Member States retain the right to adopt more stringent protective measures following Article 193 TFEU. This would seem to indicate a great freedom for the Member States in imposing for example green taxes. However, as is often the case with the legal system of the European Union, things are more complicated than they seem. First, it is not always apparent whether a particular area is harmonized or not. This issue will be explored in Section 3.2 below. Furthermore, even if the area is truly not harmonized the adoption of green taxes is limited in a number of ways due to the concept of

---

[71]   TFEU, Article 193, which provides that measures introduced under the Environmental Title may only include minimum harmonization, was introduced as a reaction to fear among the Member States that EU law would offer a lower level of protection than national law. Brus, *op. cit.*, page 640.

[72]   *See* above Part 2.3.

the internal market. Section 3.3 below will outline the various ways in which green taxes can be subject to review due to the provisions of the internal market. Section 3.4 will then contrast these difficulties with the limits imposed by EU law on other forms of environmental regulations. Throughout Part 3 numerous examples from the case law of the European Court of Justice will be discussed.

3.2   The Effects of Harmonization

It might appear reasonable to believe that the existence of harmonization can be expressed as a binary value – on or off, yes or no. An area is either harmonized or not. However, matters are normally more complicated. The most obvious complication is the extent of the harmonization. The possibility for a Member State to act in an area of shared competence between the Union and the States might depend on whether the Union legislation exhaustively regulates the area or not.[73] However, harmonization may be problematic also in other aspects. In this section we will demonstrate how existing Union legislation can have far-reaching and sometimes rather surprising effects.

The effects of harmonization are illustrated by the Braathens case.[74] In this case Sweden wanted to introduce a special environmental tax on emissions created by domestic commercial aviation. The tax was calculated on fuel consumption and emissions of hydrocarbons and nitric oxide.[75] Directive 92/81 had harmonized excise duties on mineral oils and Article 8.1 exempted mineral oils used for fuels for air navigation from excise duties. However, Sweden argued that the charge did not constitute excise duties but a special environmental tax, beyond the scope of the Directive. The Swedish Tax Authorities emphasized that the tax was not charged on the fuel per se, but rather on the polluting emissions created by aviation.[76] This line of reasoning, however, did not persuade the European Court of Justice. The Court found a "direct and inseparable link between fuel consumption and the polluting substances". Hence, the Swedish environmental tax was within the scope of the Directive and was therefore not allowed.[77] While the Court of Justice has an obvious point in that

---

[73]   For an introduction to these issues, *see, e.g*, Chalmers, D., and Tomkins, A., *European Union Public Law*, Cambridge University Press, 2007, pages 188–93. *See* also the discussion in footnote 16 above.

[74]   Case C-346/97, *Braathens Sverige AB v Riksskatteverket* [1999] ECR I-3419.

[75]   *Ibid.*, para. 8.

[76]   *Ibid.*, para. 16.

[77]   *Ibid.*, paras. 23–24.

a different interpretation would render the Directive ineffective,[78] this approach makes the effects of the Directive very far-reaching.

The European Court of Justice has in some situations taken a very strict approach to harmonization by interpreting the scope for Member State action narrowly. This is demonstrated by the *Brenner* case.[79] Here Austria wanted to change the toll system for the Brenner Motorway, one of the transalpine links. In short, the changes had the effect of increasing the tariff for vehicles with more than three axles when driving longer distances, so-called full itineraries.[80] The toll system was regulated by Directive 93/89[81] and therefore the Austrian government informed the Commission of the changes. The Commission put forward a number of objections to the new tariffs. One of these objections was that the increase in tariffs was not proportional to the costs of the Brenner Motorway.[82] According to Article 7 (h) of the Directive the toll rates applied should "be related to the costs of constructing, operating and developing the infrastructure network concerned". Austria argued environmental reasons for the increase in tariffs. The aim of the increase was to transfer goods traffic from the motorways to the rail network, thereby reducing the adverse effects on the environment. However, the Commission took the position that environmental effects could not be considered a "cost" according to Article 7 (h) of the Directive. Thus, the tolls could only be used to cover economic costs related to the motorway in question. This restrictive interpretation of Article 7 (h) would, according to the Austrian government, have paradoxical consequences. High tolls would be allowed on roads with light traffic, in order to cover the construction and operation costs, while only limited tolls would be allowed on roads with heavy traffic, where many vehicles would contribute to cover the costs. This could lead to a downward spiral, where increasing traffic would lead to falling tariffs, leading to even more traffic, and so on. Austria argued that this would clearly violate the protection of the environment.[83] The European Court of Justice sided with the Commission. Regarding the environmental arguments put forward by the Austrian government the Court concluded as follows:

---

[78]   *Ibid.*, para. 24.
[79]   Case C-205/98, *Commission v Austria* [2000] ECR I-7367.
[80]   *Ibid.*, paras. 7–23.
[81]   Council Directive 93/89/EEC of 25 October 1993 on the application by Member States of taxes on certain vehicles used for the carriage of goods by road and tolls and charges for the use of certain infrastructures, OJ L 279/32 12.11.1993.
[82]   *Commission v Austria* [2000], paras. 24–30.
[83]   *Ibid.*, paras. 116–129.

As regards the Austrian Government's argument that the requirement of a direct link between toll rates and costs associated with the infrastructure concerned would give rise to successive decreases in toll rates on heavily used motorways which, by reason of the subsequent increase in traffic, would have more and more damaging effects on, in particular, the environment, it need only be pointed out that, if such a consequence were to ensue, it would be the result of a mechanism intentionally created by the Community legislature, upon which it would then, if necessary, be incumbent to take appropriate measures to remedy the situation.[84]

In other words, so be it. Even if the adverse environmental effects would arise that would be for the Union legislator to remedy, not Austria. While this approach cannot be faulted as being in violation of the Directive, it demonstrates how limited the scope for environmental charges initiated by the Member States can be.

3.3 The Internal Market as a Potential Obstacle for Green Taxes

3.3.1 Introduction – the concept of the internal market

The European Union is not only a customs union (employing a single customs policy against third countries) but also an internal market, enabling the free movement of the factors of production. The Union Treaties guarantee the free movement of goods, persons, services and capital – famously known as the four freedoms. The wording of the basic Treaty provisions gives the impression of prohibiting only discrimination. For example, Article 45.2 TFEU states that the free movement of workers "shall entail the abolition of any discrimination based on nationality between workers of the Member States as regards employment, remuneration and other conditions of work and employment". However, in its extensive case law the European Court of Justice has made it clear that not only discrimination but also restrictions on the freedom of movement violate the Treaty and have to be justified. Sections 3.3.2 to 3.3.6 below will outline how the European Court of Justice can review green taxes and similar measures as potential violations of the internal market.

3.3.2 The ban on discriminatory taxes

Following Article 110 TFEU Member States cannot use the tax system to discriminate against foreign products or to protect domestic production. Article 110, while placed in a different part of the Treaty, is part of the rules on the internal market and the free movement of goods. Article 110

---

[84] *Ibid.*, para. 134.

only concerns taxation of products; the rules relating to taxation concerning persons and services are discussed in Section 3.3.5 below. The idea behind Article 110 is to supplement the other rules on the free movement of goods. In short, it would make no sense to regulate the use of customs duties as well as practical obstacles to trade if the Member States could still protect domestic product by way of the tax system. Article 110 might appear uncontroversial, in the sense that it only prohibits discrimination, leaving the choice of taxation system to the Member States as long as domestic and imported products are treated alike. However, as will be demonstrated above, the effect of environmental charges can sometimes be discriminatory, thus bringing them within the scope of Article 110, despite the absence of discriminatory intentions on the part of the lawmaker.

A flurry of Article 110 cases before the European Court of Justice has concerned taxation of vehicles. As discussed above, many Member States have imposed different forms of taxes on passenger cars and other vehicles for the (explicit or implicit) purpose of reducing CO_2 emissions.[85] These cases can be roughly divided into three different categories; the connection between vehicle power rating and taxation, the special problem of imported used cars and particular effects of vehicle taxation.

Many judgments of the Court of Justice have centered on national vehicle taxation systems where the tax to be paid was in some way determined by the power rating of the vehicle. The first, and most well known of these, was the *Humblot* case.[86] Here France had imposed an annual car tax and the amount to be paid depended on the so-called fiscal power rating (CV) of the car. Below 16 CV a variable rate was applied up to a maximum of 1100 francs, depending on the exact power rating of the car, but above 16 CV a flat rate of as much as 5000 francs was applied.[87] The twist was that no French cars were rated above 16 CV. Thus, the higher tax in fact only applied to imported cars. The Court of Justice found that the tax system consisted of two separate parts – one below 16 CV which were proportionate and one above 16 CV which had only a flat – and very high – rate of tax. Combined with the fact that the system was created so that only foreign cars suffered from the much higher tax, this constituted discrimination. The competitive advantages that certain imported cars might have were in effect cancelled out by the taxation scheme.[88]

---

85   *See* the discussion above Part 2.3.1.
86   Case 112/84, *Humblot v Directeur des services fiscaux* [1985] ECR 1367.
87   *Ibid.*, paras. 3–4.
88   *Ibid.*, paras. 14–15.

Following *Humblot*, France changed the taxation of cars to encompass nine different bands, depending on the fiscal power rating of the car. The first band included cars with a fiscal power rating of up to 4 CV; the last band included cars with a fiscal power rating of 23 CV or more. This system was challenged in the *Feldain* case.[89] According to the Court of Justice this new system also violated Article 110. Even with the changes, only imported cars ended up in the most heavily taxed category, encouraging consumers to buy domestic products instead.[90] The Greek system for vehicle taxation has similarly been tested before the European Court of Justice. In 1990 the Court of Justice tried an action brought by the Commission concerning two Greek taxes imposed on passenger cars, one payable when purchased and the other at the time of registration. Both taxes were progressive and based on the cylinder capacity of the car in question. The progression was not constant but increased more sharply for cars with a cylinder capacity exceeding 1200 cc and then again at 1800 cc.[91] The Commission argued that the Greek taxation system violated Article 110 on the ground that the difference in tax was not based on objective criteria. The Court stated that the Greek law was only in violation of EU law if it was capable of discouraging consumers from purchasing foreign produced cars in such a way that it benefits domestically produced cars. In the case at hand it was irrelevant that only foreign produced cars were affected by the increase in tax in the third tier (no cars produced in Greece exceeded 1800 cc). According to the Court, even if it was assumed that the tax discouraged prospective consumers from buying a foreign-built car belonging to the third tier, those consumers would buy a model in the first tier (all cars of foreign manufacture) or the second tier (cars of foreign or Greek manufacture) and "[c]onsequently, the Commission has not shown how the system of taxation at issue might have the effect of favouring the sale of cars of Greek manufacture."[92] While this attitude of the Court might appear rather generous, in particular in comparison to *Humblot*, it demonstrates the need to establish actual – as compared to only potential – discrimination of imported products.[93]

---

[89]   Case 433/85, *Jacques Feldain v Directeur des services fiscaux du département du Haut-Rhin* [1987] ECR 3521, paras. 5–7. *See also* Joined Cases 76, 86 to 89 and 149/87, *G. Seguela and A. Lachkar and others v Administration des impôts* [1988] ECR 2397, referring to *Feldain*.
[90]   *Feldain*, paras. 18–19.
[91]   Case C-132/88, *Commission v Greece* [1990] ECR I-1567, paras. 3–4.
[92]   *Commission v Greece*, para. 20.
[93]   Barnard, C., *The Substantive Law of the EU – The Four Freedoms*, (2nd ed.), Oxford University Press, 2007, page 54.

In other words, as the likely alternative to the most heavily taxed cars were other imported cars, actual discrimination against foreign products could not be demonstrated.

The taxation of imported used cars has posed particular problems. Several countries have tried a system with a registration tax for vehicles. Such a tax is levied on vehicles only once, normally when they are placed in circulation in the Member State in question, no matter if the vehicle is sold as new or imported. Naturally, such a tax would tend to disadvantage imported vehicles unless depreciation of value is taken into account when calculating the tax. The Member States have tried a number of different solutions to this.

In the *Tadeu* case Portugal levied a one-time motor vehicle tax based on cylinder capacity on light motor vehicles imported new or used or assembled in Portugal. The tax on imported second-hand vehicles was reduced by 10 per cent as compared to new vehicles.[94] The Court of Justice found this practice to discriminate against imported cars, thus violating Article 110. The Court observed that, as the tax was only levied once, a part of it remained incorporated in the value of domestic second-hand vehicles. In comparison, imported second-hand cars had to carry no less than 90 per cent of the tax, regardless of age. The system thus clearly favored second-hand cars on the domestic market.[95] Greece employed a similar system, with minor modifications.[96] A special one-time consumer tax was levied on the purchase of new and imported vehicles. In order to avoid disadvantaging imported second-hand cars the tax was reduced, given the age of the imported second-hand car. The reduction was 5 percent per year, up to a maximum of 20 percent. One of the reasons behind the limited reduction in taxation was environmental; Greece wanted to avoid older cars (being dangerous and polluting) being put into circulation.[97] However, the European Court of Justice was not satisfied. It agreed with the Commission that imported used cars and domestically purchased cars were similar or competing products according to Article 110. The amount of tax borne by these different categories of cars should therefore be compared. The imported used cars were clearly in a less favorable position, due to the fact that the annual depreciation of value for cars is normally considerably more than 5 percent; depreciation is not linear but normally higher in the first years and obviously depreciation of value

---

94   Case C-345/93, *Fazenda Pública and Ministério Público v Américo João Nunes Tadeu* [1995] ECR I-479, para. 13.
95   *Ibid.*, paras. 10–20.
96   Case C-375/95, *Commission v Greece* [1997] ECR I-5981.
97   *Ibid.*, paras. 1–11.

continues after four years. In conclusion, the Greek system violated Article 110.[98]

In a recent case the Greek system for vehicle taxation was tried again.[99] Now Greece had reformed its system so that the taxable value was reduced with 7 percent yearly, up to a maximum of no less than 80 percent. However, perhaps to the surprise of Greece, the Court of Justice was still not satisfied. The Court emphasized that what is now Article 110 "seeks to ensure the complete neutrality of internal taxation as regards competition between products already on the domestic market and imported products".[100] It went on to emphasize that Article 110 would be infringed if the taxation system did not take the vehicle's actual depreciation of value into account. In other words, the taxable value of an imported second-hand vehicle may not be higher than the real value of the vehicle.[101] In the case at hand the Court of Justice took issue *inter alia* with the fact that the Greek system employed a single criterion in determining the taxable value: age. The Court pointed out that many criteria might determine the value of a vehicle, including age, mileage, general condition, propulsion method and make or model. In particular, the failure of the Greek system to take mileage into account meant that imported second-hand vehicles were treated less favorably as compared to vehicles on the domestic market. The Court stressed that the value of the vehicle would be considerably affected by whether it was subject to intense or normal use in its first few years. In conclusion, the Greek system infringed Article 110 (again) by discriminating against imported products.[102]

A final, very interesting, case concerning Article 110 will be discussed here. The *Nádasdi* case concerned the Hungarian vehicle taxation system.[103] The Hungarian system was different in the sense that the registration tax was not based on the value of the car but on environmental classification. The latter was in turn based on emission norms, type of fuel used and engine size.[104] However, despite the fact that the taxation was not based on the value of the vehicle the European Court of Justice found the

---

[98] *Ibid.*, paras. 14–30.
[99] Case C-74/06, *Commission v Greece* [2007] ECR I-7585.
[100] *Ibid.*, para. 24.
[101] *Ibid.*, paras. 26–28.
[102] *Ibid.*, paras. 37–43 and 61.
[103] Joined Cases C-290/05 and C-333/05, *Ákos Nádasdi v Vám- és Pénzügyőrség Észak-Alföldi Regionális Parancsnoksága* (C-290/05) and *Ilona Németh v Vám- és Pénzügyőrség Dél-Alföldi Regionális Parancsnoksága* (C-333/05) [2006] ECR I-10115.
[104] *Ibid.*, paras. 7–13.

system to infringe Article 110. The fact remained that, since the tax was levied only once, it would be just as high for imported second-hand cars as for new cars purchased on the domestic market. Consequently, consumers of second-hand cars would be encouraged not to buy an imported vehicle.[105]

Some of the car taxation cases touch on more specific issues. One such case concerned the French taxation system for vehicles.[106] The calculation of the engine rating, which formed the basis for taxation, was unfavorable for vehicles incorporating new technology, such as a six-speed manual gearbox or five-speed automatic transmission. Again it turned out that a clear majority of the vehicles with these technologies were imported. Thus, the French system encouraged consumers to purchase French cars and thereby infringed Article 110.[107] In a similar case, Greece had implemented legislation that lowered the rate of vehicle tax to be paid for vehicles incorporating "new" or "anti-pollution" technology.[108] This reduced rate was also extended to vehicles with traditional technology. However, imported vehicles had to fulfill a number of conditions in order to get the benefit of the reduced rate. Thus, the legislation obviously protected the domestic industry. The argument of the Greek government that the preferential treatment was necessary in order to offset the competitive disadvantage of the Greek car industry and thereby enable it to adapt to new environmental rules did not sway the Court of Justice. The legislation was deemed to be in violation of Article 110.[109]

Another example of special issues is the *Commission v Italy* case.[110] This is similar to the general vehicle taxation cases discussed above, with the modification that instead of introducing a separate registration or consumer tax Italy had used the harmonized rules concerning value added tax. Diesel-engine cars with a cubic capacity of no more than 5000 cc were subject to normal VAT, while diesel-engine cars with higher cubic capacity were subject to a higher rate of VAT. The Commission took issue with the fact that only imported vehicles were subject to the higher rate of VAT. However, the Court of Justice did not share the Commission's concerns. It pointed out that while the complaint of the Commission was technically true, most models of imported diesel cars were subject to normal VAT and only one (!) model fell under the higher rate. Furthermore, when also taking petrol-

---

105   *Ibid.*, paras. 55–57.
106   Case C-265/99, *Commission v France* [2001] ECR I-2305.
107   *Ibid.*, paras. 40–51.
108   Case C-105/91, *Commission v Greece* [1992] ECR I-5871, para. 3.
109   *Ibid.*, paras. 16–23.
110   Case 200/85, *Commission v Italy* [1986] ECR 3953.

engine cars into consideration, the higher rate of VAT was applied to Italian cars as well. Thus, the Italian VAT legislation did not infringe Article 110.[111]

Before leaving the application of Article 110 the possibility of justifying differences in taxation systems should be mentioned. While direct discrimination (based directly on nationality)[112] cannot be justified, a *prima facie* case of indirect discrimination can be saved by objective justification. The Court of Justice has recognized a number of different interests as being able to constitute objective justification for a difference of treatment.[113] Environmental protection can serve as such objective justification. For example, protection of the environment was one of the arguments put forward by the Greek government to defend the vehicle taxation system in the case discussed above.[114] However, as no discrimination was established it was not necessary to enter into the issue of justification. It should be remembered though that environmental protection is by no means a *carte blanche* for Member State legislation. This has already been demonstrated in several of the judgments discussed above.

It is further illustrated by the *Outokumpu* case.[115] In *Outokumpu* the European Court of Justice examined a Finnish excise duty on electricity. Domestically produced electricity was charged a duty at a rate depending on the method of production (based on environmental concerns), while imported electricity was charged at a flat rate, equal to the average rate charged for domestic electricity. The flat rate was thereby higher than the lowest rate charged on domestic electricity but lower than the highest rate.[116] The Court of Justice observed that environmental protection constituted an important Union objective and that it could justify the application of varying rates on electricity. However, environmental concerns could not justify levying a flat rate on imported electricity, without taking the method of production into account, given that the flat rate was higher than the lowest rate charged on domestic production. The Finnish government tried to defend the flat rate for imported electricity by arguing

---

[111]   *Ibid.*, paras. 13–25.

[112]   *See, e.g.*, Case 57/65, *Lütticke v Hauptzollamt Saarlouis* [1966] ECR 205. All the above discussed cases are, however, examples of indirect discrimination, where the difference in treatment between domestic and imported products depended not directly on nationality but rather on other factors, such as power rating.

[113]   Two examples include Case 196/85, *Commission v France* [1987] ECR 1597 and Case 46/80, *SpA Vinal v SpA Orbat* [1981] ECR 77. The former concerned regional development and the latter the preservation of rare resources (petroleum) for important uses.

[114]   Case C-132/88, *Commission v Greece* [1990] ECR I-1567, para. 9.

[115]   Case C-213/96, *Outokumpu Oy* [1998] ECR I-1777.

[116]   *Ibid.*, paras. 1–11.

that the method of production could not be assessed once the electricity had entered the distribution network. The Court admitted that it might indeed be extremely difficult to determine the method of production of imported electricity, but this did not excuse a system where the importer did not even have the chance to demonstrate which method had been used. Consequently, the excise duty infringed Article 110.[117]

In summary, Article 110 TFEU imposes obvious restrictions on the Member States when it comes to green taxes. Neither direct nor indirect discrimination will be allowed, but complete fiscal neutrality is required. The demands of the Court of Justice can be far-reaching, which is demonstrated not least by the cases concerning imported second-hand vehicles. However, actual – not simply potential – discrimination must be demonstrated, and marginal effects (such as in *Commission v Italy*) are not sufficient. Environmental protection can justify differential treatment, but only when the differences are unrelated to the origin of the products.[118] In *Outokumpu* environmental protection could not justify the Finnish excise duty, as environmental concerns, while underlying the varying rate charged on domestic electricity, did not motivate the flat rate charged on imported electricity.

3.3.3   Customs duties and charges having equivalent effect

While the issues of harmonization and the ban on discriminatory taxes are the most obvious limitations on green taxes imposed by the Member States a number of other aspects of the internal market can also be relevant. Article 30 prohibits customs duties and charges having equivalent effect to customs duties (CEEs). The European Court of Justice has taken a very strict stance when it comes to customs duties and CEEs. In the seminal *Commission v Italy* case the Court defined CEEs as "any pecuniary charge, however small and whatever its designation and mode of application, which is imposed unilaterally on domestic or foreign goods by reason of the fact that they cross a frontier, and which is not a customs duty in the strict sense".[119] A customs duty or a CEE cannot be justified; it will always be a violation of Union law.[120] This strict stance is understandable, given

---

117   *Ibid.*, paras. 31–41.
118   Barnard, *op. cit.*, page 54.
119   Case 24/68, *Commission v Italy* [1969] ECR 193, para. 9.
120   However, certain charges may fall outside of the definition above. For example, in Case 158/82, *Commission v Denmark* [1983] ECR 3573, para. 19, the Court of Justice stated that if "the charge in question represents payment for a service rendered to the importer, of a sum in proportion to the service" it would escape what is now Article 30.

that the abolition of inter-State charges is a crucial aspect of the internal market.

Naturally, the Member States would prefer that green taxes are not considered customs duties or CEEs according to Article 30, as such a categorization would effectively close the door on the measures. As regards the relationship between Article 110 and Article 30 the Court of Justice has made it clear that the Articles cannot be applied together.[121] In other words, a national charge constitutes either a customs duty/CEE or internal taxation. Furthermore, the Court of Justice has on numerous occasions defined the demarcation line between customs duties/CEEs and taxation, stating that financial charges which are part of a general system of internal taxation applying systematically to domestic and imported products according to the same criteria are taxes following Article 110, not customs duties/ CEEs following Article 30. This holds true even in the absence of similar domestic products, on the condition that the charge is levied on whole classes of products in the same position.[122] The Court of Justice has upheld the conditions of this definition of internal taxation rigorously. Claims by the Member States that charges on imported goods should be regarded as internal taxation since domestic production is subject to similar levies have largely been unsuccessful. It follows from the case law of the Court of Justice that absolute equivalence is required, so that the charges are levied according to the same criteria and at the same stage of production.[123]

In the area of green taxes the demarcation line between customs duties/CEEs and taxation is illustrated by the recent *Commission v Italy* case.[124] Sicily had imposed an environmental tax on the ownership of gas pipelines crossing the territory of Sicily and containing methane gas. The aim of the tax was to fund investments to reduce and prevent environmental risks associated with the pipelines.[125] The Commission pointed out that only one pipeline was affected by the legislation; a part of the trans-Mediterranean gas pipelines transporting natural gas from Algeria. Furthermore, the Commission argued that the aim of the Sicilian

---

[121]   *See, e.g.,* Case C-266/91, *Celulose Beira Industrial SA v Fazenda Pública* [1993] ECR I-4337, para. 9.

[122]   *See, e.g.,* Case 78/76, *Steinike & Weinlig v Federal Republic of Germany* [1977] ECR 595, para. 30.

[123]   *See, e.g.,* Case 87/75, *Conceria Daniele Bresciani v Amministrazione Italiana delle Finanze* [1976] ECR 129, para. 11. *See* further Craig, P., and de Búrca, G., *EU Law – Text, Cases, and Materials*, (4th ed.), Oxford University Press, 2008, pages 643–4.

[124]   Case C-173/05, *Commission v Italy* [2007] ECR I-4917.

[125]   *Ibid.,* para. 6.

legislation was not to tax the infrastructure (the pipelines) but rather the content (methane gas). This was demonstrated *inter alia* by the fact that the basis of assessment was the volume of pipelines containing methane gas. Thus, the Commission argued that Sicily imposed a pecuniary charge on goods due to the fact that they crossed the frontier. The charge therefore constituted a CEE, in violation of what is now Article 30.[126] The Italian government on the other hand argued that the tax should not be regarded as a CEE. It claimed that the tax was motivated by environmental principles inherent in Union law, in particular the precautionary principle. According to the Italian government the sole purpose of the tax was environmental protection, thus it could not be regarded as a customs-related charge. Finally, Italy argued that the tax was not levied on goods, as such, but only on the infrastructure.[127] Despite the Italian efforts the Court of Justice followed the arguments of the Commission, finding that the tax represented a CEE. Following a long line of case law the Court concluded that as the charge was a CEE the purpose of the legislation was immaterial.[128]

3.3.4   Measures having equivalent effect to quantitative restrictions

Article 34 TFEU prohibits quantitative restrictions and measures having equivalent effect to quantitative restrictions (MEQRs). In particular, the latter concept has spawned a vast case law from the Court of Justice as well as an almost incredible amount of books and articles. Briefly put, the concept of MEQRs prohibits not only *de jure* discriminatory rules but also national measures restricting the access to the domestic market for imported goods.[129] At first sight these rules, aimed at practical obstacles to trade, would seem to have little to do with green taxes, given that the latter are pecuniary obstacles to trade. Technically, the wide definition of MEQRs could also include pecuniary measure. However, the Court of Justice has established that Articles 30 and 110 constitute *lex specialis* in relation to Article 34. In the *Compagnie Commerciale* case the Court explained that obstacles of a fiscal nature covered by what is now Article 30 and 110 did not fall within the scope of Article 30.[130]

---

126   *Ibid.*, paras. 13–15.
127   *Ibid.*, paras. 20–26.
128   *Ibid.*, paras. 35–42.
129   *See* Derlén, M., and Lindholm, J., "Article 28 E.C. and Rules on Use: A Step Towards a Workable Doctrine on Measures Having Equivalent Effect to Quantitative Restrictions", *The Columbia Journal of European Law*, Volume 16, 2010, page 191, with further references.
130   Joined Cases C-78/90, C-79/90, C-80/90, C-81/90, C-82/90 and C-83/90,

Obviously, in some situations practical and pecuniary obstacles to trade can coincide. For example, in the *Bernhard Schloh* case Belgian legislation imposed two roadworthiness tests on vehicles imported from other Member States, each time imposing a fee for the test.[131] The roadworthiness test is a typical example of a practical obstacle to trade, while the fee obviously is a pecuniary obstacle. When it comes to the relationship between these two obstacles the Court of Justice concluded that if the test infringed what is now Article 34 the fee would be unlawful as well. If the test did not infringe Article 34 the fee was lawful, under the condition that it fulfilled the requirements of what is now Article 110 TFEU.[132] On the other hand, a practical obstacle can also be consumed by a fiscal obstacle. The *Brzezinski* case offers an example of this.[133] This case is similar to many of the vehicle taxation cases discussed above in connection with Article 110 TFEU. Poland imposed an excise duty on vehicles before they were registered. Furthermore, a simplified declaration had to be handed in to the customs authorities, if the vehicle was imported from another Member State.[134] The Court of Justice found the excise duty to be part of the internal system of taxation, to be tried according to Article 110.[135] The issue then arose of whether the requirement of a declaration should be regarded as a separate issue, to be tried as a practical obstacle to trade according to what is now Article 34. However, the Court concluded that the declaration, while not a fiscal obstacle per se, was inextricably linked to the excise duty, being a mere corollary of that duty. Thus, Article 34 could not be employed.[136]

The big issue when it comes to green taxes and Article 34 is whether the latter can be used when Article 110 (for some reason) cannot be applied. The Court of Justice had opened the door for this already in the *Commission v France* case, where a previously existing tax benefit for newspaper publishers was removed in respect of publications printed in other Member States.[137] The Court of Justice established that the issue could not be resolved on the basis of the free movement of services. Printing work

---

Compagnie Commerciale de l'Ouest and others v Receveur Principal des Douanes de La Pallice Port [1992] ECR I-1847, para. 20.

[131]   Case 50/85, *Bernhard Schloh v Auto contrôle technique SPRL* [1986] ECR 1855, paras. 1–7.

[132]   *Ibid.*, paras. 21–24.

[133]   Case C-313/05, *Maciej Brzeziński v Dyrektor Izby Celnej w Warszawie* [2007] ECR I-513.

[134]   *Ibid.*, paras. 7–13.

[135]   *Ibid.*, paras. 20–25.

[136]   *Ibid.*, paras. 42–53.

[137]   Case 18/84, *Commission v France* [1985] ECR 1339, paras. 1–3.

leads directly to a physical product and therefore the legislation should be considered according to the free movement of goods rules. The Court concluded that the French legislation encouraged newspaper publishers to have publications printed in France and not in other Member States. It therefore constituted an MEQR and infringed what is now Article 34 TFEU.[138] The French measures under consideration were taxation legislation, but it was hardly a case of imported products being taxed more heavily than domestic products. Neither was it a case of imported products being subject to a special charge when crossing the border. In this situation Article 34 provided a handy solution as a fallback option. At the very least the French rules made the free movement of goods more difficult.

The door was opened even wider in the seminal *Commission v Denmark* case.[139] The case concerned a Danish registration duty for private vehicles. The duty was calculated by reference to the purchase price including VAT. The rate was 105 percent up to a certain threshold and 180 percent on the price exceeding the threshold.[140] The Commission argued that the registration duty was so high that it compromised the free movement of goods, thus violating Article 110. The twist was that Denmark did not produce any cars, or any competing products. The Court concluded that Article 110 could not be used to assess the registration duty for new vehicles.[141] Article 110 prohibits discrimination and discrimination presupposes domestic products similar to or in competition with the imported products. In the absence of discrimination, Article 110 cannot be used to challenge a high rate of duty.[142] So far the reasoning of the Court is hardly surprising. However, the Court then added, with a reference to a case from 1968,[143] that even in the absence of similar or competing domestic products the Member States are not allowed to impose on imported goods "charges of such an amount that the free movement of goods within the common market would be impeded as far as those goods were concerned".[144] Employing this test would mean applying Article 34 to the national taxation rules. However, as the Commission

---

[138]   *Ibid.*, paras. 12–16.
[139]   Case C-47/88, *Commission v Denmark* [1990] ECR I-4509.
[140]   *Ibid.*, paras. 1–3.
[141]   The effects of the registration duty on imported second-hand vehicles did, however, constitute an infringement of Article 110, along the same line of argumentation as in many of the other cases concerning taxation of imported second hand vehicles discussed above. *See Commission v Denmark*, paras. 15–22.
[142]   *Ibid.*, paras. 5–11.
[143]   Case 31/67, *Firma August Stier v Hauptzollamt Hamburg-Ericus* [1968] ECR 235.
[144]   *Commission v Denmark*, para. 12.

had not based its action on Article 34 the issue was not explored further.[145]

In 2003 the opportunity to explore this issue presented itself in the *De Danske Bilimportører* case.[146] The case concerned the same Danish registration duty. The Court of Justice reiterated the arguments from *Commission v Denmark*; stating that Article 110 could not be used to censor national taxation legislation when no similar or competing domestic products existed.[147] Regarding the possible use of Article 34 the Court observed that the information provided demonstrated that a considerable number of vehicles were registered every year. Consequently, the registration duty did not appear to impede the free movement of goods within the Union.[148] In conclusion, it is indeed possible to challenge even a non-discriminatory tax by using Article 34. The tax would then be re-classified, no longer being viewed as internal taxation according to Article 110 but instead as an MEQR according to Article 34.[149] However, following the *De Danske Bilimportører* case it is clear that it is not enough that the tax is very high. Presumably it will have to be demonstrated that the tax leads to a significant reduction in imported goods.[150]

3.3.5   Free movement for persons and services

The ban on discriminatory taxes applies not only to taxation of goods but also in other aspects of the internal market. However, the structure is somewhat different. Article 110 TFEU explicitly concerns issues of taxation. When it comes to other forms of discriminatory taxes the general rules on free movement for persons, services and capital apply. However, these Articles do not explicitly concern issue of taxation. When the Court of Justice started examining national tax law provisions using these freedoms the Member States objected, arguing that the European Union has no competence when it comes to direct taxation. In the well-known *Avoir Fiscal* case the Court of Justice answered, stating as follows:

---

[145]   *Ibid.*, para. 13.
[146]   Case C-383/01, *De Danske Bilimportører v Skatteministeriet, Told- og Skattestyrelsen* [2003] ECR I-6065.
[147]   *Ibid.*, paras. 34–39.
[148]   *Ibid.*, paras. 40–43.
[149]   *Ibid.*, para. 42.
[150]   The Danish government and the Danish Tax Authorities argued that only taxation leading to trade in the product in question ceasing or becoming insignificant would qualify for examination according to Article 34, *ibid.*, paras. 21 and 28. The Court of Justice simply stated that the free movement of goods had not been "impeded", *ibid.*, para. 41.

> It must first be noted that the fact that the laws of the member states on corporation tax have not been harmonized cannot justify the difference of treatment in this case. Although it is true that in the absence of such harmonization, a company's tax position depends on the national law applied to it, article [49 TFEU] prohibits the member states from laying down in their laws conditions for the pursuit of activities by persons exercising their right of establishment which differ from those laid down for its own nationals.[151]

In other words, the Member States retain great freedom when it comes to issues of direct taxation, but this discretion cannot be used to discriminate against persons, corporations, services or capital from other Member States. Consequently, the Court of Justice has employed the rules of the internal market to combat such discrimination.[152] For example, in the *Manninen* case the Court concluded that the free movement of capital prevented a tax credit on dividends restricted to dividends from Finnish companies.[153] In the *Baars* case Dutch rules on exemption from wealth tax, which did not apply for assets invested in shares in companies in other Member States, were declared contrary to the freedom of establishment.[154] In the *Schumacker* case the Court concluded that German rules denying non-residents deductions on income from employment were contrary to the free movement of workers.[155]

A number of cases in this category concern green taxes. Most interesting is perhaps the recent *Sardegna* case, where the region of Sardinia had imposed a regional tax on stopovers for tourist purposes, aimed at aircrafts and certain ships.[156] However, the tax was only imposed on operators with

---

[151]   Case 270/83, *Commission v France* [1986] ECR 273, para. 24.

[152]   There is some debate in the literature as to whether the Court of Justice sometimes goes even further, prohibiting not only discrimination but all taxation making cross-border trade less appealing. Suzanne Kingston argues that the Court of Justice seems to limit itself to discrimination analysis in issues of taxation. *See* Kingston, S., "A light in the darkness: Recent developments in the ECJ's Direct Tax Jurisprudence", *Common Market Law Review*, 2007, Volume 44, page 1321, at pages 1358–9. Karen Banks disagrees, finding no definitive direction in the case law of the Court of Justice. Banks, K., "The Application of the Fundamental Freedoms to Member State Tax Measures: Guarding against Protectionism or Second-guessing National Policy Choices?", (European University Institute (EUI) Working Papers, RSCAS 2007/31), pages 44–6.

[153]   Case C-319/02, *Petri Manninen* [2004] ECR I-7477.

[154]   Case C-251/98, *C. Baars v Inspecteur der Belastingen Particulieren/ Ondernemingen Gorinchem* [2000] ECR I-2787.

[155]   Case C-279/93, *Finanzamt Köln-Altstadt v Roland Schumacker* [1995] ECR I-225.

[156]   Case C-169/08, *Presidente del Consiglio dei Ministri v Regione Sardegna* [2009] not yet published.

tax domicile outside of Sardinia.[157] On the face of it the legislation was discriminatory, impeding the free movement of services.[158] Sardinia tried to justify the legislation by reasons of environmental protection. It argued first that no discrimination existed since domestic operators and operators outside Sardinia were not in objectively comparable situations. Residents of Sardinia contributed, by way of general taxation, to regional measures aimed at preserving the environment while non-residents "behave like environmental 'free-riders', by using the resources without paying towards the costs of those activities".[159] The Court of Justice did not accept this argument. According to the Court no objective differences existed between domestic operators and operators outside of Sardinia. The fact that the former contributed by way of general and income taxation to environmental protection was irrelevant, as the aim and nature of the special stopover tax was different from the aim and nature of general taxation. While the former was specially designed to protect the environment the latter financed the State budget and thereby all activities of the region. Consequently, as no objective differences existed the Sardinian legislation discriminated against operators in other Member States.[160] Sardinia then tried to justify this discrimination, again on environmental grounds. Sardinia had implemented a new regional policy on the protection of the environment, including levies to finance expensive restoration of coastal areas. However, the Court of Justice was once more unimpressed. It stated that even if the reasons presented by Sardinia could justify the tax they could not justify the implementation thereof, where only operators outside of Sardinia were liable to pay the tax. The pollution caused by the vehicles affected by the tax is independent of the origin of the operator and it was therefore neither appropriate nor necessary to limit the tax to operators outside of Sardinia.[161]

While the *Sardegna* case may appear rather straightforward, at least in the sense that the discrimination was apparent, it illustrates an important point. Member States may certainly have an interest in penalizing environmental free riders, polluting but not contributing by way of taxation. However, in order to avoid infringing the free movement of services, or other aspects of the internal market, an environmental tax has to be general in application. Claims that residents of the State in question contribute in other, more general ways, to the State finances, will obviously not sway the Court of Justice.

---

157 *Ibid.*, para. 7.
158 *Ibid.*, paras. 29–32.
159 *Ibid.*, para. 33.
160 *Ibid.*, paras. 34–39.
161 *Ibid.*, paras. 40–45.

3.3.6   State aid

Finally, the rules on state aid should be introduced. Article 107 TFEU prohibits the Member States from granting aid that distorts competition on the internal market by favoring certain undertakings or the production of certain goods. Following the case law of the Court of Justice a measure is categorized as state aid if four conditions are fulfilled:

> [F]irst, there must be an intervention by the State or through State resources. Second, the intervention must be liable to affect trade between Member States. Third, it must confer an advantage on the recipient. Fourth, it must distort or threaten to distort competition . . .[162]

The concept of state aid is not determined by the nature or aim of a measure. Consequently, measures of a fiscal nature can also be defined as state aid.[163] Discriminatory taxes may be subject to Article 107 as well as Article 110 TFEU. Thus, the fact that a tax can be described as state aid will not save it from being scrutinized according to Article 110.[164] In many situations green taxes can be classified as state aid, in the sense that certain products or certain methods of production are granted tax reliefs.[165] The *Air Liquide* case provides an example.[166] The case concerned a local tax on motive force, according to which undertakings were required to pay an annual tax on motors used in the business. However, motors used in natural gas compression stations were exempted from the tax.[167] The Court of Justice emphasized the four conditions required for a measure to be classified as state aid. It observed that the concept of aid was wider than that of a subsidy. Not only positive benefits but also measures mitigating the effects of charges, such as tax exemptions, are included in the concept aid. The Court also added that the limited size of the aid, or indeed the limited size of the undertaking receiving the aid, does not exclude the existence of state aid. Consequently, the Belgian tax exemption regarding motors in natural gas stations could constitute state aid according to Article 107 TFEU.[168]

---

[162]   Case C-237/04, *Enirisorse SpA v Sotacarbo SpA* [2006] ECR I-2843, para. 39, references omitted.

[163]   Case 173/73, *Italy v Commission* [1974] ECR 709, para. 13.

[164]   Case 73/79, *Commission v Italy* [1980] ECR 1533, para. 9.

[165]   Ståhl, K, and Persson Österman, R., *EG-skatterätt*, (2nd ed.), Iustus, 2006, page 314.

[166]   Joined Cases C-393/04 & C-41/05, *Air Liquide Industries Belgium SA v Ville de Seraing* (C-393/04) and *Province de Liège* (C-41/05) [2006] ECR I-5293.

[167]   *Ibid.*, paras. 6–7.

[168]   *Ibid.*, paras. 27–38.

The prohibition of state aid is, however, not absolute. A Member State measure which is prima facie considered to be state aid can be justified on a number of grounds, set out in Article 107. Environmental protection can be such a ground, according to which a state aid measure can be justified.[169] When it comes to environmental protection special guidelines are available, according to which state aid for environmental purposes can be approved by the Commission.[170] The Member States will notify the Commission of the aid scheme, whereupon the Commission will perform a balancing test, weighing the positive impact of the measure against its potentially negative side-effects.[171]

The Commission has considerable discretion and the Union courts will not readily interfere with its assessment.[172] However, this is by no means a *carte blanche* for the Member States or the Commission. For example, in the *British Aggregates* case the European Court of Justice did take issue with a Commission decision not to raise objections against a certain British measure.[173] The United Kingdom had imposed a levy on aggregates. However, certain aggregates were excluded from the levy, in order to encourage resource efficiency. The Commission found the levy to constitute a tax with a very narrow scope, targeting so called virgin aggregates due to their adverse effect on the environment.[174] The decision of the Commission not to raise objections against the British levy was challenged by the British Aggregates Association before the General Court of the European Union on a number of grounds. The General Court dismissed the action, following which the British Aggregates Association brought the case before the Court of Justice.[175] The Court of Justice upheld the action on a number of grounds and therefore set aside the judgment of the General Court.[176] The Court of Justice took, inter alia, issue with

---

[169] Case C-143/99, *Adria-Wien Pipeline GmbH and Wietersdorfer & Peggauer Zementwerke GmbH v Finanzlandesdirektion für Kärnten* [2001] ECR I-8365, paras. 30–31.

[170] Community guidelines on State aid for environmental protection, Official Journal C 82/1, 1.4.2008.

[171] *Ibid.*, para. 16.

[172] *See* for example Craig and de Búrca, *op. cit.*, pages 1084–6 and Schütte, M., "The Notion of State Aid", in M. Sánchez Rydelski, *The EC State Aid Regime – Distortive Effects of State Aid on Competition and Trade*, Cambridge University Press, 2006, pages 23–53, at pages 49–51.

[173] Case C-487/06, *British Aggregates Association v Commission of the European Communities and United Kingdom* [2008] ECR I-10505.

[174] *Ibid.*, para. 2.

[175] *Ibid.*, paras. 3–8.

[176] *Ibid.*, paras. 196–198.

the application of the concept of state aid. It emphasized that the classification of a measure as state aid is not based on its objective but on its effects. The General Court, as well as the Commission, incorrectly concluded that the British measure could not be regarded as state aid as it was motivated by reasons of environmental protection. The Court of Justice admitted that it is for the Commission to take account of the goal of environmental protection when employing the Union rules on state aid. Furthermore, the protection of the environment is an essential objective of the Union. However, environmental protection does not play a part in determining whether a measure constitutes prima facie state aid. When a state measure is selective, that is, favoring certain undertakings or certain goods without objective reasons, it constitutes state aid. The measure can then be justified by reason of environmental protection, as a later step in the process.[177]

In other words, the Commission and the General Court had jumped the gun, excluding the very existence of state aid due to the objectives of the British rules. Such casual acceptance of environmental measures is obviously not accepted by the Court of Justice.

3.4   Imposing Non-Economic Environmental Measures – Out of the Frying Pan and into the Fire!

Section 3.3 above has demonstrated the numerous obstacles Member States have to navigate when introducing green taxes. Significant restrictions exist, most notably when it comes to measures discriminating against foreign goods or otherwise impeding the normal functioning of the internal market. However, it is important not to lose perspective. This section will demonstrate that the restraints imposed by Union law are actually greater when it comes to non-economic environmental measures. From the Member State perspective economic and non-economic environmental measures might be completely interchangeable. Thus, a Member State can limit the consumption of a particular product, deemed hazardous to the environment, by way of taxation or by imposing practical restraints, such as bans, quotas or special requirements when it comes to packaging, labeling and handling.

However, from the point of view of Union law the choice is vital. Union law prohibits not only discriminatory rules but also non-discriminatory restrictions on the free movement on the internal market. While such restrictions can be justified by important societal needs the measures have

---

[177]   *Ibid.*, paras. 79–93.

to be both suitable and necessary, that is, fulfill the requirements of the proportionality test.

The following example will illustrate the extent of the review conducted by the Court of Justice. In the *Danish bottles* case Denmark had introduced a system where manufacturers of beer and soft drinks had to sell their products in re-useable containers.[178] The choice of container had to be approved by a National Agency. Since the containers would have to be technically suitable for the system of returning containers such approval could be denied for certain containers. Non-approved containers could be used only if a deposit-and-return system was established, and only for quantities not exceeding 3000 hectoliters per year and producer.[179] It was undisputed that the Danish rules constituted practical obstacles to trade, prohibited by what is now Article 34 TFEU. However, Denmark argued that the measures were justified, as they were necessary to protect the environment. The Court of Justice admitted that environmental protection constituted a mandatory requirement, capable of justifying practical obstacles to trade. The Danish rules, however, did not pass the proportionality test. The Court observed that the rules ensured a "very considerable degree of protection of the environment" by making sure that empty containers could be returned to any retailer, not just the importer. However, other measures could also protect the environment, without posing the same difficulties for imported containers. Thus, the Danish rules were disproportionate.[180]

The issue of taxation of imported second-hand cars, discussed in section 3.3.2 above, can be contrasted with the measures adopted by the Czech Republic when entering the Union. The Czech Republic had implemented legislation prohibiting the import of second-hand vehicles older than 8 years. The aim of the legislation was road safety as well as protection of the environment. However, the Commission quickly took action against these measures as they constituted an obstacle to the free movement of goods. The Czech legislation was swiftly amended.[181] A ban on imports would constitute a quantitative restriction, prohibited by Article 34 TFEU and very difficult to justify.

---

[178] Case 302/86, *Commission of the European Communities v Kingdom of Denmark* [1988] ECR 4607.

[179] *Ibid.*, paras. 1–3.

[180] *Ibid.*, paras. 7–22, the quote from para. 20.

[181] Infringement procedure 2004/5151 and Bobek, M., and Kühn, Z., "What about that 'incoming tide'? The application of EU law in the Czech Republic", in A. Lazowski, *The Application of EU Law in the New Member States – Brave New World*, T.M.C. Asser Press, 2009.

Finally, the *Attanasio* case is a recent example of the freedom of establishment and environmental protection.[182] Italian legislation concerning the construction and operation of service stations stipulated a minimum distance of 3 kilometers between stations. The legislation was motivated by several reasons, including public health, environmental protection and road safety.[183] The Court of Justice examined the legislation in the light of the freedom of establishment, protected in Article 49 TFEU.[184] The Court stressed that Article 49 precluded not only discriminatory national measures but all measures "liable to hinder or render less attractive the exercise by Union nationals of the freedom of establishment".[185] The rule on minimum distance between service stations was, according to the Court, such a restriction, prohibited by Article 49.[186] When discussing whether the restriction could be justified the Court observed that public health, environmental protection and road safety could constitute overriding reasons in the public interest. However, the national measures would also have to be proportional. In this regard the Court expressed grave doubts. The fact that only new service stations fell within the scope of the legislation was particularly problematic and put the consistency of the policy into question.[187]

In summary, it is certainly possible to implement non-economic measures to protect the environment, even when these measures restrict the free movement on the internal market. However, the extent of the review is significantly greater as compared to the fiscal measures discussed above. Even non-discriminatory measures can be caught by EU law and to justify such measures the principle of proportionality has to be fulfilled. The latter practically involves demonstrating to the Court of Justice that the chosen regulation is not only suitable but the best solution imaginable.

4.   SUMMARY AND CONCLUSIONS – ILLUSTRATING THE PROBLEM

At the beginning of this chapter we introduced four regulatory options available within the European Union for the purpose of protecting and

---

[182]   Case C-384/08, *Attanasio Group Srl v Comune di Carbognano* [2010] not yet published.
[183]   *Ibid.*, paras. 1–6.
[184]   *Ibid.*, paras. 36–41.
[185]   *Ibid.*, para. 43.
[186]   *Ibid.*, paras. 44–45.
[187]   *Ibid.*, paras. 51–57.

enhancing the environment: (A) EU green taxes, (B) other EU measures, (C) national green taxes and (D) other national measures.[188] We have subsequently examined under what conditions the EU law framework allows for legislation to be enacted under each regulatory option.

The ability of the European Union to achieve environmental goals by enacting green taxes is quite limited. The Environmental Title of the TFEU is capable of supporting an EU measure introducing a green tax but only if all of the twenty-seven Member States support the measure.[189] The fact that each Member State may veto any proposal is important. In many cases it will be difficult to gain unanimous support for a proposed green tax that would have extensive effect on the national level.[190] In addition, any such measure can only encompass minimum harmonization, not maximum harmonization.[191]

Other Treaty provisions grant the EU significantly greater power to introduce green taxes. One example is the frequently used Article 113 TFEU that does not require Member State unanimity and allows for maximum harmonization. However, any measures introduced under those provisions, including green taxes, must primarily improve the functioning of the internal market and only secondarily promote the environment. This significantly affects how useful such measures can be for the purpose of achieving environmental goals.

While the Treaties significantly restrict the European Union's ability to enact green taxes, they afford it comparatively generous power to enact other measures intended to promote the environment. With regard to non-tax measures, the Environmental Title is capable of supporting a broad range of actions and only requires the support of a qualified majority of the Member States.[192]

---

[188]   *See* above section 1.

[189]   TFEU, Article 192 (2).

[190]   This is demonstrated by the failed attempt to introduce a carbon tax on the EU level. In the early 1990s the Commission suggested a harmonized carbon and energy tax. However, even after extensive discussion and amendments to the proposal unanimity was out of reach. The Commission had to scrap the proposal and instead opt for a system limited to excise duties on mineral oils. *See* "information from the Commission", http://ec.europa.eu/taxation_customs/taxation/excise_duties/energy_products/index_en.htm, May 16, 2010. Recently, the Commission has resumed planning for an EU carbon tax, but it remains to be seen whether the Member States can agree on such a proposal. There is still political resistance, most notably from the United Kingdom, *see* http://news.bbc.co.uk/2/hi/8552604.stm, May 16, 2010.

[191]   TFEU, Article 193.

[192]   TFEU, Article 191 (1).

Thus, due to the basic legal framework of the Union, it is more difficult for the European Union to enact green taxes than it is to enact other measures. By comparison, the EU law framework operates in the other direction with regard to Member States, steering them towards green taxes and away from other types of measures.

When it comes to environmental measures adopted by the Member States Part 3 above demonstrates a significant discrepancy when it comes to the limits imposed by EU law. Green taxes can be challenged by a number of different Articles related to the internal market. However, non-discriminatory taxes will normally be beyond the reach of EU law. This is illustrated by the Swedish experience. Before Sweden entered the European Union a carbon tax had already been adopted. The tax was enacted following a proposal from the Commission of Environmental Charges, appointed in 1988.[193] The carbon tax entered into force in January 1991, amounting to 0.25 SEK per kilogram of emitted CO_2. The tax was part of an extensive reform of the Swedish taxation system, where income taxes were significantly reduced while energy and environmental taxes were increased. The carbon tax was highly controversial and considered especially problematic for the significant Swedish export industry. Gradually, exemptions have been introduced, resulting in significantly lower rates of taxes for certain products and industries while the general rate of the tax has increased.[194] The Swedish carbon tax is still applied for a number of products, 15 years after the entry of Sweden into the European Union. For example, in 2010 the carbon tax is 2,44 SEK per liter of petroleum. This tax is added to the harmonized energy tax.[195]

As a general tax on CO_2 emissions the Swedish carbon tax does not constitute a discriminatory tax according to Article 110 TFEU. Nor can it be said to be a customs duty/CEE or an MEQR. The discussion concerning the carbon tax has, from an EU perspective, mostly concerned the exemptions granted to various products and industries. As explained in Section 3.3.6 above, such exemption will normally constitute state aid. Sweden has notified the Commission of derogations from the general carbon tax and the

---

[193] *See* primarily Official Governmental Report (SOU) 1990:59 *Sätt värde på miljön. Miljöavgifter och andra ekonomiska styrmedel*, Allmänna förlaget, 1990.

[194] *See, e.g.*, Brännlund, R., "Green Tax Reforms: Some Experiences from Sweden", in K. Schlegelmilch, *Green Budget Reform in Europe: Countries at the Forefront*, Springer, 1999, pages 67–91, at pages 71–73, and Harrison, G.W., and Kriström, B., *Carbon Taxes in Sweden*, Final Report to the Commission, 1997, at pages 4–8.

[195] Swedish Law (1994:1776) on the Taxation of Energy (Lag om skatt på energi), Chapter 2, paragraph 1.

Commission has employed the rules on state aid to scrutinize the Swedish measures. In 2003 the Commission examined a number of reductions in energy tax and carbon tax, granted by the Swedish government.[196] One of these was the reduction in carbon tax by 75 per cent granted to the manufacturing industry. The Commission found the reduction to constitute state aid following what is now Article 107 TFEU, as it reduced taxation income for Sweden (this being equal to aid) and as it benefited only certain sectors (it was selective). However, the aid was allowed according to Article 107.3 and the Community Guidelines on State aid for environmental protection.

National measures are more susceptible to challenge on EU law grounds if they are not of a fiscal nature. Even if such measures are not discriminatory in nature, they will still frequently be captured by EU law for having an adverse effect on the internal market. The fact that actions taken by the Member States for the purpose of protecting the environment are prone to affect the internal market and how small the effect on the market can be and still violate EU law is well illustrated by the Court of Justice's decision in *Mickelsson*.[197] In 2004, Sweden enacted a law making it unlawful to ride jet skis outside general navigable waterways and such waters defined as suitable for use by local authorities.[198] One of the main aims of the law was to protect the environment against the perceived harmful effects of jet skis. Soon after the law was enacted, two men were stopped by the Swedish Coast Guard for navigating waters not specifically designated as appropriate for jet ski use and were eventually criminally charged for violating the Swedish jet ski regulation. While admitting their conduct violated the Swedish regulation, the men challenged the validity of the law, arguing that it violated EU law, more specifically the free movement of goods.[199] The European Court of Justice agreed that a national measure such as the one in question constitutes an obstacle to the free movement of goods contrary to EU law if it restricts the consumers' use of the product – here jet skis – to such an extent that it has considerable influence on the interest of consumers to buy the product.[200]

That does not mean that all such national measures are unacceptable under EU law. As long as the measure does not discriminate against

---

[196]　Invitation to submit comments pursuant to Article 88(2) of the EC Treaty, concerning aid C 42/03 (ex NN 3/B/01), Official Journal C 189, 9.8.2003/6.

[197]　Case C-142/05, *Åklagaren v Mickelsson* [2009] not yet published.

[198]　Förordning om användning av vattenskoter (Svensk författningssamling [SFS] 1993:1053) (Swed.).

[199]　*Åklagaren v Mickelsson* [2009], paras. 9–14.

[200]　*Ibid.*, paras. 24–8. The European Court of Justice left it to the national court to determine if this was the case in *Mickelsson*.

persons or goods from other Member States, it may be justified for reasons such as the protection of the environment. However, in order to justify the measure, the Member State must show that it is both necessary and appropriate. The ECJ requires that the measure in question will lead to the intended end result and that it is the best possible solution for achieving this result.[201] The rigorousness of this process can be exemplified by *Toolex*, an ECJ judgment concerning a set of Swedish rules that together constituted a ban on the industrial use of a certain chemical, trichloroethylene. Toolex Alpha AB, a producer of compact discs whose application for an exception to use trichloroethylene to remove grease residue had been denied, brought the claim arguing *inter alia* that the national rules constituted an unlawful obstacle to the free movement of goods.[202] Only after Sweden produced numerous medical studies linking trichloroethylene and cancer were the Swedish rules found to be necessary and appropriate for the purpose of protecting human health.[203]

In conclusion, the framework of EU law is structured in such a way that Member State environmental measures will be subject to stricter scrutiny if they are not of a fiscal nature. If a Member State wants to take action for the purpose of protecting and enhancing the environment and it wants to limit possible challenges, it is well advised to choose green taxes over other measures. The framework of EU law has a similar effect on the European Union that should seek to protect and enhance the environment through the adoption of measures other than green taxes. It is likely that forceful environmental measures that are controversial in one or more Member States will not be adopted if framed as a tax.

EU green taxes and national non-tax environmental measures are by no means impossible occurrences. However, the framework of EU law promotes the adoption of EU non-tax environmental measures and national green taxes. This can be problematic if such measures are not the optimal instrument for achieving environmental goals. To return to the example used initially in this contribution, whether Europe chooses emission taxation or emission trading does not merely hinge on which is the better regulatory solution for the purpose of reducing CO_2 emissions but also on the framework of EU law.

---

[201] *See generally* Craig and de Búrca, *op. cit.*, pages 81–6.
[202] Case C-473/98, *Kemikalieinspektionen v Toolex Alpha AB* [2000] ECR I-5681, paras. 13–24.
[203] *Ibid.*, paras 38–45.

8. Behavior modifying taxes, emissions trading and tax expenditure reform: market-based responses to climate change in Australia

Wayne Gumley and Natalie Stoianoff

1. INTRODUCTION

This chapter will consider recent regulatory responses to climate change in Australia with a view to providing guidance for policy makers in the East Asia region. In particular, it will review the reasoning behind the choice of emissions trading ahead of other market-based instruments such as behavior modifying taxes and tax expenditure reform. It will firstly describe the key international agreements on climate change. Secondly, it will provide a review of the key literature in support of market-based instruments including the relative merits of carbon taxes and emissions trading. Thirdly, the chapter will review the history of regulatory responses in Australia at both Federal and State government levels, leading up to and including the proposed Australian emissions trading scheme, known as the Carbon Pollution Reduction Scheme (the CPRS). Fourthly, the chapter will review features of the underlying taxation system which constitute significant "barriers to change" which are very likely to undermine the intended objectives of the CPRS. The chapter concludes with some suggestions for emerging economies of the East Asia region on how taxation rules can be integrated with climate change objectives.

2. INTERNATIONAL RESPONSES TO CLIMATE CHANGE

The first major international agreement on climate change was the *United Nations Framework Convention on Climate Change* (UNFCCC), which was opened for signature at the Rio Earth Summit in 1992.[1] The UNFCCC states as its ultimate objective:

> . . . to achieve . . . stabilization of greenhouse gas concentrations in the atmos-phere at a level that would prevent dangerous anthropogenic interference with the climate system. Such a level should be achieved within a time frame sufficient to allow ecosystems to adapt naturally to climate change, to ensure that food production is not threatened and to enable economic development to proceed in a sustainable manner. [2]

The UNFCCC does not specify how stabilization of the climate system is to be achieved but merely lays the basis or "framework" within which the parties can work towards the objective. This framework consists of guiding principles[3] and various commitments of the parties, which includes general commitments applicable to all parties[4] and additional commitments appli-cable only to developed countries.[5] The UNFCCC envisaged that a series of "Conferences of the Parties" would later strengthen the obligations through protocols to impose more specific obligations.

The first binding protocol was that agreed at Kyoto, Japan, in 1997, after five years of negotiation.[6] The Kyoto Protocol set binding national emission reduction targets for developed nations to meet by 2012, and also established certain flexibility mechanisms to assist the meeting of these targets, in particular, emissions trading, joint initiatives and clean development mechanisms. The Kyoto Protocol included several clauses which were quite favorable to Australia, including a rule which allowed reductions in land clearing to be counted as an offset against actual emis-sions (which became known as "the Australia clause").[7] Ironically, after negotiating fiercely over its terms the Australian government followed the lead of the Bush administration in the United States and refused to ratify the Kyoto Protocol throughout the next eleven years, due to the perceived negative impacts upon the Australian economy. This "coalition of the

---

[1]   The UNFCCC was initially signed by 155 States and came into force on the ninetieth day after 50 States had signed and ratified its terms, which was 21 March 1994. By Dec 2009 it had been adopted by 192 parties.
[2]   Article 2 and the preamble to the UNFCCC.
[3]   UNFCCC, Article 3.
[4]   UNFCCC, Article 4 (1).
[5]   And any other countries (listed in Annex I) that wish to voluntarily commit to them. UNFCCC, Art 4 (2).
[6]   The Kyoto Protocol to the United Nations Framework Convention on Climate Change was adopted in Kyoto, Japan, on 11 December 1997 and entered into force on 16 February 2005 (henceforth "Kyoto Protocol").
[7]   Kyoto Protocol, Article 3.7.

unwilling" helped prevent the Kyoto Protocol from coming into force until early 2005.[8] One of the first major developments under the Protocol was commencement of the European Union Emissions Trading Scheme in January 2005.[9]

In 2007 the Intergovernmental Panel on Climate Change (IPCC) released its Fourth Assessment Report which indicated that global emissions would need to be reduced by somewhere in the order of 80 to 90 per cent by 2050 in order to restrict the average increase in global air temperature to 2°C or less (which is broadly considered to be the upper limit for a safe climate outcome).[10] In the same year the comprehensive Stern Review on the Economics of Climate Change carried out by the UK Treasury concluded that the economic cost of delayed greenhouse gas reductions would be far greater than the cost of early emission reductions.[11]

These two reports provided the basis for a growing international consensus that a strong post-Kyoto agreement was urgently needed, with far more stringent emission reduction targets for the periods to 2020 and 2050. This was the main agenda for the UNFCCC's 15th Conference of the Parties (COP15) at Copenhagen in December 2009. The Copenhagen meeting was the first COP where United States and China took leading roles, but ultimately no binding agreement was reached. The resultant "Copenhagen Accord" provided only a "soft" commitment to keep the global temperature increase below two degrees and a scheme to protect tropical rainforests known as Reducing Emissions from Deforestation and Forest Degradation (REDD).[12] On a more positive note, the Copenhagen meeting demonstrated a general trend towards increasing

---

[8] Article 25 of the Kyoto Protocol specifies that the Protocol enters into force 90 days after the date on which not less than 55 Parties have ratified the Convention, including included Annex I Parties responsible for at least 55 per cent of the total carbon dioxide emissions in Annex I countries. This threshold was not reached until Russia ratified the Protocol on 14 November 2004.

[9] The European Union Greenhouse Gas Emissions Trading Scheme (EU ETS) is based on Directive 2003/87/EC, which entered into force on 25 October 2003. *See* EU ETS website, http://ec.europa.eu/environment/climat/emission/index_en.htm, November 12, 2010.

[10] This corresponds to a target of restricting atmospheric concentrations of CO_2 to 450ppm. *See* Metz, B. et al. (eds.), *IPCC:, Climate Change 2007: Mitigation. Contribution of Working Group III to the Fourth Assessment Report of the Intergovernmental Panel on Climate Change*, Cambridge University Press, 2007, at Figures SPM 7 and SPM 8.

[11] Stern, N., *The Economics of Climate Change: The Stern Review*, Cambridge University Press, 2007.

[12] United Nations, *The Copenhagen Accord* (FCCC/CP/2009/L.7), 18 December 2009.

engagement with climate change issues in both developed and developing countries. On the assumption that most nations will eventually set themselves some form of emission reduction targets under the UNFCCC process, the question to be addressed in this chapter is what regulatory strategies will be most appropriate to achieve those targets, and what lessons can the emerging economies of East Asia take from the recent regulatory responses in Australia?

3.   THE CASE FOR MARKET-BASED INSTRUMENTS

There are a variety of regulatory strategies available to achieve environmental objectives such as the reduction of greenhouse gas emissions. These range from environmental education and voluntary agreements to the use of market-based instruments and "command and control" regulations. Fauchald uses the term "informational strategies" rather than environmental education and notes the utility of this strategy as supplementary to the other strategies.[13] In short, such a strategy is aimed at informing individuals and both private and public bodies of the environmental problems, of ways of dealing with those problems and generally providing information that can be used to produce a positive environmental impact. While the intention would be to influence behavior, education tends to be perceived as a long-term strategy.[14] However, such environmental education paves the way for a greater acceptance of new "command and control" mechanisms and market-based instruments aimed at addressing environmental problems.[15]

Voluntary agreements can be used by governments with industry groups to achieve agreed standards, or, in this case targets, for lowering emissions.[16] While voluntary agreements may produce higher industry compliance, agreed targets may be much less than would be otherwise

---

[13]   Fauchald, O. K., *Environmental Taxes and Trade Discrimination*, Kluwer Law International, 1998, page 29.

[14]   Riethmuller, S. H. and Buttriss, G. J., *Closing the Gap between Pro-environmental Attitudes and Behaviour in Australia*, Australian National University, 2008.

[15]   Wuertenberger, T. D., "The Regulation of CO_2 Emissions Caused By Private Households – An Analysis of the Legal Situation In The European Union and Germany", *Missouri Environmental Law and Policy Review*, Volume 16, Number 1, 2009, page 55.

[16]   *See* for example European Environmental Agency (EEA), "Market-based Instruments for Environmental Policy in Europe" EEA Technical Report, Number 8, 2005 (henceforth "EEA Technical Report"); and the U.S. Environmental

required when using "command and control" regulations.[17] It should be noted that the voluntary agreement concept has been used successfully in Australia when implementing different environmental policies, such as in the case of biodiversity conservation. For example, South Australia effectively used such agreements to abate land clearing and conserve native vegetation during the 1980s and 1990s but these were supported by "financial assistance, advice and local government rate relief to landholders".[18]

The more common regulatory option to deal with environmental problems has been the use of normative strategies, namely, "command and control" mechanisms.[19] These generally involve public authorities imposing rules that either require individuals or organisations to do something or prohibit individuals or organisations from doing something. For example, a particular industry may be required to use specific technologies or equipment, such as filters, in order to abate pollution.[20] These are referred to as technology based regulations.[21] Alternatively, the instrument may simply designate acceptable levels of pollution and leave it to the industry to determine what method will be utilised to achieve those levels.[22] Such performance-based regulations provide greater flexibility for compliance.[23] However, "command and control" mechanisms have received much criticism as an effective tool in the quest to reduce emissions.

Protection Agency (EPA), *The United States Experience with Economic Incentives for Protecting the Environment*, 2001.

[17]   Kerret, D. and Tal, A., "Greenwash or Green Gain? Predicting the Success and Evaluating the Effectiveness of Environmental Voluntary Agreements", *Pennsylvania State University Journal of Environmental Law*, Volume 14, 2005, pages 31–84.

[18]   Stoianoff, N. P. and Kelly, A. H., "Conserving Native Vegetation On Private Land: Subsidizing Sustainable Use Of Biodiversity?" in Deketelaere, K. et al. (eds.), *Critical Issues in Environmental Taxation,* (Vol. IV), Oxford University Press, 2007, pages 299–315, 306.

[19]   Fauchald, *op. cit.*, page 27; Stewart, R., "Economics, Environment, and the Limits of Legal Control", *Harvard Environmental Law Review*, Volume 9, 1985, page 9.

[20]   For instance, the fitting of anti-pollution devices in vehicles as required under Part 3 Division 3 Clause 11 of the Protection of the Environment Operations (Clean Air) Regulation 2002 (NSW).

[21]   Hahn, R. and Stavins, R., "Incentive-based Environmental Regulation: A New Era from An Old Idea?", *Ecology Law Quarterly*, Volume 18, 1991, page 18.

[22]   *See* for example the emission standards set in Part 4 of the Protection of the Environment Operations (Clean Air) Regulation 2002 (NSW).

[23]   Borck, J., Coglianese, C. and Nash, J., "Evaluating the Social Effect of Performance-Based Environmental Programs", (Corporate Social Responsibility Initiative (CSRI) Working paper, No. 48, 2008), page 1; Fauchald, *op. cit.*, page 28.

Such mechanisms are usually backed up with sanctions for failure to comply and this means that the severity of the sanction and manner in which compliance is enforced become significant factors in determining the effectiveness of a "command and control" mechanism.[24] Further, the cost-effectiveness or efficiency of "command and control" mechanisms have been criticized with claims that such regulation will be behind the technology available or with standards achieved offer little incentive to continue improving pollution abatement.[25] However, the work of Cole and Grossman in 1999 found to the contrary when comparing empirical data.[26] Recently, Fullerton et al. confirmed this finding concluding that monitoring and enforcing "command and control" mechanisms were easier than for other environmental strategies.[27]

Even so, this brings us to the strategy utilizing market-based instruments. Such instruments have become important for the protection of the environment as the market, representing human economic activity, has been held responsible for the environmental ills the world is experiencing today. This is based on the fact that a price is not placed on the damage to the environment caused by production processes. Accordingly, where a production process results in air pollution, for instance, the damage is experienced by all of society not just the producer and accordingly the pollution comprises an external cost of that production which must be borne by society as a whole. This is considered a failure of the market to maximise social welfare and is caused by market actors not bearing the full costs of their production process. Daly and Farley point out that if these market actors bear the full costs of their decisions, in other words internalize these external costs of production, they will either produce less of the products causing the pollution or transfer the costs to the consumer, who, in turn, will consume less due to the higher price for those products.[28] This underlies the basis of the "polluter pays principle" espoused by the

---

[24]   Consider, for example, the operation of the Protection of the Environment Operations (Clean Air) Regulation 2002 (NSW).

[25]   Bohm, P., and Russell, C., "Comparative Analysis of Alternative Policy Instruments", *Handbook of Natural Resource and Energy Economics*, Volume 1, 1985, pages 395–460.

[26]   Cole, D. H. and Grossman, P. Z., "When is Command-and-control Efficient? Institutions, Technology and the Comparative Efficiency of Alternative Regulatory Regimes for Environmental Protection", *Wisconsin Law Review,* Volume 5, 1999, pages 887–938.

[27]   Fullerton, D., Leicester, A. and Smith, S., "Environmental Taxes" (National Bureau of Economic Research (NBER) Working Paper, No. 14197), 2008.

[28]   Daly, H. E. and Farley, J., *Ecological Economics: Principles and Applications*, Island Press, 2004, page 10.

Organisation for Economic Co-operation and Development (OECD) in the 1972 document, *Guiding Principles on the International Economic Aspects of Environmental Policies.*

The "polluter pays principle" is "to be used for allocating costs of pollution and control measures to encourage rational use of scarce environmental resources and to avoid distortions on international trade and investment".[29] It is based on the argument that when prices do not reflect resource use or the costs of pollution "market inefficiencies result with excessive production or consumption of products and activities that impose social costs".[30] This is in line with the Pigouvian theory that is said to underlie the economic rationale of environmental taxes such as carbon taxes. Milne describes this theory as "a theory of economic efficiency that derives from the proper allocation of costs between entities engaging in pollution and victims of that pollution in society at large".[31] In addition to carbon taxes, emissions trading schemes also set a price on the externality, namely pollution, so that the cost of the environmental damage is internalized. While Mann acknowledges that economists regard carbon taxes as the "gold standard of market-based instruments"[32], we have seen greater political emphasis on emissions trading schemes.[33] The question is whether one form of market-based instrument is better than another or whether both should operate on differing levels simultaneously. What is agreed is that market-based instruments provide a greater incentive compared to "command and control" regulations to "reduce environmentally harmful activities beyond the level prescribed or by other means than those prescribed".[34] Further, economic strategies have been shown to have greater flexibility and provide a better estimate of any effects on competitiveness compared to "command and control" regulations.[35] The

---

[29]   OECD, *Guiding Principles Concerning the International Economic Aspects of Environmental Policies,* Doc. C (72)128 (26 May, 1972), reprinted in 11 I.L.M. 1172, 1972 (henceforth "OECD Guiding Principles").

[30]   OECD, *Environmentally Related Taxes in OECD Countries: Issues and Strategies,* OECD, Paris, 2001, page 21.

[31]   Milne, J. E., "Environmental Taxation: Why Theory Matters", in Milne et al. (eds.), *Critical Issues in Environmental Taxation,* (Vol. I), Richmond Law & Tax, 2003, page 4.

[32]   Mann, R. F., "The Case for the Carbon Tax: How to Overcome Politics and Find Our Green Destiny", *Environmental Law Reporter,* Volume 39, Number 10118, 2009, page 10120.

[33]   Consider the European Union Emissions Trading Scheme and Australia's recent attempt, the Carbon Pollution Reduction Scheme.

[34]   Fauchald, *op. cit.,* page 25.

[35]   *Ibid.,* page 26.

next two sections will consider environmental taxes and emissions trading schemes in turn.

3.1 Environmental Taxes

The recent review of the Australian taxation system conducted by Dr Ken Henry ("the Henry Review"), defined environmental taxes as follows:

> To be an environmental tax — rather than just a tax — there must be a direct link between the tax and the marginal social cost of the activity damaging the environment. The tax effectively 'corrects' for the market under-pricing the loss of social value from a damaged environment.[36]

The Henry Review recognized that Australia has had few "environmental taxes", namely, Leaded Petrol Levy (1993), Aircraft Noise Levy (1995), and Product Stewardship Oil Levy (2001). However it also noted that the OECD has adopted a broader definition which includes all unrequited government levies that are of "environmental relevance".[37] Two Australian taxes concerning fossil fuels which fall within this broader definition are the federal fuel excise and the petroleum resource rent tax, which will both be mentioned in more detail later in this chapter. The Henry Review firmly endorsed greater use of taxes to address "spillover" environmental costs, provided such taxes are well designed.[38] However, in response to the "diabolical" Climate Change phenomenon, the Federal Government has previously declared its preference for an emissions trading strategy in the form of the proposed CPRS. Nevertheless, there is still considerable opposition to the CPRS in Federal Parliament, and thus the alternative of a carbon tax is worthy of consideration.

The theoretical foundation for taxing externalities such as pollution can be found in Arthur Cecil Pigou's work, *The Economics of Welfare*, first published in 1920 and revised three more times ending with the fourth edition in 1932. In essence this theory proposes the internalization of external costs such as pollution in order to maximize welfare. This is intended to be achieved by placing a tax or levy on the polluting activity such that it

---

[36] Commonwealth of Australia, *Architecture of Australia's Tax and Transfer System*, 2008, page 282 (henceforth "Commonwealth of Australia Tax System").

[37] OECD, *The Political Economy of Environmentally Related Taxes*, Paris: OECD, 2006.

[38] Commonwealth of Australia, *Australia's Future Tax System*, Report to the Treasurer, Part Two, Detailed analysis, Volume 2, December 2009, page 351.

equals the "marginal social damage it generates".[39] In 1971, Baumol and Oates recognized the difficulty of implementing this theory "because of our inability to measure marginal social damage".[40] Accordingly, they recommended an alternative in the "spirit of the Pigouvian tradition", namely, the establishment of "standards of environmental quality . . . and then [the imposition of] a set of charges on waste emissions sufficient to attain these standards".[41] Their proposal represents the "least-cost method to realise" the specified quality standards[42] and operates as follows:

> the public authority can levy a uniform set of taxes which would in effect constitute a set of prices for the private use of social resources such as air and water. The taxes (or prices) would be selected so as to achieve specific acceptability standards rather than attempting to base them on the unknown value of marginal net damages. Thus, one might tax all installations emitting wastes into a river at a rate of t(b) cents per gallon, where the tax rate, t, paid by a particular polluter, would, for example, depend on b, the BOD value of the effluent, according to some fixed schedule. Each polluter would then be given a financial incentive to reduce the amount of effluent he discharges and to improve the quality of the discharge (i.e., reduce its BOD value). By setting the tax rates sufficiently high, the community would presumably be able to achieve whatever level of purification of the river it desired. It might even be able to eliminate at least some types of industrial pollution altogether.[43]

Such environmental taxes are clearly in line with the "polluter pays principle" referred to above. When the OECD adopted this concept in 1972, the primary aim was to avoid market distortions through the use of direct and indirect environment-related subsidies.

It is expected that "the polluter should bear the expenses of carrying out . . . [these] measures" and further "the cost of these measures should be reflected in the cost of goods and services which cause pollution and/or consumption".[44]

This "cost covering" function is one of the three functions used by the European Environment Agency to define environmental taxes.[45] The

---

[39]   Baumol, W. J. and Oates, W. E., "The Use of Standards and Prices for Protection of the Environment", *Swedish Journal of Economics*, Volume 73, Number 1, 1971, page 42.

[40]   *Ibid.*

[41]   *Ibid.*

[42]   *Ibid.*, page 46.

[43]   *Ibid.*, 45.

[44]   OECD Guiding Principles, *op. cit.*

[45]   EEA, "Environmental Taxes: Implementation and Environmental Effectiveness", Environmental Issue Report, Number 1, 1996, page 8 (henceforth "EEA Issue Report").

Agency recognizes the impact of the political process in designing such taxes; for example, if the tax is truly effective, the revenue raised by the tax will diminish as the tax base (the polluting activity) diminishes[46] and so tax rates may be set at levels that will not match the marginal external cost. The second function is that of an incentive to reduce polluting behavior.[47] If new technologies are developed or available, manufacturers would be encouraged to implement such strategies and thereby avoid the pollution tax and hence reduce the price of their product in the marketplace. Accordingly, there is a constant incentive for the polluter to reduce emissions as increased profit will be the reward.[48] The third function is that of revenue raising. Certainly, any tax has the role of revenue raising for the government charging the tax. However, in the case of environmental taxes, such as a carbon tax, the question is to what use is the revenue put? It may simply form part of consolidated revenue and not be funneled into an environmental program or it could be ear-marked for a specific environmental program. Alternatively, the environmental or carbon tax may reduce a nation's reliance on other taxes. This "double dividend" is based on the OECD's emphasis on levying taxes on "bads" (pollution) rather than "goods" such as labor and capital.[49]

In the debate about responses to climate change, with the rise of free-market economists came a theoretical shift away from environmental taxes in favor of the market-based emissions trading strategy which will be discussed in the following section. Additional arguments against a carbon tax include the possible detrimental effects on national competitiveness and the regressive impact of such taxes.[50]

3.2   Emissions Trading

Ronald Coase led the movement away from environmental taxes, preferring property rights to deal with the problem of externalities. In his 1960 seminal paper, *The Problem of Social Cost*[51], Coase criticized the use of

---

[46]   EEA Technical Report, *op. cit.*

[47]   EEA Issue Report, *op. cit.*, page 8.

[48]   Pearson, M. and Smith, S., "The European Carbon Tax: An Assessment of the European Commission's Proposals", *The Institute for Fiscal Studies*, 1991, page 942.

[49]   OECD Guiding Principles, *op. cit.*

[50]   Engle, E., "Ecotaxes and the European Union", *European. Energy and Environmental Law Review*, Volume 16, 2001, pages 298, 303. But one could equally argue the possible detrimental impact on competitiveness by emissions trading schemes.

[51]   Coase, R., "The Problem of Social Cost", *Journal of Law and Economics,* Volume 3, 1960, pages 1–44.

taxes to correct market imperfections favoring the market's ability to correct itself where externalities exist.

> If factors of production are thought of as rights, it becomes easier to understand that the right to do something which has a harmful effect (such as the creation of smoke, noise, smell, etc.) is also a factor of production . . .[52]

Accordingly, through such transferable "property rights", the market can be used to value them and ensure their best possible use and hence this would lead to optimal resource allocation and a correction to market imperfections. Baumol explains the criticism of Pigouvian taxes in his 1972 paper, *On Control and the Taxation of Externalities*.[53] The problem with taxes is that such an intervention may cause their own market imperfections by absorbing more resources than are lost due to the initial market failure (the pollution for instance). However, the Coase theorem (as it has been described) relies on there being no transaction costs to the bargaining over the property rights.[54] Coase himself recognizes that quite often transaction costs in market transactions do exist and can be very costly: "sufficiently costly at any rate to prevent many transactions that would be carried out in the world in which the pricing system worked without cost".[55]

Accordingly, the Coase theorem has its limitations in that the expected "rearrangement of rights will only be undertaken when the increase in value of production consequent upon the rearrangement is greater than the costs which would be involved in bringing it about".[56] Despite Baumol's defence of Pigouvian taxes he later joins forces with Wallace E. Oates to produce *The Theory of Environmental Policy*, first published in 1975 and revised in 1988. While still focusing on the treatment of externalities and recognizing the role of Pigouvian taxes, Baumol and Oates provide a further analysis of the property rights concept espoused in the Coase theorem.

In essence, the concept of emissions trading is born out of the Coase theorem. Baumol and Oates indicate that the property right encapsulating the right to pollute at a specified level needs to be distributed to entitled parties.[57] This is achieved by the government allocating those rights to pollute

---

[52] *Ibid.*, 44.
[53] Baumol, W. J., "On Taxation and the Control of Externalities", *American Economic Review*, Volume 62, Number 3, pages 307–322.
[54] Coase, *op. cit.*, page 15.
[55] *Ibid.*
[56] *Ibid.*
[57] Baumol, W. J. and Oates, W. E., *The Theory of Environmental Policy*, Cambridge University Press, 1988, pages 180–90.

at that specified level and then leaving the parties to adjust their behavior in order to work within those rights. Hence, businesses that keep their emissions below their permitted level have capacity to trade-in their remaining rights to pollute to those who have exceeded their allocated rights. And so emissions-trading begins. Baumol and Oates consider this to be a cost-effective way of meeting predetermined environmental targets.[58] It allows those polluters who have access to low-cost emissions reduction equipment or methods to reduce emissions until the cost equals the market price of the rights to pollute (also known as "permits"). Conversely, where a polluter exceeds their right to pollute they must buy further rights from the market. The expectation is that where the market price of these rights exceeds the cost of undertaking abatement activities, such as investment in equipment, the polluter will take the cheaper option, that is, decide to pollute less by obtaining the abatement equipment.[59] Such emissions trading regimes have been developing over recent times with the US having implemented one for the reduction of Sulphur Dioxide gases since 1990.[60] Meanwhile, the EU passed a Directive establishing a scheme for greenhouse gas emissions trading in October 2003 and is now in its second phase.[61]

Emissions trading is synonymous with tradable permit systems and, like environmental taxes, establishes a price for the relevant polluting activity such that polluters are encouraged to internalize such externalities through cost-effective means. While there are a variety of designs, the key choices are twofold, cap-and-trade versus baseline-and-credit.[62] As has been described above, where the emissions trading scheme establishes a fixed target of emissions and then allocates a fixed number of permits to the polluters based on this target, the polluters are free to trade-in the permits so as to meet the target or cap. With such a cap-and-trade regime the target can be achieved. The baseline-and-credit design instead establishes a benchmark for emissions such that if a polluter's emissions fall below that benchmark the difference is tradable but there is no compulsion to do so.[63] Accordingly, as "the baseline-and-credit model does not guarantee that a specific target will be met" leaving the benefit of such a scheme to be uncertain, it is then preferable to opt for a design that does establish an emissions target.[64] Hence the cap-and-trade design is the

---

[58]   *Ibid.*
[59]   *Ibid.*
[60]   Mann, *op. cit.*, page 10120.
[61]   Directive 2003/87/EC.
[62]   EEA 2005 Technical Report, *op.cit.*, page 19.
[63]   *Ibid.*, page 17.
[64]   *Ibid.*

preferable option. What then must be determined is the size of the total allocation and then the method of permit allocation. Once again this requires a choice between two options: free allocation of permits or auctioning of permits.

The European Environment Agency points out that there is a strong theoretical basis for auctioning the allowance rather than giving them away.[65] However, rather than describing why auctioning is good other than as a source of revenue for the government to then apply against preexisting distortionary taxes, the arguments provided are aimed at explaining why free allocation is bad; for example, making polluters wealthier and sustaining inefficient enterprises, reducing environmental effectiveness, increasing the price of tradable allowances and increasing the transaction costs is the negotiation for allowances.[66] Meanwhile, the three arguments made in favor of free allocations commence with a return to the Coase theorem. The European Environment Agency uses an elegant statement by Tietenberg to explain the first argument:

> Whatever the initial allocation, the transferability of the allowances allows them to ultimately flow to their highest valued uses. Since those uses do not depend on the initial allocation, all initial allocations result in the same outcome and that outcome is cost-effective.[67]

The second argument is based on political acceptability. By giving away the allocations free of charge this is akin to paying the polluters to support the implementation of the scheme, because they are getting a real tradable financial asset at no cost.[68] The third argument relies on this aspect of the arrangement, namely, previously unknown emitters may come forward to claim their free allowances, thereby making themselves known to the authorities that will monitor and enforce the scheme.[69] While these are all compelling arguments, it should be noted that it is possible to have a hybrid arrangement where both free allocations (enabling political "buy-ins") and auctioned permits (providing efficiency gains) exist.[70]

---

[65] *Ibid.*, page 21.
[66] *Ibid.*, page 21.
[67] Tietenberg, T. H., "The Tradable Permits Approach to Protecting the Commons: What Have We Learned?", (Paper Presented at the CATEP Workshop "Trading Scales: Harmonising Industry, National and International Emission Trading Schemes", Fondazione ENI Enrico Mattei, Venice, 3 and 4 December, 2001). As reproduced in EEA Technical Report, *op. cit.*, page 21.
[68] EEA Technical Report, *op. cit.*, page 21.
[69] *Ibid.*, page 22.
[70] *Ibid.*, page 21.

For an emissions trading system to be effective, compliance must be high; for compliance to be high, there must be an authority capable of monitoring performance and enforcing the regime. Part of this requires adequate reporting systems to be established so that there is confidence in the operation of the scheme.[71] As with any form of regulation, there needs to be some consequence for non-compliance that will encourage participants to play ball and so fines for non-compliance need to have a deterrent quality.

It is no wonder that Mann definitively states that a "carbon tax is better than a cap-and-trade (emissions trading) system because of its simplicity, transparency, efficiency and certainty (of cost)".[72] While emissions trading has been the politically favorable alternative to carbon taxes, mostly due to a firm belief that taxes are too interventionist and the market should be given the opportunity to sort out the pollution problem, there remains the fact that a carbon tax is infinitely easier to implement than an entire trading system. As we have seen above, for a carbon tax to be implemented the level of the tax must be decided; we already know what the pollutant is and most likely the measurement standards for emissions.[73] Further, the government structure for the collection of taxes is already in place.[74] By contrast, an emissions trading scheme will require the design of a regulatory system to create and monitor markets; the cap needs to be determined as well as the number of initial allowances,[75] not to mention exemptions from the scheme. What is quite evident is the significance of the design of the regime. Mann stresses that "[a]s the saying goes, the devil is in the details" emphasizing that emissions trading requires far more details than a carbon tax.[76]

As can be seen, the administrative costs of an emissions trading system will be quite high compared to simply imposing a tax on emissions across sectors. But what we must not forget is that when we choose an emissions trading system there are still tax consequences. In Australia the proposed CPRS legislation will treat dealings in "Australian emission units" in a similar fashion to trading stock for taxation purpose using a rolling balance system.[77]

---

71   *Ibid.*, page 22.
72   Mann, *op. cit.*, page 10122.
73   *Ibid.*, page 10120.
74   *Ibid.*
75   *Ibid.*
76   Mann, *op. cit.*, page 10122.
77   The Carbon Pollution Reduction Scheme (Consequential Amendments) Bill 2010 proposes insertion of a "rolling balance" system into the Income Tax

4.   AUSTRALIAN RESPONSES TO CLIMATE CHANGE

One of the most important commitments under the UNFCCC was for the parties to develop and publish national inventories.[78] The National Greenhouse Gas Inventory indicates that Australia is close to meeting its Kyoto Protocol target, to restrict emissions to 108 per cent of the 1990 level by 2012.[79] However, emissions for several key sectors have escalated dramatically in the reported period, particularly in the energy industry (up 55 per cent, primarily due to coal and gas fired power stations) and transport sector (up 26.9 per cent, primarily due to cars and commercial vehicles). Despite these substantial increases Australia can meet its Kyoto target through special accounting rules which allow Australia an offset for "land use change" due to reductions in deforestation.[80] It should also be noted that Australia's per capita greenhouse gas emissions are the highest of any OECD country, and that Australia is one of the world's leading exporters of coal. Whilst "exported" emissions are not counted under the Kyoto rules, it is estimated that they are equivalent to the whole of Australia's domestic emissions.[81] Australia is also a major importer of goods manufactured in developing countries. However, the Kyoto Protocol does not require reporting of embedded emissions in imported goods. Whilst these figures strongly suggest that Australia is one of the world's greenhouse villains, the Garnaut Review also highlighted Australia's vulnerability to climate change:

Assessment Act 1997 (Cth), under proposed new Div 240. Under these rules it is proposed that the cost of acquiring units will be deductible, hence any units allocated free of charge will not give rise to any deduction. The proceeds on sale of units will be assessable, whilst surrender of units in accordance with the CPRS requirements will result in a reduction to the rolling balance account balance at the end of the relevant year. The Bill also proposes that the sale of emission units in a secondary market will be a taxable supply for goods and services tax purposes, with GST registered sellers liable to GST and registered buyers entitled to an input credit. In general, no capital gains or losses will arise except in the case of certain cross border transactions.

[78]   UNFCCC, Article 4, para 1(a).
[79]   *See* Australian Government Department of Climate Change, *National Greenhouse Gas Inventory: Accounting for the KYOTO Target*, May 2009, http://www.climatechange.gov.au/en/climate-change/~/media/publications/greenhouse-report/national-greenhouse-gas-inventory-pdf.ash, November 12, 2010 (henceforth "Australian Government Inventory").
[80]   Kyoto Protocol, Article 3.7 (known as "the Australia clause").
[81]   *See* calculation by Rising Tide Australia: Grassroots Climate Action website, "Clean Coal", http://www.risingtide.org.au/cleancoal, November 12, 2010.

Australia has a larger interest in a strong mitigation outcome than other developed countries. We are already a hot and dry country; small variations in climate are more damaging to us than to other developed countries. We live in a region of developing countries, which are in weaker positions to adapt to climate change than wealthy countries with robust political and economic institutions. The problems of our neighbours would inevitably become our problems. And the structure of our economy means that our terms of trade would be damaged more by the effects of climate change than would those of any other developed country.[82]

The greatest impact of the Kyoto Protocol is that it imposed the first ever binding greenhouse emission targets for developed countries, which required national governments to formulate credible greenhouse reduction policies. However, the quest for effective greenhouse responses in Australia has proven to be an enormous political challenge for two successive Federal governments.

4.1 The Howard "No Regrets" Policies

When Australia signed the Kyoto Protocol in 1998, the recently elected Liberal Government led by John Howard was very concerned about the potential impacts of emission reduction strategies upon local industries, particularly in the mining and energy sectors.[83] As a consequence, the Howard Government resisted ratification of the Kyoto Protocol, and adopted a "soft" approach to greenhouse emissions in its 1998 National Greenhouse Strategy.[84] This Strategy opted primarily for "no regrets" approaches, centered on the voluntary industry partnership program Greenhouse Challenge.[85] Other measures promoted by the Strategy included improvements to monitoring of national emissions,[86] communication and education,[87] promoting efficient and sustainable energy use,[88]

---

[82]   Garnaut, R., *Garnaut Climate Change Review: Final Report*, Cambridge University Press, 2008, Summary, page xix. The variations in climate referred to by Garnaut are already evident across southern Australia through declining rainfall over the last decade and recent severe bushfire events.

[83]   After winning the 1996 federal election, the Howard Government took over from the former Labor Government led by Paul Keating, which had handled most of the early negotiations leading up to the Kyoto Protocol.

[84]   Commonwealth of Australia, *The National Greenhouse Strategy*, Australian Greenhouse Office, 1998.

[85]   *Ibid.*, at Module 3.

[86]   *Ibid.*, at Module 1.

[87]   *Ibid.*, at Module 2.

[88]   *Ibid.*, at Module 4.

efficient transport and sustainable urban planning,[89] enhancing green-house sinks and sustainable land management,[90] best practice in industrial processes and waste management[91] and adaptation strategies.[92]

One of the most notable achievements in this Strategy was the Mandatory Renewable Energy Target scheme (MRET) which took effect in 2001.[93] The MRET required wholesale purchasers of electricity to contribute towards an aggregate target of an additional 9500 Gigawatt hours (GWh) of renewable electricity per annum by 2010.[94] It is interesting to note that in mandating this requirement, the MRET has a prescriptive "command and control" approach; however, it also introduced a Coase-style property rights approach by establishing a market for "renewable energy certificates" (RECs) to give more flexibility to the scheme.[95] Prior to the announcement of MRET, Australia's renewable energy sector generated around 16 000 GWh of electricity, equating to around 10.5 per cent of Australia's electricity market. The vast majority of this renewable electricity was generated from hydro-electric sources (particularly from Tasmania and the Snowy Mountains scheme). Other minor renewable sources included landfill gas, biomass, photovoltaic and wind.[96] Thus the MRET target represented an increase in the order of 60 per cent over pre-existing renewable energy generation in Australia. However, a recent Senate Committee inquiry has revealed that the MRET scheme has been oversubscribed since 2006, and the proportion of renewable energy to total electricity production has in fact dropped since MRET commenced.[97]

---

[89]   *Ibid.*, at Module 5.
[90]   *Ibid.*, at Module 6.
[91]   *Ibid.*, at Module 7.
[92]   *Ibid.*, at Module 8.
[93]   Under the Renewable Energy (Electricity) Act 2000, electricity suppliers must surrender a prescribed amount of Renewable Energy Certificates (RECs) each year or pay a statutory penalty.
[94]   This target was originally intended to represent 2 per cent of total electricity production, but later converted to an absolute quantity. *See* Australian Parliament, House of Representatives, Combined Explanatory Memorandum to Renewable Energy (Electricity) Bill 2000 and Renewable Energy (Electricity) (Charge) Bill 2000, introduced to the House 22 June 2000.
[95]   RECs are a tradable instrument created through solar, wind, or other renewable energy systems. Electricity suppliers may generate RECs themselves or buy them on a secondary market at the prevailing market rate.
[96]   Australian Government, Renewable Opportunities, A Review of the Operation of the Renewable Energy (Electricity) Act 2000, September 2003, Chapter 2, page 11, http://www.mretreview.gov.au/report/index.html, 12 November, 2010.
[97]   The original MRET objective of increasing the overall proportion of renew-

Following the Stern Review and Fourth Assessment Report by the IPCC, the Howard Government became more engaged with climate change. In April 2007, the Federal Opposition Labor Party led by Kevin Rudd joined with the Australian State governments to commission Professor Ross Garnaut to conduct an independent review of the medium to long-term policy options for addressing climate change in Australia.[98] In June 2007, the Government announced an Australian Carbon Trading Scheme to be introduced by 2012, but this proposal lapsed when that Government was voted out of office in November 2007. However, one important legacy of this policy was the National Greenhouse and Energy Reporting Act 2007. This legislation was introduced to provide a standardized framework for the reporting of greenhouse gas emissions and energy use as a precursor for an Australian emissions trading scheme. The first annual reporting period for organizations with emissions or energy use above the relevant NGER thresholds began on 1 July 2008.[99]

4.2 The Rudd Government CPRS Proposals

The newly elected Labor Government led by Kevin Rudd received world-wide acclaim when it moved quickly to fulfill an election promise to ratify the Kyoto Protocol.[100] At this time, Australia was confident of meeting its Kyoto commitments and the more difficult challenge was to devise and implement an effective emission reduction strategy for the post-Kyoto period and, in particular, the longer-term targets considered at the Copenhagen Conference. The Garnaut Review, released

---

able energy in Australia's electricity generation effort by 2 per cent has not been met due to the conversion of the target to a set quantity of 9500 GWh, and a general underestimation of the growth in electricity demand. *See* Australian Senate Standing Committee on Economics, Inquiry into the National Market Driven Energy Efficiency Target Bill 2007 [2008] and Renewable Energy Legislation Amendment (Renewable Power Percentage) Bill 2008, May 2008; *See* the dissenting report by the Australian Democrats at page 61, http://www.aph.gov.au/senate/committee/economics_ctte/nmdeet_08/report/report.pdf, November 12, 2010.

[98] *See* "About the Review" at the Garnaut Climate Change Review website: http://www.garnautreview.org.au/update-2011/about-review.html, May 12, 2011.

[99] *See* Australian Government Department of Climate Change and Energy Efficiency, "National Greenhouse and Energy Reporting", http://www.climate-change.gov.au/government/initiatives/national-greenhouse-energy-reporting. aspx, November 12, 2010.

[100] This decision received worldwide acclaim when it was announced at the 13th Conference of the Parties at Bali in December 2007. This refers to the 13th Conference of the Parties to the United Nations Framework Convention on Climate Change, held at Bali Indonesia, from 3–15 December 2007.

in September 2008, concluded that an emissions trading scheme would be the best approach for this purpose.[101] The Government accepted this recommendation and quickly released a White Paper on the design features of a comprehensive emissions trading scheme in December 2008.[102] In May 2009 a package of bills was submitted to Parliament to establish the CPRS with effect from 1 July 2011.[103] However, there has been considerable opposition to the CPRS bills in the Australian Senate where the bills were rejected on 13 August 2009 and again on 2 December 2009. Whilst the bills were re-introduced into Parliament on 2 February 2010, Prime Minister Rudd announced on 27 April 2010 that the Government would delay the implementation of the CPRS until the end of the Kyoto Protocol commitment period in 2012.[104] A few months later Kevin Rudd lost the leadership of the Australian Labor Party and was replaced as Prime Minister by Julia Gillard. In September 2010, the Gillard Government established a Multi-Party Climate Change Committee to 'explore options for the implementation of carbon price [and] help to build consensus on how Australia will tackle the challenge of climate change', starting from the position that 'a carbon price is a necessary economic reform required to reduce carbon pollution.[105] In February 2011, the Gillard Government announced a two-stage carbon price plan with a fixed price period to commence as early as 1 July 2012, that would operate for three to five years before transitioning to emissions trading scheme.[106]

It is likely that the Gillard carbon pricing scheme will use the legislative

---

[101] Garnaut, *op. cit.,* page xxxii (Summary).

[102] Commonwealth of Australia (Department of Climate Change), *White Paper on Carbon Pollution Reduction Scheme*, December 2008, Volume 1 Policy Decisions Summary. *See also* "Australia's Low Pollution Future: The Economics of Climate Change Mitigation", 30 October 2008, http://www.treasury.gov.au/lowpollutionfuture/, November 12, 2010.

[103] *See* the Carbon Pollution Reduction Scheme Bill 2010 (Cth) and ten other related bills, http://www.climatechange.gov.au/en/government/initiatives/cprs/cprs-progress.aspx, November 12, 2010.

[104] Prime Minister of Australia, "Interview: Transcript of Doorstop, Nepean Hospital Penrith", 27 April 2010, http://www.pm.gov.au/node/6708, November 12, 2010.

[105] Prime Minister of Australia, "Prime Minister establishes Climate Change Committee" (Media Release, 27 September 2010), http://www.pm.gov.au/press-office/prime-minister-establishes-climate-change-committee, 1.

[106] Prime Minister of Australia, 'Climate change framework announced' (Media Release, 24 February 2011), http://www.pm.gov.au/press-office/climate-change-framework-announced. This media release includes attachment 'Carbon Price mechanism' (Multi Party Committee on Climate Change, 24 February 2011).

framework provided by the earlier Carbon Pollution Reduction Scheme Bill 2010 (Cth) which provides the rules for establishing and operating the CPRS, the Carbon Pollution Reduction Scheme (Consequential Amendments) Bill 2010 (Cth) which makes a host of amendments to other legislation including the Income Tax Assessment Act 1997 (Cth), and the Australian Climate Change Regulatory Authority Bill 2010 which establishes a new regulatory authority to administer the CPRS and also take over administration of the National Greenhouse Energy and Reporting Act 2007 (Cth). In summary, the scheme was proposed to operate as follows:

- the CPRS objects include a commitment to reduce Australia's greenhouse emissions by 25 per cent below 2000 levels by 2020 if the UNFCCC parties agree globally to stabilize levels of CO_2 equivalent in the atmosphere at 450 parts per million or lower;[107]
- a "price signal" will be created for greenhouse emissions by imposing obligations to acquire "eligible emission units"[108] upon certain "liable entities";[109]
- "eligible emission units" includes "Australian emission units" acquired under the CPRS as well as eligible international units (such as the Kyoto mechanisms and the European Union ETS),[110] which links the CPRS with international carbon markets;
- liable entities are to primarily include entities with operational control of a facility producing direct (Scope 1) emissions of CO_2 of 25,000 tonnes or more per annum;[111]
- some sectors will be covered indirectly. For instance, transport emissions are to be covered by making certain "upstream" fossil fuel suppliers liable;[112]
- some sectors like waste and synthetic greenhouse gases will be subject to different emissions thresholds; and
- Australian emission units will in future years be allocated through an auction system, with the total units issued progressively reduced

---

[107]   CPRS Bill 2010, Section 3.
[108]   *Ibid.*, Section 5 (definitions).
[109]   *Ibid.*
[110]   *Ibid.*
[111]   *Ibid.* The greenhouse emissions covered are identical to those covered by the Kyoto Protocol (i.e., carbon dioxide, methane, nitrous oxide, sulphur hexafluoride, hydrofluorocarbons and perfluorocarbons).
[112]   *Ibid.*, Division 4 of the CPRS Bill 2010.

to promote a "carbon market" through trading of units (known as a "cap-and-trade" approach);[113]

However certain sectors will be sheltered from the full impact of the scheme:

- certain "emissions-intensive trade-exposed" industries (e.g. aluminium smelters) will receive assistance in the form of free emission units during a transitional period.
- motorists will be initially compensated for fuel price increases by a cent-for-cent decrease in fuel excise.
- certain "strongly affected industries" will get direct assistance (e.g. coal-fired electricity generators). This assistance is in addition to separate funding for development of carbon capture and storage systems.
- agriculture will not be included at present (but will be reconsidered in 2013).
- the clearing of native forests (deforestation) is specifically excluded from the scheme.

Some of the strong features of the proposed Australian CPRS include its broad industry coverage and integration with international schemes. On the other hand, the likely impact of the scheme is softened considerably by concessions to some of the most greenhouse-intensive activities, and the adoption of a modest fallback position in the absence of international agreement, requiring only a 5 per cent emissions reduction by 2020.

The Rudd Government has also introduced a new expanded Renewable Energy Target (RET) scheme to achieve a 20 per cent share for renewable energy by 2020. The RET legislation increases the former MRET target of 9 500 GWh by more than four times to 45 000 GWh in 2020. The RET scheme also absorbs a range of existing and proposed State and Territory renewable energy schemes into a single national scheme.[114]

---

[113]   Prior to the Prime Minister's announcement on 27 April 2010, the Minister for Climate Change, Energy Efficiency and Water, Senator Penny Wong, had announced in 2009 a delay in the start date of the Carbon Pollution Reduction Scheme of one year, to 1 July 2011, in order to manage the impacts of the global recession. She also announced that a one-year fixed-price period will be introduced with permits to cost A$10 per tonne of carbon in 2011–12, and a transition to full market trading from 1 July 2012. *See* Press Release 4 May 2009, http://www.climatechange.gov.au/minister/wong/2009/media-releases/May/mr20090504.aspx, November 12, 2010.

[114]   The expanded national RET scheme is implemented through the following legislation: Renewable Energy (Electricity) Act 2000, Renewable Energy

4.3   State Government Responses

The responses to climate change by the Australian State governments is also highly significant, as they have historically exercised direct control and ownership of many key sectors producing greenhouse emissions, including electricity generation, transport, urban development, agriculture and forestry. Most of Australia's older coal-fired power stations were initially built, owned and managed by State governments. However, in the early 1990s, the Federal Government encouraged the States to adopt micro-economic reforms known as National Competition Policy, based upon the premise that State-owned monopolies were inefficient, and that "competition is a positive force that assists economic growth and job creation".[115] As a consequence, many formerly State-owned power stations were sold off to the private sector, and largely into foreign ownership, particularly in Victoria.[116] A similar effect was achieved in the transport sector through the privatization of metropolitan railways and tram networks in Victoria,[117] and the increased reliance upon public–private partnerships to build new toll-based motorways.[118] One of the most notable projects of

---

(Electricity) Regulations 2001 and Renewable Energy (Electricity) (Charge) Act 2000. The legislation above was amended by the following legislation passed by the Commonwealth Parliament on 20 August 2009: Renewable Energy (Electricity) Amendment Act 2009 and Renewable Energy (Electricity) (Charge) Amendment Act 2009. Legislation to implement the expanded national RET scheme was passed by the Commonwealth Parliament on 20 August 2009 and following Royal Assent, is now in place. *See also* the RET website http://www.climatechange.gov. au/government/initiatives/renewable-target.aspx, November 12, 2010.

[115]   Commonwealth of Australia, *National Competition Policy Report* (The Hilmer Report), 1993, page xv.

[116]   The sale of electricity infrastructure in Victoria yielded almost A$22 billion for major power stations including Yallourn, Hazelwood, Loy Yang A & B, Newport and Jeeralang, *see* Roarty, M., *Electricity Industry Restructuring: The State of Play,* Parliamentary Library, Science, Technology, Environment and Resources Group Research Paper 14, 1997–98, 25 May 1998, http://www.aph.gov. au/library/pubs/rp/1997-98/98rp14.htm#Major, November 12, 2010.

[117]   In 1999, five Victorian train and tram franchises were let to the private sector. VLine freight service was sold to an international consortium, Freight Victoria. Management of VLine country passenger trains, Bayside metropolitan trains and Yarra trams was awarded to National Express. The franchise for Yarra Trams was awarded to Metrolink and Hillside trams to Melbourne Transport Enterprises. *See* Department of Transport Victoria, *Annual Report 1998–99,* Part 3, Public Transport, 1999.

[118]   Victorian Government Public Accounts and Estimates Committee, *Report on Private Investment in Public Infrastructure,* October 2006, page 63, http://www. parliament.vic.gov.au/paec/inquiries/inquiry/129, November 12, 2010.

this type was Melbourne's CityLink toll-way completed at a cost of over A\$2 billion in 2000. The contract for this project effectively locks the City of Melbourne into a car-based transport policy for up to 54 years, including limitations upon the State government's ability to construct any competing infrastructure, such as a rail link to Tullamarine airport.[119]

Nevertheless the States have also maintained a close regulatory relationship with the electricity generation industry through traditional pollution control legislation, and they have used this relationship to promote reductions in greenhouse gas emissions. For instance, a State-based Greenhouse Gas Reduction Scheme (GGAS) commenced in New South Wales electricity sector on 1 January 2003, using project-based activities to offset emissions.[120] GGAS will cease to operate upon the commencement of the proposed CPRS. As a result the NSW Government has decided to transfer most of the incentives for energy efficiency activity in GGAS into a new Energy Savings Scheme which commenced on 1 July 2009. This Scheme has set an energy efficiency target of 0.4 per cent of total electricity sales, which will increase to 4 per cent in 2014.[121] In Victoria the Environment Protection Authority (EPA) has produced some innovative greenhouse reduction measures, through its pollution licensing powers under the Environment Protection Act 1970 (Vic), including the Industry Greenhouse Program[122] and Environment and Resource Efficiency Plans.[123]

The Industry Greenhouse Program (IGP) was developed in response to actions outlined in the 2002 Victorian Greenhouse Strategy (VGS).[124]

---

[119]   Russell, E. W., Waterman, E. and Seddon, N., *Audit Review of Government Contracts: Contracting, Privatisation, Probity and Disclosure in Victoria 1992–1999, An Independent Report to Government*, May 2000, http://www.dpc.vic.gov.au/auditreview/1_main.pdf, November 12, 2010.

[120]   The Greenhouse Gas Reduction Scheme was created in 2002 through amendments to the Electricity Supply Act 1995 (NSW) and the Electricity Supply (General) Regulation 2001 (NSW); *see* the Greenhouse Gas Reductions Scheme website, http://www.greenhousegas.nsw.gov.au/, November 12, 2010.

[121]   *See* the Energy Saving Scheme webpage, http://www.industry.nsw.gov.au/energy/sustainable/efficiency/scheme, November 12, 2010.

[122]   *See* the Industry Greenhouse Program webpage, http://www.epa.vic.gov.au/greenhouse/industry-greenhouse-program.asp, November 12, 2010.

[123]   *See* the Energy and Resource Efficiency Plan webpage, http://www.epa.vic.gov.au/bus/EREP/default.asp, November 12, 2010.

[124]   This Program is administered in accordance with the requirements of the *State Environment Protection Policy (Air Quality Management)* and its incorporated *Protocol for Environmental Management "Greenhouse Gas Emissions and Energy Efficiency in Industry"*, see EPA Victoria, *The EPA Victoria Industry Greenhouse Program – The Story So Far*, Publication No. 1035, February 2006.

This strategy required all Victorian enterprises subject to EPA's works approval and licensing system to implement cost-effective opportunities for improving energy efficiency and reducing greenhouse gas emissions. The IGP is the first regulatory greenhouse and energy efficiency program in Australia and one of the first worldwide. The Program was highly successful. When completed at the end of 2006 it had reduced greenhouse gas emissions by 1.23 million tonnes per annum and produced energy savings to businesses of A$38.2 million.[125]

Based upon the success of the IGP, the Victorian Government established a more comprehensive statutory scheme in 2007 to achieve water and waste management objectives along with greenhouse reductions. Under s 26H of the Environment Protection Act any Victorian business that uses at least 100 terajoules of energy or 120 megalitres of water in any financial year from 2006–07 must prepare an approved "Environment and Resource Efficiency Plan".[126] A plan must identify and assess actions that can reduce energy and water use and waste generation. If actions have a pay-back period of less than three years, then those actions must be implemented. The EPA has advised that business sites registered for EREP to date cover a large proportion of Victoria's energy and water use and include many companies and sectors that have not previously worked with the EPA.[127]

5.   BARRIERS TO CHANGE IN THE AUSTRALIAN TAXATION SYSTEM

Whilst the proposed CPRS has attracted an enormous amount of attention, other important findings of the Garnaut Review have been overshadowed. In particular Garnaut cautioned on the need to deal with "barriers to change":

> For the emissions trading scheme to have the desired effect of driving new consumption behaviour and investment decisions, it must be well integrated within the broader economy. Barriers to change must be removed or minimised in order that there may be an efficient economic response to the ever diminishing supply of permits.[128]

---

[125]   EPA Victoria, *Industry Greenhouse Program Key Outcomes*, Publication No. 1167, September 2007.
[126]   Details of what are scheduled activities and the various EREP obligations are set out in regulations *Environment Protection (Environment and Resource Efficiency Plans) Regulations* 2007 (S. R. No. 138/2007).
[127]   EPA Victoria, "Big Users, Big Gains", in *EPA Annual Report 2008*, page 15.
[128]   Garnaut, *op.cit.*, page 317 (Chapter 13 An Australian Policy Framework).

The Garnaut Review also explained how relevant barriers to change could be identified:

> Governments will need to review existing policies to ensure that they do not adversely interact with the objectives of successful mitigation and adaptation and, most immediately, the introduction of an emissions trading scheme. Reviews should cover federal and state taxes and subsidies, procurement policies, industry assistance programs, product and technology standards, accounting standards, taxation rules and public investment in research and development. The aim should be to identify perverse incentives that might inhibit adjustment to the effects of an emissions trading scheme or adaptation to the effects of climate change.[129]

The recommendation for a review of "federal and state taxes and subsidies" in order to identify "perverse incentives" was specifically included in the terms of reference of the Henry Review.[130] This chapter will now consider a range of "barriers to change" within the Australian taxation system that are likely to directly oppose the impact of the carbon price that is envisaged under proposed CPRS. This requires detailed consideration of how the taxation system applies to a range of greenhouse-intensive activities in sectors like natural resource extraction, agriculture, property development and transport. Before doing so, there is a need to distinguish between taxes, user charges and tax concessions. The classic definition of a tax is "a compulsory exaction of money by a public authority for public purposes, enforceable by law, and not a payment for services rendered."[131] Thus "user charges" imposed by governments for the use of natural resources are not a tax, but they are just as important as part of the price signal which influences the use of natural resources. Taxes themselves also need to be treated with caution as there are numerous exceptions and

---

[129]   *Ibid.,* page 304. Interestingly the Garnaut draft report was a little more specific: "The aim should also be to identify perverse incentives that might inadvertently inhibit investment in low-emissions technologies or promote activities associated with high emissions." *See* Garnaut Climate Change Review, Draft Report, June 2008, at para. 14.2.3.

[130]   The Australia's Future Tax System Review (the "Henry Review") was established by the Rudd Government in 2008 to examine Australia's tax and transfer system, including state taxes, and make recommendations to position Australia to deal with the demographic, social, economic and environmental challenges of the 21st century. *See* Terms of Reference, in Appendix A of Commonwealth of Australia Tax System*, op. cit.,* page 327, http://taxreview.treasury.gov.au/content/downloads/report/Architecture_of_Australias_Tax_and_Transfer_System_Revised.pdf, November 12, 2010.

[131]   Per Latham J in *Matthews v The Chicory Marketing Board* [1938] 60 CLR 263.

exemptions which moderate their effects. The Australian Treasury recognizes that such tax concessions are an alternative form of government spending and it has adopted the expression "tax expenditures" to describe them. The two key areas which need to be considered as barriers to effective carbon pricing are user charges for fossil fuels and tax expenditures which subsidize greenhouse intensive activities.

5.1 User Charges for Fossil Fuel Extraction

The Henry Review has recognized that user charges are particularly important for management of "common pool" natural resources "like fisheries, underground water and forests".[132] It recommended that such user charges should be high enough to ensure that the rate of exploitation of such resources does not exceed what is socially optimal,[133] and that there is also a strong case for the use of taxation and regulation to address market failures where environmental spillover costs arise.[134] In Australia, the State governments impose user charges on a wide range of natural resources including fossil fuels, water, timber and fisheries, often described as "royalties".[135] However, the States have historically encouraged natural resource exploitation to promote economic growth. As a result royalties for coal, oil, gas and other minerals are quite low, ranging from 2.5 per cent to 10 per cent of the resource value.[136] The Henry Review used Forestry Tasmania as an example of a government agency that often sells natural resources at a price below their "production" cost, using a formula which implicitly attaches a zero value to any environmental amenity associated with the forest.[137] Similarly, in Victoria, it has been calculated that

---

[132] *Ibid.*, page 330.

[133] *Ibid.*, page 333.

[134] *Ibid.*, page 336.

[135] There may be an argument that some State charges calculated by reference to volume of a resource used could be construed as duties of excise, which can only be validly imposed by the Federal Government under Section 90 the Commonwealth of Australia Constitution Act 1901; *see Ha & anor v State of New South Wales & Ors* [1997] HCA 34. However, this is unlikely if the charge is directly connected with the harvesting or taking of natural resources, *see Harper v Minister for Sea Fisheries* [1989] HCA 47; (1989) 168 CLR 314 (26 October 1989) and *Matthews v The Chicory Marketing Board* (1938) 60 CLR 263.

[136] Commonwealth of Australia Tax System, *op. cit.*, at 2.5 State taxes, Table 2.5 State mining royalties, http://taxreview.treasury.gov.au/content/Content. aspx?doc=html/home.htm, November 12, 2010.

[137] *Ibid.*, page 332 (Box E1-3 Does Forestry Tasmania charge users of forests appropriately?).

the commercial value of the timber extracted from the Thomson River catchment in Victoria is lower than the value of water losses caused by these forestry activities.[138] Recent research also shows that the carbon sequestration value of native eucalypt forests has been greatly under-estimated.[139] In the case of water provided by State-based water authorities the water price is generally very low by global standards, with urban water costing around A$1 per kilolitre and rural irrigators paying far less for water rights which can now be traded in rural water markets for prices in excess of A$1000 per megalitre.[140] It is relevant to note that this pattern of under-pricing of natural resources by State governments is clearly in conflict with the National Competition Principles, which prompted the States to privatize energy, water and transport utilities. One of the other key requirements of the NCP agenda is "full cost" pricing for natural resources, but there has been little evidence of progress in this area.[141]

The Henry Review drew a distinction between "common pool natural resources" and "non-renewable" mineral and fossil fuel reserves. In the latter case it argued that conventional State-based royalties failed to collect a sufficient return to the Australian community and thus a resource rent approach should be preferred, similar to the Petroleum Resource Rent Tax which has been successfully applied by the Federal Government to offshore petroleum projects since 1986.[142] This recommendation was

---

[138] The Central Highland Alliance, "An Investigation into Logging within Sites of National Significance" (the Baw Baw Report), http://www.tcha.org.au/Baw_Baw_Report/Baw_Baw_Report.html, November 12, 2010.

[139] Mackey, B. et al. (eds.), *Green Carbon: The Role of Natural Forests in Carbon Storage*, Australian National University (ANU) E Press).

[140] The Parliament of the Commonwealth of Australia, *The Value of Water: Inquiry into Australia's Management of Urban Water,* 2002, http://www.aph.gov.au/senate/committee/ecita_ctte/completed_inquiries/2002-04/water/report/report.pdf; and National Water Commission, *Australian Water Markets Report 2007–2008*, Section 3 National Summary of Trading Activity (Figure 3.4).

[141] Council of Australian Governments, *Competition Principles Agreement*, 11 April 1995 (As amended to 13 April 2007), Part 3 Competitive Neutrality Policy and Principles, Paragraph (5), www.coag.gov.au/, November 12, 2010.

[142] Henry Review, *op. cit.*, pages 221–5. The PRRT is imposed by the Petroleum Resource Rent Tax Act 1987 (Cth), which applies to the recovery of all petroleum products from Australian waters other than the North West Shelf and the joint petroleum development area in the Timor Sea. The calculation of taxable profit is prescribed by the Petroleum Resource Rent Tax Assessment Act 1987 (Cth) which currently applies 40 per cent "rent" on the "taxable profit" of a petroleum project. The PRRT raised $1.25 billion in revenue for 2009–10; *see also* Budget Paper No. 1: Budget Strategy and Outlook 2010–1, Statement 5 Revenue, Table 7 Company and Other Related Income Taxation Revenue, pages 5–21.

adopted in the 2010 Federal Budget in the form of a new "Resource Super Profits Tax" to be introduced from 2012–13. It is forecast that the new resource tax will eventually collect revenue in the order of A$9 billion per annum.[143] Although this proposal was described as a "tax" it should not be considered a true environmental tax as there is no attempt to reflect the marginal social cost of the relevant extractive industries, and much of the revenue collected is to be "re-invested" in those industries as infrastructure funding, exploration write-offs and company tax reductions.[144] The new tax is also designed to replace most of the current State mining royalty regimes, and thus it is more properly defined as a de facto user charge.

In conclusion, it seems that user charges for fossil fuels and other natural resources in Australia have not been rigorously imposed in the past, but the new Federal Resource Super Profits Tax may significantly increase the revenue collected in this way for the minerals and fossil fuel sector. Thus, the current under-pricing of fossil fuel extractions may end in 2012, and at least one significant barrier to change with respect to the CPRS may be removed.

5.2 Tax Expenditures

The Australian Treasury publishes an annual "Tax Expenditures Statement" listing the estimated value of the major tax expenditures provided through the federal taxation system each year.[145] Some of the largest tax expenditures are provided to the most greenhouse-intensive and environmentally damaging sectors of the Australian economy, namely agriculture, property development and transport.

---

[143] *See* Prime Minister Kevin Rudd and Treasurer Wayne Swan, Joint Media Release "Stronger Fairer Simpler: A Tax Plan for Our Future", Commonwealth Treasurer Media Release, No. 028, 2 May 2010. Full details of the new Resource Super Profits Tax are contained in the Final Report of the Henry Review: Commonwealth of Australia, *Australia's Future Tax System, Final Report to the Treasurer*, December 2009, http://taxreview.treasury.gov.au/content/Content. aspx?doc=html/home.htm, November 12, 2010.

[144] It may be questioned whether anything other than a completely prohibitive amount could ever be calculated in the case of fossil fuels and climate change. The Stern Review has estimated that business as usual could lead to economic losses in the order of 5–20 per cent of global per capita consumption. *See* Stern, *op. cit.*, Chapter 6 Economic Modelling of Climate-change Impacts.

[145] The latest Taxation Expenditure Statement reporting for the 2008–09 year was released on 29 January 2010, http://www.treasury.gov.au/contentitem. asp?NavId=022&ContentID=1719, November 12, 2010.

5.2.1 Agriculture

The National Greenhouse Gas Inventory shows that agriculture and deforestation contributed about 23 per cent of total Australian emissions.[146] The first comprehensive report on the "State of the Environment" in Australia was produced by the Federal Government in 1996.[147] This report found a wide range of environmental degradation had been caused by agricultural activities in Australia since the first European settlement. In particular, it found that "inland waters in southern Australia are in poor shape",[148] "soil erosion remains a problem, and other forms of degradation, such as salinisation, are not adequately addressed."[149] Other pressures include fertilizers and other chemicals used in agriculture and forestry,[150] with increased sediments and nutrients contributing to declining water quality in inshore areas of the Great Barrier Reef.[151] The most recent 2006 SoE report found that agriculture is still the main use of land in Australia, occupying some 62 per cent of the continent, and whilst it returns high economic benefits, it also contributes to a wide range of significant environmental problems, including habitat loss, surface soil loss, salinity, and soil and water quality issues.[152]

With such a wide range of adverse external environmental impacts arising from agriculture there seems to be a strong case for the application of an environmental taxation approach. However, successive Australian governments have generally adopted a wide variety of strategies to protect and subsidize this sector including tariffs, public funding of irrigation infrastructure and an extensive range of taxation concessions. Whilst there has been a significant dismantling of tariff protection under international trade agreements, subsidized infrastructure and substantial taxation concessions have continued. In response to the unpredictable Australian

---

[146] Australian Government Inventory, *op. cit.*, at Appendix 2, Table 1 and Table 6.

[147] The Environment Protection and Biodiversity Conservation Act 1999 (Cth) requires the Minister for Environment Protection, Heritage and the Arts to table in Parliament every five years a report on the State of the Environment in Australia. The first report of this type was published in 1996 and subsequent reports have been produced in 2001 and 2006.

[148] Commonwealth of Australia, *Australia: State of the Environment 1996, An Independent Report Presented to the Commonwealth Minister for the Environment by the State of the Environment Advisory Council,* 1996, Executive Summary, page 13.

[149] *Ibid.*, page 14.

[150] *Ibid.*, pages 22–4.

[151] *Ibid.*, page 39.

[152] Commonwealth of Australia, *Australia: State of the Environment 2006.*

climate and variable commodity prices, flexible income recognition rules have been provided for taxation purposes, including income averaging for primary production income,[153] and the Farm Management Deposits Scheme.[154] The need for large up-front capital expenditure to acquire land, machinery and access to water has resulted in deductions for many forms of capital expenditure including accelerated write-off for machinery, new horticultural plants,[155] the cost of establishing grapevines,[156] expenditure on water facilities[157] and timber plantations.[158] More recently, deductions have been created for environmental management expenditures, including Landcare operations,[159] environmental protection expenditure[160] and mine site rehabilitation.[161] Primary producers also benefit from a range of tax concessions under other Federal, State and local government taxation schemes. For example, the sale of farming land is exempt from the Federal Goods and Service Tax,[162] and a rebate for Federal excise duty applies to diesel fuel used in primary production.[163] Land used for primary production is also generally exempt from State land taxes,[164] and certain transfers of land used for primary production may also be exempt from stamp duty.[165] Municipal rates and water charges are also commonly lower for agricultural land use than they are for residential or industrial purposes.

Despite these numerous tax concessions, Australian agriculture has declined in importance from about 30 per cent of gross domestic product since early in the last century to less than 3 per cent in 2003.[166] In the last 15 years, this sector has suffered a prolonged decline in rainfall over southern Australia, followed by record rainfall and flooding in the summer of 2010. This pattern of weather extremes is predicted to continue and worsen under IPCC climate modelling, with continuing adverse financial

---

[153]   ITAA97, Division 392.
[154]   ITAA36, Schedule 2G (Sections 393–1 to 393–65).
[155]   ITAA97, Sections.40–515 to 40–575.
[156]   *Ibid.*
[157]   *Ibid.*
[158]   ITAA36, Sections 82KZMG.
[159]   ITAA97, Sub-Division 40G.
[160]   ITAA97, Section 40–755.
[161]   ITAA97, Section 40–735.
[162]   *See* A New Tax System (Goods and Services Tax) Act 1999, Section 38–480.
[163]   *See Excise Act 1901* (Cth), Section 78A.
[164]   *See,* e.g. Land Tax Act 1958 (Vic), Section 9 (1) (ga).
[165]   *See,* e.g., Duties Act 2000 (Vic) at s 56.
[166]   Australian Bureau of Statistics, *Australian Year Book 2005*, Chapter 13 Industry structure and performance, page 428.

outcomes in agriculture.[167] The general picture which emerges is that the Australian agriculture sector is contributing a substantial level of greenhouse emissions along with numerous other adverse environmental impacts, whilst the viability of many traditional family farms is heavily dependent upon generous taxation concessions and "off-farm" income. The Australian taxation system entrenches these problems by allowing farm losses to be used as a tax shelter for off-farm income. This has been exploited by many high-wealth individuals who enjoy farm ownership for lifestyle purposes, and also by the promoters of numerous mass-marketed agribusiness investment schemes, which are often driven by tax deductions rather than commercial viability. Such schemes are often destined to economic failure, which causes not only losses to naïve investors but also many unnecessary environmental impacts.

5.2.2 Property development

Another highly significant contributor to Australian greenhouse emissions is the residential and commercial buildings sector, which is responsible for about 23 per cent of Australia's total greenhouse emissions.[168] Census data for Melbourne shows that between 1991 and 2003 there was a significant increase in the average floor area of homes, whilst in the same period there was a steady *decline* in the average number of persons in a household. These factors have combined to produce a substantial increase in both aggregate and per capita greenhouse emissions.[169] However, the residential housing sector and a large proportion of the commercial building sector will not be directly affected by the proposed CPRS. Garnaut recommended a range of regulatory responses such as energy efficiency standards for buildings and appliances to address this problem.[170] Unfortunately, these measures do not deal with the more fundamental problem of energy intensive "lifestyle" preferences. There are several aspects of the Australian income tax system which appear to provide a perverse incentive in this context:

---

[167] *See* Martin, P., Crooks, S. and Phillips, P. "Farm Financial Performance 2009–10 – Projections for Broadacre and Dairy Farms: Broadacre Farm Incomes Lower in 2009–10", *Abare Australian Commodities December Quarter*, Volume 16, Number 4, http://www.abare.gov.au/interactive/09ac_dec/htm/farm_perf.htm, November 12, 2010.

[168] Centre for International Economics, *Capitalising on the Building Sector's Potential to Lessen the Costs of A Broad Based GHG Emission Cut,* (Centre for International Economics, Canberra), 2007, page 13.

[169] Department of Planning and Community Development, "Melbourne Atlas 2006 Housing", 2006, http://www.dse.vic.gov.au/DSE/dsenres.nsf, November 12, 2010.

[170] Garnaut, *op. cit.*, Chapter 17.

- Capital gains derived from sale of a "main residence" are exempt from capital gains tax.[171] This is one of the major tax expenditures listed in 2009, with forgone revenue estimated at A$14 billion.[172]
- Capital gains are generally taxed at *lower rates* than employment or business income, as they are only assessable upon realization and the taxable gain can be reduced by a 50 per cent "discount" in most cases.[173] The taxable gain may also be reduced by capital losses and revenue losses, with the possibility of a further 50 per cent discount in the case of "active assets" (used in a business activity). The capital gains tax discount is one of the largest tax concessions provided by the Australian government, with an estimated cost of A$5.38 billion for 2009–10.[174]
- The allowance of deductions for revenue losses on "negatively-geared" residential investment properties is another substantial tax concession in the Australian system, with the cost of forgone revenue estimated to be in the order of A$5 billion.[175] This concession encourages investors to borrow large sums with the expectation of deducting investment expenses against income from other sources in the short term, whilst a concessionally taxed capital gain will be obtained in the longer term.[176]

The broad effect of these tax concessions for property development has been to strongly encourage Australians to create private wealth through

---

[171] Income Tax Assessment Act 1997 (Cth), Subdivision 118–B Main residence.
[172] Commonwealth of Australia, 2009 *Tax Expenditures Statement,* Item E4, page 154.
[173] *See* Income Tax Assessment Act 1997 (Cth), Part 3–1 Capital Gains and Losses.
[174] Commonwealth of Australia, 2007 *Tax Expenditures Statement,* Item E9, pages 10 and 164.
[175] This revenue forgone by negative gearing is not separately quantified by Treasury as it is considered a "design feature" of the tax system and thus outside the chosen definition of "tax expenditure". According to a 2003 Parliamentary Library research paper the cost to revenue of negative gearing in Australia was in the order of $1.4 billion by 2002, which would suggest it is now costing at least $3 or 4 billion. *See* Smith, J., "Tax Expenditures: The 30 Billion Twilight Zone of Government Spending", (Research Paper No. 8), 2002–03, page 9. The Economics Editor for *The Age* Tim Colebatch, recently estimated the forgone revenue at $5 billion. *See* Colebatch, T., "Negative Gearing Top Tax Break", *The Age,* Saturday 27 March, 2010.
[176] Income Tax Assessment Act 1997 (Cth), Section 8–1. Under this provision there is generally no requirement for income derived from an investment asset to exceed the expenses allowed as a deduction.

property investments. This violates the equity principle, as these concessions clearly favor citizens with passive investment income (who tend to be wealthy) rather than citizens who derive their income from employment (commonly less wealthy). For example, wealthy homeowners in elite city districts such as Point Piper in Sydney, or Toorak in Melbourne, can generate multi-million dollar profits on selling their homes without any liability for capital gains tax.[177] The concessional treatment of capital gains also allows property investors to minimize tax through the use of interposed entities (that is, companies and trusts). In this way a taxable capital gain can be allocated (split) amongst a group of beneficiaries (for example, family members, or entities with tax losses) which can further reduce the liability, often to zero or very low effective marginal rates.

Another regressive consequence of these tax concessions is reduced housing affordability, by putting heavily geared investors in direct competition with home buyers. A recent study has shown that over one million low- to middle-income households in Australia spend more than 30 per cent of their income on housing, which is very high by OECD standards.[178] As a consequence, first home buyers find it cheaper to buy a home in the expansive new subdivisions on the outer urban fringes where the prevailing housing style is large, energy hungry, and highly automobile dependent. Local government planning laws have also evolved in tandem to support the growth of low density "auto cities".[179] These outer suburban communities impose high infrastructure costs on local and State governments as well as displacing some of Australia's most productive agricultural land.

The taxation rules also create barriers to change in the rental housing market. There are a range of incentives provided to encourage homeowners to invest in greenhouse friendly improvements such as insulation and solar panels.[180] However, landlords are unlikely to invest in these

---

[177] *See* "How One Man Makes $8200 A day by Living in Sydney's Best Street", *Sydney Morning Herald*, April 6, 2008.

[178] National Centre for Economic and Social Modelling, referred to by Michelle Grattan in "Rudd Determined to Act on Housing Affordability", *The Age,* 3 March, 2008.

[179] Newman and Kenworthy have pointed out that the adverse social and environmental impacts of auto cities has been traded off erroneously by decision makers who saw economic benefits from increased mobility. Newman, P. and Kenworthy, J., "The Problem of Automobile Dependence at the End of the Twentieth Century", in *Sustainability and Cities: Overcoming Automobile Dependence*, Island Press, 1999, page 52.

[180] *See* note 112 above. Under the Federal Renewable Energy Target program, Solar Credits are provided in the form of additional tradable Renewable Energy

energy efficiency mechanisms as the reduced energy bills will only accrue to the tenant. Similarly a tenant is unlikely to so invest in energy efficiency if the long term capital benefit will accrue to the landlord.

The Henry Review was mainly concerned with investment distortions rather than environmental consequences. Accordingly, it recommended a 40 per cent savings income discount to individuals for non-business income in the form of interest, residential rental income, capital gains (and losses); and interest expenses related to listed shares.[181] However, in conjunction with the 2010 Federal Budget the Government has stated that it "will not implement . . . at any stage", a reduction to the CGT discount, a discount to negative gearing deductions, or a change grandfathering arrangements for CGT.[182]

5.2.3   Transport

Transport emissions make up about 14 per cent of Australia's total emissions and also one of the strongest areas of emissions growth (particularly passenger cars and light commercial vehicles).[183] Garnaut recognized that "decarbonising" the transport system would require policy steps beyond the CPRS scheme. In particular Garnaut recommended a shift to denser urban form with improved public transport infrastructure, and secondly, the removal of a range of policies that distort the costs of vehicle ownership and use.[184] The urban form issue has already been mentioned above with regard to property development. With regard to ownership and usage of motor vehicles, there are two major tax concessions to be considered; the fuel tax credit scheme and the fringe benefits tax treatment of employer-provided cars.

5.2.4   The fuel tax credit scheme

Petrol and diesel are subject to a Federal excise duty of 38.143 c/L and also subject to GST at 10 per cent.[185] The petrol and diesel excises raised

---

Certificates or "RECs" for eligible small-scale solar PV, wind and hydro-electricity systems installed on or after 9 June 2009. Further incentives are provided by "feed-in tariffs" provided by State-based electricity suppliers. *See* Dooley, A."Solar Electricity Incentives", *Choice online*, 2009, http://www.choice.com.au/Reviews-and-Tests/Household/Energy-and-water/Solar/Solar-electricity-incentives/Page/Introduction.aspx, November 12, 2010.

[181]   Henry Review, *op. cit.*, Recommendation 14.
[182]   *See* Prime Minister Kevin Rudd and Treasurer Wayne Swan, Joint Press Release, note 141 above.
[183]   Australian Government Inventory.
[184]   Garnaut, *op. cit.,* Chapter 17.
[185]   *See* Commonwealth of Australia, *Budget Paper No. 1: Budget Strategy and Outlook 2010–11*, Statement 5 Revenue, Table 9 Excise and Customs Duty

over A\$13 billion in 2009–10.[186] However, despite the large sums collected, Australia's fuel taxes are the fourth lowest of all OECD countries.[187] Consideration of the tax rate alone is misleading in this context, as over A\$4 billion in fuel excise is reimbursed through the fuel tax credit scheme.[188] The petrol excises were originally hypothecated for road construction purposes, and thus it is difficult to argue that they are environmental taxes in the Pigouvian sense. When the GST was introduced in 2000, the system was reformed to remove fuel taxes from business inputs, so that its incidence falls primarily upon private consumption of fuel.[189] The CPRS proposals will provide a cent-for-cent reduction in the fuel excise to offset fuel price increases upon households and heavy vehicle users. This household compensation, together with the fuel tax credit available to the business sector, considerably undermines the supposed objective of the CPRS, of putting a price on carbon emissions. The Henry Review has recommended that fuel taxes should be replaced by a system of targeted road user charges, taking into account urban congestion, energy content and road damage caused by heavy vehicles,[190] and that the fuel tax credit should be retained but limited to genuine off-road use.[191]

5.2.5   FBT car concessions

The private use of employer-provided cars is referred to as a "car benefit" under the Australian Fringe Benefits Tax (FBT) rules.[192] Concessional

---

Revenue, pages 5–24. Aviation fuels are subject to a lower excise rate of 28.54 per cent.

[186]   *Ibid.*, Table 10.

[187]   Commonwealth of Australia Tax System, *op. cit.*, page 212 (Chart 5.12: Taxes as percentage of unleaded petrol price in 28 OECD countries).

[188]   Australian Taxation Office (ATO), *Taxation Statistics 2006–07*, Canberra.

[189]   As part of the arrangements for introduction of a Federal Goods and Services Tax from 1 July 2000, the Commonwealth took over a range of volume based licence fees formerly collected by the States.

[190]   Henry Review, *op. cit.,* Recommendation 65, discussed at page 377 (Section E3–3 Road pricing should reflect social costs).

[191]   *Ibid.*, page 398 (The future of fuel tax).

[192]   The Fringe Benefits Tax Assessment Act 1986 (Cth) provides that fringe benefits tax (FBT) applies to employers who provide non-cash benefits to staff in lieu of salary or wages. The system requires payment of FBT by the employer on the taxable value of the benefit, at the flat rate of 46.5 per cent, whilst making the benefit value exempt from income tax for the employee. The taxable value of a car benefit is determined by a formula which applies a prescribed percentage to the base value of the car. The prescribed percentage varies according to the annual number of kilometres travelled by the vehicle. The environmental anomaly is

valuation rules for a car benefit provide a strong incentive for high income employees to take a company car in lieu of salary (that is, a "salary sacrifice" arrangement). This valuation formula actually *reduces* the FBT payable as the annual kilometers travelled increases. Not surprisingly, car benefits are the most common of all fringe benefits.[193] The cost of this concession in forgone revenue is estimated to be A$1050 million for the 2009–10 year.[194] The value of this concession is also considerably enhanced by an associated exemption of car running expenses such as petrol, registration and insurance.[195] In practical terms these concessions generally provide a total subsidy of several thousand dollars per year to recipients of a company car. Employer-provided car parking is also preferentially taxed under the FBT rules.[196] The Federal Government completed a review of the automobile industry in 2008, which recommended a new FBT statutory rate table to reform this anomaly.[197] The Garnault Review also endorsed the Bracks Report, concluding that:

> . . . the current treatment of vehicles and parking spaces distorts decisions towards private vehicle use and greater demand of transport overall. These provisions could be improved by ensuring the salary sacrifice arrangements are mode neutral, and amending the statutory fraction method to ensure it is distance neutral.[198]

From a greenhouse reduction perspective, the car benefit concession is clearly inconsistent with policies to minimize the use of private vehicles for commuting and traffic congestion in central business districts. Cities like London and Singapore have introduced congestion taxes to reduce

---

that the percentage starts at 26 per cent for vehicles which travel less than 15,000 kilometres per annum and then it progressively *reduces* to as little as 7 per cent for vehicles travelling over 40,000 km.
    [193] The ATO, *Taxation Statistics 2006–2007* reported that 34 820 car benefits were provided in for the 2007–2008 FBT year, *see* Table 3.
    [194] Commonwealth of Australia, *2007 Tax Expenditures Statement,* at D26, page 150.
    [195] Fringe Benefits Tax Assessment Act 1986 (Cth), Section 53.
    [196] The 2007 Taxation Expenditure Statement identifies a range of tax concessions for car parking including exemption from FBT for small business employers ($17 million in 2007–08), discounted FBT valuation ($22 million) and car parking provided by scientific, religious, charitable or public education institutions or for certain disabled employees (not quantified, categorised as over $10 million). *See 2007 Tax Expenditure Statement*, items D28, D34 and D44.
    [197] Commonwealth of Australia, *Review of Australia's Automotive Industry: Final Report* (Bracks Review), Canberra, 2008, page 72.
    [198] Garnaut Climate Review, *op. cit.*, page 527.

congestion and improve environmental conditions.[199] City parking levies have been introduced in recent years in Sydney, Perth and Melbourne.[200] One of the few arguments in favor of the car-benefit anomaly is that it supports Australian car manufacturers; however, this point is not convincing as the concession also applies for the acquisition of imported vehicles.[201] The Henry Review considered that the car-benefit valuation formula was anomalous mainly from an equity perspective and accordingly it recommended that the formula be changed to value car benefits using a uniform statutory fraction of 20 per cent regardless of how many kilometers are travelled.[202]

5.2.6 Tax expenditure analysis

The role of tax expenditures in the context of the proposed CPRS was one of the matters to be considered by the Henry Review.[203] The Canadian tax scholar Neil Brooks presented a very comprehensive paper on the history and importance of the tax expenditure concept to a business tax reform colloquium during the consultation period.[204] Brooks outlined the major theoretical objections to the tax expenditure concept and noted the connection between tax expenditures and the role of government in a market economy. Significantly, he argued that tax expenditures are in essence spending programs which have nothing to do with the tax system, and hence they should not be evaluated by the traditional taxation criteria of equity, neutrality and simplicity.[205] The importance of this point is underlined by the fact that measured tax expenditures in Australia now represent over A$100 billion of the Federal Budget Government or 8.5 per

---

[199]   *See* London Congestion Charge website, http://www.tfl.gov.uk/roadusers/congestioncharging/default.aspx, November 12, 2010.

[200]   *See* e.g., Office of the Premier of Victoria, "City Car Parking Levy to Ease Congestion", Media Release, Friday 22 April, 2005.

[201]   Commonwealth of Australia, *Review of Australia's Automotive Industry, Final Report*, 22 July 2008, page 105.

[202]   Henry Review, *op. cit.*, page 47 (Recommendation 9(b)).

[203]   The Terms of Reference for the Henry Review include a number of environmental considerations including the interaction between the tax system and the CPRS, *see* Appendix A of the Commonwealth of Australia Tax System, http://taxreview.treasury.gov.au/content/Content.aspx?doc=html/home.htm, November 12, 2010.

[204]   Brooks, N., "The Importance of the Tax Expenditure Concept to Australia's Future Tax System Review Panel", (Notes for a Presentation to Business Tax Reform Colloquium at Sydney), 23–25 February, 2009.

[205]   *Ibid.*, page 3.

cent of GDP.[206] It follows that tax expenditures must be evaluated using the same budgetary criteria used in assessing other government spending programs. Brooks advocates that this would normally involve at least a four-stage inquiry, including consideration of: [207]

i)   whether the measures are meeting a valid government objective;
ii) whether the program is fair and efficient;
iii) whether other policy instruments would better achieve the program objectives; and
iv) if the tax system is to be used, what is the most appropriate design of the instrument?

The Henry Review did not contradict this view, but its conclusions on tax expenditures were modest, including recommendations that the Budget rules should recognize the spending character of tax expenditures by encouraging trade-offs between tax expenditures and spending programs,[208] the publication of detailed information on tax expenditures should be separate from the Mid-Year Economic and Fiscal Outlook (MYEFO),[209] that reporting standards be developed for identification and measurement of tax expenditures as a basis for reporting the broader economic and distributional effects of tax expenditures in a periodic Tax and Transfer Analysis Statement,[210] and that the Council of Australian Governments should examine the ways in which the States could uniformly report tax expenditures.[211]

6. LESSONS FOR EAST ASIA

This chapter has reviewed regulatory responses to climate change in Australia with a particular focus on a range of tax expenditures which in effect, operate as "barriers to change" that may significantly undermine the intended objectives of the proposed CPRS emissions trading scheme. In considering what lessons emerge for East Asia, it should be recognized that Australia is one of the world's most energy-and-greenhouse-emission intensive nations on a per capita basis, and also an Annex 1 party to

---

[206] Australian Government Treasury, *2009 Tax Expenditures Statement*, at 4 (Table 1.1).
[207] *Ibid.*, pages 22–3.
[208] Henry Review, *op. cit.*, Recommendation 135.
[209] Henry Review, *op. cit.*, Recommendation 136.
[210] Henry Review, *op. cit.*, Recommendation 137 (*see also* Recommendation 132).
[211] Henry Review, *op. cit.*, Recommendation 138.

the Kyoto Protocol.[212] By contrast, per capita greenhouse emissions for Asian nations are significantly lower.[213] However, the industrialization of many East Asian nations continues at a great pace, with the International Monetary Fund predicting continued growth at the rate of 8.5 per cent in 2010.[214] Much of that economic growth is manifest in rapid urbanization with increasing use of energy and consequential greenhouse emissions. The World Energy Outlook predicts that non-OECD countries, will account for 81 per cent of the growth in energy use in cities to 2030.[215] China, India, and South Korea are already all in the top 10 nations in terms of aggregate emissions.[216] Thus there will be increasing pressure on the nations of East Asia to commit to emission-reductions strategies, and this is already influencing greenhouse policy decisions, with China, India and Korea having pledged significant emission reductions following the 2009 Conference of the Parties at Copenhagen.[217]

Within this context, the recent experiences with greenhouse reduc-

---

[212] Annex 1 refers to developed country parties listed at Annex 1 to the UNFCCC in accordance with Article 4 (2) of that Convention. Only Australia, Japan and New Zealand are Annex 1 countries in the East Asia region. Annex 1 countries are committed to meeting specified greenhouse reduction targets within the Kyoto Protocol commitment period ending in 2012.

[213] The per capita greenhouse emissions of Annex 1 parties averaged 11.1 tons per person in 2001, compared to 1.6 tons per person in Asia. UNFCCC, *United Nations Framework Convention on Climate Change, The First Ten Years*, 2004, page 34 (Table 2.3 Key macroeconomic and greenhouse gas indicators, 2001).

[214] Lipsky, J., "Realizing the Potential of Asia's Developing Economies", (a speech by First Deputy Managing Director, International Monetary Fund, Hanoi), 22 March, 2010, http://www.imf.org/external/np/speeches/2010/032210. htm, November 12, 2010.

[215] International Energy Agency, *World Energy Outlook 2008 – Global Energy Trends to 2030*, Chapter 8: Energy Use in Cities, page 184.

[216] Australian Government Inventory, *op. cit.*

[217] UNFCCC, "Appendix II – Nationally appropriate mitigation actions of developing country Parties" in Press Release "UNFCCC receives list of government climate pledges", 2 February, 2010, http://unfccc.int/home/items/5265. php, November 12, 2010. China will endeavor to lower its carbon dioxide emissions per unit of GDP by 40–45 per cent by 2020 compared to the 2005 level; *see* Su, W.,"Letter to UNFCCC" from Director-General, Department of Climate Change, National Development and Reform Commission of China (National Focal Point), January 28, 2010. India will endeavor to reduce the emissions intensity of its GDP by 20–25 per cent by 2020 in comparison to the 2005 level; *see* Rajani Ranjan Rashmi, "Letter from Joint Secretary Ministry of Environments and Forests", 30 January, 2010. South Korea has advised its intention to reduce national greenhouse gas emissions by 30 per cent from business as usual emissions by 2020, *see* "Memorandum from Ministry of Foreign Affairs and Trade, Republic of Korea to UNFCCC", 25 January, 2010.

tion measures in Australia can provide useful guidance to the nations of East Asia. In particular, the recent attempts to introduce market-based mechanisms and the recognition of various barriers to change are highly relevant. The first lesson that emerges is that "no regrets" voluntary and information-based strategies initially adopted in Australia have had little effect in reducing greenhouse emissions since the 1990 base year. The national inventory shows that Australia's national emissions have increased by around 30 per cent in this period, with energy-related emissions increasing by 42 per cent.[218] It is very clear that meaningful emission reductions cannot be achieved under a "business as usual" approach.

The second lesson is that reliance upon market-based instruments to reduce greenhouse emissions is unlikely to succeed where there are deeply entrenched barriers to change in the form of tax concessions and subsidies which tend to support "business as usual". Australia's highly complicated taxation system and strong industry lobby groups have contributed to many forms of industry support delivered through the tax system as "tax expenditures". For instance, capital gains tax concessions, negative gearing, car fringe benefits and fuel tax credits, have created distortions in favor of greenhouse-intensive activities in sectors like agriculture, property development and transport. The latest proposals are intended to create a "carbon price" to discourage greenhouse emissions across the whole Australian economy, but a wide range of underlying tax expenditures in these key problematic sectors will significantly counteract this objective. This weakness will be exacerbated by political compromises; to shelter and compensate "emissions-intensive" and "strongly affected" industries and to exclude agriculture and deforestation.

The third lesson from Australia is that robust systems for reporting and removal of tax expenditures need to be put in place to make tax expenditure programs transparent and reviewable. It is important to recognize the true character of tax expenditures as government spending programs. Normally, government spending is clearly quantified and carefully scrutinized within the budget process. By contrast the value of tax expenditures is often unknown and benefits continue indefinitely with very little public scrutiny. Accountability and transparency can only be achieved if tax expenditures are evaluated using the same budgetary criteria used in assessing other government spending programs.

---

[218]   Australian Government Inventory, *op. cit.*, at Appendix 3, Table 1.

9. Green taxation: the New Zealand story

Shelley Griffiths*

1. INTRODUCTION

When I began background research for this chapter, I went to the website "Google New Zealand" and entered a search for pages from New Zealand matching the search term "behaviour modification and green tax". The first "hit" was to the New Zealand Green Party's youth affairs policy where "green" and "tax" and "behaviour modification" happened to appear in the co-leader's policy statement but in a totally unlinked way. Subsequent "hits" were of no more relevance. Not to be deterred, I altered the search to "behaviour modification and tax". Here, the first two hits were references to a US case appearing in New Zealand websites and thereafter the subsequent hits were of no more relevance. I share this anecdote, not to demonstrate my haphazard research skills, but to highlight the fact that behaviour modification and tax are strange bedfellows in the New Zealand context.

Since 1984, successive New Zealand governments have remained committed to a broad-base low-rate income tax model. The main focus of reform in the 1980s was on broadening the tax base and lowering marginal rates. It was a move toward bringing the tax base closer to the economic concept of income. Previously, the system was one that could be described as narrow-base high-rate, and a major cause of that was the provision of incentives or concessions for activities that were seen as having social or economic merit. The reforms of the 1980s were predicated in large measure on a rejection of that policy.[1] Notwithstanding the broad-base low-rate model, there has never been any appetite in New Zealand for a comprehensive capital gains

* The author gives her thanks to research assistants Josh Williams and Peter Barnett at the Faculty of Law, University of Otago.

[1] Tax Review 2001, *Final Report*, October 2001, http://www.treasury.govt. nz/publications/reviews-consultation/taxreview2001, November 11, 2010. Pages 5–17 describe the pre-1984 regime and the changes to it. *See also* Inland Revenue Department, *Briefing Papers to the incoming Government*, Volume 1, December

tax. The three main tax bases are personal income, company income and expenditure on goods and services. The reform of the tax system occurred at speed throughout the 1980s and then the pace slowed somewhat in the 1990s (with more emphasis on the administration architecture). In 2001, a committee was formed to conduct a far-reaching stock take of the tax system. The 2001 Tax Review (commonly referred to as the McLeod Committee) was overtly an occasion to consider whether the "architecture" of the tax system was appropriate and it concluded that it was. By 2009 it seemed it was time for another stock take. In the briefing to the incoming Minister of Finance following the 2008 election, the Inland Revenue Department warned that although the tax system was widely believed to be fair, and compliance costs were low by international standards,[2] there were some "growing pressures" because to an "increasing extent, the tax paid by an individual depends on the way in which income is earned".[3] The Department urged the new Minister that reforming the tax system to create greater coherence was necessary. A few months later, the Minister welcomed the establishment of a Tax Working Group, co-ordinated by Victoria University of Wellington and including experts from the private sector and academia as well as the Treasury and Inland Revenue to consider the medium-term direction of the tax system and assess policy options. Over the course of 2009, the Working Group has released several background papers encompassing the broad range of tax policy issues. The Working Group was due to release a report on 1 December 2009,[4] and in the event managed to keep close to a very tight timetable with release of the Report in January 2010. Both the 2001 and 2009 Reviews considered environmental taxation. Sandwiched between those two events was New Zealand's ratification of the Kyoto Protocol and development of policy responses to meet New Zealand's commitments. The story of green taxation in New Zealand has two strands to it. The first is the rejection of eco-taxation as a behavioural modification instrument. This stance has more than anything been

---

1999, page 35, http://www.taxpolicy.ird.govt.nz/publications/index.php?catid=3, November 11, 2010.

  [2] A World Bank report put New Zealand in the top ten countries in terms of ease of paying taxes. The World Bank and PricewaterhouseCoopers, *Paying Taxes 2008: The Global Picture*, page 17, http://www.doingbusiness.org/features/taxes2008.aspx, November 11, 2010.

  [3] Inland Revenue, *Briefing for the Incoming Minister*, November 2008, page 5, http://www.taxpolicy.ird.govt.nz/publications/files/IRBIM2008.pdf, November 11, 2010.

  [4] *See also* New Zealand Treasury, *Challenges and Choices: New Zealand's Long-term Fiscal Statement,* October 2009, pages 25–29, http://www.treasury.govt.nz/government/longterm/fiscalposition/2009/ltfs-09.pdf, November 11, 2010.

shaped by the low-rate broad-base model accompanied by rejection of concessions and incentives. There has been some limited use of fees and charges to influence behaviour, but this has not been widespread. New Zealand policy makers have evidenced a preference for education and only limited use of direct incentives to encourage such things as home insulation.[5] The second is the acceptance and then rejection of carbon tax as the appropriate instrument for meeting Kyoto targets.

This chapter therefore looks at the 2001 and 2009 reviews, which serve as bookends to the Kyoto debate. It also considers, based on the categorization by the 2001 Review, the use of eco-charges. Finally, it reviews those instances, principally but not exclusively in the Income Tax Act 2007, where specific tax rules deal with environmental protection measures and conversely with the tax treatment of activities that might have adverse environmental outcomes.

2. NEW ZEALAND AND CLIMATE CHANGE

New Zealand's emissions profile is unique among developed countries, as Table 9.1 shows:

Table 9.1   New Zealand greenhouse gas emissions 2007

By gas:	%	
Carbon dioxide	47	
Methane	35	
Nitrous Oxide	17	
Other	1	
By sector:	%	% increase/ (decrease) since 1990
Agriculture	48	12
Energy	43	39
Industrial Processes	6	(25)

Note: Ministry for the Environment, *New Zealand's Greenhouse Gas Inventory 1990–2007: An Overview,* April 2009, http://www.climatechange.govt.nz/carbon-reports/reports. html#greenhousegas, November 11, 2010.

---

[5]   The government website "energy wise" encourages home insulation, the use of solar water heating, using motor vehicles less frequently, encourages the purchase of energy rated (ENERGY STAR®) appliances, and provides for various subsidies to facilitate such changes, http://www.energywise.govt.nz/, November 11, 2010.

In other developed countries, agricultural emissions are typically around 11 per cent of emissions. Agricultural emissions are primarily from the methane produced by 33 million sheep and 10 million cattle. This predominance of agricultural emissions demands that the New Zealand approach to greenhouse gas reduction is rather different from anywhere else. However, it is also noteworthy that the increase in total greenhouse gas emissions of about 22 per cent between 1990 and 2007 is largely reflective of the growth in emissions from the energy sector. The energy sector includes transport, for example the combustion of fuels in cars and trucks, and its emissions are no doubt influenced by the very high rate of personal car ownership in New Zealand. Much of the remainder of the energy sector is electricity generation, although 60 per cent of electricity generation is from renewable sources, primarily hydro and wind. This relatively high proportion of energy from renewables is widely recognized as posing New Zealand a particular challenge in making relatively fast gains in emissions reduction because replacing, for instance, coal-fired power stations with wind farms, while desirable, would make no significant impact.[6]

In itself, climate change is predicted to have a less severe impact on New Zealand than many other parts of the world. Current predictions are that although New Zealand will be warmer and wetter in some parts and drier in others than currently, the direct impact of climate change is not expected to be at a level that will have a major negative impact on the primary sector. While the coastline is vulnerable to increasing sea levels, the outlook for New Zealand is not as severe as for many other places. However, while New Zealand is a minor contributor to global emissions, it is the second most emissions-intensive economy in the world and in the top five OECD countries for per capita emissions.[7]

At the same time, New Zealand trades heavily on its "clean green image". There is an imperative to maintain this image and resist any international move that would see New Zealand's agricultural products shunned because of the distance they must travel to market, or indeed to see tourists dissuaded from travelling such distances to see and enjoy the

---

[6]   Environmental standards are primarily regulated through the Resource Management Act 1991, where *inter alia* Section 15 forbids the discharge of contaminants (defined by Section 2 as including greenhouse gases) unless specifically allowed by a district plan or a resource consent, *see Greenpeace New Zealand Inc v Genesis Power Ltd* [2008] NZSC 112.

[7]   Skilling, D. and Boven, D., "We're Right Behind You: A Proposed New Zealand Approach to Emissions Reduction", (The New Zealand Institute Discussion Paper, 2007/2), pages 7–11, http://www.nzinstitute.org/Images/uploads/Were_right_behind_you_-_Full.pdf, November 11, 2010.

"clean green" environment. Changing consumer preferences internationally will continue to inform the New Zealand response. But further than that, the clean green environment is a source of national pride. While there has been some considerable debate as to whether New Zealand should be a leader in climate change policies or a "fast follower",[8] there is no doubt that New Zealand has a commitment to engage in the international debate. While it seems the direct effects on New Zealand are unlikely to be as significant as they are in some other places, the indirect effects are likely to have a significant economic impact on a small trading nation. There has been and there continues to be some political divide in New Zealand on the appropriate response. However, as between the two major political parties that divide has been about being a world leader or doing a "fair share". The discussion in New Zealand has unsurprisingly had two strands. First, an international commitment to play our part, and secondly, a halting journey to find an economically (and politically) acceptable solution. By 2009 emissions were significantly higher than their 1990 level and with few opportunities for abatement. The existing high proportion of renewable energy and the relatively limited options for reducing agricultural emissions make rapid improvement a particular challenge. However, by 2009 the political consensus, informed by international moves, is to implement an emissions-trading scheme (ETS), albeit with quite significant differences of opinion as to the proper structure of the trading scheme. What is equally clear is that the principal policy tool to tackle emissions reduction will be an ETS, augmented by an education campaign and some selected direct incentives, the non-use of eco-tax and the very limited use of tax charges.

3.   TAX REVIEW 2001

In 2001 a group of experts were invited by the government to consider "whether the architecture of our tax system is adequate for today's needs."[9] The functions of the Tax Review were to examine and inquire into the structure and effects of the tax system in New Zealand; to formulate proposals for improving that system, either by way of making changes to the system, abolishing any existing form of tax, or introducing new forms of tax; and to report to Parliament through the Minister of Finance, the Minister of Revenue and the Minister of Economic Development. The essential questions for review were the level of tax, the appropriate bases

---

8   *See*, for example, Skilling and Boven, *ibid.*
9   Tax Review 2001, *op. cit.*, page i.

for tax and the definitions of those bases, and the rates that should apply. The Committee endorsed the broad-base low-rate model of the previous decade and a half and took as its starting point the position that a "well-functioning tax system works best the lower the revenue level it is required to collect, the broader the base to which it applies, and the lower the rates at which it is levied."[10] As part of its broad remit, the Committee considered the use of "eco-taxes" generally, and carbon taxes specifically, to meet commitments under the Kyoto Protocol, the government having already signaled an intention to ratify the Protocol.[11]

3.1 Eco-taxes and Eco-charges

The Committee considered that "eco-taxes"[12] are appropriate where three conditions are broadly satisfied:

- The environmental damage of each unit of emissions is the same across the geographic area to which the tax applies;
- The volume of emissions is measurable; and
- The marginal net damage of emissions is measurable.

New Zealand forms one market but the incidence of external damage from negative environmental effects is very localized. Air and water problems are very localized in nature and, as noted above, the most serious issues result from agricultural activity. This lack of co-incidence of damage across the country makes an eco-tax, by definition levied nationally, inefficient. Further, there are very high costs of measuring adverse impacts in order to tax them. Therefore, eco-taxes would need to be levied on some product proxy such as an input to (for example fertilizer) or output from (for example butterfat) the production process. These factors led the Committee to conclude that it was unlikely that an eco-tax levied nationally would produce net benefits to New Zealand.[13] The Committee

---

10 *Ibid.*, page 2.
11 New Zealand ratified the Protocol in December 2002, before the first three of its major trading partners which are, rank ordered: Australia, the United States and the People's Republic of China. The next three are Japan, Singapore, and Germany who ratified about the same time, with the exception of Singapore which did not ratify until 2006.
12 The Committee drew the distinction between "eco-taxes" levied through the national tax system and "eco-charges" which are local authority usage fees, such as for waste disposal and water supply.
13 Tax Review 2001, *op. cit.*, pages 46–7.

acknowledged the OECD view that there was still some behaviour modification benefit from such taxes even if they were set at a relatively low rate. The Committee considered that in practice "the case for very low taxes is weakened" once account is taken of the disproportionate cost burden imposed by such selective taxes. The Committee also dismissed the "double dividend" argument put to it by some submitters. This argument is in essence a variant of the OECD argument, its proponents maintaining that there are social benefits from the lower consumption of the good that is taxed and from using the revenue thus raised to reduce other distortionary taxes. The Committee's view was that this was only achieved because "the eco-tax effectively appropriates property rights previously enjoyed by users of the eco-taxed good." While such expropriation cannot always be avoided, it ought to be counted as a disadvantage of such a tax. An argument for eco-tax in those terms was identical to an argument that advocated for concessionary tax treatment for any activity or sector. The "initial presumption" in tax design was always against the introduction of selective tax. For the Committee the bedrock position was opposition to selective taxes; on that ground alone, an eco-tax was undesirable.

The Committee thus rejected the introduction of an eco-tax for two broad reasons. The case for it being an effective means of addressing New Zealand's environmental issues was weak. This conclusion has to be considered against the backdrop of the prevailing view that Kyoto would be good for New Zealand. Calculations done in the early years of the decade suggested that New Zealand was likely to receive large greenhouse gas credits in the first commitment period.[14] Secondly, the Committee was philosophically opposed to using the tax system on a selective basis to grant concessionary privileges to selected activities. By 2001, that opposition was firmly entrenched in the prevailing orthodoxy in New Zealand.[15]

The Committee did, however, consider that there was a much stronger case for eco-charges levied at the local level. Localized environmental concerns could be addressed through carefully designed eco-charges, so long

---

[14] *See*, further, below at 4.1.

[15] The government was quick to reject any politically unacceptable suggestions in the McLeod Committee's Final Report, particularly those surrounding the taxation of investments and capital gains, but the overall thrust of "broad-based low-rate" and simple and efficient taxation remained intact. Ironically, but unsurprisingly, it is the same imperfections that the 2009 review is currently addressing. (For the interesting comment made at the time in the business press, *see*, for example, Morgan, G., "McLeod II: Cowardice Under Fire", October 31, 2001, available at http://nbr.infometrics.co.nz/mcleod-ii--cowardice-under-fire_252.html, November 11, 2010.

as they satisfied the criteria set out above. Waste levies and water levies were instruments that might potentially meet the criteria and have positive impacts. The Committee had also received some submissions supporting the use of eco-taxes or -charges to extract rents from the users of natural resources, such as levies on mineral mining and charges on commercial fishing landings. The Committee was not supportive of these, for reasons very similar to the rejection of eco-tax generally. A tax that efficiently extracted resource rents would be necessarily designed to have no impact on investment decisions, that being the *sine qua non* of tax efficiency. Therefore such resource rents would have a minimal environmental impact.[16]

Thus overall the McLeod Committee did "not see a comprehensive program of ecological tax reform as suited to New Zealand" but "strongly" supported the "continuing movement towards greater use of eco-charges at the local and regional level."[17]

3.2   A Carbon Tax

As noted above, the Final Report of the Committee was released in the period prior to New Zealand's ratification of the Kyoto Protocol but when it seemed certain the government would ratify. The Review concluded that the best way for New Zealand to meet its obligations was through the introduction of a broad-based carbon tax, aligned to international carbon prices and including the agricultural sector.

In the period after New Zealand's ratification, the government worked on policy options for meeting these obligations and it is to that we now turn our attention. However, before doing so it is worth reiterating that a major tax policy review committee had rejected eco-taxes and behaviour modification on the basis that they were inconsistent with principles of efficient taxation. Behaviour modification was dismissed from the mainstream agenda and through the course of the decade it never regained its place.

4.   CONFRONTING KYOTO

4.1   Carbon Tax versus ETS

In 2002, the New Zealand government signed the Kyoto Protocol and in the same year developed a strategic climate change goal. Climate change

---

[16]   Tax Review 2001, *op. cit.*, page 49.
[17]   *Ibid.*, page 50.

matters to New Zealand because of the potential impact on a nation with such a proportionately large coastline and because of the primacy of the agricultural and tourism sectors of the economy, both of which rely on the quality of the environment and the ability to market on the basis of a "clean green" image. As part of the policy to meet the objective of making "significant greenhouse gas reductions" toward "a permanent downward path for total gross emissions by 2012",[18] a decision was made that a carbon tax would be introduced. Details of the tax were confirmed in April 2005.

The carbon tax was to apply to fossil fuels and to other large geo-thermal developments and manufacturing processes. It was to be set at NZ$15 per tonne of carbon dioxide or carbon dioxide equivalent emissions. The tax would not cover nitrous oxide and methane from the agricultural sector. If the international price for carbon changed significantly the rate would be changed, but in any event to no more than NZ$25 per tonne. The New Zealand government estimated that this would lead to an increase in expenditure for electricity and other fuels of NZ$4 per household per week. The government stated that the NZ$360 million of revenue expected to be raised by the carbon tax would lead to offsetting changes in the 2005 budget, so that the carbon tax would be fiscally neutral.

The tax was intended to reduce emissions in two ways. First, it discouraged the production of carbon by penalizing firms with large emissions profiles. Secondly, it encouraged consumers to choose more efficient and cleaner products. It aimed to create a price differential between clean and polluting energy sources so that the price of the different energy forms reflected their true costs and their negative externalities were impounded into their price and therefore not ignored in production and consumption decision-making. The government also proposed Negotiated Greenhouse Agreements (NGAs) as a way of shielding trade-exposed activities for New Zealand firms. Where a carbon tax would reduce the international competitiveness of domestic output relative to output of foreign competitors, NGAs were intended to provide relief so that New Zealand producers would not be disproportionately disadvantaged in global markets. In return for a commitment to move to international best practice for emissions management, NGA firms were relieved of an obligation to pay the carbon tax on inputs and were offered rebates on the tax content of

---

[18] Ministry for the Environment, *Review of Climate Change Policies*, 2005, para 7.2.2, www.mfe.govt.nz/publications/climate/policy-review-05/index.html, November 11, 2010.

the prices of their inputs. Further, the government clearly expected that a carbon tax would be a "transitional path toward full or partial emissions trading"[19] which would likely become a better option as world markets in emissions trading developed.

Several themes can be noted in the 2005 carbon tax. The first is the troubled position in respect of agricultural emissions. In 2003, the government had proposed a tax on all livestock for their methane emissions. Labelled a "fart tax", it was vehemently opposed by the farming industry, notwithstanding the fact that the revenue raised was to be spent on research into ways of reducing the methane emissions from ruminant animals.[20] The tax was withdrawn but the government had learnt a difficult lesson with an industry that is both responsible for the majority of New Zealand's greenhouse gas emissions and the generation of much of its wealth. The proposed carbon tax was truly a tax on carbon. Further, the agricultural sector would have been protected from the full force of the tax by NGAs. The second theme is that an environmental tax was not a revenue-raising device. Fiscal neutrality was fundamental. Any revenue raised would be "recycled through a package of changes to the business tax regime."[21]

However, in 2005, Cabinet decided to commission a review of New Zealand's climate change policies.[22] A cross-departmental team from the Treasury, the Ministry for Economic Development, the Ministry of Agriculture and Forestry, the Ministry of Transport and the Ministry for the Environment was assembled to conduct the review. When New

---

[19] Inland Revenue Department, *Implementing the Carbon Tax: A Government Consultation Paper*, May 2005, Foreword, http://taxpolicy.ird.govt.nz/publications/files/carbontax.pdf, November 11, 2010.

[20] Haggerty, J., and Campbell, H., "Farming and the Environment": Te Ara – the Encyclopedia of New Zealand, www.TeAra.govt.nz/en/farming-and-the-environment/6/4 (accessed October 2009); there were numerous protests in 2003 against the "fart-tax", *see* "MP runs into strife on tractor", *New Zealand Herald*, September 5, 2003, www.nzherald.co.nz/nz/news/article.cfm?c_id=1&objectid=3521866, November 11, 2010 (reporting the story of a farmer MP driving his tractor up the steps of Parliament at the end of a rally at which a petition against the tax signed by 64,000 people was presented).

[21] Ministry for the Environment, *Review of Climate Change Policies, op. cit.*, para 3.2.2.

[22] There was some evidence that carbon tax would have potentially politically unacceptable impacts on households and prices, and although the distributional effect of the carbon tax was ambiguous there was some evidence households with relatively low total expenditure spent a disproportionate amount on carbon intensive commodities; this regressivity was no doubt concerning, *see* Creedy, J., and Sleeman, C., "Carbon Taxation, Prices and Household Welfare in New Zealand", (New Zealand Treasury Working Paper 04/23, Wellington, December 2004).

Zealand had signed up to Kyoto in 2002, it seemed that meeting its commitments would be relatively easy. However, by 2005 some fundamentals had changed. Underlying emissions growth was higher and forestry planting was lower than had been expected in 2002 and less of New Zealand's forests could be counted as "Kyoto forests". To this point, the government had been developing climate change policies based on the assumption that it would meet its Kyoto obligations, mainly because of the large tracts of forests. When it became apparent that these forests did not satisfy the definition of forests under the Protocol, the most likely scenario for the first commitment period was 36 million tonnes of excess CO_2 emissions, requiring the government to purchase carbon credits at an estimated cost of NZ$1.2 billion.

Against these changed policy assumptions, the Review looked at the long-term view and how New Zealand should approach the task of meeting its commitments under the Kyoto Protocol. Price-based measures (carbon tax and emissions trading schemes), regulatory policies and support-based policies were discussed as alternative ways to address the issues. Overall, the Review concluded that there was general international agreement that price-based mechanisms were more cost-effective than regulations. Other commentators reviewed had noted that price-based measures were well suited to addressing carbon dioxide pollution. But where agriculture and NGA firms are excluded from a carbon tax, unequal incentives to reduce emissions are created. This, we remember, is precisely the position that New Zealand had arrived at in the 2005 carbon tax proposals.

The Review considered the two price-based measures that assign costs to pollution and create financial incentives to reduce emissions, that is, emissions-trading schemes and carbon taxes. It criticized tax policy for not being able to set a sufficiently certain target for emissions reduction. Under a permit-based emissions-trading scheme, the Review noted that it is possible to set a target and leave the market to determine the price for the permit. However, the price would be influenced by a variety of factors in the international market, leaving the appropriate course of action for domestic firms somewhat uncertain. Further, the Review stated that a permit-based scheme is likely to yield better results than taxes because it can instantaneously adjust to international changes in the price for carbon permits. Firms will be able to quickly respond to changes in world price under emissions trading, but under a tax policy they will be forced to wait for legislative price changes, subject in the interim to an inefficient disparity between the world price and the domestic tax rate.

The Review concluded that it was important that a sustainable regime be established as soon as possible and that it was preferable not to retain the carbon tax and associated NGAs. The short term and rather static nature of the carbon tax would not be a useful stepping-stone to an emissions-trading scheme. The Review therefore proposed that "the Government should consider formulating an alternative climate change goal"[23]; in short, it was time for a rethink.

In December 2005, the government announced that the carbon tax would not proceed and instead it would consider other ways for New Zealand to meet its commitments to cut greenhouse gas emissions.[24] In September 2007, the government announced the result of the rethink: New Zealand would adopt a cap-and-trade emissions-trading scheme. The scheme would cover all six greenhouse gases and sectors of the economy would be progressively phased in to the scheme. The primary domestic unit of trade would be a New Zealand Unit (NZU) and the market for NZUs would be linked to international markets, allowing both sales to, and purchases from, those markets. Legislation was passed in 2008 just prior to the 2008 election. The 2008 Act has been in force since September 2008 and the forestry sector, the first to which the scheme applies, began operating under it from 1 January 2009. It has effect for the stationary energy and industrial processes sectors from 1 January 2010, liquid fuels from 1 January 2011 and agriculture and waste from 1 January 2013. The 2008 election resulted in a change of government and the new National Party-led government had maintained in opposition that there were design faults with the ETS as enacted and that the scheme be referred to a special parliamentary committee for review.

The National Party had indicated a clear preference for an ETS but its coalition and support partners in government[25] were less convinced, and when the ETS was referred to the committee it was a back-to-basics review with a carbon tax returned to the agenda. The current Minister for Climate Change Issues has said that the ETS is a more flexible tool than a carbon charge and that it has a natural corrective element with carbon prices likely to fall during periods of economic weakness, and additionally

---

[23] Ministry for the Environment, *Review of Climate Change Policies*, *op. cit.*, chapter 7, *passim*.

[24] Media Statement, "Minister Responsible for Climate Change Issues", December 21, 2005, www.taxpolicy.ird.govt.nz/news/archive.php?year=2005 &view=410, November 11, 2010.

[25] The nature of the New Zealand electoral system, mixed member proportional representation, makes it highly unlikely that one party will ever govern alone. The current government is a mixture of the National Party, the ACT Party, the United Future Party and the Maori Party. As the largest party in the grouping, National had entered into a variety of agreements with the various parties and representatives of each of the parties are Ministers outside Cabinet.

that alignment with Australia, which is also currently developing an ETS, is a motivation for keeping an ETS in New Zealand.

However, a number of large New Zealand companies and some political parties prefer a carbon tax. For instance Air New Zealand has a strong preference for a carbon tax. The company's estimate of its 2011 liability from the ETS is between NZ$13.8 million and NZ$27.5 million and it has indicated that it would rather pay a carbon tax with the revenue generated from such a tax going to emission reduction projects.[26] The general thrust of business opposition is that an ETS has uncertainty that will have an adverse effect on business and investment decisions.

The 2008 scheme remained in force while the select committee conducted its Review. Some 279 submissions were received and the committee issued its report in August 2009. The Committee concluded that an ETS is the preferable policy instrument, but this was opposed in two minority reports from the ACT party and the Maori Party. It preferred an ETS because of its ability to link to international schemes, the ability to track the international price of emission units and the greater flexibility for managing price risks for participants.[27] Still up for determination were, *inter alia*, sector entry dates,[28] transitional assistance (especially because of the effect on domestic prices for electricity), points of obligation and implementation issues.[29] Two of the National Party's support partners prefer a

---

[26] Air New Zealand, *Submissions to the Emissions Trading Scheme Review Committee on the Review of the Emissions Trading Scheme and Related Matters,* February 27, 2009, pages 12–13, http://www.parliament.nz/en-NZ/PB/ SC/Documents/Evidence/c/0/a/49SCETSSCevidenceETSR_176-Air-New-Zealand. htm, November 11, 2010.

[27] Emissions Trading Scheme Review Committee, *Review of the Emissions Trading Scheme and Related Matters,* August 2009, page 8 and pages 30–34, http://www.parliament.nz/en-NZ/PB/SC/Documents/Reports/f/4/f/49DBSCH_SCR 4485_1-Review-of-the-Emissions-Trading-Scheme-and-related.htm, November 11, 2010.

[28] For example, while stationary energy and industrial processes are due to be part of the scheme from 1 January 2010, regulations that are necessary for full implementation are not yet finalised.

[29] Of particular concern are questions around forestry. Under ETS, a liability arises if there is deforestation of pre-1990 forestry. This liability arises if pre-1990 forest-land is not reforested but is used for other (potentially more lucrative) purposes. This has a significant effect on land values and is complicated in particular by the fact that Maori have significant holdings of pre-1990 forests. Maori have pointed out that reduction of value of pre-1990 forested land has the effect of diminishing the value of settlements made between the Crown and iwi (tribes) for historic grievances under the Treaty of Waitangi.

carbon tax, albeit for different reasons,[30] and further political negotiation was needed to effect the completion of the scheme. An Amendment Bill was introduced to Parliament in September 2009. Entry dates were revised with energy and transport entering the scheme on 1 July 2010 and the agriculture entry date extended to 2015 from 2013, and the Bill provided for a range of transitional support mechanisms.[31] One of the significant changes is the establishment of a "transitional phase" for industry compliance with only a 50 per cent obligation and a NZ$25 price cap applying to liquid fossil fuels, stationary energy and industrial processes until 2013. This halves the burden on these sectors. Alterations are also proposed to ease the burden on emissions-intensive trade-exposed entities, those businesses that would be adversely impacted because their competitor firms in other jurisdictions might not be exposed to the cost of carbon. This is particularly apposite in the case of agriculture where New Zealand is alone in proposing the inclusion of agriculture in an ETS. Unsurprisingly, the measures that are capable of characterization as supporting polluters during the transition phase have drawn criticism.[32] In November 2009, the Finance and Expenditure Select Committee, after hearing submissions, decided to return the Bill to Parliament unchanged because the Committee could not reach a consensus. The Committee had failed to agree on whether it should be passed.[33] However, the Maori Party agreed to support the changes and legislation was passed in December 2009.[34] The principal changes were the revised entry date of 1 July 2020 for transport, energy and industrial sectors and I January 2015 for agriculture. The Act also implemented the transitional phase until 1 January 2013 with a 50 per cent obligation and a NZ$25 fixed price option for the transport,

---

[30]   Emissions Trading Scheme Review Committee, *op. cit.,* see the ACT Party's minority view page 103 and the Maori Party's minority view page 113.

[31]   Climate Change Response (Moderated Emissions Trading) Amendment Bill 2009; the modifications include a transition phase for the following three years with a half-obligation and a fixed price option of NZ$25 a tonne; additionally, there are support mechanisms for trade-exposed emission intensive industry.

[32]   *See,* for example, "Climate Subsidies Worth $225K for Each Tiwai Pt Job", *New Zealand Herald*, October 27, 2009, http://www.nzherald.co.nz/business/news/article.cfm?c_id=3&objectid=10605697, November 11, 2010. Tiwai Pt is the site of an aluminium smelter controlled ultimately by Rio Tinto, and it has warned of the impact on the smelter which will be the first in the world to come under an ETS. *See also* Fitzimons, J. (Green MP), "Kiwis and Businesses Overwhelmingly Reject ETS Changes," November 2, 2009, http://www.greens.org.nz/press-releases/kiwis-and-business-overwhelmingly-reject-ets-change, November 11, 2010.

[33]   Climate Change Response (Moderated Emissions Trading) Amendment Bill 2009, Report of the Finance and Expenditure Select Committee, November 2009.

[34]   The Climate Change Response (Moderated Emissions Trading) Act 2009.

energy and transport sectors. Debate is likely to continue, especially since New Zealand's closest neighbour was unable to pass an ETS. However, as only 3 per cent of New Zealanders say they understand the ETS and how it will work, debate is unlikely to take place in the wider population and will remain confined to policy developers. The particular problem facing New Zealand is that unless agricultural emissions are tackled it will prove almost impossible to reduce greenhouse gas emissions, but being the only country to include the agricultural sector is feared to have unacceptable consequences for trade-exposed agriculture.

It is clear, however, that a carbon tax is unlikely to be implemented in New Zealand in the foreseeable future.[35] Two other tax issues remain. First, what other more specific uses of tax and tax policy might there be to make more localized green initiatives, and, secondly, how might the tax consequences of the ETS be dealt with.

4.2 Tax Consequences of the ETS

When the ETS was first developed as a climate change policy tool in 2007, officials in the IRD and Treasury released a paper on the tax consequences of the ETS. Some changes to the goods and services tax (GST) legislation were also required.

The 2007 proposals on the income tax treatment of ETS-related issues suggested that expenditure incurred by a participant in the scheme in meeting obligations under the scheme ought to be a deductible expense. Income from the allocation of emissions units (NZUs) ought to be recognized as taxable income on an emerging basis over time. Income would thus be recognized on a systematic basis in the same periods as the expenditures for which the NZUs intended to compensate the recipient. Market values ought to be used to determine the value of any accrued income at the relevant balance dates. This was the proposed treatment for all but the forestry sector.

The position of the forestry sector was somewhat different. As noted above, removal of pre-1990 forests will result in a liability if there is a

---

[35] Despite economic evidence preferring a carbon tax or a tradable permit scheme in New Zealand and Australia, New Zealand, mirroring Europe, appear committed to an ETS. On the economic case for preference for a carbon tax in the New Zealand context, *see* Freebairn, J., "Carbon Tax Vs Tradable Permits: Efficiency and Equity Effects for a Small Open Economy", given at a conference New Zealand Tax Reform – Where to Next? Victoria University of Wellington, 11–13 February 2009, http://www.victoria.ac.nz/sacl/cagtr/tax-policy-2009-abstracts.aspx, November 11, 2010.

change of land use, that is, if forests are not replanted. The Government proposed a one-off allocation of NZUs to owners of such forests to partially compensate them for the potential loss in the value of their land. The 2007 Paper suggested that as this allocation was effectively compensation for loss of capital value, the allocation ought to be treated as a capital gain and therefore not be taxable. The situation was different for post-1990 forests and any units received as a result of carbon sequestration ought to be taxable as they are earned. Both of these proposals are logical within the existing framework of income taxation in New Zealand and the non-existence of a comprehensive capital gains tax.

The key GST proposals were equally logical in terms of the application of GST in New Zealand. The NZUs would be treated as a supply of services, NZUs allocated at no charge would be a supply for no consideration and registered persons acquiring NZUs for the principal purpose of making taxable supplies would be entitled to claim input tax deductions.

The Climate Change (Emissions Trading and Renewable Preference) Act 2008 made changes to the Income Tax Act 2007 and the Goods and Services Tax Act 1985 consistent with these proposals. Emissions units, including those related to post-1990 forests, are normally treated as being on revenue account. However, those related to pre-1990 forests are treated as being on capital account.[36] However, for those taxpayers who hold forestry land on revenue account, such as property developers and land dealers,[37] emissions unit transactions will be on revenue account. This indicates how clearly the tax consequences of ETS transactions are consistent with the objectives of the tax system. Thus any tax consequences of ETS transactions follow conventional tax treatment. The amendments to the GST legislation also followed a predictable path.[38]

5.   2009 REVIEW AND ENVIRONMENTAL TAXES

For more than 20 years, successive New Zealand governments have remained committed to a broad-base low-rate model. The mantra has been a system that is "fair, simple, and efficient".[39] There is no current suggestion that this will change, but in May 2009 a Tax Working Group

---

[36]   Income Tax Act 2007, Sections CB 36 and CW 3B.
[37]   Income Tax Act 2007, Sections CB 6 – CB 15.
[38]   Goods and Services Tax Act 1986, Section 11A.
[39]   Minster of Finance, "Speech to New Zealand Institute of Chartered Accountants", October 17, 2009, http://www.taxpolicy.ird.govt.nz/index.php?view=707#speech, November 11, 2010.

of private sector and academic experts and tax policy officials was set up to consider what key tax policy challenges currently face New Zealand. Its purpose is to assist the Government in considering medium-term options of tax policy design. As part of the review the policy division of the Inland Review Department have prepared papers on a raft of possible initiatives on the fiscal framework, personal taxes, GST and transfers, revenue raising and base broadening, and corporate taxation.[40] The group is due to report to the government in December 2009. Among the papers on revenue raising and base broadening, the question of environmental tax was addressed.[41]

This paper addressed environmental tax in a manner largely consistent with the conceptual perspective of the McLeod Committee. Environmental taxes ought to be used where they are identified as a policy tool useful for furthering environmental outcomes. It is environmental, and not tax, policy that ought to drive their implementation. Environmental taxes that were fiscally motivated, that is, implemented to raise revenue, could "run contrary to the principle of a broad-based low-rate tax system". Therefore tax, as an instrument of environmental policy, ought to be developed only to further a defined environmental objective and not to raise revenue. This reasoning has been implicit in all stages of the debate in formulating New Zealand's response to Kyoto obligations; any revenue to be raised from the carbon tax was to be "recycled" by some equivalent reduction through business tax reform. That was again made explicit in the September 2009 document. However, the paper did suggest that where the current system (presumably predominantly the income tax system) had the effect of supporting economic activities that had detrimental environmental effects, it might be appropriate to address such biases in the system where those effective subsidies were favouring activities that are environmentally damaging. This is a small but subtle change, but the analysis is still couched in terms of removing positive biases rather than overtly using tax to modify behaviour.

The document described how environmental taxes are one of several options available to address environmental issues and the economic consequences of negative externalities not being appropriately impounded in price. Other methods include regulation, the "command-and-control"

---

40 The background papers are available at http://www.victoria.ac.nz/sacl/ cagtr/twg/, November 11, 2010.

41 Policy Advice Division of Inland Revenue Department and New Zealand Treasury, "Other Base Broadening and Revenue Raising Ideas," (Background Paper for Session 3 of the Victoria University of Wellington Tax Working Group, September 2009), http://www.victoria.ac.nz/sacl/cagtr/twg/Publications/3-other-base-broadening-ird_treasury.pdf, November 11, 2010.

option, and economic instruments such as the ETS. Environmental taxes can be justified on the basis that market mechanisms have failed to factor-in the total costs to society and it is appropriate to use an intervention such as a tax to correct that market failure. Such a tax would need to be evaluated against the usual tax proposal evaluation benchmarks: efficiency, equity and administrative impact. Currently, there appears to be little knowledge of how effective such taxes might be in modifying behaviour. In addition the paper noted that there appears to be some evidence that environmental taxes are regressive, although with the regressivity appropriately ameliorated they can "end up being progressive". But looking to the future, it is clear that the policy response by New Zealand to the imperatives of climate change has been the ETS. The paper accepts this as preferable to a tax, but raises the possibility that the specifics of how and where taxes as a policy tool might be used to assist environmental outcomes requires a "detailed assessment of environmental priorities and policy mixes currently in place". The review thus leaves open the possibility that environmental detriment could be addressed by means of taxes, but it makes it clear on repeated occasions that any resulting revenue "should be directed towards funding the reduction of other taxes such as income tax reductions." Environmental taxes should be chosen if they are the most effective environmental policy instruments, but they ought not to be used for revenue raising. That, as a policy choice, is one for environmental rather than tax policy and there would appear to be no particular appetite in New Zealand to use such instruments. It is the Ministry for the Environment which is responsible for the development and implementation of policy in this area and a review of its website shows a range of policy initiatives, such as education, grants to those investigating marine-based electricity generation and those researching ways to reduce emissions from animals.[42] However, the 2009 paper, and it must be emphasized that this is only a background paper to an advisory group, does raise the possibility of using tax more deliberatively as an instrument to further environmental policy goals.

The Tax Working Group reported in January 2010.[43] The Report endorsed the broad-base low-rate model and made several recommenda-

---

[42]   Ministry for the Environment, "Government Sustainability Initiatives with Climate Change Benefits," June 12, 2009, http://www.mfe.govt.nz/issues/climate/policies-initiatives/government-initiatives-climate-benefit/index.html, November 11, 2010.
[43]   "A Tax System for New Zealand's Future: Report of the Victoria University of Wellington Tax Working Group", January 2010, http://www.victoria.ac.nz/sacl/cagtr/pdf/tax-report-website.pdf, November 11, 2010.

tions to return New Zealand to that paradigm, concluding the misalignment of top marginal rates and the exclusion from the tax base of certain activities (primarily real property investment) had had the consequence of New Zealand's tax system drifting from this ideal. The Report discussed that in general there are two types of tax: revenue and corrective taxes. The Group had focussed on revenue taxes, but suggested that although beyond its scope the Report did consider that "there may be circumstances where corrective taxes are warranted to address externalities, such as pollution".[44] This is a very mild statement but it is still a subtle shift because it would in the New Zealand context be one of the stronger statements that tax might have a desirable instrumental effect. At the same time, as the implementation of the ETS grew closer, more commentators began to label the ETS itself a "tax". There are some suggestions in those two things that the New Zealand attitude might change. Only time will tell.

However, there already are two areas where instruments that can be collected under the general rubric of environmental tax have been introduced already: a waste disposal levy in 2009 and a fuel excise duty.

6. SOME LIMITED USE OF ENVIRONMENTAL CHARGES

6.1 The Waste Disposal Levy

Under the Waste Minimisation Act 2008, a NZ$10 per tonne levy is charged on all waste sent to landfill after 1 July 2009. The purpose of the Act is to encourage waste minimization and a decrease in waste disposal to protect the environment and provide economic, social and cultural benefits.[45] Half of the levy will go to territorial authorities to be spent on achieving the objectives set out in their obligatory waste management and minimization plans. The other half will go to a central fund to be used in waste minimization projects established by the Waste Advisory Board.[46]

6.2 Water Charges

Internationally New Zealand is ranked fifth in terms of water availability. That is to say, New Zealand has the fifth highest amount of internal

---

44   *Ibid.* page 14.
45   Waste Minimisation Act 2008, Section 3.
46   Waste Minimisation Act 2008, Sections 30–32, and Part 7.

renewable water (average annual surface runoff and groundwater recharge generated from endogenous precipitation) available per person. Urban household water supply in New Zealand is mostly run through local government. A few local authorities contract out aspects of water, wastewater and storm water services to private companies. Others have established business units within the local authority structure to manage water; still others create council-owned companies to run the service.

Once simply a component of progressive rates, house owners now also pay one flat fee for being connected to the water supply, called the Uniform Water Charge. According to Water New Zealand, a not-for-profit organization for those involved in the water sector generally, 11 out of 73 councils meter domestic water supply and households pay for water according to how many cubic metres they use. Thus the support for an eco-charge seen as far back as 2001 has not translated into extensive action. No doubt the relatively plentiful supply of water in New Zealand has meant there has been no policy pressure to restrict access to and use of water, particularly in the domestic sphere.

6.3   Fuel Excise Duty

There is an excise duty on motor spirits, compressed natural gas and liquefied natural gas. The rate on motor spirits is 45 cents per litre plus a further 8 cents per gram of lead. There was an increase of 3 cents per litre effective from 1 October 2009 with a further 3 cents in 1 October 2010. This increase was specifically earmarked for development of the transport network and for allocation to public transport. In 2007, the then government developed a regional fuel tax to pay for the electrification of the rail network in Auckland, New Zealand's largest city. Later regional fuel tax was made available to all regions that wished to take advantage of the scheme. The government elected in November 2008 decided to remove the regional fuel tax in favour of a phased increase in fuel excise duty to fund increased expenditure on State highways and the electrification of passenger transport in Auckland and Wellington.[47]

---

[47]   Office of the Minister of Transport, "Replacement of Regional Fuel Tax with Increases to Fuel Excise Duty and Road User Charges" (Cabinet Paper), http://www.transport.govt.nz/ourwork/Land/Documents/ Replacement%20of%20 regional%20fuel%20tax.pdf, November 11, 2010; and "Cabinet Minute of the Decision to Endorse the Minister's Recommendation", CAB Min (09) 8/11–14, March 9, 2009, http://www.transport.govt.nz/ourwork/Land/Documents/ Transport%20funding%20package%20%20Cabinet%20minute.pdf, November 11, 2010.

7. OTHER MATTERS

The 2009 discussion paper raised the possibility that there might be instances where the tax system was encouraging activity that was environmentally undesirable. Conversely, we might also find situations where the tax system operates to dissuade practices that have positive environmental consequences. What the chapter now turns to is a brief discussion of three different activities and the way in which they are treated for tax purposes.

7.1 Taxation of Petroleum Exploration

A recent review of the deductibility for income tax purposes of expenditure on exploration and development of petroleum mining is instructive on the approach taken in New Zealand to policy development in taxation. In September 2007, tax policy officials reported at the request of the Ministers of Revenue and Finance on the "uncertainty and disincentives" in the then current rules on deduction for petroleum mining exploration.

In 2004, the Government had announced a series of measures designed to encourage oil and gas exploration in New Zealand. This was driven by concerns about the rate of depletion in the Maui gas reserves off the coast of the North Island and the moves were reflective of an identified need to encourage the development of new fields to meet future energy needs.[48] The government then changed the petroleum royalty rules to make them more internationally competitive in order to stimulate a higher level of exploration. In 2005, income from drilling exploratory or development wells was exempted from income tax for a period of six years ending on 31 December 2009. The activities must be carried out by non-resident companies and the exemption was confined to offshore petroleum fields.[49]

The second prong to this strategy was a review of the deductibility rules for petroleum exploration. In September 2007, tax policy officials reported at the request of the ministers of Revenue and Finance on the "uncertainty and disincentives" in the then current rules on deduction for petroleum mining exploration. As the consultation paper prepared by Treasury and IRD officials noted, "underlying the changes was the principle that

---

[48] On New Zealand petroleum exploration generally, *see* Ministry of Economic Development, *Petroleum Investment Strategy*, http://www.crownminerals.govt.nz/cms/petroleum/publications, November 11, 2010.
[49] Income Tax Act 2004, Section CW 45B (now Income Tax Act 2007, Section CW 57).

the tax system should not create barriers or obstacles to an increase in exploration."[50]

The legislation drew a distinction between onshore and offshore development expenditure. Development expenditure was normally deductible over the seven years beginning with the income year in which the expenditure was incurred. However, expenditure incurred in offshore developments could only begin to be deducted in the later of the year in which the expenditure was incurred or the first income year of commercial production. This meant, of course, a timing difference in the deductibility of onshore and offshore expenditure. The seven-year amortization period was arbitrary, concessionary for some developments, penal for others, but a proxy for the true economic decline in value. The policy review held that the distinction between the timing of the deductibility of onshore and offshore expenditure was untenable and that taxpayers ought to have more choice in the method of writing-off expenditure so as to more accurately reflect the reduction in economic value. Tax ought "not to influence investment decisions"[51] and so it recommended the removal of the distinction between onshore and offshore developments and also favoured taxpayers being able to use a reserve depletion method of expenditure allocation. Thus with effect from 1 April 2008 the distinction was removed and taxpayers have the choice of a straight line or a "units of production" method of allocation. In addition, development expenditure allocated to future years will become fully deductible in the income year in which the relevant permit is relinquished or disposed of. Costs of failed production wells are deductible in the year of abandonment. Before 2008, failed wells were also subject to the seven-year amortization rule and this change can be readily identified as a tax-friendly attitude to petroleum exploration.[52]

From the perspective of the policy to reduce carbon emissions, using the tax system to support, if not overtly encourage, petroleum exploration might seem rather odd. As the September 2009 discussion document noted, there might be rules within the tax system that favour environmentally damaging activities, and it would seem that those governing petroleum exploration are instances of them.

The New Zealand government has taken the position that it is desirable

---

[50] "Suggested Changes To The Petroleum Mining Expenditure Tax Rules: Consultative Paper Prepared by the Policy Advice Division of Inland Revenue and by The New Zealand Treasury", November 26, 2007, http://www.taxpolicy.ird.govt.nz/publications/files/petroleumcp.pdf, November 11, 2010.

[51] *Ibid.*, para 19.

[52] Income Tax Act 2007, Sections DT1 to DT8 and EJ12 to EJ 20.

to encourage the exploitation of petroleum reserves.[53] This has led to a policy response to make the tax rules certain and to minimize "disincentives" that might flow from particular tax treatment. The overt purpose of the petroleum deductibility provision review might have stopped short of using tax as a positive instrument to create incentives, those who see a need for the world to move away from reliance on fossil fuels as necessary for a greener world, might well identify these deductibility provisions as having environmentally adverse consequences. However, they are the direct consequence of a political decision made to "unlock" petroleum reserves and the tax treatment is consistent with the theory of how tax policy is developed in New Zealand.

7.2   Fringe Benefit Tax on Motor Vehicles

A fringe benefit arises when a motor vehicle is made available to an employee for their private use.[54] The value of the benefit is calculated on the basis of the value of the vehicle that is made available. The taxpayer has the choice of electing either 20 per cent of the vehicle's cost or 36 per cent of the vehicle's tax (that is, depreciated) value. The amount of tax payable is then dependent on the number of days the vehicle is available and the rate of tax.[55]

Fringe benefit tax therefore includes no incentives to provide employees with more fuel-efficient or lower cc vehicles. Indeed, insofar as, for example, hybrid vehicles are more expensive than petrol-fuelled vehicles, the fringe benefit tax system would discourage use of the more expensive hybrid vehicle.

7.3   Deductions for Business Environmental Expenditure

The rules regarding deductibility for environmental expenditure designed to avoid, remedy or mitigate the discharge of contaminants were clarified

---

53   This position has been shared by the Labour-led government (until 2008) and the National-led government (after 2008), see for instance the speech by the Minister of Energy in November 2009 when he outlined the government's desire to "unlock" the country's petroleum resources, http://www.beehive.govt.nz/speech/unlocking+our+petroleum+potential, November 11, 2010.

54   Income Tax Act 2007, Section CX6.

55   Income Tax Act 2007, Section RD26: the employer has a choice of paying a flat rate of 64 per cent or electing a multi-rate system, it being one that taxes fringe benefits that can be attributed to individual employees at rates related to the all-inclusive remuneration of individual employees.

in 2005.[56] Previously, to meet the requirements for deduction as "capital environmental" expenditure[57] the expenditure had to be deductible under the normal deductibility criteria,[58] or satisfy the requirements of depreciable capital expenditure. Notwithstanding the apparent breadth of these provisions, there were still instances of such expenditure that was not deductible. For instance, s DJ 10 predated the Resource Management Act 1991[59] and costs incurred in complying with environmental standards required in that Act sometimes fell into a hole as neither immediately deductible or depreciable.[60] Insofar as the provision referred to "industrial waste" there was some uncertainty about what the ambit of that expression was. To facilitate certainty, s DB 37 was enacted in 2005. It, accompanied by the provisions in Schedule 6A to the Act, set out categories of deductible environmental expenditure: testing and feasibility expenditure, restoration expenditure and monitoring expenditure that are deductible immediately. Construction or improvement expenditure is deductible over the lesser of 35 years or the length of any granted resource consent. Further, previously a deduction had been available for those dealing with "industrial waste". There was no definition of that term so there was inevitably ongoing uncertainty as to whether a deduction thereof was allowed. The word "industrial" was removed so that a deduction is now clearly available for the removal of all types of waste and this amendment applied retrospectively.[61] This is certainly more taxpayer friendly and at the same time more environmentally friendly. The new 2005 environmental rules introduced a matching mechanism so that site restoration and monitoring costs could be matched against prior business income. Section EK 1 of the Income Tax Act 2004[62] established a Crown Bank Account called the

---

[56]   Income Tax Act 2004, Section DB 37 (now Income Tax Act 2007, Section DB 46).

[57]   Income Tax Act 2004, Section DJ10.

[58]   Income Tax Act 2007, Section DA1, expenditure is generally deductible if it is incurred in deriving assessable income or incurred in carrying on a business for the purpose of deriving assessable income. Expenditure is usually deductible in the year in which it is "incurred", *see CIR v Mitsubishi Motors* [1995] 3 NZLR 513; the general permission is subject to general limitations in Section DA2, the most relevant of which, in this context, being the capital limitation – deduction is denied "to the extent to which it is of a capital nature".

[59]   The age of the provision being an interesting point to note in itself, Income Tax Act 1976, Section 124.

[60]   On the general difficulties with "black hole" expenditure, *see Milburn NZ Ltd v CIR* (2001) 20 NZTC 17,017.

[61]   Inland Revenue Department, *Tax Information Bulletin,* Volume 17, Number 7, September 2005, page 31.

[62]   Now Income Tax Act 2007, Section EK1.

Environmental Restoration Funds Account (ERA) into which businesses can make payments towards their restoration and environmental monitoring liabilities. Thus a person who carries on business and expects to incur in a later income year expenditure that is "not on revenue account property" and is expenditure related to the effects of the discharge of a contaminant[63] and has provided for this future liability in its financial statements, may make deposits into an ERA. A taxpayer is allowed a deduction for a payment to an ERA.[64] In essence the effect of these provisions is to allow the bringing forward of deductions and to override the disallowance for capital expenditure and the usual rules of timing of deductions.

There are also some provisions in the Income Tax Act 2007 that encourage the planting of trees. For example, s DO3 specifically overrides the capital limitation to allow deductions for tree planting where the trees are planted on farms but not for shelterbelts or for the purposes of harvesting produce from the trees.[65]

There is therefore some support for positive environmental initiatives in the Income Tax Act 2007 but again the debate has been couched in terms of tax certainty following policy initiatives developed outside the tax system itself.

8. CONCLUSION

Since the 1980s, tax policy in New Zealand has been developed with reference to the principles of efficiency, fairness and simplicity, and successive governments have remained committed to a broad-base low-rate model. There has been a reluctance to use the tax system as either an incentive for behaviour or activity and equally there has been no appetite to use the tax system as disincentive. The McLeod Committee explained this in this way: the benefits of such mechanisms were uncertain, but the costs were clear. Thus it could never be sufficiently certain that the benefits would outweigh the costs and cost/benefit analysis was a key plank of efficient tax policy development and implementation. Meanwhile, through the first decade of this century, the New Zealand government has grappled with ways to meet Kyoto obligations and develop policy responses to climate change.

---

[63] Income Tax Act 2007, Section EK2 and Schedule 19: liabilities for environmental damage may arise under the Resource Management Act 1991, either as a condition of a resource consent or as a consequence of having to deal with the effects of a contaminated site.

[64] Income Tax Act 2007, Section EK 4.

[65] *See* further at Income Tax Act 2007, Sections DO 2 – DO 6.

Tax is not currently identified as a prime, or even significant, policy instrument. The Green Party has suggested shifting the tax base off work and enterprise and on to "waste pollution and scarce resources",[66] but there is no widespread support for or indeed interest in, such a change. Although there is increasing support for taxing capital rather than labour, and a growing recognition of the distortionary effect of the way certain things, for example land, are taxed, there has been no apparent inclination to use tax in an overtly instrumental way to tackle "green" issues. Whether this will change in the immediate future seems unlikely. There are, however, some small and subtle shifts in discussion that hint the argument might be re-calibrated. Only time, of course, will tell.

---

[66] Green Party of Aotearoa New Zealand, "Green Taxation and Monetary Policy", http://www.greens.org.nz/policy/green-taxation-and-monetary-policy, November 11, 2010.

10. Concluding thoughts: a greener future?

Jefferson VanderWolk

The information presented in the foregoing chapters might easily be interpreted negatively, feeding the pessimism of cynics who search, apparently in vain, for signs that the human race – or more precisely the world's governments – will act effectively to reduce greenhouse gas (GHG) emissions before it is too late to prevent a global environmental catastrophe. Can green taxation in East Asia make a difference? The history of the various efforts made in recent decades to use tax measures to reduce GHG emissions in countries in Europe and North America, and more recently in Australia and New Zealand, is hardly encouraging. Tax impositions on the use of fossil fuels, and also tax subsidies for investment in environmentally friendly plant and equipment, appear to have done little or nothing to prevent steady growth in per capita carbon emissions in certain industrialized countries such as Canada, the United States and Australia (although the experience in northern European countries is somewhat more encouraging).[1]

Now that China and other Asian countries have become leading

---

[1] For example, researchers have concluded that if the Swedish tax system in 1990 had remained unchanged, Sweden would have produced 20 per cent more CO_2 than the current level. Its sulphur tax also helped reduce SO_2, NO_x and CO_2 emissions by 94 per cent, 20 per cent and 54 per cent respectively, compared with 1970 levels. Between 1990 and 2006, CO_2 emissions in Sweden dropped by 9 per cent while GDP increased by 44 per cent. In Denmark, sulphur tax helped achieve an 84 per cent decrease of sulphur emissions within the ten year period from 1995 to 2004. In Germany, green tax measures helped reduce CO_2 emissions by 2–3 per cent from 1999 to 2003. Related tax reforms reduced some other tax rates, which helped to create 250,000 jobs in Germany during the same period. *See* China Council for International Cooperation on Environment and Development (CCICED) Policy Research Report, *Economic Instruments for Energy Efficiency and the Environment*, 2009, page 8, www.cciced.net/encciced/media/publication/PubProcessofAGM/2009agmpp/tfreports/200911/P020100310337908430760.pdf, November 15, 2010.

emitters of GHG, is there any realistic hope that the countries of East
Asia will be able to use tax policy effectively to reduce pollution and GHG
emissions in a way that has eluded the other industrialized nations to date?
Despite the record of the past in other parts of the world, the answer is yes
– there are grounds for believing that green taxation will be adopted with
at least some success in East Asia over the next twenty or thirty years. The
reasons lie in the social, economic, and geographic differences between
the newly industrialized East Asian countries and the developed economies of Europe, North America, Australia and New Zealand. Indeed, it
is not unrealistic to expect that China and other East Asian jurisdictions
will take the lead among the global community of nations in reducing the
carbon intensity of industrial activities, using green taxation among other
governmental tools to do so.

The differences between newly industrialized East Asian countries and
the developed economies of the West may be highlighted by looking at
the factors enumerated by Professor Arthur Cockfield, in Chapter 6, on
Canada's experience to date, as explanatory of that country's poor record
of controlling per capita carbon dioxide emissions growth. First, he notes
that Canada has a huge amount of land which is sparsely populated. In
those circumstances, "global warming concerns may be perceived by many
Canadians to be less of a problem [than other concerns], given the amount
of habitable space available to the current and forecast population."[2] In
contrast, industrialized countries in East Asia are relatively densely populated and urbanized. There is simply nowhere one can go to escape the
environmental effects of industrial plants, construction sites, traffic jams,
and so forth, unlike Canada or Australia where the possibility of living in
an undeveloped wilderness is very real.

Second, in Professor Cockfield's words, "Canada is a northern country
and the fear of 'global warming' may not appear too troublesome to many
Canadians . . . If global climate change was labeled 'global cooling', as
it was under a scientific theory from the 1970s, then Canadians might
be searching for more effective tax policies."[3] On this point, the contrast
with much of East Asia is stark. Hong Kong, Singapore, and everything
in-between lie in the tropics and are warm – and getting warmer – all year
long. At least half of China's 1.3 billion people also live in warm weather
most of the time. Moreover, most of them are near the coast. Rising sea
levels could wreak havoc in mega-cities such as Shanghai and the Hong
Kong-Shenzhen-Guangzhou conurbation. In addition, extreme weather

---

[2]   *See* Chapter 6.
[3]   *Ibid.*

events such as typhoons and floods have been occurring regularly in southern China and neighbouring regions in recent years, with devastating consequences. Unlike Canadians, the people of East Asia have every reason to fear the effects of global climate change.

Third, Professor Cockfield points out that, in Canada, "resource exploitation [ie the mining of coal and other minerals, and oil and gas extraction] plays an important part in provincial and national economic development, creating jobs and bringing in government tax revenues."[4] The opposite is true of jurisdictions such as Taiwan, Hong Kong, South Korea, and Singapore, where natural resource exploitation plays no part at all in the economy. Larger countries in the region, such as China, have significant extractive industries, but as a percentage of the national economy, the exploitation of natural resources in those countries is less important than in Canada (with the possible exception of Indonesia). Moreover, as global manufacturing becomes increasingly concentrated in East Asia, natural resource exploitation in countries such as Canada and Australia is growing in importance in those countries, whereas in East Asia it is becoming less important as manufacturing and services grow rapidly. China's recent moves to acquire the rights to natural resources in Africa and Australia illustrate the trend: increasingly, the East Asian manufacturing economies will be supplied with raw materials by other parts of the world and will convert those raw materials into products that are then exported globally.

The fourth and last factor mentioned by Professor Cockfield is that "the alleged uncertain science of global warming may be playing a role in reducing political support for effective tax policy solutions."[5] The lack of political will to use tax laws or other regulations to impose a price on carbon exists not only in Canada but also in the United States, Australia, and other Western democracies. Whether or not the same will be true in East Asian democracies such as South Korea and Taiwan remains to be seen. However, in a number of countries in the region, including the largest country, China, as well as advanced economic centres such as Singapore and Hong Kong, the government is able to enact tax measures in accordance with policy decisions taken by the central government authorities, without the need to go through a democratic political process such as that in Canada, the United States, or Australia. Therefore, several key East Asian jurisdictions are in a position to adopt green tax measures that might not be politically acceptable in countries where new taxes must be approved by legislators who fear the wrath of the voters in their home

---

4 *Ibid.*
5 *Ibid.*

constituencies who may be unhappy with the idea of increased taxation. This is not to say that green tax measures in China, Singapore, and Hong Kong should be instituted without considering the political consequences. Political acceptability is always an important consideration in the design of a new tax. But it is less likely to defeat a proposal at the start in most East Asian countries than in the U.S. and other Western democracies.

Thus, it can readily be seen that many of the factors that have impeded the successful use of green tax measures in North America, Australia, and, to a lesser extent, Europe, are far less likely to derail green tax proposals in East Asian countries. The prevailing conditions are simply different. In particular, the urbanization of China and other East Asian countries is likely to create additional pressure for action by governments to tackle air pollution and other forms of environmental degradation. It is no secret that health problems result from breathing polluted air in crowded cities, day in and day out. The cost of providing health care to large urban populations must be borne by the community at large through taxation. Therefore, policy makers can be expected to reach the sensible conclusion that it is better to impose taxes on activities that cause air pollution, thereby discouraging those activities and helping to prevent widespread health problems in the community, than it is to allow the pollution to grow unabated, exacerbating health problems that will have to be paid for through increased taxation down the road. The stakes are high in cities such as Hong Kong, Taipei, Seoul, and Singapore, where the populations are aging and the life expectancy of both men and women is lengthening. This will also be true, before long, in Chinese cities on the mainland.

Another factor supporting the view that East Asian countries are likely to take the lead in green taxation globally is the financial condition of the governments in the region. The richer jurisdictions such as Singapore and Hong Kong have amassed huge cash surpluses. China, too, appears to have come through the global financial crisis of 2008–09 with its massive cash reserves intact (assuming the United States government's Treasury bonds are still safe investments when this book is published). Thus, the well-funded governments in East Asia are under less financial pressure than governments in the West, where legislative initiatives addressing climate change have been relegated to the back burner while policymakers and legislators focus on restarting the national economy. Many East Asian countries, in contrast, have the financial resources to subsidize the cost of requiring businesses and families to switch to environmentally friendly practices. Also, the adoption of green taxes may involve a corresponding revenue cost in the form of reduced taxes on non-polluting productive activities in compensation for heavier taxation of polluting activities. The ability to bear these costs is a very helpful factor when green tax measures are being considered.

To the extent that green tax measures raise additional revenue, the money can be earmarked for spending on green initiatives such as the upgrading of public bus and taxi fleets, the construction of additional public transport facilities, the clean-up of toxic waste dumps, and the like. Well-designed and targeted publicity regarding the use of new revenue for environmental projects that enjoy public support can go a long way to overcoming political resistance to new taxes. Public education and awareness of environmental issues, with particular emphasis on the costs of *not* dealing with them, are crucial, especially in societies that have been focused, until now, on purely economic development. The concept of sustainable development has to be introduced and consistently reinforced by governments throughout East Asia if environmental protection measures are to succeed.

Another consideration, as noted by Professor Stephen Phua in the conclusion of his chapter on Singapore's green tax measures in respect of land transportation, is that

> . . . the incorporation of sustainable development into a nation's policy goal is not necessarily a zero sum game. By participating in the development of green energy technologies, nations stand to reap long term benefits. Technology acquisition and transfer would typically entail a transfer of skills to the domestic labour market. The discovery of new technologies through investments in research and development would eventually enable some nations to export green goods and services to the rest of the world.[6]

In other words, the greening of an economy can be good for business. Given that the businessmen of East Asia are competing very successfully in the global economy, it is reasonable to expect that they would adapt successfully to new laws or regulations involving mandatory adoption of green technologies and business practices. As Professor Phua suggests, this could lead to a position of dominance in the provision of the relevant goods or services globally, resulting in economic growth and an upward move along the value chain for the national economy. The well-known American journalist Thomas Friedman has been hammering at this point in his columns in the *New York Times* for some time.[7]

---

[6] *See* Chapter 4.

[7] *See*, e.g., Friedman, T., "Their Moon Shot and Ours", *New York Times*, Septemper, 25, 2010; "Aren't We Clever?", *New York Times*, September 19, 2010; "We're Gonna Be Sorry", *New York Times*, July 25, 2010; "No Fooling Mother Nature", *New York Times*, May 5, 2010; and "Failure Is Not an Option",

Considering all of the reasons for optimism about the future of green taxation in East Asia, it may be asked why governments in the region have not adopted more green tax measures to date. The answer would appear to be that we are at or near a turning point, where such measures will start to be adopted more frequently, and will be more meaningful. For example, there are signs that China will adopt a national carbon tax within the next few years, along with various other green tax measures. Up to now, such measures have not been a practical possibility, given that China has been in the process of putting the foundations of its tax system in place. Also, the imperatives of economic development have generally taken precedence over environmental protection considerations as the countries of East Asia have risen out of poverty over the past thirty years or so.

Now, as we enter the second decade of the 21st century, the economies of China, South Korea, Taiwan and other East Asian jurisdictions are among the most dynamic in the world, putting those countries on track to surpass the rich countries of the West in economic power in due course. For the reasons noted earlier, there will be sound policy reasons for their governments to adopt green tax measures in addition to other measures aimed at ensuring sustainable development and the reduction of environmental degradation. Energy efficiency and clean technologies will gain steadily in importance, not only in the region but throughout the world. The regional businesses that devote the necessary effort and resources to becoming innovators in these fields will acquire a competitive advantage. A virtuous cycle of investment in research and development followed by successful exploitation of resulting technology, leading to reinvestment of profits in further R&D, could be established in a number of companies based in the region that will grow to become global leaders in clean technology, renewable energy, smart grid systems, and the like. The resulting benefits for the world, both environmentally and economically, could be enormous.

Of course, economic competition between the powerhouses of East Asia has the potential to interfere with the adoption of sensible policies regarding environmental protection and sustainable development. The existence of regional organizations such as the Association of Southeast Asian Nations (ASEAN) may reduce the risk of harmful competition and enhance the possibility of fruitful cooperation in the area of coordinated environmental policies. Agreement on a carbon tax to be applied

---

New York Times, April 28, 2010, http://topics.nytimes.com/top/opinion/editorial sandoped/oped/columnists/thomaslfriedman/index.html, November 15, 2010.

consistently to all industries in all countries throughout the region would certainly be desirable. If a powerful country such as China were to take the lead on an issue of this kind and succeed in obtaining the agreement of its trading partners in the region, the rest of the world might follow over time. Wishful thinking? Perhaps. But, for the reasons mentioned above, the wish is not baseless. The cynics are free to make their predictions of doom; the rest of us must do what we can to avoid it.

Index